By the same author

Winter War: The Falklands with John Witherow

The Provisional IRA with Eamonn Mallie

Famous Victory: The Gulf War

The Irish Empire

Fighter Boys: Saving Britain 1940

Bomber Boys: Fighting Back 1940–1945

3 Para

A Good War

Ground Truth: 3 Para Return to Afghanistan

ritain: A Day-to-Day Chronicle, 10 July–31 October 1940

Follow Me Home

Tirpitz: X-Craft, Agents and Dambusters – The Epic Quest to Destroy Hitler's Mightiest Warship

Wings: The RAF at War, 1912–2012

Reckoning: Death and Intrigue in the Promised Land

ler King: The True Story of William Ash – The Greatest Escaper of World War II

Air Force Blue: The RAF in World War Two

Who Was Saturday: The Extraordinary Life of Airey Neave

Praise for O_p

Operation Jubilee

Dieppe, 1942: The Folly and the Sacrifice

PATRICK BISHOP

SIGNAL

McCLELLAND
& STEWART

To Bob and Angela

Contents

List of Illustrations and Maps

Illustrations

1. Mountbatten meets the troops. (Bettmann/Gettyimages)
2. 'Jock' Hughes-Hallett. (Keystone/Hulton Archive/Gettyimages)
3. 'Ham' Roberts made the perfect scapegoat for the Jubilee disaster. (Mirrorpix/Gettyimages)
4. Andy McNaughton excelled as a soldier and a scientist. (Popperfoto/Gettyimages)
5. Monty gives a good impression of being Harry Crerar's best friend. (Keystone-France/Gettyimages)
6. Trafford Leigh-Mallory saw Jubilee as the chance to win glory. (Imperial War Museums CH 13289)
7. Lord Lovat after 4 Commando's triumph. (Imperial War Museums H 22583)
8. 3 Commando's CO John Durnford-Slater with second-in-command, Peter Young. (Image courtesy of the National Army Museum, London)
9. Lt Col Cecil Merritt VC of the South Saskatchewans. (Mirrorpix/Gettyimages)
10. Captain John Foote VC, RHLI. (Toronto Star Archives/Gettyimages)
11. Captain Denis Whitaker, RHLI. (Mirrorpix/Gettyimages)
12. Lt Col Dollard 'Joe' Menard. (History and Art Collection/Alamy Stock Photo)
13. Lt Col Fred Jasperson. (Private collection)
14. The Rileys, with CO Bob Labatt at front and centre. (Royal Hamilton Light Infantry officers, photographs taken inside POW Camp Oflag VII B. CWM 20160239-006_4. George Metcalf Archival Collection, Canadian War Museum)
15. Lt Col Hedley Basher of the Royals with his successor, Douglas Catto. (Dieppe Blue Beach Every Man

Maps

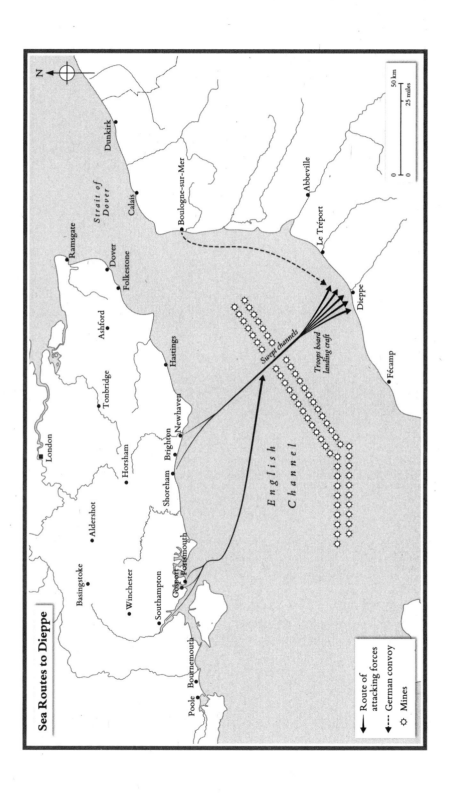

Sea Routes to Dieppe

N

London

Basingstoke

Winchester

Aldershot

Southampton

Bournemouth

Poole

Gosport
Portsmouth

Horsham

Shoreham

Brighton

Newhaven

Tonbridge

Ashford

Hastings

Folkestone

Dover

Ramsgate

Strait of
Dover

Calais

Dunkirk

Boulogne-sur-Mer

Abbeville

Le Tréport

Dieppe

Fécamp

English
Channel

Swept channels

Troops board
landing craft

→ Route of
attacking forces

----- German convoy

✧ Mines

50 km
25 miles

0
0

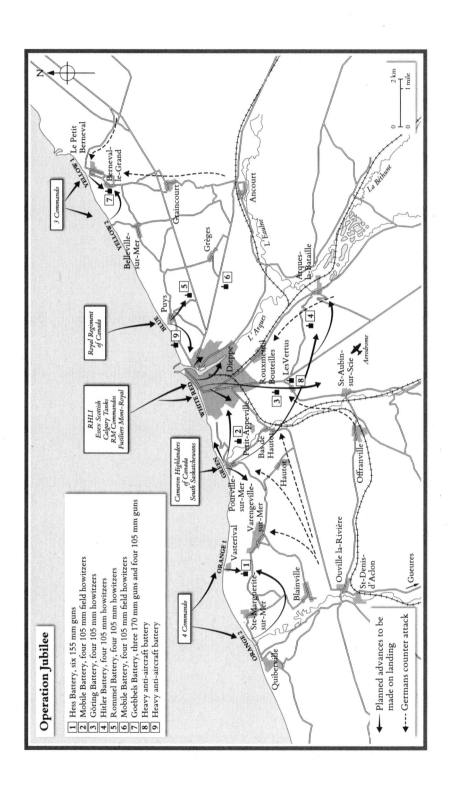

Operation Jubilee

1. Hess Battery, six 155 mm guns
2. Mobile Battery, four 105 mm field howitzers
3. Göring Battery, four 105 mm howitzers
4. Hitler Battery, four 105 mm howitzers
5. Rommel Battery, four 105 mm howitzers
6. Mobile Battery, four 105 mm field howitzers
7. Goebbels Battery, three 170 mm guns and four 105 mm guns
8. Heavy anti-aircraft battery
9. Heavy anti-aircraft battery

Planned advances to be made on landing

--- Germans counter attack

N

0 ____ 2 km
0 ____ 1 mile

3 Commando

YELLOW 1 Le Petit Berneval

Le Petit Berneval

YELLOW 2

Berneval-le-Grand

7

Belleville-sur-Mer

Graincourt

Gréges

Ancourt

La Béthune

L'Eaulne

Arques-la-Bataille

5

6

Royal Regiment of Canada

BLUE Puys

9

Dieppe

Rouxmesnil Bouteilles

LesVertus

L'Arques

8

St-Aubin-sur-Scie

Aerodrome

WHITE RED

RHLI
Essex Scottish
Calgary Tanks
RM Commandos
Fusiliers Mont-Royal

Petit-Appeville

2

Bas de Hautot

3

Cameron Highlanders of Canada
South Saskatchewans

GREEN

Pourville-sur-Mer

Varengeville-sur-Mer

Hautot

Offranville

ORANGE 1 Vasterival

1

Ste-Marguerite-sur-Mer

Blainville

Ouville la-Rivière

St-Denis-d'Aclon

Gueures

4 Commando

ORANGE 2

Quiberville

Introduction

The war had been over for thirteen years when at breakfast tables around the country a small group of former comrades opened the morning post to find a letter from their old chief. He had a favour to ask. The Admiralty was preparing a report on a controversial operation in which they had all been intimately involved when they worked together at Combined Operations Headquarters. He enclosed a draft of the text concerning their part in the drama. 'I cannot help feeling that this does not tell the whole story,' he wrote. He invited suggestions as to how it might be amended 'to put the responsibility . . . fairly and squarely where it belongs', which, he made clear, was not with him or them.[1] He signed off, 'Yours ever, Dickie'.

The writer was Louis Mountbatten and the action in question was Operation Jubilee, the August 1942 raid on Dieppe. The appeal got a generous reception. The old comrades rallied round, and under the supervision of Lord Louis produced a version to his liking. When the Admiralty published its report, the account followed closely the Mountbatten team's narrative of events.

These exchanges took place in the summer and autumn of 1958 when Mountbatten was First Sea Lord and in charge of the Royal Navy. He was officially a great man, created Earl Mountbatten of Burma for his services to victory in South East Asia, and the uniforms he loved to wear were almost ludicrously encrusted with decorations and orders. He was about to take over the newly created post of Chief of the Defence Staff, making him the professional head of the armed forces at a time of great upheaval, and it might be thought that he had little time to waste on the historiography of what in the context of a world war has been seen as only a minor episode.

This was just one example of Mountbatten's attempts to hijack the Jubilee narrative. From the day the operation ended until the close of his life, he hammered away at the construction of a legend that presented Dieppe as a calculated sacrifice in which the losses (which he routinely downplayed) taught hard lessons which were triumphantly justified on D-Day. He made the case so often that it sometimes seemed that the main person he was trying to convince was himself.

Bernard Montgomery, another key player, also kept his sharp blue eyes focussed on accounts of his role in the story, intervening brazenly when he thought his reputation was threatened. In books and interviews he often expressed astonishment at the decision to do without an aerial bombardment before the raid, a move which was later held to have helped to doom the enterprise. Yet it was he who chaired the meeting at which the fateful choice was made.

Mountbatten and Montgomery believed themselves to be men of destiny and had been building their own myths virtually since the day they first put on uniform. Dieppe marred the heroic canvas depicting their wartime achievements, and it was perhaps to be expected that they would take every opportunity to touch up the picture.

Yet their interest concealed deeper concerns. Dieppe was more than just another painful station on the calvary of failure that preceded the Allies' change of fortunes. It was a defeat but also a great human tragedy that to those most closely involved in it seemed to require not just vindication but absolution.

In the summer of 1942 the last thing the Allies needed was another disaster. In the Dieppe raid, that is what they got. The news of the attack produced first surprise, then dismay and finally bewilderment. 'What I don't understand is why Dieppe?' puzzled Major General Percy Hobart in a letter to the military historian and expert Basil Liddell Hart. 'A raid is either "to obtain information" and destroy some worthwhile objective or it is to train one's own troops. In the latter case one would not select a strongly defended sector. In the former, what was the objective? Evidently we did not reach it. It all sounds pretty Passchendaele to me.'[2]

The reference was to the notorious 1917 battle on the Western Front when thousands of Allied troops, many of them Canadians, floundered to their deaths in an ocean of mud. Some of the Jubilee survivors reached for a different episode from British military history to describe what they had endured. It was, they said, 'just like the Charge of the Light Brigade'. The difference was that in this case 6,000 – mostly Canadians – had been sent into the jaws of death, rather than the 670 or so who had charged the Russian guns at Balaclava in 1854. Soon no comparisons were necessary and Dieppe stood in its own right as a metaphor for bloody futility.

Hobart's questions have never been properly answered. In the thousands of official documents generated by the preparations for Jubilee the military objectives of the raid are laid out clearly enough. There is very little that reveals the higher purpose. Almost all the explanations and justifications supplied by those who planned and mounted it came afterwards.

The hole in the story where a clearly stated intention should be has subsequently been filled by several theories. Some have sought to uncover a secret motivation that clears up the mystery, or to explain it through the malign behaviour of a principal actor or actors. This book, while making its own contribution to what we know about why things happened as they did, offers a broader explanation.

Dieppe provides in miniature a display of the way that human qualities, failings and passions that are held in check by the constraints of peacetime tend to run free in times of war. Those at the top were driven by a complicated and sometimes contradictory combination of motives of the sort that only the strange moral ambience of wartime can produce: patriotism and duty, yes, but also reckless ambition.

Jubilee might have been small compared with what was to come but it was big at this stage in the conflict, the largest amphibious assault that Britain had attempted since being driven from the continent. Much more than straightforward military considerations were at stake. Britain was at a crucial new phase of its war, seeking to both impress and restrain its new American allies while managing a tortuous partnership with the Soviet Union. It was having to learn the deference due to powers on whose resources victory ultimately depended.

Jubilee was intimately linked to those realities. Its outcome showed how the pressures of high politics could override military common

sense to generate action at almost any price. In Jubilee the line connecting Churchill's need to keep Stalin and Roosevelt happy and a
shambles of smoking tanks and crumpled bodies on a French beach is
stark and clear.

The losses at Dieppe were, proportionately, among the worst suffered in a single operation in the Allied war in Western Europe. Of
roughly 6,000 ground troops who took part, 3,625 were killed,
wounded or captured. This would have been considered nothing on
the Eastern Front. During the months of July, August and September 1942 the Red Army lost through death, capture, injury and
sickness an average of 27,256 *every day*.[3]

That did not make the Dieppe losses less shocking. The scale of
the operation meant it carries an intimacy and imaginability that the
Russian battles can't convey. They are just too enormous, too distant
and too horrendous to comprehend. But standing on a summer
morning by the sea wall beneath the gardens that run down to the
narrow little beach at Puys where the Royal Regiment of Canada
came ashore, it is very easy to summon up the horror of that day; the
demonic rip of bullets pouring from the defenders' MG34 machine
guns at a rate of fifteen rounds a second, the whistle and thud of
mortars and the humped khaki shapes, swaying face down in waves
clouded with blood.

That the victims were mostly Canadians is one of the elements
that gives the story its heavy tinge of tragedy. The deference which
the British were forced to show to the Russians and Americans did
not apply to Dominion family members. Despite the blood debt
owed by Britain to Canada for its support in the previous war, the
old habits of condescension and the assumption of unquestioning
obedience died hard. Just as at Passchendaele, the Canadians would
pay the price for British mistakes. Their leaders too had a share in the
blame. If, as some said, the troops were martyrs, then those who
commanded them had done much to determine their fate.

In this book, as with all my books, my primary interest is in the
participants and their experience, be they British, Canadian, American, French or German. Each project is an attempt at resurrection.

The challenge is to bring back to life the faces smiling out from the monochrome snaps and show them as they were. We can't know the story without knowing the actors; the stuff they were made of and the forces that drove them on.

I come to the task with some knowledge of war from a former life as a foreign correspondent reporting on conflicts around the globe. The first war I covered was the 1982 recapture by British troops of the Falkland Islands. I went ashore with 42 Royal Marine Commando huddled in a Second World War-style landing craft. Mercifully there were no Argentinian machine-gunners waiting for us as the bow door clattered down and we stepped thigh-deep into the sea. But I can still recall the slap of spray on my face and the metallic tang of fear on my tongue as we ran in, a tiny taste of what the attackers must have felt as they closed the fatal shore.

PART ONE

Prologue
'Tommy kommt'

That Friday morning Georges Guibon did what he did most mornings. He left his house at 41 rue Jean Ribault and set off on a tour of the town. It was 14 August 1942 and the summer was flagging. The air was heavy and the leaves on the trees were coated with dust. He turned left along the terraced street and headed north up rue du Général Chanzy towards the seafront.

Guibon's shrewd eyes took in all around him. He was fifty-six years old and before the Germans came was director of the local chamber of commerce. He was 'Dieppois' born and bred but he also knew the wider world. His father once owned the Hôtel de Paris, one of the best in town, and as a young man he had been sent to Switzerland, England and Germany to learn the trade and the languages. His knowledge of German came in useful for eavesdropping as he made his daily round, not too fast to miss anything and not too slow to attract attention, looking and listening, writing it all down in the diary he kept to record 'the stuff they don't tell you about in the newspapers'.[1]

He paused at the junction of the place Carnot waiting for the jeeps and trucks to pass. To the left stood a memorial put up after the Franco-Prussian War of bronze infantrymen clutching rifles, bracing to repel the invader. But the invaders were here now and had been for more than two years. Every day they looked down on the monument from the windows of an old school on the west side of the square, now requisitioned as a military headquarters and festooned with swastika flags. The occupation no longer seemed like an aberration that would one day pass. It had started to feel normal.

Guibon crossed to the rue de Sygogne and entered the Old Town. The streets here were narrow with brick houses rising above bars, restaurants and shops, most of them shuttered and empty. They backed onto a broad promenade, nearly a mile long and lined with hotels and boarding houses. Beyond that was the beach, a steep pebbly rampart that shelved down to the English Channel.

In summers before the war Dieppe would have been crammed with tourists. It was very popular with the English, who arrived by the hundreds every day on the packet boat from Newhaven sixty-eight miles across the Channel to play golf, go to the horse races, drink an apéritif in the cafés on the old port and dine in one of the many restaurants before perhaps stopping off for a flutter at the casino before bedtime.

That seemed like a dream now. Dieppe was half empty and the town had been turned into a fortress. The beach where holiday-makers swam and sunbathed was strung with barbed wire and the promenade studded with concrete pillboxes bristling with machine guns. According to the collaborationist newspapers, the only ones on sale, the 'Anglo-Saxon' tourists who once thronged the place were now the enemy. It was the Germans who were France's real friends.

The Germans had marched in unopposed on the morning of 8 June 1940. The occupiers at first promised to act 'correctly' but expected total obedience. They spread themselves across the town and villages, requisitioning houses, businesses, factories and vehicles. Everything was ordered for their convenience. Bars and restaurants were closed to local people after 9 p.m. but stayed open to serve the garrison as they came off watch. In Madame Lili's brothel next to the fish market, country girls whose fathers and brothers were locked up in German prisoner-of-war camps attended to the needs of the occupiers.

On every wall was a proclamation in heavy Gothic type ordering the population to do this or forbidding them to do that, threatening dire penalties if disobeyed. The punishment for any serious act of resistance was death.

The occupiers were digging themselves into the landscape. Since the start of the year they had been covering the coast with concrete, building new positions and strengthening existing ones. Nature had done much of the Germans' work for them. The town was easy to defend. It lay in a mile-wide cleft in a natural rampart of chalk cliffs up to 200 feet high. Everywhere there were vantage points from which to observe all approaches from which the enemy could launch an amphibious attack and bombard them when they arrived.

The east and west headlands were barnacled with artillery batteries and machine-gun and mortar posts. Caves in the cliff faces hid guns mounted on rails that were difficult for an attacker to spot and virtually impossible to hit. Down below, streets leading from the town to the promenade were barred by roadblocks mounted with machine and anti-tank guns.

The Germans were not yet satisfied with their preparations. As Guibon walked down the rue de Sygogne heading for the sea the sound of explosions rolled towards him. They came from the casino, at the western end of the promenade where engineer teams had started to demolish the colonnaded pleasure dome to widen the field of fire.

Guibon got as close as he could, loitering by a pair of German officers long enough to hear their conversation. 'They were smiling as they looked at the houses round about,' he wrote in his diary. 'The tiles on the front had all been smashed by the blasts from the dynamite they were using to destroy the west wing of the casino. I heard one of them say, "Everything's going to be blown up." '

He reached the front and turned right to walk along the strip of the promenade, which was open to civilians during the day. A rifle range was set up on the beach and a row of soldiers lay belly down, blasting at the targets. All around, work parties lugged boxes of ammunition to the machine-gun posts.

Something was rattling the Germans' usual composure. 'It's obvious that they are really worked up and are expecting the "Tommies",' Guibon noted that night. 'There's a lot of alarming chatter running about – "the English have landed at Saint-Valery" [a port twenty miles to the west], "the Americans have landed 8,000 men" etc. . . . They are constantly on the alert, carrying out manoeuvres and marches from which they return exhausted. At night the villages round about are closed off by tank traps and rolls of barbed wire.'

But the weekend passed without incident. Then on the afternoon of Monday 17 August, American bombers struck Rouen, the regional capital forty miles to the south. Their target was the railway junction and surrounding stations but inevitably bombs went astray killing and wounding civilians.

It was, Guibon wrote, a 'terrible bombardment . . . all these tragic happenings are shaking the population who are expecting some serious event'. So too, it was clear, were the Germans. He saw them 'pointing at the sky repeating to each other "*Tommy kommt.*" [Tommy is coming.] They are running about everywhere, always on the alert. They never put down their rifles and are always looking upwards.' They were convinced a landing by the British was imminent, 'telling each other: "they must – they have no other choice"'.

Though they desperately wanted this to be true, Guibon and his friends were not convinced. 'It is possible,' he wrote before going to bed on the night of Tuesday 18 August. The British prime minister had after all just ended a five-day conference in Moscow with Stalin whose angry appeals for help from his allies to relieve pressure on the Eastern Front had been broadcast to the world. 'After Churchill's trip to Russia it's plausible, but we don't believe it.'

A few hours later he was proved wrong. At four o'clock, unable to sleep, he heard 'gunfire, probably coming from the sea which went on for half an hour. Then towards 04.50 the increasing growl of aero engines and the racket of furious anti-aircraft fire.' He looked out of the window to see the German official who was billeted with him standing in the street, gazing up at glittering fountains of anti-aircraft fire. He 'dodged back indoors and as I came down the stairs he asked me: "*Haben sie ein Keller?*" [Do you have a cellar?]' It was with some satisfaction that Guibon replied '*Nein.*' Thus began what Guibon called the 'most terrible awakening that we have ever known'.

1.   Now or Never

The Chief of the Imperial General Staff (CIGS) General Sir Alan Brooke looked out at the world through heavy, horn-rimmed glasses. He was always inclined to pessimism but Britain's situation in the spring of 1942 filled him with something close to despair. On the evening of 31 March he confided to his diary: 'During the last fortnight I have had for the first time since the war started a growing conviction that we are going to lose.' It was 'all desperately depressing . . . There are times when I wish to God I had not been placed at the helm of a ship that seems to be heading inevitably for the rocks.'[1]

Brooke had been the professional head of the army for four months and had inherited a daunting situation. In the two and a half years since the war began British troops had failed to win a single battle against the Germans. There was nothing to suggest that their fortunes were about to change. Having been thrown out of Norway, Belgium, France, Greece, Hong Kong and Singapore they were now struggling to defend Egypt against the numerically weaker but militarily superior Afrika Korps led by Erwin Rommel.

The year had opened with a succession of disasters. Singapore was the strategic cornerstone of Britain's eastern empire. It was supposed to be impregnable but in the middle of February the garrison surrendered to a Japanese attacking force half its size. As the bastion fell, three of the German navy's principal warships left their berths at Brest on the French Atlantic coast and, under the noses of the Royal Navy, dashed up the English Channel to safety in home ports. These episodes were not just defeats but humiliations, engendering a national mood of pessimism and self-doubt.

Brooke's malaise was felt everywhere in Britain that season. The elation of survival had faded, replaced by a realisation of the huge difficulties and sacrifices that lay ahead. 'What is wrong with the nation's spirit may be a matter for diagnosis, but that the wrong is there is incontestable,' declared an editorial in the conservative *Spectator*.[2] 'Virtue somehow, for some reason, has gone out of us. The national fibre is unmistakably different from what it was in those days in 1940 which the Prime Minister could speak of, in accents that carried universal conviction, as our finest hour. No one can pretend we are living through our finest hour today.'

Faith in Churchill and his coalition government was waning. A Gallup poll published on 1 April suggested that half the voters were dissatisfied with the way the war was being run.[3] The fact that Britain was locked in a fight for its life had not changed the savage rules of politics. Some inside the prime minister's own party sensed his waning strength and were wondering whether the time had come to make their move. Churchill knew very well the danger he was in. The black dog of depression was a frequent visitor now and those closest to him watched with concern as he swung between noisy ebullience and troughs of pessimism and doubt. 'Papa is at a very low ebb,' wrote his daughter Mary in her diary, two weeks after Singapore fell. 'He is not too well physically and he is worn down by the continuous crushing pressure of events.'[4]

The Singapore disaster, 'the greatest in our history' as he admitted to President Roosevelt, sapped his will to go on. Weeks afterwards, his physician Sir Charles Wilson found him 'stupefied' by the event, discovering him wrapped in his towel in his bathroom staring at the floor and muttering, 'I cannot get over Singapore.'[5] At times he seemed to think that the game he had played so well for so long was almost up. 'I am like a bomber pilot,' he told Malcolm MacDonald, the British High Commissioner to Canada. 'I go out night after night, and I know that one night I shall not return.'[6]

Churchill was starting to look like yesterday's man. His performance in 1940 might have won him his place in history but was he fitted to steer the country from survival to victory? For that perhaps a different style of leader was needed, someone who pointed the way to the creation of a more equitable post-war Britain rather than the preservation of a status quo ante that for many held few happy memories. In the spring of 1942 people were ready to look beyond conventional candidates to articulate their mood. They found one in the unlikely figure of Sir Stafford Cripps.

In appearance and style he could scarcely have been more different to the prime minister. Churchill was stout and Cripps bony. This was unsurprising. Cripps was a vegetarian and ate one meal a day, typically vegetables, sour milk, wholemeal bread and butter and an occasional baked potato, and he neither drank nor smoked. Churchill started the day with a cooked breakfast accompanied by a weak whisky and sometimes finished it in bed with a bowl of consommé, even if he had just got back from dinner. In between he liked the plain but expensive fare he was brought up on: roast beef and chicken, grouse, pheasant, venison and the occasional lobster. All this was washed down with champagne, claret, burgundy, port and brandy and finished off with a ten-inch Havana cigar.[7]

Churchill behaved like a prima donna. He could humiliate a subordinate one minute and love-bomb them the next, switching moods to dominate all around him. Cripps was dry and preacherly and his apparent sincerity carried its own strong charge. And whereas Churchill's appeal was rooted in a vision of Britain's past, Cripps's persona and beliefs seemed to speak to the future.

Richard Stafford Cripps was born in 1889 into an upper-middle-class family with progressive ideas. Between the wars he made a fortune at the Bar, enjoyed luxury cruises in the Mediterranean and owned a country estate. Yet he was also a revolutionary Marxist, a position he somehow squared with intense Christian beliefs. Ramsay MacDonald had appointed him Solicitor General in the 1929–31 Labour government but his steady move to the left and pro-communist sympathies got him expelled from the party in 1939. These same beliefs commended him to Churchill and when he formed his coalition government in May 1940 he had made Cripps Britain's ambassador to Moscow where he played a crucial role in forging the Anglo-Soviet alliance of 1941.

When Cripps left for Moscow he was relatively unknown and not much admired. When he returned to London in January 1942 public interest in him and his mission was intense. He described his

experiences in a series of broadcasts praising the spirit he witnessed in
Russia and contrasting it with the attitude he found at home. He
wanted to make his listeners understand 'the differences between
the fortunes of war as you have experienced them and as they have
been suffered by millions of our Russian allies'.[8] The Soviet masses
had responded with 'self-sacrificing heroism . . . giving their lives
and their labour' and rejecting black marketeers – a contrast to the
'tolerance which is shown in this country . . .' Since his return he
had felt 'a lack of urgency. I may be wrong but I feel it in the atmosphere in contrast to what I felt in Russia.' He urged his listeners to
'unstinted sacrifice' without 'slackness or selfishness' in order to win
a war that was 'the brutal negation of every teaching of our Christian
civilisation'.

His first talk was on the BBC's *Postscript* programme broadcast just
after the nine o'clock news and was listened to by half the country's
adults. Almost all approved of the content.[9] The language he used
was plain, the rhetorical opposite of Churchill's. It seemed that
people were no longer in the mood for the florid and the grandiose.
Their ears were tuned for a simpler message and Cripps appeared to
have found the right wavelength to reach them.

Since his return his standing had soared. A poll taken in April 1942
put him just behind the Foreign Secretary Anthony Eden should
Churchill for any reason quit the scene.[10] Much of his appeal came
from his association with Russia. In his *ushanka* fur hat, Cripps
seemed almost like an honorary member of the Politburo. Direct
experience had tempered some of his early enthusiasm for commun-
ism but blind spots still remained. In an address to the nation for the
Pathé Gazette newsreel he set out to calm the fears of 'some people in
this country who are still afraid of the spread of the Russian ideol-
ogy', telling them: 'As a matter of fact, the Soviet Union [has] no
idea and no wish to interfere with the internal affairs of any other
country. I know that from the lips of Stalin himself . . .'[11]

Cripps's admiration was increasingly shared by the British public.
Russia's grip on the public imagination was becoming a source of
concern in high places. The fact that for the first twenty-two months
of the war the Soviet Union had been Germany's de facto ally did not

seem to matter and the two were enemies now only because Hitler had turned on Stalin. Yet as Brooke noted drily 'many seemed to imagine that Russia had only come into the war for our benefit!'[12] Nonetheless the public recognised that the Red Army was now doing most of the fighting and suffering enormous losses as they struggled to push the Germans back.

Public morale was monitored by Ministry of Information teams. In the early months of 1942 they were struck by both the depth of public disillusionment and the rising regard for Russia. The Home Intelligence Division weekly report for 9–16 March on the 'general state of confidence and reaction to news' recorded that 'a depression verging on apathy appear[s] to predominate . . . neither civilians nor members of the Services "know for what aims they are sacrificing their labour and their lives" '.[13]

This contrasted with the 'continued admiration for Russia, confidence in her ultimate victory, and a continued tendency on the part of the public to compare Russia's achievements with our own setbacks'. The censors who spied on private mail reported that: 'The majority of writers seem to pin their faith almost entirely on the Russians – "the chaps who don't talk but keep on killing Huns" '. A 'large number of writers' expressed the view that 'if we had some of the Russian spirit and some of the Russian generals we would win this war in half the time'.

Spirit alone though was not enough. Winter had slowed but not stopped the fighting on the Eastern Front. The thaw was coming and with it the inevitable resumption of the German onslaught. Russia's situation was desperate. To hold out it needed all the help that Britain and America could give.

From the late summer of 1941 British convoys had been shipping tanks and fighter aircraft via the Arctic Ocean to Archangel and Murmansk. Whatever was given was never enough and instead of gratitude the government received ever shriller demands.

Stalin wanted much more than materiel. He was insisting, not just in private messages but in public statements, on a military intervention in the West – the opening of a 'second front' which would force the Germans to divert major resources away from the East. Behind the appeal was a warning. If help was not forthcoming, he hinted, he was prepared to consider making a separate peace with Hitler.

Moscow's demands were amplified by politicians and the press not just in Britain but in America and Canada. As the weeks passed, the clamour grew for a 'Second Front Now!' Leading the chorus in Britain was one of Churchill's closest cronies, the mischief-making Canadian press baron Lord Beaverbrook, until recently minister of aircraft production in the War Cabinet and owner of the mass circulation *Daily Express*, which he used to promote an early invasion of the continent. The pre-war arch appeaser was now Russia's best friend. 'Beaverbrook came in the evening,' noted the Soviet ambassador to London Ivan Maisky in his diary on 2 March. 'If there's anything Stalin wants, Beaverbrook is always at his disposal . . .'[14]

A fortnight later Maisky had lunch at Chequers with Churchill and the Foreign Secretary Anthony Eden. There he relayed an urgent appeal from Stalin for action. Moscow believed that the war would be decided in 1942 and Maisky spelled out the reasoning simply and starkly:

> A crucial moment in the course of the war really is approaching . . .
> How do things stand? Germany is preparing an enormous offensive
> this spring. She is staking everything on this year. If we succeed in
> defeating the German offensive this spring, then in essence we will
> have won the war . . . It would only remain for us to finish off the
> crazed beast . . . Now, suppose we fail . . . Suppose the Red Army is
> forced to retreat again, that we begin to lose territories once more,
> that the Germans break through to the Caucasus – what then? For
> Hitler will not stop at the Caucasus . . . He will go farther – to Iran,
> Turkey, Egypt, India. He will link hands with Japan somewhere in
> the Indian Ocean and stretch out his arms towards Africa. Germany's
> problems with oil, raw materials and food will be resolved. The Brit-
> ish Empire will collapse . . . What would be our chances of victory?
> And when? . . . That is the choice before us! It's now or never![15]

Churchill and his military chiefs needed no convincing of the credibility of this scenario. Something would have to be done. But the truth was that the slim resources available to them made it impossible to mount an operation of the scale needed to force a significant switch of German resources away from the Eastern Front. To be effective it would have to be aimed at somewhere of vital strategic importance to Germany and that meant France or the Low Countries. The enemy coast was only twenty-one miles away. The obvious place to strike was somewhere in northern France, the Pas de Calais or Normandy. The truth was that Britain had nothing like the quantities of trained men, guns and equipment required to launch such an operation and would not have them for many months to come. 'This universal cry to start a western front is going to be hard to compete with,' wrote Brooke on 30 March, 'and yet what can we do with some ten divisions against the German masses?'[16]

Despite the pessimism at the top, Britain was now in a much better strategic position than it had been five months before. Churchill's main object since the war began had been to get the United States to join the British Empire as a belligerent in the fight against Hitler. He had used every wile and blandishment to lure them in but in the end it was Japan that decided the issue. Since the attack on Pearl Harbor in December 1941 Britain and America had been partners, and in the space of four months had achieved a remarkable degree of agreement. However, there were still fundamental differences over timing and geography that blocked the formation of a mutual long-term strategic plan. By the spring of 1942 the gratitude that Churchill and the military felt towards the Americans was tempered by frustration at their new ally's reluctance to passively accept British proposals for when and where the war should now be fought.

The magical change in Britain's fortunes came at a cost. Henceforth, US interests, desires and strategic appreciations would play an increasing role in shaping the big decisions. The US would be providing the bulk of the troops, the materiel and the money to make victory possible. Britain was saved but the price of her salvation was autonomy and when America spoke, she had to listen.

Churchill found it hard to accept the new reality. Six days after Pearl Harbor he invited himself to Washington and took a battleship across the Atlantic to meet President Roosevelt. He was in a hurry to get to him before Roosevelt and his team had time to settle on their own policy for running the war. An informal agreement had already been reached in early 1941 at a secret conference between American, British and Canadian senior staff officers held in Washington known as 'ABC-1'. It assumed that if war broke out between the USA and Germany, America would probably also find itself at war with Italy and Japan. In that case, it made geographical sense to join forces with Britain to concentrate on beating Germany and Italy first. The logic was that defeating Japan would not make that much difference to the war against Germany. Beating Germany, though, would mean the rapid end of Japan. The strategic focus should therefore be on the 'Atlantic Theatre' of Europe and Africa. The argument was cemented when Churchill and Roosevelt met for their first face-to-face encounter at Placentia Bay in Newfoundland in August 1941 and the 'Germany first' doctrine was reaffirmed.

But that was then. The devastation done to the Pacific Fleet by the Japanese bombers at Pearl Harbor four months later had inflamed public opinion. Churchill worried that Roosevelt would fold under pressure from the public, politicians and the military to forget Europe for the time being and set about dealing retribution to the perpetrators.

As the *Duke of York* butted into south-westerly gales, Churchill prowled the mess decks, wreathed in cigar smoke, apparently deaf to the cacophony of groaning metal and shrieking wind. The British were in no position to withstand a delay while America dealt with the Japanese. 'We were conscious of a serious danger,' wrote Churchill afterwards, 'that the United States might pursue the war against Japan in the Pacific and leave us to fight Germany and Italy in Europe, Africa, and in the Middle East.'[17]

Churchill and his entourage arrived in Washington on 22 December. The prime minister stayed at the White House and made himself at home, rejecting the Lincoln Bedroom awarded him by the president's wife Eleanor in favour of the Rose Suite and alienating the domestic staff with his rudeness and demands. With the president he was on his best behaviour. After a banquet on the first evening the two retired with their close advisers to the Oval Office to get down to business. By the time they went to bed, two major issues had been resolved and Churchill's worst fears had subsided. America, it seemed, would stick to the 'Europe first' plan. And Roosevelt appeared to have agreed to Churchill's proposals that they open their joint campaign with an Anglo-American invasion of French-held North Africa, an operation code-named Gymnast.

Beneath the surface bonhomie lay a seam of mutual disregard and suspicion. The US generals and admirals found the British strangely self-satisfied given they had so far suffered mainly defeats in the war and were there to seek American help. They also suspected that their new allies regarded them primarily as a bottomless reservoir of men and materiel that would be used to pursue the selfish interests of Britain and its empire.

The senior army, navy and air-force officers accompanying the prime minister looked on their hosts with affectionate condescension. 'The country has not – repeat not – the slightest conception of what the war means, and their armed forces are more unready for war than it is possible to imagine' was the verdict of Sir John Dill, lately sacked as army chief by Churchill to make way for Brooke but present as an adviser.[18]

The Arcadia Conference lasted more than three weeks and on the whole was a remarkable success. By the end the two sides had worked out a rough plan for how they would pursue the next two years of the war. They agreed a system of united command in each theatre of the war and an overall control mechanism to allow those commands to function in the shape of a single Combined Chiefs of Staff committee sitting in Washington. They ramped up American industry to its maximum war-making capacity and agreed how the results should be allocated.

But although most of Churchill's agenda had been accepted, a crucial point of contention remained: when and where would the Allies start the reconquest of Europe?

On the voyage over Churchill had produced a paper called 'the campaign of 1943' in which he ventured to 'hope, even if no German collapse occurs beforehand, to win the war at the end of 1943 or 1944'.[19] There were three stages to the strategy. The first was 'closing the ring' by gaining control of French West Africa and the whole of the southern Mediterranean coastline from Tunis to Egypt, by the end of 1942. Next came 'liberating the populations', by encouraging revolt among the conquered nations and inside Germany itself. The third phase was the 'final assault on the German citadel', when Allied forces would make 'three or four' landings around the edges of Europe to join up with resistance forces, who would 'supply the corpus of the liberating offensive'. These operations were to be timed to coincide with the uprisings.

Roosevelt appeared to have supported the first proposition by seeming to approve of Operation Gymnast. But Churchill and his team soon learned it was unwise to treat an initial agreement by the president on anything as final. He might be commander-in-chief of the armed forces but he showed more deference to the American service chiefs than Churchill did to his. The man whose opinion mattered most to him was General George Marshall, the army chief of staff. Marshall was stern, ascetic and dedicated, a paragon of duty and honour. He had a reputation for utter candour, a trait that at times had seemed likely to terminate his early career.

In 1917 he was serving in France as a major on the staff of the American 1st Infantry Division when the Expeditionary Force commander General Pershing came to inspect them. Pershing was dissatisfied and humiliated the divisional commander in front of his subordinates. Marshall protested and when Pershing ignored him and tried to depart, he grabbed his arm and forced the general to listen, telling him it was Pershing's own headquarters which was the source of the problems. Instead of sacking him as all around expected, Pershing listened. He began to seek Marshall's advice on 1st Division matters and eventually chose him as an aide.[20]

Marshall was never persuaded by Gymnast, thinking it a waste of time and resources. He was also deeply sceptical of Churchill's second proposition and strongly opposed to the third. He simply did not believe that people living under Nazi rule would be willing or able to mount a serious threat to the conquerors. The Allies would have to liberate Europe unaided, and not by a strategy of scattered invasions but in a single, overwhelming attack that would drive on to Berlin. The sooner it came the better.

Marshall took the Russians' warnings very seriously. The longer a continental invasion was delayed, the greater the likelihood that the Soviet Union would either collapse or be forced to seek terms with Hitler. Despite Britain's patent unpreparedness and the fact that the first American troops had only just arrived in the United Kingdom, a major operation had to be launched to relieve the Red Army. The enemy had to be struck at the closest point and that meant a cross-Channel invasion, preferably before 1942 was out. Marshall had recently reorganised the War Department to create an engine room for action called the Operational Plans Division. It was commanded by Major General Dwight D. Eisenhower, whom Marshall now tasked with drawing up proposals.

When the Prime Minister and his advisers left for home on a flying boat on 16 January 1942 the British and American positions were unbridged. Churchill had gone to Washington to 'show the president how to run the war', wrote his personal physician on the trip, Sir Charles Wilson. 'It has not worked out quite that way.'

The Americans had confirmed the crucial principle of 'Germany first' but their acquiescence came with a proviso. What they really meant was 'Germany first, and soon'. They were in a hurry, and their impatience filled Churchill and his military chiefs with anxiety. Defeat after defeat had at least taught them one vital lesson: overwhelming force was needed to beat the Germans. Going into battle with anything less than the most favourable odds was certain to end in disaster. Physically and psychologically Britain was in no condition to withstand another setback. They were therefore dead set against a premature invasion, which they were sure would end in failure resulting in a collapse of morale and a lengthy – perhaps permanent – postponement of final victory. They were determined to go at their own pace, but if they were to keep their new allies tied to the grand strategic principle of prioritising Europe over the Pacific, the Americans would have to be played along, reined in and then let down gently. It was, Churchill mused when in his cups, 'like wooing a woman'. But America was still a long way from melting into his embrace.

★

The chiefs of staff understood that words alone would not silence the demands for action from Moscow and Washington. They would have to come up with options for some sort of major operation that year, no matter how wasteful or illogical. At the least it would serve as a gesture of good faith and a proof they were serious about launching a proper invasion as soon as circumstances allowed. By early spring the prospect of Russia breaking with the Allies had become a real concern. It was the chief topic of conversation at a dinner on 5 March at Downing Street. Present were the Churchills, Brooke, Anthony and Clarissa Eden and the production minister Oliver Lyttelton. Brooke noted that Eden was 'apparently nervous lest Russia should make peace with [the] Germans'.[21] After dinner there was 'discussion of [an] offensive in France to relieve pressure on [the] Russians'.

This was the signal for a flurry of action. Churchill followed up the next day with an urgent memo demanding to know 'what could be done if it became imperative to carry out a holding operation in France in, say, July 1942 with the object of keeping Russia in the war'.[22] At that day's Chiefs of Staff Committee – the cerebral cortex of the British war-making machine where the heads of the army, navy and air force came together every day to review progress and take the big decisions – the Commander-in-Chief, Home Forces, General Sir Bernard Paget, was brought in to discuss 'preparations for a very large-scale raid in France in May or June'.

The Russian situation had already prompted a proposal from the War Office for an emergency landing of at least six divisions in France to relieve pressure on the Eastern Front. Paget, whose command would supply the troops, and the chief of RAF Fighter Command Sholto Douglas, whose squadrons would provide the air power, argued that it should take place in the Pas de Calais. Other strong voices insisted that that coast was too strongly protected and it must be launched much further west in Normandy where defences were weaker and troops thinner on the ground. Either proposition was high-risk, bordering on suicidal. It was essentially a sacrifice, offering up Britain's skeleton army in the higher cause of keeping Russia in the war. Under the code name Operation Sledgehammer this project would grow in scope and duration in the next few months. The Americans were more positive about its chances, however, and Sledgehammer would become a cause of friction.

Another possibility emerged when the chiefs met on 10 March to examine 'the problem of assistance to Russia by operations in France, with a large raid or lodgement'.[23] With so few trained divisions on hand they could not afford to throw any of them away on an enterprise like Sledgehammer.

A more modest attack might still do the Russians some good. Fighter Command was strong and in daily action over the French coast trying to force the Luftwaffe to come up and engage in a battle of attrition. A large raid launched at an objective in easy reach of the fighter bases in south-east England could generate a major clash that would severely weaken the Germans' air strength and compel them to bring in reinforcements. The chiefs concluded that the 'only hope was to try to draw off air forces from Russia and that for this purpose [the] raid must be carried out on the Calais front' and Brooke directed 'investigations to proceed further'.

The matter was not settled there. Sledgehammer kept resurfacing along with other proposals and from mid-March the question of the size, shape and location of a cross-Channel operation was continually debated. Were the raiders to hit and run or try to establish a permanent lodgement? Should they focus on the Pas de Calais where large-scale air support was possible, or the Cherbourg Peninsula in Normandy which was further from German troop concentrations but where it would be harder to provide fighter cover?

The debate carried a note of desperation that was evident in a proposal code-named Imperator. This was a plan to launch a division of assault troops supported by armoured units to take and hold Boulogne or a similar port, then drive a large mobile force towards Paris where they would destroy German military headquarters before falling back to be evacuated from a different port. It was a fantastic scenario, which to succeed would have required outstanding skill, phenomenal good luck and extraordinary incompetence on the part of the enemy, none of which had been at all in evidence in Britain's war to date.

The news that Marshall was coming to Britain to thrash out an agreed joint military timetable brought the issue to a head. He was bringing with him a memorandum for action largely based on recommendations produced at the Planning Division by Eisenhower. Like his boss, Eisenhower was spurred by fear of a Russian collapse, noting in his diary, 'we've got to do it – go after Germany's vitals – while Russia's still in the war'. On 25 March, he presented his proposal to Marshall, who gave it his approval. It called for a full-scale invasion of the continent on 1 April 1943 by thirty American and eighteen British divisions who would be carried across the Channel in 7,000 landing craft. The target area was between Boulogne and Le Havre. It was a highly ambitious plan. American troops had only just begun to cross the Atlantic, the landing craft had yet to be built and their construction was still low on the US Navy's priority list. Marshall nonetheless gave Roundup, as the plan was code-named, his backing. His support for it was perhaps less a realistic aspiration than a wish to jolt the British out of a caution that to American eyes sometimes looked like complacency. Eisenhower also backed a Sledgehammer-style emergency scheme to be launched by an Anglo-American force of five divisions if Russia looked close to collapse or – a very unlikely scenario – the Germans' position suddenly critically weakened.

Marshall was due to arrive in Britain on 8 April, together with President Roosevelt's closest adviser, Harry Hopkins. Clearly a major amphibious assault of some sort was on the horizon. Fortunately there was an organisation whose business it was to plan, mount and launch such operations, and that was proving to be rather good at it.

2.   Lord Louis

Visitors to the Combined Operations Headquarters building at 1a Richmond Terrace, just off Whitehall in the centre of London, were frequently impressed by the atmosphere of bustle and purpose that seemed to swirl through its corridors. One new recruit arriving in late March 1942 noted 'a refreshing breeziness and a feeling that at last the war was getting somewhere'.[1] The staff were still basking in the afterglow of a successful operation. A few days before, a commando force had attacked the French Atlantic port of Saint-Nazaire, blowing up a gigantic dry dock and denying Hitler a repair berth for his last remaining battleship. The raid had been planned and mounted by COHQ. Its effects on the battle to keep the Atlantic sea lanes open would turn out to be slight, but in the meantime it provided a morale boost for a public battered by setbacks and failures. It was, purred the prime minister, a 'brilliant and heroic exploit'.[2]

The coup was the most spectacular yet in a series pulled off by Combined Ops since it had come under the command of Lord Louis Mountbatten the previous autumn. Its new standing was reflected in an extraordinary boost to the status of the new chief. A few weeks previously Winston Churchill had made Mountbatten the fourth permanent member of the Chiefs of Staff Committee. The appointment came with a promotion. Mountbatten leapfrogged two levels from his current rank of commodore to acting vice admiral, which, as he delightedly told his daughter Patricia, made him the youngest vice admiral in the Royal Navy since Horatio Nelson.[3] And in generous recognition of the fact that Mountbatten's organisation embraced all three services, the prime minister was throwing in the honorary ranks of lieutenant general and air marshal for good measure.

Wartime collapsed conventional notions of seniority but this was still quite a jump. Mountbatten was only forty-one and a greenhorn compared to the men he was joining. The current committee chairman was his old chief, the First Sea Lord and professional head of the Royal Navy Sir Dudley Pound who at sixty-four had a lifetime of staff and active service experience. Air Chief Marshal Sir Charles Portal, Chief of the Air Staff, was at forty-eight the closest to Mountbatten's age, though he was a veteran of the Western Front where he flew light bombers. His last appointment had been as head of Bomber Command and in service and Whitehall matters was vastly more experienced than the newcomer. Pound was about to be replaced in the chair by the CIGS Alan Brooke, whose good opinion Mountbatten most needed if he was to survive and prosper.

Brooke was then fifty-eight, and had commanded the guns in some of the great Western Front battles of the 1914–18 war. He was from a grand Ulster landowning family, steeped in centuries of Protestantism and soldiering. In public he was abrupt and demanding, expecting everyone to come up to his own standards of application and efficiency, a rather forbidding figure whom 'men admired, feared, and liked . . . in that order, perhaps'.[4] In private he was surprisingly emotionally needy and hated being parted from his adored wife Benita. Nature provided a refuge from the world of men and he studied and photographed birds obsessively. His life's passions were distilled in a single diary entry. 'This morning I went to a demonstration of booby traps prepared by the 4th Div[ision],' he wrote to Benita from France on 16 April 1940 while waiting for the Germans to attack. 'In the afternoon I went for a walk in the woods nearby and imagined you were at my side. We discussed the lovely carpet of anemones, and all the nice green young shoots. In the garden M. Rosette has found a blackbird's nest that I am watching. I wish I could take photographs of it.'[5]

Neither Brooke nor any of the other chiefs disliked Mountbatten. They knew him well from his frequent attendance at their meetings in his previous capacity as adviser on Combined Operations and were as susceptible as everyone else to his famous charm. That did not mean they altogether welcomed his great leap forward. Pound had advised Churchill against the appointment, warning that it would undermine his own authority as navy chief. Brooke 'enjoyed Dicky's presence' at meetings, even though he was apt to waste 'both his own time and ours'.[6] He feared his permanent inclusion in the Chiefs of

Staff Committee would be a drag on the smooth working of the machine and felt 'there was no justification for this move'.

Resistance, they all knew, was futile. Churchill had added a note to the memo announcing the change stating that while they were welcome to discuss the appointment as much as they liked, 'I trust they will find themselves generally able to agree.'[7] So it was that from 5 March 1942, Louis Mountbatten could count his membership of Britain's highest military council as another conquered peak on his epic ascent of the heights of power and command.

Mountbatten was wealthy and high-born but as hungry for success and fame as the lowliest *arriviste*. He was the second son of Prince Louis of Battenberg, and his mother, Princess Victoria of Hesse and by Rhine, was the granddaughter of Queen Victoria. The branches of his family tree were intertwined with most of the royal houses of Europe. Yet all his life he was gripped by an ambition that seemed insatiable. Some explained it as a desire to avenge his father who was forced to step down as First Sea Lord in 1914 because of anti-German feeling. Mountbatten pursued his upward trajectory long after he had avenged the slight. The truth, more likely, was that he was simply made that way.

He was obsessed with titles, ranks, uniforms and decorations and no distinction was too small to matter. In 1943, as he was leaving Combined Operations to take charge of South East Asia Command, he asked Brooke for a small favour. The honorary ranks bestowed on him by Churchill had given him the idea of adorning his tropical uniforms with army and air-force buttons as well as navy ones. He had approached the king for permission and 'HM . . . gave his approval and was kind enough to say he liked the idea very much.'[8] However, for Mountbatten, ordinary buttons would not do. 'I should, therefore, be so grateful,' he wrote, 'if you would send me one of your own buttons that I might wear. Luckily colour, shape and size are sufficiently like the naval uniform not to draw attention.' He added: 'You can, of course, rely on me to avoid making any sort of "stunt" of this.'

Such things mattered to Mountbatten. The foible might be

considered unimportant or funny. It was also a small sign of the self-regard that coloured all his thoughts and actions, private and public. In wartime, in a position of great authority which gathered the lives of thousands of men in his hands, the consequences could be fatal.

Mountbatten was married to Edwina Ashley who when they wed in 1922 was the richest heiress in Britain. Her money bought them fine houses in town and country, fast cars, yachts, speedboats and polo ponies. She was tall and raw-boned, lively and sensuous. He was lean and athletic, his good looks slightly marred by eyes that as one of his senior officers at COHQ Robert Henriques bitchily observed were 'smallish' and 'too close together by only a fraction'.[9] Between them the pair were the incarnation of glamour, a quality that the interwar world could not get enough of. Their friends were not just the rich and the smart on both sides of the Atlantic, but the brightest talents in show business, stars like Charlie Chaplin, Douglas Fairbanks and Noël Coward. Being gay or left wing was no bar to the couple's company providing you were amusing or attractive, or preferably both.

Edwina was not much interested in her two daughters. In the interwar years she led a purposeless existence filling the void with love affairs and endless travel. Dickie was a doting father but his navy career meant long absences. He eventually took lovers of his own. Each accepted the other's infidelities and accommodated their priorities in life, and the marriage, despite rocky patches, on the whole worked well.

Beneath the surface nonchalance Mountbatten was serious and phenomenally energetic. Writing in March 1941 to his twelve-year-old daughter Pamela in New York where she had been sent with her elder sister Patricia for safety, he offered his recipe for a happy existence. 'By all means get all the fun out of life too,' he told her – 'ride as much as possible, go to museums, plays and cinemas – but remember that in the years to come your chief pleasure in life will be in honest work. I have certainly found it my chief pleasure.'[10]

Mountbatten joined the navy as a cadet at the Royal Naval College at Osborne on the Isle of Wight in May 1913, shortly before his thirteenth birthday. He served as a midshipman in the war just missing – to his intense disappointment – the 1916 Battle of Jutland. When peace came he did two terms at Cambridge University where contemporaries were surprised to note that this serviceman of royal blood was sympathetic to the Labour Party. His first ship was the battle cruiser HMS *Renown*. Between postings he served as an aide to his second cousin the Prince of Wales, joining him on foreign tours and cementing a close friendship. The abdication crisis split court and nation but Mountbatten managed to remain on good terms with both the outgoing Edward VIII and the incoming George VI. In time the new king too would treat him as a confidant.

Mountbatten's naval career was greatly helped by these royal connections but he was also diligent and hard-working. The navy was a highly technical service and he bent himself to mastering the vital science of signals. He brought the Mountbatten touch to his speciality, decorating the bonnet of his cream-coloured limousine with statuettes of silver signallers waving semaphore flags.

In 1934 he got his first command, taking over a new ship, the 1,375-ton destroyer HMS *Daring*. Destroyers were stylish and satisfied his love of speed on land and sea. A ship's happiness depended to a great extent on the personality of the captain and every vessel Mountbatten commanded was a happy ship. He appreciated early on the necessity to make everyone on board, from his number one to the engine-room stokers, feel part of the same great enterprise. Before taking over *Daring* he memorised the details of every member of the ship's company so that when they mustered for the first time he could drop some personal reference that humanised the encounter.

In 1938 he joined the ship with which his name would be for ever linked. HMS *Kelly* was a Javelin-class destroyer of the latest design with a top speed of thirty-two knots. From its bridge as 'Captain (D)' he would lead the eight vessels of the new 5th Destroyer Flotilla. When the war began *Kelly* did some useful work, rescuing British troops in Norway, bombarding the Germans after they seized Maleme airfield during the Crete disaster of 1941 and possibly sinking a U-boat. Overall, though, her contribution would turn out to be minimal. Accidents and disasters followed her around her service in home waters, Norway and the Mediterranean. For the first fourteen months of hostilities *Kelly* was on operations for less than two weeks, and spent most of the rest of the time in shipyards undergoing repairs.

On an unsuccessful mission to intercept a captured merchantman in the early autumn of 1939 the ship's upper works were partially wrecked by an enormous wave as it raced home to Scapa Flow at high speed in heavy seas. Shortly afterwards she hit a mine in the Tyne Estuary. No sooner were repairs completed than she collided with another destroyer in a snowstorm. On the night of 9/10 May she clashed with a German E-boat while on patrol in the North Sea. *Kelly* was struck under the bridge by a torpedo which tore a great hole in the hold, ruptured the boiler and killed twenty-seven men. Miraculously she stayed afloat and after being taken in tow for ninety-one hours arrived safely back in the Tyne.

While *Kelly* was repaired Mountbatten led the flotilla from other destroyers. On 29 November 1940 it attacked three German destroyers off the Lizard Peninsula in Cornwall. Mountbatten was on board HMS *Javelin*, which was hit by two torpedoes, detonating the aft magazine and killing forty-six men.

When *Kelly* was at last ready to return to service the flotilla joined the Mediterranean Fleet and in spring of 1941 was sent to evacuate British and Commonwealth forces from Crete. On the morning of 23 May, she was sunk by Stuka dive-bombers and half the crew killed. It was the end of the ship but the start of an enduring legend.

Some of these calamities could be put down to bad luck. Others were due to human error, with Mountbatten carrying much of the blame. The near-capsize in the autumn of 1939 would not have been so devastating if the captain had not been driving the ship at twenty-eight knots, twice the appropriate speed in the conditions. The torpedoing of May 1940 was at least partly due to the fact that he broke away from the rest of the patrol in darkness in a foolhardy attempt to hunt a U-boat.

Any other sailor might have expected such escapades to cripple his career prospects. Mountbatten's powerful patrons ensured that he emerged from them undamaged. Churchill tried to upgrade the 'mention in despatches' he was awarded for the May 1940 exploit to a Distinguished Service Order. The commander-in-chief of the Home

Fleet, Admiral Charles Forbes, was having none of it. *Kelly*, he ruled, had 'only been to sea fifty-seven days during the war, and that any other captain would have done the same in bringing the ship home'. Mountbatten took this as evidence that the admiral bore him a grudge. He told his second cousin the king that Forbes disliked him for 'talking too much and not being sufficiently humble'.[11]

The fiasco of 29 November 1940 provided more evidence of Mountbatten's ability to survive setbacks that would have sunk another career. He set off in *Javelin* with a force of five ships to intercept three German destroyers off the Cornish coast. Dawn was still two hours away when he sighted them and closed at full speed. Alerted by the noise of the engines as well as their own radar, the Germans had plenty of time to react. Mountbatten greatly reduced his chances of success by an eccentric choice of tactics. The conventional manoeuvre would have been to carry straight on with all guns blazing. Instead, to the dismay of *Javelin*'s commander Anthony Pugsley, he ordered the ship to swing onto a parallel course, throwing the guns off target and presenting a flank to the German torpedoes which duly struck home, crippling but not sinking the destroyer.

This conduct could not be overlooked. In the subsequent inquiry Mountbatten insisted that his tactics gave a better chance of bringing all guns to bear on the enemy, as would indeed have been the case if it had been daylight. However, the consensus was that Mountbatten had blundered, with the Vice Chief of the Naval Staff commenting: 'It is elementary that one should open fire first at night.'[12] No punishment followed. Mountbatten was not only Churchill's protégé but a national hero and this was no the time to lower public morale by denting his reputation. Somehow the episode was spun to the newspapers as a British victory, and shortly afterwards he was gratified to get his DSO, awarded not for any specific action but for 'wholehearted devotion to duty'. In his eyes it was long overdue and his many allies in the press agreed. 'No one even suggested that the fact that he had royal relatives had anything to do with it,' wrote Quentin Reynolds, an American war correspondent based in London. 'Instead, sailors in wardrooms said, "About time, too."'[13]

No blame attached to Mountbatten's handling of *Kelly*'s last voyage. On 21 May 1941 the 5th Flotilla left Malta with orders to assist in stopping the Germans reinforcing the airborne invasion of Crete launched the previous day. Air support was minimal and the destroyers would be at the mercy of the German bombers operating from southern Greece. The guns of *Kelly* and her sister ship *Kashmir* skilfully supported the Australian and New Zealand forces around Maleme aerodrome and sunk an enemy supply ship. On the morning of 23 May they were spotted by a German reconnaissance plane. Well-rehearsed evasion tactics saved them from the first attack by Junkers 88s but there was no escaping the swarm of more accurate Stuka dive-bombers that followed. *Kashmir* sank almost immediately. *Kelly* stayed afloat long enough for Mountbatten to see the survivors off. He almost drowned when swimming free himself, then narrowly missed being chopped up by the destroyer's propellers.

Once aboard a life raft he led three cheers for the old ship as she sank beneath the warm sea. More than half of the crew of just over 200 were dead. The rest were eventually picked up by HMS *Kipling* and Mountbatten moved among his men, encouraging and consoling. The affection and concern were heartfelt and devoid of condescension. It was displays of humanity like this rather than his capabilities as a warrior that explained the lifelong devotion he inspired among most of his crew.

The sinking of *Kelly* would provide the supreme example of Mountbatten's ability to extract glory from disaster. The story would go into legend thanks to the 1942 film *In Which We Serve*. Directed by Noël Coward and David Lean it told the story of HMS *Torrin* and its quietly heroic and humane captain, E. V. Kinross – whom Coward also played. It was obviously all based on *Kelly*. Mountbatten worked closely with Coward at every stage of the production, intervening to make changes to the script to make Kinross more middle class than the toff portrayed in the original, a shrewd adjustment to the more democratic temper of the times.

Mountbatten's active service record exposed him as a poor battle commander. His craving for glory made him impatient, overconfident and rash. In this area of his life, if in no other, he seemed also prone to bad luck. It did not seem to matter. When he returned from Egypt after *Kelly*'s last voyage he found a plum job waiting. Dudley Pound offered him command of a new cruiser. Mountbatten was hesitant. A cruiser sounded wonderful but an aircraft carrier would be even better. He instructed Edwina to invite the First Lord of the Admiralty and political chief of the navy, A. V. Alexander, to lunch to make his case. By the end of the summer he had got his way. The offer was upped to command of the carrier HMS *Illustrious*. Launched only two years before she had been badly damaged by dive-bombers in the Mediterranean and was now in the US Navy shipyard at Norfolk, Virginia where repairs were due to complete in November. Churchill decided to send Mountbatten out early to work up the ship but also to serve as an ambassador for the British war effort. Edwina, who had thrown herself into war work and now held a senior position in the St John's Ambulance Brigade, was to go with him on a goodwill tour to thank the American Red Cross for its help.

Why were the likes of Pound and Alexander so keen to humour Mountbatten and advance his career? The hope of personal gain clearly played a part. Mountbatten's royal and political connections gave him extraordinary access. In 1940 he could, if he wanted, pick up the phone and speak directly to the king or the prime minister. A good turn to him might well result in a good turn to them. Mountbatten understood perfectly how the favour market worked. His word was his bond and if he was asked to perform a service he would do his utmost to deliver.

Churchill's affection and admiration perhaps sprang from his weakness for men in his own mould. Both had an enormous appetite for life and a broad generosity of spirit. They were bold to the point of foolhardiness but rarely learned from their mistakes. Both were driven by a conviction that they were bound for greatness. Churchill shared his protégé's hunch, was prepared to forgive him almost anything and gave him his head.

Mountbatten proved the soundness of his patron's judgement often enough to ensure his continued support. The American trip was a triumph. Despite giving massive material aid to Britain the United States showed no enthusiasm for joining her on the battlefield. Churchill used Mountbatten to sell the British war to Americans high and low. He charmed the public with multiple newspaper and radio interviews, courted Roosevelt over dinner at the White House while making his number with the US Navy brass. Mountbatten was attuned to America in a way that most Englishmen of his class and background were not. He loved the world of the movies and somehow found the time to ask Walt Disney to design a mascot for his new ship. Disney came up with a sketch of Donald Duck in admiral's uniform, holding a miniature aeroplane trailing a Union Jack.

Mountbatten's hosts saw the core of seriousness beneath the genial exterior. 'His knowledge of his profession, his keen observation of our methods, his frank statements of his thoughts of them . . . have not only won our liking, but also our deep respect,' wrote the Chief of Naval Operations, Admiral Stark, in a letter to Dudley Pound.[14]

In early October, with *Illustrious* almost ready for battle again, Mountbatten went off on a quick visit to the US naval base at Pearl Harbor. On way back to rejoin the ship at Norfolk he passed through Los Angeles where the British consul showed him signals from the Admiralty and the prime minister ordering him to hand over his ship and return home immediately. Mountbatten was dismayed. *Illustrious* had suited him perfectly, offering the chance of the lasting glory that had eluded him so far.

On the evening of 25 October 1941 he arrived at Chequers, the prime minister's official country retreat. Over dinner Churchill laid out in detail the new job he had chosen for him. He was to take over as head of the recently created Combined Operations Headquarters, replacing the elderly incumbent, Admiral Sir Roger Keyes. Mountbatten protested that he 'would rather go back to *Illustrious*'.[15] The prime minister's indulgence had its limits. 'You fool!' he snapped. 'The best thing you can hope to do there is to repeat your last achievement and get yourself sunk!' Chastened, Mountbatten sat back to listen as Churchill laid out his plans for the organisation and its new leader.

Combined Operations evolved from the grim strategic realities facing Britain following the disasters of 1940. After Dunkirk, the priority was survival and the defence of the island. Though Churchill made it immediately clear that the long-term objective was to return to the continent and liberate Europe, that day was a long way off. In the meantime, some way had to be found to demonstrate to the British public and the world the nation's aggressive spirit and its determination to fight on. The RAF's growing bomber fleet was the prime means of striking back but it was only with the first 1,000-bomber raid on Cologne on 30 May 1942 that they began to make any real impact on the enemy. On land the pitiful lack of resources restricted Britain to a policy of hit-and-run amphibious raids whose value, initially at least, was going to be more psychological than military.

A proposal from a Transvaal-born lieutenant colonel called Dudley Clarke which reached Churchill early in June 1940 was guaranteed to excite his freebooting instincts. It called for a specialised raiding force, similar to the South African 'kommandos' who had plagued the British during the Second Boer War of 1899–1902. The prime minister quickly ordered the raising of 'specially trained troops of the hunter class' and urged a 'vigorous, enterprising, and ceaseless offensive against the whole German-occupied coastline'.[16]

The commandos would go on to be one of the great success stories of the war, but their early days were marked with bathos and in their first year they managed only two raids. Lord Lovat, an early volunteer, remembered: 'Without the benefit of a Combined Planning Authority to provide maps, intelligence, transportation, air cover, signals and specialist weapons, the outcome of each sortie became a comedy of errors.'[17]

In the first operation launched three weeks after Dunkirk a hundred-plus men in four groups were dropped by launch south of Boulogne to capture prisoners and seize intelligence documents from a military HQ in a requisitioned seaside hotel. During the crossing one group was machine-gunned by the RAF who had not been warned of the operation. Another party ran aground. The hotel HQ was empty and no prisoners were captured. Many of the party arrived back in England insensible having drunk the rum ration on the return voyage.

There was a second bungled raid on Guernsey in mid-July. 'Let

there be no more silly fiascos,' ordered Churchill and appointed
Admiral Sir Roger Keyes to take charge of the new Combined Operations Command. It was a sentimental choice. Keyes was sixty-seven
years old and retired. Churchill admired him for his reckless bravery,
famously demonstrated during a pyrrhic raid on the Belgian port
and U-boat base of Zeebrugge in April 1918 which won Keyes the
Victoria Cross (VC). As an MP in the years before the war he vigor-
ously opposed appeasement and supported Churchill's rearmament
campaign.

Under Keyes the commandos managed a few minor successes and
one more substantial one. In March 1941 they launched Operation
Claymore, aimed at destroying fish-processing factories in the Lofoten
Islands off the coast of Norway which supplied the Germans with
nutrients as well as the glycerine used in TNT. There was also a hidden objective, as the Canadian historian David O'Keefe has revealed.
Britain had made a start on cracking the Enigma-machine-encrypted
codes used by the German military. In March 1940 the Code and
Cypher School at Bletchley Park began using bulky electromechan-
ical machines called 'bombes' that mimicked the Enigma technology
to sift the quadrillions of possibilities the machine generated. The top-
grade intelligence it laboriously obtained was known as 'Ultra'.

The product gleaned from German naval transmissions was particularly vital. It helped the Naval Intelligence Division (NID) at the
Admiralty plot the movements of U-boats and surface raiders and
route transatlantic convoys away from ambushes. But Enigma never
stood still. Encryption was made even more impenetrable by constant
alteration of the machine's settings and code words and the addition
of rotor arms which greatly increased complexity. To keep abreast of
the changes the cryptanalysts needed to get their hands on machines
and code books. The only way to do that was to capture them, but
overt operations to seize the hardware would inevitably alert the
enemy who would respond with yet more security-enhancing refine-
ments. 'Pinch' operations, as they were known, therefore had to be
camouflaged. Operation Claymore provided the NID with excellent
cover to launch an operation to grab machines and code books known
to be carried on even the smallest German vessels.

A fleet of two landing ships and five destroyers – with about 500 commandos plus Free Norwegian troops and Royal Engineers on board – left Scapa Flow early on 1 March. They arrived at their destination just before dawn three days later. Surprise was complete. The German garrison was still in bed, sleeping off a party the night before and offered virtually no resistance. When the raiders departed the sky was black with the smoke from 3,200 tons of burning oil and the harbour littered with the sunken ships. They took with them 228 German prisoners and some 300 islanders who volunteered to join the fight against the occupiers. A search of the armed trawler *Krebs* yielded Enigma machinery and code books which enabled the cryptanalysts at Bletchley Park to break radio traffic for the next five weeks.

The Lofoten Raid was the high point of Keyes's time at Combined Ops. Apart from the nascent commando force the organisation had very few resources and relied largely on the goodwill and cooperation of the army, navy and air force to get anything done. The army was instinctively opposed to the idea of elite units which seemed to implicitly denigrate the qualities of the regular battalions. The navy and air force were reluctant to divert precious resources to what they sometimes regarded as little more than stunts. Keyes was temperamentally incapable of learning the diplomacy and guile required in bureaucratic warfare. 'The increased complexities of war meant nothing to him,' wrote the official historian of Combined Operations.[18] 'Planners were grit in the machine; the professional heads of the three services a trio of comparatively junior officers.' Any hesitation on their part was treated as evidence of gutlessness. He once told the assembled chiefs of staff they were 'yellow'. Even a VC could not expect to get away with this for long.

It pained Churchill to tell him it was time to go. However, Keyes was plainly not the man for the much expanded role the prime minister planned for Combined Operations. In the autumn of 1941 the war somehow had to be moved forward. The threat of invasion had dwindled but Britain was still recovering its strength and the arrival of America on the battlefield was still a fervent desire, not an expectation. Nonetheless Russian appeals for help and domestic agitation for a second front already demanded a response. In September the Ministry of Information was forced into a discreet public-relations offensive, holding confidential briefings with newspaper editors to explain why an invasion in the current circumstances would be suicidal and plead with them to tone down the pro-Russian campaigning. 'To rush onto the continent before we are ready is to invite another Dunkirk,' warned the briefing paper prepared by the tri-service Joint Planning Staff.[19]

It was nonetheless recognised that these arguments would not check public opinion and the Russians for long. Something would have to be done and the best on offer with the resources available was some sort of large-scale raid. The chiefs of staff believed that nothing short of an invasion was likely to persuade the Germans to shift aircraft, men or armour from the East. Churchill, while vehemently opposed to an early attempted return to the continent, was more optimistic about what a limited operation could achieve. A memo dated 14 September 1941 called for plans to be made 'forthwith for a raid of a major nature on one of the ports of northern France' preferably before the end of October.[20] His preferred target was Cherbourg in Normandy. A brigade of tanks landed on neighbouring beaches 'could effect a surprise attack in temporarily overwhelming strength on the port itself. The dockyards, port installations and ships in the harbour could be destroyed and the attacking force evacuated before the enemy could react in any strength.'

The action, he predicted, 'would have effects of major importance. It would surprise the enemy and encourage our friends. It would be evidence to the Russians of our good faith and to the world of our growing strength. And it might well force the Germans to withdraw first-class troops from the Eastern Front in anticipation of future more extensive operations.'

This was the first in a succession of proposed cross-Channel adventures, emanating from several quarters, that would preoccupy planners on the Home Front for the next eleven months. As Mountbatten sat down to dinner with Churchill at Chequers on 25 October, he learned what his part was to be in this new chapter of the war.

★

The picture that has come down to us of the meeting was painted by Mountbatten for Bernard Fergusson, the official historian of Combined Operations. According to him, Churchill began by telling Mountbatten: 'Up to now there have hardly been any commando raids. I want you to start a programme of raids of ever-increasing intensity, so as to keep the whole of the enemy coastline on the alert from the North Cape to the Bay of Biscay. *But your main object must be the re-invasion of France* [original italics].' His ultimate challenge was to 'create the machine which will make it possible for us to beat Hitler on land. You must devise the appurtenances and appliances which will make the invasion possible. You must select and build up the bases from which the assault will be launched . . . I want you to select the area in which you feel the assault should take place and start bending all your energies towards getting ready for this great day.'[21]

This was, as Mountbatten noted in his diary, a 'staggering' remit. He was being asked to start work on the reconquest of north-west Europe, even though Britain was still alone and America had yet to enter the war as a belligerent. Whether Churchill's orders were quite so emphatic is open to question. The formal directive issued to Mountbatten was narrower. It stated he was to act as technical adviser on all aspects of planning and training of combined operations. He was given responsibility for joint training for all three services. He had to study tactical developments in all forms of combined operations, varying from small raids to a full-scale invasion of the continent. Finally he was charged with overseeing and driving on research and development into all types of technical equipment and sea craft suitable for combined operations.[22]

This suggests a more limited role for the organisation and its new leader than recorded in the official history. Fergusson was a professional soldier, a Scottish aristocrat and a huge admirer of Mountbatten. His hero took a close interest in the writing of the book, annotating drafts as they were written.[23] The resulting narrative drew a straight line between Mountbatten's leadership of COHQ and the Normandy landings, reinforcing the story repeated continuously by Mountbatten to justify the tragedy that haunted his time at Combined

Operations and went on rematerialising like an unlaid ghost for the rest of his life. That was, that far from being a catastrophic blunder the Dieppe raid was part of a grand plan. From the outset it was intended as a 'rehearsal for D-Day' and the bitter lessons learned on the beaches of Dieppe saved many lives when the real performance began. The truth was rather different.

3. HMS *Wimbledon*

When Mountbatten's reign began Combined Operations Headquarters had a staff of twenty-three, including typists and messengers.[1] Six months later it had expanded to 400. The organisation was remade in the image of its new leader and his presence was felt everywhere. Arthur Marshall, who worked as a security officer at Richmond Terrace, 'had sometimes to report, quaking a little, to Mountbatten himself. A succession of orders and instructions were crisply rapped out (there were never any repetitions to make sure that you had got it right), followed by that sensational smile and the words "Now, Marshall, will you run along and do that for me?" One departed in a haze of hero-worship, a worship that was common to the entire headquarters.'[2]

As in his navy days, Mountbatten noticed everybody, high and low, and took an extraordinary interest in their welfare. Marshall once 'had to spend twenty minutes with [him] while we decided where the marine sentries could stand so that they would be out of a draught, although draughtless nooks and corners tended to mask their field of view and diminish their usefulness as sentries'.

For all his self-belief Mountbatten wanted to be liked, and flattered everyone with attention and little courtesies. Every officer at HQ was invited usually in pairs, to lunch with the Mountbattens at their house in Chester Street, where they 'could not have been easier or more welcoming and they made one feel that this had, for them, been the Treat of the Week'. Though he thought of himself as a man of destiny he would go to great lengths to avoid being perceived as high and mighty. Long after the war he sent a worried letter to his former number two at COHQ, Charles Haydon. 'My dear Charles,' he wrote, 'In the rush before Christmas a muddle occurred over Christmas cards for when they had all been signed and put into envelopes one card signed "Dickie" was left over and was not discovered until the others had been posted. Some detective work has failed to discover exactly which card went astray, but one of my staff who was helping me has an uneasy feeling it may have been the card destined for you. If you got a pompous one signed "Mountbatten of Burma" you will know this was unintentional and please forgive me.'[3]

Such solicitousness displayed either touching humility or a well-camouflaged concern for his image, depending on whether you were a fan or a detractor.

It was certainly true that Mountbatten was fully alive to the benefits of publicity and adept at manipulating the press to gild the reputation of himself and his organisation. Richmond Terrace and its inhabitants fascinated the press and Mountbatten was happy to invite them in. Inevitably, the focus of interest was on its leader, and worldly hacks melted under the chief's laser charm. When Quentin Reynolds, a left-leaning, New York Irish former sports writer, now a war correspondent for *Collier's* magazine in London, visited HQ he found Mountbatten 'sat behind a big desk but he fitted it well. He arose, smiling, and shook hands the way a sailor shakes hands. His handclasp was hard and firm. [He] is tall, with dark hair and eloquent eyes which narrow in concentration and then open wide when he laughs.' He left the meeting 'completely captivated by the man. There wasn't a false note in him.'[4]

He created a high-pitched ambience around him, and Goronwy Rees, a writer and mover in left-wing London intellectual circles before the war who was attached to the planning staff in the spring of 1942, noted the 'atmosphere of sustained drama and crisis . . . of continuous improvisation, of meetings and conferences hurriedly called and as hurriedly cancelled, of brilliant and unorthodox ideas adopted with enthusiasm and abandoned when found to be impracticable . . .'[5]

He was not the only one to wonder if all the activity was to much purpose. Lord Lovat, a Highland toff from the Fraser clan, noted during a visit in the spring of 1942 that it 'swarmed with red-tabbed gentlemen. The bee-hive illusion was enhanced by busy passages, honeycombed with rooms filled with every branch of the services, including the powder-puff variety, who looked elegant in silk stockings. There was said to be a fair proportion of drones among the inmates . . .'[6]

Mountbatten was the busiest bee of all. He brought with him the same blazing energy he applied to every project he tackled. Though the term had not yet been invented, he was a workaholic, rarely spending fewer than twelve hours a day at his duties and sometimes sleeping in the office.

He needed deputies from the army, navy and air force whose loyalty to him and to COHQ was at least as strong as their devotion to their parent service. This could not be taken for granted. Inter-service staffs were a novelty at the time and COHQ was the first independent one ever. Few had positively welcomed its existence, and according to Bernard Fergusson much 'dirty work . . . went on in the service ministries to undermine COHQ during the first six months of Mountbatten's tenure'.[7]

He was lucky in finding loyal lieutenants. His vice chief was an Irish Guardsman, Major General Charles Haydon, who after leading a battalion in France had gone on to command the Special Service Brigade in which the new commando units were grouped. Haydon was sometimes exasperated by his boss's methods but later looked back nostalgically at the 'sustained enthusiasm that was remarkable when one recalls how often [Combined Operations] were regarded – and *treated* – as trespassers on the preserves of one or other of the service ministries'. The result was that 'out of the labours grew a highly skilled staff – brimful of ideas, prepared to think and plan on a generous inter-service basis, and surprisingly little trammelled by purely service foibles and customs'.[8] Air Vice Marshal James Robb RAF and Commodore Robert Ellis RN who served as deputy and assistant chief of Combined Operations were equally efficient and dependable lieutenants.

But Mountbatten looked for something more from his entourage. He was naturally drawn to mavericks, and other key appointments reflected his taste for the risky and unorthodox. As his naval adviser he chose a controversial RN captain whose verve and intelligence were offset by a knack of putting colleagues' backs up. John Hughes-Hallett, usually known as Jock, was a forty-year-old bachelor, tall and jug-eared, with a challenging look in his sloping eyes and a self-satisfied set to his mouth.

He came from a service family and after officer training at Dartmouth served in the Great War aboard the battlecruiser HMS *Lion* before studying for a year at Cambridge. Like Mountbatten, Hughes-Hallett was technically minded, spending the interwar years specialising in torpedoes, mines and radar. Like Mountbatten, who enjoyed devising innovative solutions to technical problems, he had a flair for invention. Among Hughes-Hallett's conceptions was a night deck-landing system for aircraft carriers which won plaudits from senior officers at the Admiralty. In 1940 he was executive officer on the cruiser *Devonshire* during the disastrous Norway campaign, where he earned a mention in despatches. On his return he was thrown into anti-invasion preparations overseeing mine-laying to protect likely landing areas in the south-east and getting another mention in despatches for his efforts. He also chaired an interdepartmental committee charged with improving Britain's low-level radar cover.

In December 1941 he joined Mountbatten's staff as naval adviser. Mountbatten picked him on the principle that as both a sailor and an expert in repelling seaborne invasions Hughes-Hallett should be equally good at mounting them. He would play a central part in all the great Combined Ops enterprises of the coming year, culminating in Jubilee which he not only helped to plan but led as naval force commander.

Jock Hughes-Hallett admired his new boss to the point of infatuation. Mountbatten's personality, his 'boundless energy and enthusiasm infused a new spirit', which was only heightened by his elevation to the Chiefs of Staff Committee, after which his staff felt 'for the first time that their work was real and earnest: that the raids they were working on would in all probability be carried out'.[9]

In some ways Hughes-Hallett was Mountbatten's alter ego. He shared his drive but also his impatience with anyone who pointed out the flaws in an outwardly brilliant scheme. He also had a tendency to take the credit for any successes while evading responsibility for the duds. In other ways the two were poles apart. 'Dickie' circumvented opposition by a combination of chutzpah, flattery and charm. Hughes-Hallett appeared not to give a damn what people thought of him and bulldozed opposition, an approach that earned him the nickname 'Hughes-Hitler'. He was unlikely to be found at the centre of a genial throng in the wardroom.

His superior during the original planning for Dieppe, Rear Admiral Tom Baillie-Grohman, did not bother to hide his dislike. 'He is not my money, nor is he the money of a very large number of naval officers,' he wrote to Mountbatten.[10] 'He is considered, and I think with some reason, as too loud-voiced, overbearing, and too cocksure of himself without adequate reason.' Mountbatten stood up for his man. 'I quite agree about his loud voice [and] his overbearing and cocksure manner,' he replied, 'but I entirely disagree that it is without reason. It is just because he is right 99 per cent of the time that he does annoy so many people.'

Confidence was a virtue in Mountbatten's eyes and it was abundantly on display among the senior members of the planning staff who had the vital job of evaluating and selecting targets and driving projects forward. The military adviser was Colonel Antony Head, who had all the assurance that came with an Eton education and the ribbon of the Military Cross (MC) on his tunic, won in France in 1940. Head was assisted by Major Robert Henriques, an Old Rugbeian from one of Britain's grandest Sephardic Jewish families and a pre-war professional soldier who also wrote novels. They were men in Mountbatten's mould, risk-takers who were eager to get on with their exciting new task and impatient with objections and hindrances. Their self-assuredness could grate with those not in the COHQ club. Lovat for one was irritated when Henriques 'tried to do my thinking for me' and had been unimpressed by his 'too clever to learn' attitude, first noted when the two crossed swords at a commando training centre.[11]

Beyond Mountbatten's military inner circle were ever-widening rings of civilian helpers. Mountbatten loved the stimulus provided by expert outsiders and Richmond Terrace was well stocked with exotic specialists, including John Desmond Bernal, the Irish-born communist professor of physics at London University who pioneered X-ray crystallography, the South African zoologist Solly Zuckerman and Geoffrey Pyke, a highly unorthodox adventurer and inventor of 'Pykrete', designed to turn icebergs into aircraft carriers.

Their schemes seemed to some as evidence of a lack of seriousness at COHQ and cynics dubbed it 'HMS *Wimbledon*' as it was 'all rackets and balls'. More damning was the accusation that its chief valued friendship over competence when making key appointments. The charge of cronyism particularly attached to his choice of senior intelligence officer.

The Marqués de Casa Maury was a forty-five-year-old Cuban-Spanish aristocrat who at the start of the war owned the upmarket Curzon Cinema in Mayfair. After divorcing a society beauty, Paula Gellibrand, he married Freda Dudley Ward, the former mistress of the Prince of Wales. This connection and the fact that his stepdaughter Angela married Brigadier Robert Laycock, commander of the Special Service Brigade, placed him firmly in the same milieu as Mountbatten. In the interwar years he was a well-known racing driver and an amateur aviator and a member of the RAF Volunteer Reserve. In late 1941 he was serving as an intelligence officer in West Country fighter stations when Mountbatten invited him to come aboard COHQ.

The duties of an RAF 'spy', as intelligence officers were popularly known, were basic: briefing aircrew on known enemy dispositions before they set off on operations and debriefing them on their return. This was not a serious qualification for the crucial work of building up the best possible intelligence picture to assist the planning and execution of raids. As it was, COHQ had no intelligence-gathering capacity of its own and had to glean what it could from the service and professional intelligence agencies. The community was riven by internal feuds and the jealousy and hostility they felt towards each other was multiplied when it came to outsiders. Casa Maury was personable and eager to succeed but to the professionals of wartime spookery he was an amateur and a foreigner to boot. It was inevitable that cynics should attribute his promotion to his friendship with the boss rather than his competence, and assign him to the category of 'chum of Dickie's' – of whom there were a number at COHQ.

Despite his lavish complement of staff, Mountbatten had precious few assets. Keyes had made some progress in squeezing from the authorities the men and materiel needed for Combined Ops to fulfil its *raison d'être*. Five former Channel ferries were prised from the navy to serve as troop landing ships for long-distance raiding projects. In the spring of 1942 there was still a dire shortage of landing craft to get men and armour from landing ship to shore but at least the problem was receiving serious attention. Most of the shipbuilding effort went into replacements for the huge tonnages lost in the Battle of the Atlantic. By now, though, capacity had been diverted to start building the invasion fleet that would one day be needed for the return to the continent and a major specialised construction programme was underway that would allow at least a division to be lifted by the summer.

As to manpower, Mountbatten had an abundance of resources. As chief of Combined Operations he had control of the commando units of the Special Service Brigade and also the Combined Training Centres that carried out the inter-service training for amphibious operations.

Mountbatten had no need to look beyond the commandos to provide the ground troops for the small-scale raids of his first few months at COHQ. Increasingly ambitious operations were planned for 1942, however, requiring larger forces as well as armoured units. The chiefs of staff had directed that the regular troops, both British and Canadian, of the Home Forces Command – which since June 1940 had been defending the island from an invasion that never came – would be closely involved in these new undertakings.

The commandos were made for combined operations. Every man was a volunteer and each had to be super-fit, both physically and mentally, and willing to endure endless discomfort uncomplainingly to pass muster. Recruiting began immediately after Dunkirk when notices went up at barracks across the country calling for volunteers for special duties. Jimmy Dunning was languishing in a training establishment when he saw the announcement on the regimental orders board. He was born in Southampton in 1920 and after deciding that a career in the family butcher's shop was not for him had joined the 12th Lancers in search of 'adventure and travel'.[12] He was left behind when his unit went to France. He had been brought up on notions of 'empire and right and wrong' and the defeat hurt.

'The notice said volunteers wanted for special duty, able to swim, prepared to parachute, able to drive and to serve in whatever capacity was needed,' he remembered. He was 'young and venturesome and naïve . . . [I] thought, well, here's a chance to do something daring, bold, exciting.'

Dunning thought his prowess at water sports might be a help but that did not seem to matter to the captain from the Bedfordshire and Hertfordshire Regiment who interviewed him: 'It seemed to be just whether the officer liked my face and general bearing and attitude, and I was told I was in.' A few days later he was posted to Weymouth as a sergeant and founder member of 4 Commando, charged with counter-attacking when the expected German invasion was launched. Nothing suited him better. 'There was a tremendous spirit,' he remembered. 'Instead of having to carry on our onerous guard duties on the beaches we would be called upon to strike back. And that's what really, I think, dominated our thoughts. Having a go at Jerry.'

Private Bill Portman of the Royal Engineers was one of thirty who volunteered from his company on their return from Dunkirk, 'feeling a little browned off. I thought we'd had our backsides kicked all the way back from Brussels and I was more or less feeling a bit disgruntled and I thought we should have had a better chance to have a go at them.'[13] Only six of his comrades were selected and Portman joined 3 Commando.

The commando ethos made a refreshing change from the military milieu the volunteers had left behind. George Cook came from Manchester. His father was an engineer in a cotton mill. He left school at fourteen and was apprenticed as an electrician. He got fourteen shillings a week, often went hungry and had to walk five miles to work. War seemed to offer an escape. As soon as he was old enough he joined up and in 1940 was posted to the Royal Welch Fusiliers. Life in barracks soon got him down. He 'wasn't all that keen on the RWF to be honest . . . We'd done our basic training and the first thing we did of any importance was to go on aerodrome defence. But they gave us no ammunition. I asked an officer do we shout "bang" if the Germans attack by air drop?'[14] One day when his spirits were low he saw the fateful notice. Called for interview he was interviewed 'by this big captain and he was in 4 Commando'. Cook 'of course marched in, attention, saluted, the usual thing. And he said sit down, do you smoke, have a cigarette? Well that had never happened to me. You had to stand to attention for a lance corporal and here was a captain giving me a fag and chatting to me as though I was a human being.' After putting him at ease the captain asked Cook if he understood what he was letting himself in for. 'He said very simply, what you'll be doing is you'll be landing on the enemy shore and the chances are you won't come back. Now are you interested? So I said yes. And that was it.'

For many volunteers it had taken war for their country to give them the opportunity to show what they were worth. John Carney had grown up poor in Liverpool in the 1930s, which at the time 'was not exactly a city of milk and honey'. He left school at fourteen and later joined the King's Liverpool Regiment. By the end of 1941 he was a sergeant and rather bored of his life teaching conscripts how to handle a Vickers machine gun and drive a Bren-gun carrier. When a commando recruiting officer arrived at the barracks at Formby offering the prospect of a life where 'we weren't going to be sitting still', he volunteered. 'They said you'll have to lose your stripes to become a commando and I said that's no problem.'[15]

For those at the other end of the social spectrum the commandos offered a different sort of liberation. To Lord Lovat the life 'meant a welcome freedom from class, money or position, in a close fellowship of total involvement'.[16] For many, high and low, the fellowship of the green beret would provide the most fulfilling time of their lives.

The volunteers had signed up for one of the most brutal physical training regimes ever devised and only the toughest and most determined survived. The Scottish Highlands provided suitably harsh terrain and an early commando training centre was based at Inverailort House, a gloomy granite mansion on Loch Ailort, north-west of Fort William. Cook remembered: 'on the very first morning we marched down to the lochside and we got in a whaler with all our equipment on. We rowed out and there was this big sergeant and he said right: you've all said you can swim. Over the side and swim ashore.' Several in the boat refused but Cook jumped in and struggled through the freezing water to safety.

It felt like a real achievement and as the days passed he found himself looking forward to whatever cruel challenges the training staff had devised. It helped that everyone was in it together. Exercises were called 'schemes' and 'if you went on a scheme with an officer and you went in the water with all your equipment the officer went in with all his equipment as well'. This made an interesting contrast with the Royal Welch where 'if you were sent on a route march fully loaded the officer walked in front with a little swagger cane, stepping out'. In the commandos everyone helped everyone else. If on a long slog, carrying a mortar and laden with extra bombs, 'you were jiggered, suddenly a big pair of hands would come over and say, right mate. I'll take that off you.'

Better still, you were treated as an individual and encouraged to think for yourself, no matter what your rank or background. This was quite a departure from the British military tradition which held that only those with private educations were capable of initiative, decision or command.

As you'd volunteered for the commandos, they realised that you were human beings and you had a bit of sense. You didn't have to be roared at and shouted at all the time. Not only that, if you did anything in training, everything was explained to you. If you had a different idea, even as a lowly private, you could say, well sir, don't you think that if we went that way instead of this way it would be easier? And if you were right, that was the method adopted. Everybody relied on everybody. Everybody trusted everybody. Everybody had faith and confidence in each other. They made you realise that you were somebody. You mattered and they cared. In the Royal Welch you were just a number.

Commando training was revolutionary and much of it improvised. According to Jimmy Dunning, before the war

all physical training in the army was based on competitive games or PT . . . It invariably took place in gymnasiums or on barracks squares. But we of course had no barrack square or gymnasium. When we first started, the drill was every morning we would muster at 6.30 on the beach, do physical jerks, have a swim, then go back to our billets for breakfast, get into battledress and equipment and carry on normal training.

What was obvious was that PT was divorced from actual fighting. We started to think about this and thought we haven't got a gymnasium and vaulting horses and all that but what do we need that for? Do we need to play games? What we've got to do is relate our PT to fighting . . . We've got to learn to do PT in our ordinary gear. Instead of horses we've got fences to jump over. Instead of dumb-bells we've got rifles for arm-strengthening exercises. So that was a radical change . . . breaking away from training people to excel at sports and competition on the playing field to excelling on the battlefield.

The system was formalised at the Commando Basic Training Centre, seventeen miles from Ben Nevis in the western Highlands. It was set up early in 1942 in the grounds of Achnacarry Castle, ancestral home of Donald Cameron of Lochiel, chieftain to Cameron clan members around the world. Some 25,000 men would be trained there, from Britain, the United States, France, Belgium, Norway and Holland as well as German Jews who had escaped the Nazis. It was commanded by Lieutenant Colonel Charles Vaughan who at first sight seemed the wrong person to lead an organisation dedicated to turning out fit, free-thinking soldiers. He was forty-nine, tall and heavily built and earlier in his career he had been regimental sergeant major in the East Kent Regiment (The Buffs), a role usually associated with the roaring of spittle-flecked drill commands. But Jimmy Dunning found 'he was much more than a bawling barrack square man, although he could do that if needed'. Vaughan had fought in the ranks in the last war and had seen how little the training they had received at home prepared the new arrivals for battle and trench life. He was a father figure to his charges, reassuring them in his unofficer-like London accent and supervising their welfare while in return 'accepting nothing but the best whether it be in fitness, training, weaponry and musketry, fieldcraft or tactics' – the factors that made up the 'self-disciplined and reliant commando soldier, "fit to fight and fighting fit"'.

They were tested to the limit on fourteen-mile speed marches which a troop was expected to cover in two hours – though no one ever quite managed it. 'The whole troop had to finish together,' remembered Donald Gilchrist, a bank clerk from Paisley who joined the territorials before the war and served as an officer instructor at Achnacarry. By the end 'you had some men running like zombies more or less being held up by their companions'.[17] As they staggered up to the camp gates they were expected to pull themselves together and march in parade-ground order to a shooting range where, with arms like wet spaghetti, they had to shoot down all the metal targets on the hillside before they could return to their huts. They lived rough for days on end in the rain-soaked hills, learned concealment and fieldcraft, honed their shooting skills so that every man was a marksman and demolition expert.

Everything was as true to life – and death – as possible. The bullets flying overhead during the large-scale exercises, such as the 'opposed landing' staged as the finale to the course on Loch Lochy, were real. Forty men were killed during wartime training and the instructors emphasised that this was a deadly business. One side of the road leading to the camp was lined with fake wooden grave markers inscribed with cautionary details of how the fictional occupants had met their ends: 'This man stood on the skyline', 'This man looked over cover not round it'.[18]

The training was based on the principle enunciated by one commando officer, Derek Mills-Roberts, that 'sweat saves blood'. But equally important was the truth that to avoid death you had to become expert at dealing it, either impersonally at long distance with a sniper rifle or up close and intimate with a spine-snapping twist of the neck or a thrust of the Fairbairn–Sykes knife, the double-edged dagger specially designed for the commandos by two ex-Shanghai policemen.

The brigade's command encouraged press coverage of the goings-on at Achnacarry. The reports helped to correct an idea that had taken hold that the new units were not much more than officially sanctioned desperadoes. Donald Gilchrist reckoned 'the popular impression of a commando had hitherto been of someone who would just as soon wreck a peaceful British village as an enemy gun battery, someone who was just as liable to stick a knife into a civvie barman as a German sentry, someone from whom pretty wives and daughters should be safely locked away'.[19] Gilchrist was a commando yet 'anyone less like a hell-raising desperado than myself would have been hard to find'. Though there were a handful of 'swashbuckling characters', the great majority were 'men like me, plain, ordinary chaps', not born but made by the ethos and system enshrined at Achnacarry and elsewhere.

About one in five of those who started the course did not finish. They were 'returned to unit' having failed to make the grade whether in fitness, skill or discipline. For most this was not a cause of relief but of eternal regret. The rest were awarded their green beret, chosen because in heraldry green was the colour of hunting, then joined their new units. A commando unit comprised 450 men made up of a headquarters and six troops of sixty-six men each. This was half the size of a conventional battalion, small enough for each one to develop its own character, often shaped by the personality of the commander. Instead of barrack life they lived informally in towns where there were plenty of hotels and bed and breakfast accommodation. No. 4 Commando were based at Troon, a genteel seaside resort west of Glasgow. Each man was given a daily allowance – thirteen shillings and fourpence for officers and half that for 'other ranks' – for board and lodging which they were expected to fix up for themselves. As long as they were on parade in the morning or turned up at whatever rendezvous they were given for the day's exercises they were free to do as they pleased, with non-coms and privates socialising together in the pubs on first-name terms. The training never ceased. What was missing was action. For all their hard-won skill and fitness, the commandos had been given little employment since their birth. By the end of March 1942 they had taken part in fifteen operations, of which only six could be counted as successes.

There were many other underemployed troops in Britain that spring of 1942. Of the six trained divisions in the army's Home Command, two were Canadian. It would later be said that the Canadian troops were 'eager for action' as if they could not wait to kill Germans regardless of the risk of being killed or maimed in return. This was a convenient misrepresentation. What they did want was to get on with the war. Most were non-professional citizen soldiers and every one was a volunteer. Some had been overseas for thirty months without a whiff of action but they could not go home until the war was over.

Their impatience was shared by the commander of the 1st Canadian Corps, General Harry Crerar. Since the beginning of the year he had been lobbying Brooke, Mountbatten and General Bernard Montgomery under whose command the Canadians operated. Crerar was anxious for his men to be given a large slice of the action when future raids were mounted, regardless, it seemed, of what the operation might entail.[20] The responses were reassuring. All that was needed was a large-scale project.

4. An Unpleasant Military Problem

One thing the British were not short of was plans. In early 1942 a stream of proposals for offensive continental operations flowed over the desks of the chiefs. They varied enormously in size, intent and location from thirty-man smash-and-grab raids to full-blown armoured landings, and many were doomed to die on the drawing board. Taken together they chimed with the air of expectancy gripping Britain, the feeling that the time had come to hit the Germans hard on their own ground.

The chiefs looked on the minor projects with favour. Little harm and some good might come from a steady tempo of tightly-targeted raids potentially delivering practical benefits as well as lifting national spirits.

The major ones they viewed with foreboding, overlaid with resignation. All the big plans on the table were driven by political rather than military considerations. Given the continuing enormous imbalance in forces, all were risky in the extreme. The material situation was not about to change soon for it would be some months before America could contribute troops to a big amphibious operation. A major cross-Channel expedition was therefore seen as an operation of last resort to be launched with a heavy heart only when grand strategic pressures became too great.

Nevertheless, all the scenarios for 1942 envisaged by the Joint Planning Staff, who sifted strategic data for the Chiefs of Staff Committee, pointed to a continental landing of some description. The most optimistic foresaw the Germans collapsing on the Eastern Front and being forced to move many of their French divisions to Russia. The second envisaged stalemate, and the third the Russians being pushed to the brink of defeat.

The first possibility – highly unlikely to British eyes – would open the door to an American proposal for a joint invasion of France against significantly weakened opposition before the end of the year or early in 1943. This was Roundup, a code name disliked by Churchill for its boastful overtones which seemed to him to tempt fate. The other two also prompted some sort of action in response. Whatever happened, the Russians would need all the help they could get and the Allies were duty-bound to offer it, even though the operation might amount to little more than a goodwill gesture and token of serious future intent.

Sledgehammer – the plan for a large-scale, cross-Channel emergency invasion if the Eastern Front seemed on the point of collapse and which had the enthusiastic backing of the Americans – lay unappetisingly on the table. Originally it had been conceived as a short-term operation aimed at the Pas de Calais, on the grounds that this was the only place where Fighter Command could supply a measure of air cover. Mountbatten's advice as Combined Ops chief was firmly against it, arguing for landing much further west. In the end attention had settled on the Cherbourg Peninsula, with a large force capturing and holding it in the autumn of 1942 then breaking out in the spring. It was a fantastic scheme. The peninsula was beyond the effective range at which the RAF could provide air cover and the resupply problems would be nightmarish.

Sledgehammer was outdone in improbability by Imperator, a quixotic proposal to land an armoured force in northern France which would race to Paris, destroy the German military headquarters in the Crillon hotel then speed back to the coast for re-embarkation. Commenting to the chiefs on various versions of the Imperator plan, Mountbatten remarked that 'none of the above . . . can be classified as normal "operations of war" since they are largely devised for the purpose of achieving a political object.'[1] It was 'important to avoid embarking on an operation which the enemy can make appear as a total defeat'. However, something was needed that would provide 'the best solution to an unpleasant military problem'.

Responsibility for the big cross-Channel show, if it ever came, would lie in the hands of the commander-in-chief of Home Forces, General Sir Bernard Paget, who took over from Brooke at the end of

1941. Paget had a short fuse. According to Goronwy Rees, who met him in the course of his liaison duties, he displayed a 'brusque manner, that seemed to combine rudeness and bad temper', the consequence it was said of the constant pain from a 1918 wound that rendered his left arm virtually useless.[2] He made it clear from the beginning that he regarded these schemes as a waste of time, lives and resources.

The home-based divisions had since 1940 been braced to repel a German invasion. As the threat dwindled they were now needed for an eventual landing on the continent, a day that in Paget's view was still a long way off. In the meantime any sideshows could only disrupt preparations and delay the advent of the main event, and he struggled against being dragged into them, questioning directives ordering him to draw up interim plans.

In November 1941, when Britain's resources were minimal and America had not yet joined the war, he was told by the chiefs to prepare 'a large-scale raid of some duration in the Low Countries and France' for the spring. He settled reluctantly on Brest as the target but at the end of January reported that shortage of shipping and inadequate air cover made the project impracticable and asked that it be put off until September. Even then he considered 'the chances of success are uncertain'.[3]

He went on to suggest some criteria for judging the value of such enterprises. 'The sole object of killing Germans is not worthy of a large-scale raid since they are in good supply and of comparatively low propaganda value,' he wrote. 'The destruction of material objectives must have lasting results on enemy operations or war production and the objectives themselves must not be such as can be more easily or less expensively destroyed by: a) air bombardment b) naval bombardment c) minor sea or airborne raids d) local patriots.'

These were sound enough rules to the conventional military mind but the emphasis on caution and sobriety struck no chord at Combined Operations. Raiding was their business and they approached each project great and small with the same hectic enthusiasm. The activity suited the personality of their chief and his team. It was a very British form of warfare reflecting temperament as much as geography. One of the proudest moments in British naval history came in 1587 when Sir Francis Drake launched fireships into the Spanish fleet at Cadiz, 'singeing the king of Spain's beard' and delaying the sailing of the Armada for a year. The instinct was just as strong on land. On the Western Front in the First World War commanders kept the troops on their toes by ordering regular 'trench raids'.

A handful of men crept in darkness across no man's land, dropped over an enemy parapet, shot or bludgeoned to death whomever they found there, sparing a few to take back as prisoners. The enemy did not think the exercise worthwhile. Although the British had launched regular provocative raids across the Channel since the start of the current war, the Germans had not bothered to mount a single one in return.

The same impulse was also on show in the air. Since the Battle of Britain, the Spitfires of Fighter Command had been flying across the Channel daily to try to provoke the enemy to come up and fight, a challenge the Luftwaffe usually declined unless the odds were strongly in their favour.

Combined Ops was a new cog in the war-planning machine. As such it had to mesh with the other service mechanisms driving military activity. The foundation directive handed to Mountbatten had given COHQ the long-term task of preparing, along with multiple other organisations, for the eventual invasion of the continent. In the meantime, though, its primary activity was all aspects of the planning and mounting of raids.

COHQ planners were charged with advising on big existing projects like Sledgehammer but they were also commissioned to devise specific raids requested by the army, navy and air force. They were also expected to come up with schemes of their own in accordance with the prime minister's desire to keep the Germans off balance by constant harassment of the enemy-held coastline.

The process began at Richmond Terrace with a nucleus of officers discussing requests and proposals. It was usually led by Jock Hughes-Hallett and his naval colleagues on the basis that there was 'no use suggesting places which could not be reached by the appropriate landing craft or other vessels'.[4] Helping him were commanders David

Luce and 'Dick' de Costobadie. Both were career officers who had seen plenty of action. Luce commanded a submarine in the early part of the war winning a DSO for his exploits, and de Costobadie had earned a DSC at Dunkirk. The COHQ military and air advisers were then brought in and once an embryonic plan looked viable it was taken to Mountbatten, who seems to have almost invariably given his approval. Every operation depended on the help of the navy and air force and as the project gathered pace their representatives joined the team. In the case of larger raids requiring more troops than the commandos could provide, the planning team would be reinforced by officers from Home Forces HQ.

Anything other than very minor raids were referred to the Chiefs of Staff Committee which approved the outline plan and reviewed onward progress. Thus they could control the pace of projected operations like Sledgehammer for which they felt little enthusiasm but felt compelled to keep alive in the interests of Anglo-American harmony, while giving the green light to less contentious schemes. Churchill was also kept informed. Despite his fierce opposition to a premature return to the continent he was all in favour of modest-scale cross-Channel adventures, the more dashing the better.

On 21 January 1942 Hughes-Hallett sat down with Luce and de Costobadie to 'make tentative proposals for one raid every month up to and including August'.[5] Some were in response to outside demands and others were in-house productions. The first on the list was a parachute raid, scheduled for the end of February, to seize equipment from a radar station in Normandy. It had been requested by the RAF, who feared that the Germans had dramatically improved their anti-bomber electronic defences. Next came a major seaborne attack on the port of Saint-Nazaire. The target was the huge dry dock whose destruction the Admiralty had long desired as it would deprive the Germans of the only facility on the French Atlantic coast capable of repairing their largest warship, the battleship *Tirpitz*.

These operations had clear objectives and obvious military value. The purpose of others on the list was less precise. They included Operation Myrmidon, a long-range expedition to land a large force near Bayonne in south-western France to blow up war factories and disrupt rail traffic to Spain which was scheduled to take place immediately after Saint-Nazaire. Operation Blazing, timed for May, was an ambitious plan to seize and hold the small Channel Island of Alderney. From there, Hughes-Hallett explained, 'we hoped it would at least be possible to cut the German coastal route to the Atlantic ports by which they had sustained much of the U-boat campaign'.

No clear reason was offered for selecting the next target on the list. 'For June we chose Dieppe,' he wrote, 'as by that time we expected to have sufficient landing craft to lift an entire division.' They would attack Dieppe, it seemed, simply because they could. It was a curiously limp explanation for the event that would stain the entire history of Combined Operations Headquarters.

The early months of 1942 were a happy time for Mountbatten and his team. A string of successes seemed to more than justify the faith Churchill had invested in them. Their debut was a triumph. In late December 1941 they pulled off an operation that saw the commandos going into serious action for the first time. The objective was once again Norwegian islands and their fish-oil factories and other worthwhile targets.

In many ways the raids were a rerun of the Roger Keyes exploit of the previous March. This time though the Germans put up a proper fight. The ensuing battle showed what the new units were capable of and proved the value of the Achnacarry curriculum.

Operations Anklet and Archery were a two-pronged attack on widely separated Norwegian islands. Anklet, the smaller of the two, was aimed at the Lofoten Islands. Once again the objectives were to destroy enemy assets, take prisoners and seize any code books and Enigma material they could find. It was also intended to divert attention from Archery, the bigger raid, on Vaagso, an island between Trondheim and Bergen 300 miles to the south. Both raids had the added benefit of contributing to a grand strategic deception being played by Churchill. The return to the islands, it was hoped, would persuade Hitler that the Allies intended a landing in Norway and prompt him to boost troop numbers, thereby relieving pressure on the Eastern Front.[6]

With Archery, combined operations took a great step forward. This was a properly tri-service effort with the navy providing the troop carriers plus a cruiser and four destroyers, the army the troops, and the RAF contributing air support in the shape of nineteen Blenheim twin-engine fighters and ten Hampden bombers. Each service nominated a force commander and staff to work together on a combined plan, setting the pattern for the raids that were to follow.

The Anklet force, a mix of commandos and Free Norwegians, was embarked on the landing ship HMS *Prince Albert*, one of the requisitioned Belgian cross-Channel ferries available for Combined Ops missions. It was supported by the light cruiser HMS *Arethusa* and a phalanx of destroyers and corvettes. They landed early on Boxing Day morning when it was hoped the defenders would be lying in after the previous day's festivities. They met no resistance and set about blowing up radio transmitters, capturing prisoners and quislings and sinking ships. On one patrol vessel the raiders discovered an intact Enigma machine with rotor wheels, part of a rich haul of intelligence material gathered in the twin operations. On 27 December the force was attacked by a German seaplane and *Arethusa* damaged. In the absence of any protection from the air, the commander, Rear Admiral L. H. K. Hamilton, decided to head for home, mission by and large accomplished.

Vaagso was well defended with coastal guns, 200 regular troops, anti-aircraft batteries and four squadrons of fighters. A fight was expected and so it turned out. This was to the liking of John Durnford-Slater, commander of 3 Commando which provided the core of the land force. He and his men had been on the original Lofoten raid which 'everyone had enjoyed . . . and felt that they had done useful work'.[7] However they 'were disappointed at not seeing more action. All ranks had a burning desire to get at the enemy . . .' Durnford-Slater was thirty-two and born in Devon to a military family. His father was killed in the first few weeks of the previous war. Despite strong encouragement from his mother he had shown little inclination to follow the colours, dreaming instead of emigrating to Argentina and breeding horses. Mother's will prevailed and he ended up training as a gunner at the Royal Military Academy, Woolwich before being posted to India where he eked out his pay by training and betting on racehorses.

His fellow commando Lord Lovat admired him as a 'genial sportsman . . . All his faults were of a lovable kind. No beauty in appearance, going bald, stocky and of medium height with a jerky, short-stepping kind of action [he] spoke in a high voice, but the restless energy and drive were immediately apparent'.[8] Durnford-Slater 'knew what he wanted' and 'got the best out of his men'. He also enjoyed a party and could 'drink all night in the mess, parade the next day as fresh as a daisy, train for the morning and play a good game of rugger in the afternoon'.

At the end of November 1941 he had been summoned to Richmond Terrace to hear a proposal for 3 Commando's next job. He was given a thorough intelligence summary of the formidable German defences on Vaagso and the neighbouring small island of Maaloy to study before meeting the chief. The raid was Mountbatten's operational debut and he seemed uncharacteristically cautious, wondering out loud whether it might not 'be better to take on something not quite so strong?' He was particularly concerned about the shore batteries covering the approaches. Durnford-Slater assured him that if the cruiser *Kenya* leading the raid flotilla and its escort of destroyers closed to 3,000 yards of the shore just before the landing, they could give the batteries 'a real pounding' that would dispose of the problem. As for the opposition, Mountbatten could 'rely on our men to look after the German garrison'. With this response Mountbatten became 'most enthusiastic. Knowing that it was desperately important at this stage of the war to have a success, he had just wanted to be convinced.'

The timetable gave Durnford-Slater a few weeks to put his men through an intense preparation programme at their base at Largs, a seaside resort near Glasgow. COHQ provided a large model of the target area, location unidentified to maintain security, to familiarise them with their objectives. The force numbered nearly 600 men. It included the whole of 3 Commando, two troops of 2 Commando and a dozen Free Norwegians. They set sail from Scapa on Christmas Eve, seen off by Mountbatten who told them: 'I regard you as my test pilots. Nobody knows quite what is going to happen and you are the ones who are going to find out.' On 27 December, before dawn, the troops climbed into their landing craft and were lowered into the icy waters of the Vaagsfjord. As they approached the shore the first broadsides from the escorts slammed into the coastal battery on Maaloy. Four troops headed for the village of Sor Vaagso and two for Maaloy, with two troops of 2 Commando held back as a floating reserve.

Just before they touched down, three Hampdens flashed overhead and dropped smoke bombs to mask the approach. One was hit by flak and as it went down a bomb fell away and hit a landing craft. The phosphorus inflicted terrible burns among the men and detonated grenades, demolition charges and small-arms ammunition 'in a mad mixture of battle noises'.

Durnford-Slater led the attack on the settlement, a line of unpainted wooden buildings which straggled along a narrow street three-quarters of a mile long. His account gave a taste of the frantic energy of a raid where everything depended on maintaining momentum and denying the defenders the initiative. The example was set by the troop commanders. Durnford-Slater watched as Captain Johnny Giles of 3 Troop yelled 'Come on!' and raced at the head of his men into the smoke. Fifteen minutes later he was dead, shot by the last survivor of a house they were storming. Captain Algy Forrester commanding 4 Troop 'went off like a rocket' up the street 'leaving a trail of dead Germans behind him'. The two officers with him were soon wounded and out of action but 'Algy waded in, shouting and cheering his men, throwing grenades into each house as they came to it and firing from the hip with his tommy gun. He looked wild and dangerous . . . He had absolutely no fear'. When the party reached the German HQ in the Ulvasund Hotel he darted forward to hurl a grenade but was shot by someone firing through the front door. As he fell he landed on his own bomb.

With Forrester's death the pace faltered and the attack threatened to stall. Martin Linge, a well-known actor before the war, now commander of a Free Norwegian unit, tried to smash open the hotel door but fell back dead in a burst of gunfire. Durnford-Slater had passed him as they left the beach, smiling and happy and promising 'We'll have a party . . . when we get back.'

By now the air was thick with the smoke of burning buildings and filled with the crack and stutter of rifle and machine-gun fire, the boom of the ships' guns and the answering salvos of the batteries, and further away the echo of cannon shells and anti-aircraft barrages as German fighters attacked the flotilla. Despite the mayhem they had brought with them, the raiders were welcomed by the inhabitants, some of whom risked their lives ferrying grenades to the advancing troops.

The deadlock on the main street was broken with the arrival of 6 Troop who had finished their work on Maaloy. Captain Peter Young and Lance Sergeant George Herbert launched themselves at the hotel hurling grenades through windows and doors, killing or disabling everyone inside. The attack moved on only to be baulked again by a sniper. Durnford-Slater was pinned down with half of 6 Troop in a timber yard. One man fell dead beside him. Then another. Later he recalled that 'this was the first time in warfare that I truly felt fear.' The sniper was perched in an upper window in a nearby house, firing whenever anyone showed themselves. They were saved by the initiative of Sergeant Herbert who discovered a can of petrol in a shed behind the yard. While the others sprang to their feet to rake the building with covering fire he ran up to a window and tossed in the can. A shower of grenades set the house instantly ablaze, 'a funeral pyre for the sniper'.

This was what the commandos had spent long months and endless hardships training for. Despite their sophisticated skills they knew that battle still came down to a killing competition and there was no room for pity or time for reflection. As the commandos advanced further up the street, a door opened and a German lobbed a grenade which badly wounded Durnford-Slater's batman. Thirty seconds later 'the same door opened and the German who had tossed the grenade came out with his hands up and expressing his earnest desire to surrender'. He was 'a small man, yellow and scared' and Durnford-Slater was prepared to let him live. However 'one of my men . . . was so angry that he shot the German dead, through the stomach.' He later considered whether a man who had lobbed a death-dealing grenade one minute should be allowed to surrender the next before concluding 'I hardly think he [could] expect much mercy.'

While the battle blazed the navy had been sinking the ships in the anchorage. The intention had been to seize some of the larger ones but the Germans scuttled most of them. The defenders were unable to prevent one of the great coups of the operation. On board the destroyer HMS *Onslow* was Lieutenant Commander Allon Bacon from the Naval Intelligence Division, which led the hunt for Enigma material. With him was Dick de Costobadie from COHQ. After *Onslow* cornered the armed trawler *Fohn*, they gathered a boarding party and stormed the boat, capturing a precious list of Enigma daily settings plus a copy of the current encryption tables.[9] Other parties were busy elsewhere and the final haul amounted to two Enigma machines and a wealth of coding tables that four days later were in the hands of the Bletchley code breakers.

The raiders departed at 15.00 leaving 120 German dead. They took with them nearly a hundred prisoners as well as a party of Norwegian volunteers. Durnford-Slater reckoned their own losses 'reasonably light' at seventeen dead and fifty-seven wounded. The action had been captured on film by two movie cameramen and a stills photographer who earned Durnford-Slater's admiration for staying continuously at the forefront of the battle. Their material boosted the rapturous publicity that followed. It was, *The Times* declared, 'the perfect raid'.

The next operation brought more glory to Richmond Terrace. Operation Biting was mounted to capture key components from a Würzburg radar station perched on a cliff at Bruneval, north of Le Havre. After analysing reconnaissance photographs and intelligence reports, some from French Resistance agents, the COHQ planners thought the defences too strong for a commando attack from the sea and decided to use paratroops instead. On the night of 27 February 1942, 120 men from C Company of the 2nd Parachute Battalion dropped a few miles from the villa where the radar was installed.

They overcame the defenders and an RAF signals expert dismantled the vital parts. Then, having captured one of the technicians, they retreated to the beach where landing craft ferried them to motor gun boats which sped them back to Britain. Examination of the equipment revealed the system was impervious to conventional jamming and opened the way to the use of 'window', aluminumised paper strips which created a blizzard of signals on radar screens effectively blinding the defences.[10]

Then came the coup that really made COHQ's name. The Admiralty had been pressing for a raid on Saint-Nazaire for months. In the autumn of 1941 fears rose that Hitler's last remaining battleship, *Tirpitz*, would soon be heading to the Atlantic.[11] The Naval Intelligence Division began working with COHQ on a plan to cripple its ability to operate by denying it the use of the only dry dock on the French Atlantic seaboard large enough to accept it for maintenance and repairs. Operation Chariot was a broad collaborative effort with input from all the service intelligence agencies as well as MI6 and civilian engineers. Together they constructed a full picture of the topography, defences and port facilities.

Their contribution gets little mention in Hughes-Hallett's often immodest and self-serving memoir, which makes it sound as if it were largely a Combined Ops affair. He claimed that after the initial approach from the Admiralty it took him and David Luce only an hour to sketch an outline plan. COHQ certainly played an important part in shaping the operation, including the proposal to use HMS *Campbeltown*, an obsolete destroyer packed with explosives, to ram the lock gates before being blown up. During February the outline plan was finalised and the date set for 28 March.

Mountbatten took a close interest in the details, particularly the air support available to the raiders. The plan called for Bomber Command to carry out continuous attacks on the dock area before the assault began, shifting to the town once it had started. Laying on a bombing raid in occupied France raised political difficulties. Churchill had forbidden major operations that risked serious civilian casualties unless weather conditions guaranteed a high degree of accuracy, a vain hope given the technical abilities of Bomber Command at this point in the war. However, Mountbatten insisted and the chiefs of staff agreed that 'the success of Operation Chariot depended very largely on the success of the diversion created by the bombing'.[12] In the event, low cloud forced the aircraft to circle overhead without dropping their bombs, leaving the defenders unmolested. The episode nonetheless showed the importance Mountbatten placed on aerial bombardment as a vital component in a large raid.

The Saint-Nazaire proposal got the immediate approval of the chiefs. Here was an operation that made sense and whose undoubted risks were greatly outweighed by the potential benefits. Commanders were appointed. Commander Robert Ryder, 'Red' to his friends, a thirty-four-year-old career sailor whose two brothers had already died in the war, would lead the naval force. The military force commander was Lieutenant Colonel Charles Newman, thirty-seven, a genial, pipe-smoking former Territorial with four children and a fifth on the way, and commanding officer (CO) of 2 Commando who made up the bulk of the troops.

According to Hughes-Hallett things went smoothly until a meeting on 28 February when Mountbatten and he, together with Ryder and Newman, met Rear Admiral Sir Arthur Power and Admiral of the Fleet Sir Charles Forbes to discuss the plan. Power was Assistant Chief of the Naval Staff, supervising home operations. Forbes was Commander-in-Chief, Plymouth, where the fleet would assemble, train and depart from. Both men thus had a say in the project and Forbes made it clear he regarded it as akin to a suicide mission.

Hughes-Hallett claimed that when they walked in he greeted them with the words: 'Well I congratulate you gentlemen. As long as you don't mind having every ship in the raiding force sunk and every soldier and sailor killed, I am sure it will be a great success.'[13]

Mountbatten and Forbes had history. When commander of the Home Fleet in 1940 Forbes had turned down Churchill's suggestion that Mountbatten should be awarded the DSO for nursing the *Kelly* back to port after being torpedoed in the North Sea, declaring it was only what any captain would have done. Time had not made the admiral any more amenable. He was 'strongly opposed' to the COHQ proposal to blow up HMS *Campbeltown* soon after arrival, while the ship's company and soldiers took cover alongside nearby air-raid shelters. Experts had told him that the blast would kill everyone within half a mile. Hughes-Hallett assured him that his own advisers were confident that the troops would be safely protected by the earth and masonry of the shelters. The admiral stood his ground, insisting that the explosion be delayed until after the force had withdrawn. In the end he got his way.

There was worse to come. The force commanders now began raising objections. Newman said he disliked having 'all his eggs in one basket' with the bulk of the force embarked on the destroyer. He wanted them to be spread out among a larger number of launches and landed at different points around the dockyard. Ryder began to question the wisdom of using the *Campbeltown*, fearing it might run aground. Hughes-Hallett recalled that 'it was in vain that we pointed out that motor launches were made of wood and driven by petrol and the chances of achieving surprise with an armada of . . . coastal craft were slim'. The likelihood was that 'they would all be blazing wrecks before they got alongside at all'.

To Hughes-Hallett's indignation, 'such was the deference paid to Newman and Ryder simply because they were going to *do* the job that they nearly got their way'. Opposition collapsed only when Mountbatten 'made it clear that COHQ would have nothing more to do with the operation unless the expendable ship remained its central feature'. In the end a compromise was reached with some of the commandos sailing on the *Campbeltown* and the others split between an expanded flotilla of eighteen launches.

Chariot largely followed the script written for it by Hughes-Hallett and his team. The raiders bluffed their way to within striking distance of the port, rammed the lock gates, then leapt ashore to start demolishing facilities. Resistance was fierce and only a remnant made it back to the launches. Eight hours after the *Campbeltown* hit the gates the explosives erupted, tearing away the caissons and killing a party of forty German soldiers and civilian officials who had gone on board. The dry dock was put out of action for the rest of the war.[14] There were medals galore, including five VCs with Ryder and Newman among the recipients.

For Mountbatten and his team the operation was above all a vindication. There were still some of the old school who failed to see the point of the organisation, or like Admiral Forbes, doubted the qualities of its chief. With Saint-Nazaire, Mountbatten and his team had shown them. The things that went right, like the idea of using a destroyer to ram the gates, were Combined Ops ideas. The things that went wrong, like increasing the number of launches, were someone else's and done against their advice. The price of success had been high. Of the 622 sailors and soldiers who took part, 168 were killed and 215 taken prisoner.

This was a staggering casualty rate but COHQ planners could disclaim responsibility for it, insisting losses would have been lower if their proposal that fewer craft should be used had been followed. The episode had not only boosted the planning staff's already considerable self-esteem; it had also reinforced its belief in the soundness of its judgements, even when they clashed with established service wisdom and the objections of conventionally minded colleagues including those like Newman and Ryder whose own lives were at risk.

With Saint-Nazaire, the run of luck Combined Ops had enjoyed since Mountbatten's takeover came to an end to be replaced by a period of failure, frustration and setback. Operation Myrmidon was meant to follow hard on its heels. It was a large seaborne attack around Bayonne in south-western France and conceived as an alternative to a tentative proposal for another raid in Norway which was abandoned when it seemed German dispositions in the target area were too strong.[15] The Chiefs of Staff Committee reviewed it on 22 February when its objectives were described as 'the destruction of coastal shipping . . . the destruction of an important explosives factory at the mouth of the River Adour and the severing of the rail connection from France to Spain which is vulnerable in this area'. The proposal failed in every respect the tests suggested by General Paget for judging the merits of a raid. All the targets could be attacked more cheaply by bombing, and any damage to the railway was likely to be repaired within days. It was approved nonetheless, probably because it had the enthusiastic backing of the prime minister.[16]

Myrmidon was an unredeemed flop. At the end of March about 3,000 commandos and Royal Marines with supporting armour boarded the former Dutch ferries HMS *Queen Emma* and HMS *Princess Beatrix* and sailed for the mouth of the River Adour which led to Bayonne. They arrived at the estuary without trouble. It was only when the landing craft had been lowered to carry the force ashore that the officer in charge decided that a sandbar across the mouth of the river was probably impassable. An emergency flare summoned all craft back and the force departed for home having, as Hughes-Hallett admitted, 'achieved nothing whatsoever'.[17] This was just the start of 'weeks of frustration'. Myrmidon was supposed to be followed in May by the projected landing on Alderney, code-named Operation Blazing. It faced trouble from the start, and Hughes-Hallett's enthusiasm was constantly dampened by the objections of those who would have to carry it out. Unlike Chariot and Myrmidon, this was not a commando operation. The raiding force was made up of the 1st Guards Brigade and a battalion of airborne troops. The aim was to capture and hold the small, rocky island which lies west of the tip of the Cherbourg Peninsula for use as a base to attack German shipping supplying the Atlantic ports. The plan proposed a 'saturation' bombing raid before the paratroops dropped and the guards hit the beaches.

It was obvious from the outset that the hearts of the soldiers and airmen were not in it. Hughes-Hallett suspected that the military commander was 'reluctant to chance his arm'.[18] Bomber Command were only prepared to operate in darkness whereas the Airborne Division commander General Browning insisted his troops could only be dropped in daylight. Blazing was stopped in its tracks at a chiefs of staff meeting on 11 May attended by Churchill who warned that they could not 'in the present circumstances afford the risk of heavy casualties to our bomber force'.[19] Brooke was very sceptical about what effect the bombing would have on the German defences. As was often the case, the project was not pronounced dead there and then but put on life support until the autumn when it would be evaluated again. So it was that as summer arrived COHQ had only two major schemes on its books. One, Imperator, was still a work in progress with wide disagreement on the form it should take. The other was Dieppe.

'Why choose Dieppe?' That was the first question on everyone's lips when the news of the raid became known. The second was: 'And what for?' There is little in official records to provide answers. As the Canadian Army's official historian Colonel Charles Stacey noted after being given free access to all the files when writing his account post-war, 'Although the Dieppe raid is in general a very well documented operation, the documentation with reference to its *origins and objects* − points of special importance − is far from complete.'[20] As a result 'the historian is obliged to rely to a considerable extent upon the memories and the verbal evidence of informed persons'. These recollections brought their own difficulties. If Dieppe had been a success, the victory would have had many fathers. As a failure it was an orphan and the key participants fell over each other in the rush to deny paternity.

The responsibility for choosing Dieppe lay primarily with Hughes-Hallett as chair of the planning group which in January 1942 drew up a list of suggested operations for the first eight months of the year. Mountbatten also bore some liability as he oversaw the proposals, agreed them in principle and asked 'for outline plans to be prepared and discussed with him as soon as possible'.[21]

In his memoirs Hughes-Hallett gives a few words to justify the inclusion of the other targets on the list. About Dieppe he is strikingly reticent. On the face of it nothing linked Dieppe to the imperatives of the day. Unlike Saint-Nazaire, Brest and the other U-boat bases on the Atlantic, it had no military significance and was merely a port of call for coastal convoys. Destroying it completely would do nothing to reduce Germany's war-making capacity. Nor was a division-strength raid of short duration likely to result in any significant shift of enemy troops away from the Eastern Front. His vague statement on the subject − 'For June we chose Dieppe, as by that time we expected to have sufficient landing craft to lift an entire division' − tells us nothing.

Elsewhere, he claimed that there was no particular significance to the location, telling an American TV interviewer in 1967:

> Dieppe was chosen really for no particular reason originally except that it was a small seaport and we thought it would be interesting to capture a small seaport for a short time and then withdraw. It was just about the extremity of the range at which Fighter Command could give us cover in those days. It was not thought to be of any particular military importance and it was known at the time when we chose it early in the year not to be very strongly defended. And it appeared, so we were told by the military adviser, that it would be about the scale of objective that would be suitable for a divisional attack. That, in a nutshell, were the reasons for choosing Dieppe ... we were raiding for the sake of raiding – that was the strategy really.[22]

But a few seconds later he corrected himself. There was, after all,

> an object within an object in the special case of Dieppe. We were desperately anxious – or the senior military officers were – to get some experience to carry out what might be called an armed reconnaissance – to try and find out the sort of conditions that would be met in carrying out a fairly large-scale landing operation against determined resistance. It was something that had never been done since Gallipoli ... so it was very important to gain experience and that really was the main object of Dieppe as such.

A fuller explanation was laid out for the public in the official history of Combined Operations *The Watery Maze*, written under Mountbatten's close supervision by his friend Bernard Fergusson, and published in 1961. Fergusson wrote that in all the discussions that spring about attempting a temporary lodgement on the continent, like Sledgehammer, or a permanent one, like Roundup, 'there was always one constant accepted by everybody: a good port, in working order, must be seized early on, and before the enemy could have time to carry out demolitions'.[23] The view was that 'generally speaking one division, with two brigade groups in the assault and one in reserve, would suffice to capture a continental port, provided that it was supported by bombardment from sea and air, and that it included an element of tanks.' It was widely accepted that before such an exercise could be mounted the proposition 'must be tried out in practice'.

It was true that attention had focussed on the feasibility of capturing a major port which could supply the needs of an invading army. The only ones within reach big enough to handle the huge flow of stores needed to keep the force in the field were Antwerp, Cherbourg and Le Havre. Dieppe was modest by comparison. That, said Fergusson, was one of the reasons why it was chosen. The planners had 'already ruled it out as a desirable place to capture in the early stages of a real invasion, and we should therefore be giving nothing away by raiding it now'.

There were other considerations that made it a good choice. 'It quickly became obvious,' he wrote, 'that of all the targets up and down the Channel coast Dieppe was by far the best prospect.' The defences were believed to be 'tough, but not too tough'. There was a range of attractive targets in the shape of the airfield three miles inland and a harbour full of shipping including barges left over from 1940 when an invasion of Britain was still in prospect which could be seized and brought back across the Channel. Dieppe was near enough to England to allow the passage over to be made under cover of darkness in summertime. Crucially it was also within range of the many fighter bases sited in Sussex, Kent and Dorset, allowing a high level of fighter cover during much of the operation.

Beyond testing the feasibility of capturing a port intact, Fergusson offered a higher goal. 'The real purpose,' he declared, 'was to gain experience: to test certain tactical conceptions, and to learn more of the technique required to breach . . . the Atlantic Wall.' Thus it 'would be a raid, certainly, in the sense that the force, having got ashore, would re-embark and return to base; but it was in reality a rehearsal for re-invasion'.

The claim that Dieppe was 'a rehearsal for re-invasion' was advanced repeatedly by Mountbatten and his lieutenants and those most closely associated with the raid to defend themselves against the accusations and recriminations that would pursue them down the years. It was the rationale given by Churchill when he stood up in the House of Commons three weeks after the raid on 8 September to offer an explanation for what was by then regarded as a disaster. The operation was, he said, 'a reconnaissance in force', a term that he had just invented, with the object of getting all the information necessary before launching operations on a much larger scale, and 'an indispensable preliminary to full scale operations'.[24]

It was popularised in the title of the first book-length account to appear, *Dress Rehearsal: The Story of Dieppe* by the American journalist Quentin Reynolds who sailed with the attacking force. Far more expert military observers like Captain Stephen Roskill, the official historian of the Royal Navy in the Second World War, repeated it in his history of the war at sea, in which he stated: 'the War Office was insistent that, before a full-scale invasion was launched in Europe, it was essential to gain up-to-date experience by making a raid in force against the enemy-held coastline.'[25]

But the people who most needed convincing that the operation had a real purpose were the troops who before long would be called on to do something similar. To them, Dieppe would be presented as a tragic but necessary sacrifice, the cost of which was justified by lessons learned which resulted in many fewer lives being lost in the invasion to come. The justification was memorably laid out by General Crerar, the commander of the 1st Canadian Corps, who told the men of 3rd Canadian Infantry Division on the eve of the Normandy landings: 'The plan, the preparations, the method and technique which will be employed are based on knowledge and experience bought and paid for by 2 Canadian division at Dieppe.'[26] Mountbatten went as far as to quantify the ratio between lives lost and lives saved, telling Canadian veterans at a gathering thirty-one years after the event that 'the effect on the OVERLORD casualties was fantastic . . . twelve times as many men . . . survived the D-Day assaults and I am convinced that this was directly the result of the lessons we learned at Dieppe.'[27]

Repetition did not make these claims true. Neither did the frequency and vehemence with which they were uttered. Instead they only deepened the impression that whichever way you looked at it, little about Dieppe made sense.

PART TWO

5. *Les Doryphores*

Dieppe's very familiarity made it seem a strange place to launch an attack. Its name evoked memories of sunlit summer holidays. 'Little did I ever think in the old days of my regular journeys of Newhaven-Dieppe that I should have been planning as I was this morning!' was the reaction of Alan Brooke when the raid first came before the Chiefs of Staff Committee for approval on 13 May.[1]

It lies in a dip in a solid rampart of chalk, stretches of which are 200 feet high. The cliffs are a dingy white and streaked with ochre from the rich topsoil of the fields and woods above. Seventy or so miles across the Channel in East Sussex you find an identical coastline. It's as if a giant meringue has been snapped in half, and little imagination is needed to understand that aeons ago the two land masses were one.

The British knew it as a mildly exotic holiday destination. Since the 1850s when the ferry service began, the town filled up each summer with holidaymakers who came to bathe, gamble at the casino, watch the latest Paris plays and entertainments in the Theatre Royal, play golf on the links and go to the races at the hippodrome at Rouxmesnil-Bouteilles. Famous British and French artists set up their easels there. Sickert, Turner, Monet, Pissarro and Renoir were all drawn to the crystalline light and subtle colours of the port, the beaches and the seaward vistas from the clifftops.

As well as the visitors there was a core of permanent expatriate residents, the '*colonie anglaise*', many of them military and Civil Service widows who found that pensions went further and the risk of social embarrassment was lower on this side of the Channel. At the posher end of the spectrum were some grand families, including Lord Salisbury, three times Conservative prime minister between 1885 and 1902. His stone and brick villa in the Normandy style completed in 1872 stood above the beach at Puys, just to the east of Dieppe. As a girl, Clementine Churchill knew Dieppe well as her mother moved the family there in the summers, and after marriage she and Winston visited often.

The welcome the British received was in keeping with the cosmopolitan outlook of the Dieppois. The town owed its existence to the sea. It is omnipresent in Dieppe. Even when out of sight it makes its presence felt in the cry of gulls, the tang of salt and seaweed and the kinetic rumble of the waves. The sea brought opportunity. Dieppe men sailed the oceans in small ships to plant the flag of France in Asia and the New World. They helped colonise Florida, the Carolinas and Canada, a link commemorated in the Bassin du Canada, in the docks.

The sea also brought danger. In 1694 the town was bombarded by an Anglo-Dutch fleet and almost completely destroyed. It was rebuilt under the supervision of Louis XIV's great military architect-engineer Vauban. His assistant Monsieur de Ventabren designed a townscape of narrow streets lined with tall houses enclosing courtyards, pierced by brick arch windows and adorned with wrought-iron balconies that brought a touch of elegance to the utilitarian port.

In the spring of 1942 Dieppe was about to start its third year under German occupation. It fell in the Zone Interdite, the band of coastline running from Dunkirk in the north to Hendaye in the south subject to special anti-invasion measures and restrictions. The town had become a ghostly sketch of its pre-war self. Gradually the pre-war population of 23,000 ebbed away so that only about a half remained. To one inhabitant, Madame Ménage, it 'was like living in a house with no windows, black everywhere' and with no light on the horizon.[2]

The occupiers promised to be magnanimous in victory. They would conduct themselves 'correctly' and if the French behaved nobody – apart from the Reich's racial and ideological enemies – would get hurt. In practice, that meant acting according to a rulebook they had written to suit themselves. They took what they wanted, requisitioning public buildings, hotels and private houses and scarce food, issuing worthless receipts in return.

The conquerors stamped their identity on everything. The town was festooned with giant swastika flags and each crossroads was a forest of signposts in German directing the troops to barracks, offices and bases. Dieppe had become an outpost of the Reich and even the clocks were set to Berlin time.

The local authorities had no choice but to conform. There was no protection from the government because the Vichy regime's commitment to collaboration was wholehearted from the start. An article of the armistice signed with the Germans stated: 'The French government will immediately order all French authorities and administration services in the occupied zone to follow the regulations of the German military authorities and to collaborate with the latter in a correct matter.' Vichy dismantled the political architecture and symbolism of the Third Republic, abolishing the National Assembly and all elected bodies. It banned the tricolour and the 14 July national holiday. The bust of Marianne which used to sit in the *mairie* of every commune was replaced with one of Marshal Philippe Pétain and his pale blue eyes looked down on his *'enfants'* from portraits hung in every schoolroom. Newspapers and radio stations all spoke with the voice of Vichy.

Pétain presented himself as a shield against the invader. It was soon clear that his protection did not extend to everyone. In the autumn of 1940, with the full backing of Vichy, proclamations were issued announcing 'measures' against the Jews. Jewish-owned shops and businesses were forced to display signs identifying themselves as such. In the department of Seine-Inférieure to which Dieppe belonged, the prefect René Bouffet decreed that every public employee from high officials to workers in the municipal abattoir must sign a declaration stating they were not Jews or Freemasons. There was much worse to come.

At first the speed of the catastrophe left most people too numb to react. More than 100,000 Frenchmen died in the seven weeks between the start of the German attack in May 1940 and the 22 June armistice. A million and a half more were in prisoner-of-war camps. Defeat was followed by economic collapse. In Dieppe, much of the local economy was based on fishing and related industries which provided a living for 6,000 people. The Germans banned fishing at first and when the ban was lifted there were heavy restrictions. Factories, brickworks and coal depots were destroyed in the German air raids that struck the town in the first week of the war and the British ones that followed, and economic activity dwindled to almost nothing.

The first months of the occupation brought widespread destitution. The local courts filled up with previously respectable people reduced to thieving to stay alive. The pathetic story revealed at the Tribunal Correctionel for 7 August 1940 was typical: 'Marie Hervy, 47, unemployed, of 3 rue Bouzard and Angèle Prudent, 53, day labourer, of 7 rue David-Lacroix, three months' imprisonment for theft of an overall . . . Auguste Arnaud, 66, retired, two months' imprisonment, suspended, for theft of foodstuffs from the Prisunic store . . .'[3]

Among the population were supporters of the ideologies that had pulled France apart in the years before the war. The far right were anti-democratic, anti-Semitic, anti-communist and nationalist. To some of them defeat was almost welcome. It offered a catharsis and a leader who would guide the nation back to the virtues of an imagined past. Marshal Pétain's most fervent supporter in Dieppe was the editor of the local newspaper, *La Vigie*. Louis-Marie Poullain used its columns to promote the 'National Revolution' and its values of '*Travail, Famille, Patrie*'. He was also violently anti-British, claiming England – as both the Germans and the French persisted in calling Britain – had always been the real enemy. 'The day of her annihilation,' he wrote, 'will surely be liberation day for the whole world.'[4]

Facing them across the ideological front line were the communists. They won 15 per cent of the vote in the 1936 general election and supported the Popular Front government from the outside. They took their orders from Russia and in August 1939 backed the Soviet–Nazi non-aggression pact resulting in the party being banned and its leaders fleeing to Moscow. When the Germans arrived in June 1940 the communists found themselves loosely on the same side as the conquerors and Vichy refrained from overzealous repression. A year later Germany invaded the Soviet Union and persecution resumed, this time with Nazi assistance.

There were about fifty communist activists in Dieppe, many of them dock workers. Clandestine activity mostly consisted of distributing anti-Vichy, then anti-German tracts. Sometimes things went further. In November 1940 Charles Pieters, a docker, and a companion tried to grab the weapons of two German NCOs as they left the Tout Va Bien café, a popular German hangout overlooking the port. Pieters was caught running away but his friend escaped. Pieters claimed he was an innocent bystander caught up in the commotion but was still sentenced to nine months in prison in Rouen, from where he subsequently escaped. Three months later, unknown assailants attacked two soldiers on the seafront, wounding one of them. The attackers escaped and the mayor René Levasseur warned the population of the 'very heavy and severe punishment that will hit everyone without exception' if it happened again. This was no deterrent to a schoolteacher, Valentin Feldman, and a young woman called Lucienne Lemaire who while out distributing communist tracts one night in the winter of 1941–2 saw two Germans staggering out of a brothel in the port. They followed them and pushed them into a dock. When the bodies were recovered the Germans suspected nothing, as it was not unusual for drunken soldiers to come to grief in this way after a night on the town.[5]

After June 1941 the communists joined supporters of Charles de Gaulle in a loose coalition called the National Front. Their underground news-sheet *L'Avenir* called for 'all-out action to smash the German war machine'. Before a campaign could develop the French and German security services moved to crush the fledgling resistance. Among those captured was Feldman, a Russian-born Jew and a brilliant philosophy student, who was eventually shot in July 1942. Organised resistance was ended and the small nuisance it had caused the occupiers eliminated.

Most Dieppois had voted for centrist parties before the war. There was little enthusiasm now for Vichy. Their attitude was reflected in the response – or lack of it – to Poullain's attempts to promote the pro-Pétain 'Amis du Maréchal' organisation in his newspaper. A local branch was set up in February 1941 with membership restricted to those 'born of French parentage' and who were 'neither Jew nor Freemason'.[6] Within two months it attracted 500 members, some quite prominent including a shipowner, the director of the local hospital and most of the town's booksellers, and also a fair number of workers, shopkeepers and farmers. In October they held a conference attended by 800 people. That was the high point. Despite the best efforts of Poullain and *La Vigie*, the marshal seems to have attracted no more friends and mentions of the 'Amis' faded from the paper's pages.

Most stood back from politics and ideologies, minding their own business and keeping their heads down, absorbing themselves in the full-time work of keeping food on the table. Life was an obstacle course of bureaucratic hindrances. The authorities, both French and German, operated an *'administration paperassière'* requiring everyone to go everywhere armed with identity card, certificate of employment, ration cards and tickets, military identity documents for former soldiers and a laissez-passer (*Ausweis*) if you ventured out of the immediate area.

For the Germans there were frequent reminders that resentment and hatred seethed beneath the veneer of compliance. Some anonymous patriots risked the death penalty by acts of sabotage, repeatedly cutting military communications cables and bringing down communal punishments on the local male population who were ordered to stand guard for twelve-hour stints to protect the cables. Some mornings the town woke up to see walls covered with graffiti declaring *'Vive La France Libre!'*, *'Vive de Gaulle!'*, *'À bas Vichy'* and *'Hitler au poteau!'* ('Hitler to the firing squad!').

On 11 May 1941, in response to calls broadcast from the French service of the BBC in London, many took to the streets to stroll in the spring sunshine wearing red, white and blue, the colours of the tricolour. A month later a police agent reported an incident at the Kursaal cinema in the rue Aguado during a showing of *Paramatta, bagne de femmes*, a German period melodrama set in nineteenth-century Britain and Australia. The soundtrack carried a few bars of the British national anthem. 'The crowd recognised it and applauded frantically, despite the presence of German soldiers,' he wrote.[7]

Yet human nature still had a way of finding weak points in the wall between the conquerors and the conquered. In contrast to their attitude towards the Slav *Untermenschen* in the East, the Germans had nothing against the French. For many the war was just business. Now the Battle of France was over they wanted a minimum of trouble and the enemy's attempts at fraternisation were often successful.

The unclouded eyes of eleven-year-old Gérard Cadot saw something to admire in the first German he met. He was stranded at the home of some friends who were sheltering refugees when a soldier walked up the path and gave the front door a kick. He was 'tall and strong-looking. His sleeves were rolled back . . . a hand grenade was shoved into his belt and another in one of his incredible black leather boots . . . for a while he examined us French, all paralysed by fear, then left the house telling us not to go out.'[8] The boy was impressed. 'The German had not been aggressive. He was just doing his job as a soldier and paying due respect to civilians. We all of us felt a little reassured and had to admit that the *boches* were not the barbarians we had been expecting.'

Gérard lived in the hamlet of Vasterival, six miles west of Dieppe, with his parents Gaston and Simone. His father was the gardener at La Lézardière, a large villa looking out to sea which was the summer residence of a Parisian, Georges Painvin, a scientist, businessman and banker who in the last war had been a brilliant cryptanalyst, cracking the German military codes. The house was taken over by Luftwaffe troops who manned an observation post at the lighthouse at Cap d'Ailly a mile away. Men from the coastal battery at Varengeville, just to the south, were installed in La Maisonnette, another substantial villa.

The airmen at La Lézardière took a shine to Gérard. They gave him food for the family and took him on expeditions around the countryside, once to the radar station at Bruneval. Gérard's father Gaston despised Pétain, listened to the French broadcast on the BBC every day and welcomed the first RAF raids on Dieppe saying 'that will take the Germans down a peg or two'. But he did not turn away a French-speaking Luftwaffe airman stationed at the big house who took to dropping round at the gardener's cottage for a chat, and who apparently saw the Cadots as a substitute for the family he had left behind in Germany.

The gunners at La Maisonnette acquired local girlfriends. Gérard noted how 'each Sunday two or three bikes would be propped against the fence while the girls passed several hours with the soldiers'. Then 'mission accomplished, they returned to their weekly occupations

until the following Sunday. They came to La Maisonnette the way
that others go to evensong.'

Roger Lefebvre, the chief administrator at the *mairie* of Hautot-
sur-Mer near Pourville, noted with distaste many other cases of
'*collaboration horizontale*'. He worried in his diary that when the Germans eventually departed 'it was the France of tomorrow that would
pay the price' in the form of 'the ruination of family life, disease and
the sapping of the life force of the nation'.[9] The thought that the
Germans would one day be driven out sustained him through the
humiliations that came with his position. His job was to translate
into action the orders coming from the German administrative headquarters in Dieppe. Lefebvre was conservative, Christian and a silent
supporter of General de Gaulle. He stayed in his post because he
believed that he was doing his patriotic duty, trying to protect the
interests of the community while every now and then managing to
thwart those of the occupiers in some small way.

It was scant compensation for the fact that most of the time he was
being forced to make life easier for the enemy. When billets were
needed for troops it was he who had to find them. It was Lefebvre
who was given the job of smoothing things over with the locals when
the Germans decided to flood the pasture land on either side of the
River Scie, which ran through the commune, in order to improve
defences.

The Germans trashed everything. In the long cold winter of 1941–2
they chopped down private woodland and burned anything combust-
ible they could find in the villas along the seafront: doors, window
frames, parquet flooring and all. They were like 'termites' hollowing
out the fabric of France. Another metaphor had gained currency. By
an evil chance the occupation coincided with another invasion. In
the summer of 1941 an infestation of Colorado beetles, *doryphores* in
French, swept through the fields gorging on the crops. Gérard Cadot
and his classmates were put to work in the fields gathering the larvae,
'fat, sticky and disgusting', and like everyone saw them as the animal
equivalent of the invaders. Soon *les boches*, the old slang for the Germans, was heard less and they became *les doryphores*.

★

Lefebvre saw the Germans close up and was alive to anything that revealed the state of their morale or the progress of the war. Early in 1942 he started to notice signs of alarm that suggested faint cracks in the occupiers' facade of granite confidence. On 24 March he wrote in his diary: 'Received a circular indicating that the situation of coastal communities is going to get very complicated as the German authorities now consider the coastline as a war zone.' A few days later they issued a warning that following the raids at Bruneval and Saint-Nazaire, there would be 'heavy consequences' for local communities if any town or village was found to have given shelter to stranded enemy soldiers.

The raids were just one indication that the British were taking the offensive. On the night of 4 March the sky blazed with sustained anti-aircraft fire, aimed, he learned later, at RAF bombers on their way to devastate the Renault factory at Boulogne-Billancourt in south-west Paris. British light bombers and fighters were increasingly seen around Dieppe. In early June there were three raids in the space of a week. Lefebvre was bucked by such shows of aggression: 'Excellent visit by the RAF at noon today,' he noted in his diary after fighters shot up an artillery battery in the neighbourhood.

The Germans seemed suddenly concerned about the state of their seaward defences. Lefebvre was told to provide billets for Dutch and Belgian workers, who at the beginning of the summer started to arrive in ever bigger numbers to build a string of concrete bulwarks along the coast. At the same time, some houses along the promenade at Pourville and the high ground to the west were dynamited to provide clear fields of fire over the beach.

The echoes of the real war being fought in the East carried to the Channel coast. At the end of April Lefebvre was at Dieppe station when a unit boarded a train for the start of a long journey to the Russian front. 'They didn't seem very keen to go,' he wrote. 'The departure was stopped six times while they rounded up strays.' Some soldiers were unshaven and others still buckling up their kit bags and there was an air of doom hanging over them as the last ones climbed into the carriages. 'These ruffians were well aware that the good life in the rich land of France was now over,' he wrote with satisfaction.

What Lefebvre saw were the ripples spreading from the great

strategic changes transforming Germany's war. Now that the Americans had joined the British, the initiative in Western Europe had passed to the Allies. Sooner or later they would attempt an invasion and the units strung along the entire occupied coastline would live from now on in a state of perpetual vigilance and anxiety.

The longer the war continued in the East, the greater the danger in the West. The reality of the situation was obvious to everyone from Hitler down. On 23 March 1942 he issued Führer Directive No. 40 which declared 'in the days to come the coasts of Europe will be seriously exposed to the danger of enemy landings'. It urged that 'special attention must be paid to British preparations for landings on the open coast, for which numerous armoured landing craft suitable for the transportation of combat vehicles and heavy weapons are available'. It was one of a stream of warnings, sometimes vague, sometimes more geographically precise, that issued from the German high command that left the German units in no doubt that they were in for a fight every bit as fierce and decisive as the death grapple on the Eastern Front.

The man charged with repelling the inevitable attack was Field Marshal Gerd von Rundstedt, appointed Commander-in-Chief West in March 1942. He had been one of the main engineers of the French defeat in 1940 and gone on to direct the great German victory against the Russians at the Battle of Kiev in the summer of 1941. He came from a Prussian military family and presented himself as an honourable soldier above politics. In reality he had done his share of scheming in the Reich's perpetual military–political power struggles. He had also colluded in the campaign of mass murder of civilians and Jews in the East.

Rundstedt was now sixty-six, in poor health and a heavy drinker and smoker but alert and purposeful and as convinced as Hitler that an attack was imminent. From his Paris headquarters he pressed the pace of a massive coastal defence construction programme while stimulating an atmosphere of impending danger among his commanders and troops. In April Rundstedt issued a general order stating the principles for repelling the attack. Amphibious forces were to be 'defeated while still off the coast if possible but on the beaches at the very latest'.[10]

The coastline from Ostend in Belgium to Le Havre on the Seine Estuary was controlled by the 15th Army. It was commanded by General Curt Haase, a beefy Württemberger who had won his first Iron Cross serving as an artilleryman in 1914 and commanded a corps during the invasions of Poland and France. He was sixty years old, but according to a British intelligence assessment, 'appears to have aged prematurely' and 'could easily pass for ten or fifteen years more than his actual age'.[11] His worn-out look reflected a heart condition that would kill him the following year.

The coastline either side of Dieppe was held by the 302nd Division which took over in April 1941. It was untried in battle and had been raised in Mecklenburg and Pomerania at the end of 1940 specifically for occupation duties in Western Europe. Its area of operations stretched from the fishing port of Le Tréport in the east to the picturesque village of Veules-les-Roses in the west. At its head was the divisional commander's namesake, Major General Conrad Haase, known to the men as 'little Haase' in contrast to his boss 'big Haase'. He was born in Dresden in 1888 and fought in the First World War. He was tall and heavily built with unmilitary glasses and drooping jowls. His appearance was misleading. Haase was energetic and efficient and kept his troops on their toes with regular warnings and exhortations.

When the division arrived it was up to strength and properly equipped. As the months passed and the war in the East began to consume vast quantities of men and resources, many of the original recruits were transferred to the Russian front. From early 1942 the drafts replacing them included barely trained Poles, Czechs, Belgians and even Russians who had been lured or pressed into service. They had little appetite for fighting, and even when spread through the units reduced the division's overall effectiveness. Fortunately for Haase, only the most basic skills were required from an infantryman to adequately defend this section of the coast.

Nature had sided with the Germans. Even to the amateur eye it was obvious that Dieppe was hard to attack and easy to defend. According to one inhabitant, a Madame Ménage, no one expected an Allied attack there as 'everyone thought that this was the most difficult part of the Channel coast'.[12]

The first natural obstacle any assault would face was the beaches. They are made up of thick, smooth pebbles, some as broad and flat as demitasse saucers, that slither under foot, called '*galets*' in French. The beach in front of Dieppe town shelves quite steeply and the tides push the *galets* into a succession of undulating slopes of up to fifteen degrees, or one-in-four.[13] Assault troops would have to flounder up them, weighed down with weapons, ammunition and equipment and with bullets lashing the air before they could reach the limited cover of the sea wall and fire their first shots. Once the battle began the *galets* themselves would be shattered by exploding shells and mortar bombs, multiplying the volume of lethal shrapnel slicing the air. They offered absolutely no protection in return, as digging a shell scrape in them was impossible.

The beach was also a natural tank barrier. Haase had ordered experiments with armoured vehicles which persuaded him that the pebbles were impassable and anti-tank defences were therefore unnecessary on the shoreline.

Behind the beaches lay the cliffs. They reared up like castle walls and the few narrow ravines leading from the sea were easily blocked with concrete, wire and mines, 14,000 of which were planted at likely spots. The cliffs swooped down at two points west of Dieppe at Pourville and Quiberville where the Rivers Scie and Saâne flowed into the Channel. These were obvious landing points and easily commanded by guns on the valley slopes. There was another at the village of Puys, just a mile to the east of Dieppe port, but the beach was narrow and the sides of the valley leading up from it were steep.

Into these natural defences the Germans had installed a wide array of weaponry, much of it looted from the French army, siting the guns where they would inflict the maximum damage on any attacker. From the clifftops they had complete control of the seaward approaches to Dieppe. Two heavy-gun batteries were placed one either side of the town, capable of annihilating any naval force rash enough to launch a frontal attack as soon as it came within nine miles of the shore. One was on the cliffs at Berneval, six miles to the east of

Dieppe, equipped with three 170 mm and four 105 mm pieces. It was matched by another battery of six 155 mm cannon near Varengeville.

If the invasion fleet survived the long-range bombardment it would then face a second curtain of fire from a ring of batteries that looped in a horseshoe around Dieppe from the cliffs on either side. The eastern clifftop was dominated by the church of Notre-Dame-de-Bon-Secours. Nearby stood a battery of six 88 mm anti-aircraft guns which could also be used against sea and ground targets. Just inland was a battery of four French 105s, with an ensemble of six heavy 155s four miles from the sea on the southern edge of the town near Arques-la-Bataille. The big bluff looking seawards on the western side made a perfect gun platform, and sited around Quatre Vents farm were six 88 mm AA guns, and four 105s as well as numerous 20 and 37 mm cannon.[14] On one side it formed the western headland. Perched on top was the fifteenth-century Château de Dieppe, 'Vieux Château', which loomed over the casino and the west end of Dieppe. There were two 75 mm artillery pieces plus two heavy mortar posts in the grounds.

Thus the defenders had a wide array of artillery with which to rain down fire on an invasion fleet as it approached, then blast those troops who somehow got ashore as they struggled over the *galets*, as well as any armoured vehicles supporting them. By that point they would be exposed to another deadly scourge.

The basic weapon of the German defences was the MG34 machine gun. The MG34 was reliable and devastating. It was versatile, and at just over 12 kg and four feet in length, light and portable enough for attack or defence. It fired 7.92 mm bullets at a rate of up to 900 a minute and was effective up to 2,000 yards. The nearest British equivalent, the Bren gun, fired a similar-calibre bullet at just over 500 a minute and was effective up to 600 yards.

The machine-gun posts on the headlands could cover almost every inch of Dieppe's main beach and promenade. On the west side there were four sited near the chateau. The cliff face below provided even more advantageous positions. They were honeycombed with *gobes*, caves dug out of the chalk which were used as storehouses and at one period for human habitation. They were thus ready-made gun emplacements that were almost impervious to incoming fire and also invisible to the prying cameras of enemy reconnaissance aircraft. Below the western headland there were reinforced concrete case-mates housing a 75 mm and several 37 mm guns and flamethrowers, and there were more interconnecting bunkers to the west with steps leading up to a reinforced observation post.

The defences on the eastern headland opposite were equally well appointed with several machine guns on the heights and numerous gun positions in the *gobes* and at the base of the cliff. Immediately below lay the port entrance framed by two jetties reaching out into the sea. The mouth was partially blocked by three cargo ships sunk by the British before they left. A 37 mm gun sat near the end of the western arm, covering the entire beach, and at the landward end the turret and cannon of a captured French tank was concreted into the road.

The Dieppe seafront was bounded by the port entrance on the east and the casino and the Vieux Château on the west. In between ran a broad promenade. The boulevard Maréchal Foch ran along the seaward side. The boulevard de Verdun marked the start of the town, a mile-long row of hotels, boarding houses and villas, with a tall-chimneyed tobacco factory plonked incongruously in the middle.

These had been transformed into a bastion against frontal attack. There were sandbagged firing points for snipers and machine-gunners in the upper windows. The casino dominated the west end of the promenade. The main rooms were grouped in a block at the front with large picture windows looking out to sea. Behind it, neoclassical colonnaded wings curved out on either side. The white stucco had been camouflaged in places with green and brown paint and the whole building had been turned into a fortress with machine-gun and sniper posts on each floor and a 37 mm gun at the entrance. There were six machine-gun posts spaced evenly along the promenade running west and anti-tank guns stood at the entrances to the roads leading from the front into the town. All but two streets leading into the town from the sea were blocked by concrete anti-tank barriers.

Between the beach and the promenade was a sea wall. A timber and double barbed-wire barrier had been built along the top. Below was another thick ribbon of wire strung from metal posts concreted into the stones.

The two possible landing beaches either side of Dieppe were equally well defended. At Puys, a mile to the east, a narrow valley lined with holiday villas ran down to a cramped beach. It was overlooked by pillboxes mounting MG34s. One was sited in the garden of the last house on the right-hand side of the lane leading to the sea. It alone was capable of seeing off all but the heaviest assault. At Pourville, two miles to the west of the town, where the Scie entered the sea, the gentle eastward slopes of the river valley were dotted with pillboxes and the beach was within easy range of the strongpoint at Quatre Vents farm.

Some positions had been there long enough to start to look as if they were part of the landscape. Many had thick overhead protection. The others were well dug in. The most vulnerable were the anti-aircraft pieces which had to be able to fire upwards. Even so, the sheer volume of hardware made it unlikely the defences could be completely suppressed by bombardment by sea or air. Both the ships and attacking aircraft would anyway have to contend not only with the light and heavy flak guns but also with the Luftwaffe. The German air-force base at Abbeville was less than twenty minutes flying time away and home to the Focke-Wulf 190s of the ace Jagdgeschwader 26 fighter unit, known to their Fighter Command opponents as the 'Abbeville Boys'. All together there were 206 fighters and 107 bombers stationed in the region who could come to the aid of the defenders.[15] The Dieppe sector was the responsibility of the 571st Regiment of the 302nd Division, commanded by Oberstleutnant Hermann Bartelt. It was undermanned, with only three thin battalions numbering about 1,500 men in total spread between Berneval and Varengeville. Half the force was held in reserve at Ouville-la-Rivière seven miles to the south-west. The seafront in the town itself was held by only one company of around 150 men, while at Puys a garrison of just fifty guarded the beach.

The regimental adjutant Captain Linder was charged with overseeing the defences. Despite the weakness in numbers he was confident that it could hold the position comfortably. The spate of small-scale raids of the spring and the obvious toughness of the target led the defenders to doubt the likelihood of a major attack. They expected instead 'a commando-type enterprise as the British had done before'.[16] Linder was sure that the benefits offered by the terrain meant they could handle anything that was flung at them. The topography 'offered an advantage to the defender which you couldn't estimate too highly', he remembered. The narrow valley at Puys made it 'even easier' to defend and it was reckoned that only a 'small company' was needed to repel an attack on Pourville.

The east and west headlands bracketing the town and port were ideal for laying down 'enfilading fire', that is a sustained barrage sweeping in from the flanks that attackers would have to get through to reach the relative safety of the town. With 'heavy machine guns, your light machine guns and light cannon and anti-tank guns you could reach the esplanade from either side', he explained. If attackers did manage to make it across the killing zone to the ground below the Vieux Château they would be shielded from the guns on the headland. There was another protected spot below the east headland. However the Germans had 'tried to overcome this problem by manning some positions within the houses' on the front 'from where you could reach the dead angle'.

The Germans had thus created a near-perfect system of interlocking arcs of fire that combined to generate a maelstrom of bullets and shells that, unless preceded by a shattering bombardment, should stop dead any frontal assault on the town. Each line of defence had a role to play in the orchestrated annihilation. The gunners in the seafront buildings, for example, were ordered to shoot only at approaching and departing landing craft. In that way they would draw the attackers' fire, leaving the guns on the headlands to mow down those who managed to disembark.[17] It fitted with Rundstedt's orders to crush any attacking force before it could establish a foothold ashore. If everybody did their job, a task which only required staying at your post and firing your weapon, few attackers would get off the beach alive.

Despite the soundness of the defences, the Germans were taking no chances. By the end of April Dieppe looked very much like a battlefield in waiting. In April, the mayor René Levasseur ordered everyone on the seaward side of the town to leave their homes 'in view of the grave potential dangers facing the population and out of military necessity'.[18]

The fishing quarter of Le Pollet on the eastern side of the port emptied and the last remaining inhabitants of the tall houses in the boulevard de Verdun on the seafront departed. Dieppe was now nearly half empty. Most families had relations in the surrounding countryside and had moved out to join them. Others handed their children over to the authorities and on 4 June forty boys and girls left for a home for evacuees in Issoire, a village in the Auvergne in the Unoccupied Zone. Many of those with jobs in the town left at night, journeying to safety on a special train that ferried them back and forth to Auffay fifteen miles to the south.

Most of the activity in the emptying landscape now was ominous. Since the start of the year work had begun along the occupied coastline from Norway to the Pyrenees to create an Atlantic Wall of reinforced concrete strongpoints, ordered by Hitler to provide 'a solid line of unbroken fire' and a fortress 'which will hold in any circumstances'. At the same time the garrisons were being brought to something approaching battle-readiness.

Most of the men in the 302nd Division had not fought before. Many had undergone little beyond basic training. From his HQ at Envermeu, nine miles south-east of Dieppe, Haase worked hard to get his men up to scratch. The rawest were 'Germanised' drafts from the conquered territories. There were several field exercises to lick them into shape. In February a mock raid led by British paratroopers was staged in which the referees awarded success to the attackers.[19]

Haase raised readiness states according to the perceived threat. At level three, the lowest, only half the strength were on duty at any time. At level two, all were at their posts, and slept fully dressed and equipped. Level one meant action stations. The degree of vigilance was determined by factors ranging from the overall strategic situation to the weather conditions. If the wind was strong, units on the seafront could relax to level three. If dead calm prevailed, it was raised to level one.[20] Vigilance was also high when the moon and tide favoured the attackers. The training programme and Haase's leadership raised both efficiency and morale. '*Hase*' means 'hare' in German and in a punning reference to their chief, soldiers painted a sign on the wall of the casino and positions nearby showing the silhouette of a hare and the slogan: 'The little hares that bite'.

Despite the training and the regular alerts the troops had little to complain about. They were living easy. The food was not bad, with meat and fried vegetables for lunch, thick army '*Wehrmachtsuppe*' for supper and a daily ration of bread, butter and sausage to fill the gaps. There were occasional issues of honey and jam and tomatoes and fruit were on sale in the town and eggs and cream in the countryside. Black-market items could be had for exorbitant prices in the canteen at the Hotel Royal. A bottle of schnapps or cognac cost twelve marks and a bottle of red wine four marks (a private got thirty-five marks a month). Stockings, underwear, artificial silk, perfume and chocolate were available to send to sisters, wives and girlfriends who could not get them at home. There were plenty of bars and cafés in town, which stayed open until midnight for the off-duty troops though not for the locals. The cinema in the Grande Rue, reserved for the soldiers, showed a film every night at 7 p.m. and was always packed. Leave was reasonably frequent and long enough to allow time to visit Paris or Rouen. It was all, as everyone was fervently aware, hugely preferable to life on the Eastern Front.

Even this knowledge could not always keep boredom at bay. 'Day after day nothing,' wrote Hauptmann Joachim Lindner in his diary. 'We had a problem with the men guarding the coast, the poor man walking with his rifle along the cliffs. Nothing happened but the waves coming and going, coming and going.'[21] It was only a matter of time. 'We wait, every night we wait for Tommy,' wrote another watcher over the Channel coast, Gefreiter Heinrich Böll, to his wife Annemarie in Germany, 'but he doesn't seem to want to come yet . . .'

6. Rutter

At the beginning of April Hughes-Hallett and his team got to work on the Dieppe plan. They were keen to get things moving. The failure of the Bayonne venture after a string of achievements was a jolt to their self-esteem, and pride, as much as any strictly military consideration, demanded another success. Dieppe was now at the top of the target list with a proposed launch date of June. Nothing had been done to develop the project since it was first mentioned at the end of January and there was no time to lose.

The first thing the planning syndicate needed was precise information on the topography and defences of the area. This was the province of the senior intelligence officer, Wing Commander the Marqués de Casa Maury, who acted as liaison with the various intelligence organisations. The merits or otherwise of 'Bobby' Casa Maury, the pre-war socialite, racing driver and friend of the Mountbattens, were a subject of dispute at COHQ and elsewhere. He was almost certain to raise the hackles of old-school naval officers like Tom Baillie-Grohman, and sure enough the rear admiral disliked him on sight. Baillie-Grohman joined the Dieppe team as naval force commander late and at his first meeting at Richmond Terrace to discuss the raid he 'asked who would be assisting us in Intelligence [and] was referred to a foreign-looking officer in RAF uniform . . . I recognised him as a polo player and a foreign grandee of some sort.'[1] He was 'most surprised for a foreigner to be in this position'. His prejudices were confirmed for he 'never saw him or heard from him again during the whole planning period and certainly there was very, very little intelligence to be obtained'.

A bigger problem was that Casa Maury was resented by some of the very people on whom he most relied for help. According to Hughes-Hallett 'of all those serving at COHQ [Casa Maury] came in for most criticism from the Admiralty and the War Office, not so much on personal grounds but rather because the Naval and Military Intelligence Staffs strongly objected to having an intermediary between themselves and COHQ.'

There were other reasons for their animosity, laid out by Brigadier Robert Laycock, the dashing and efficient head of the Special Service Brigade and a friend of the Mountbattens. Writing to Casa Maury in an attempt to console him after the fusillades of criticism which followed the raid he wrote: 'although you undoubtedly produced the very best finished article from the sources at your disposal . . . the raw material fed into your department was of a poorer quality, and it appeared to me that much was being withheld from you . . . because you . . . are not on really intimate terms with the Naval Intelligence Division, the Director of Military Intelligence and [the RAF's] Assistant Chief of Staff for Intelligence or accepted as 100% *persona grata* by "C" [the head of the Secret Intelligence Service or MI6].'[2] Their hostility was 'prompted by jealousy and a refusal to believe that anyone outside their immediate acquaintance and sphere of life could do their job just as well as they can. Also, I think, they are biased by a wholly irrational prejudice against you in that you are a marquis and your name is Casa Maury and not Smith, Jones or Robinson.'

Casa Maury could not help his exotic background and, excepting Mountbatten himself, worked as hard as anyone at COHQ. Hughes-Hallett reckoned he performed his duties 'with considerable despatch displaying considerable skill, artistry and imagination'.[3] The fault lay with Mountbatten for choosing him. Casa Maury's problem was that he was an outsider in the jealous and conspiratorial intelligence world. The material he was able to obtain was the standard data available from conventional sources and he had to go through the formal channels to get it rather than using the short cuts that would have been available had he been a member of the club. There was therefore some truth in Baillie-Grohman's description of his department as a mere 'postbox' for intelligence gathered elsewhere.

Despite these handicaps, the planners soon had a fairly comprehensive picture of the target area and enemy dispositions. From 3 April information on the Dieppe defences started to arrive from the service intelligence departments as well as the odd snippet from MI6 and the Special Operations Executive which operated its own networks on the continent.

The basic lie of the land was mapped out by the Inter-Services Topographical Department (ISTD), a very efficient set-up which like many successful wartime organisations had emerged from early failures. The disastrous Norwegian campaign of 1940, in which RAF crews went into action with maps obtained from old Baedeker guidebooks, brought home the necessity for an agency that amassed up-to-the-minute geographical intelligence that all the services could draw on. The driving force behind the ISTD was the director of naval intelligence, Admiral John Godfrey. It began work in October 1940 and was based in Oxford where the university press was on hand to print reports and surveys.[4]

The starting point for all raid planning was the images provided by the RAF's Photographic Reconnaissance Unit (PRU) based at Benson, Oxfordshire. Its aircraft flew routine sorties that included the Dieppe area about once a week. Beyond that they could be tasked with special missions to gather the images needed to construct 'mosaics' of the coastal approaches and target sites. Photographs were analysed at the Photographic Interpretation Unit at nearby Medmenham which was by now expert at identifying the smallest details of military infrastructure. In one case it was noticed that cows in fields on the flanks of coastal towns in northern France had avoided grazing certain patches of grass, thus revealing the presence of barbed wire.[5]

Almost any image of the target had some value. Goronwy Rees, an intelligence officer at South-Eastern Command headquarters who was attached to the planning staff for the raid, remembered how 'for much of our knowledge . . . of the town and the beaches we had to depend on picture postcards and family snapshots . . . How strange it seemed sometimes, as one studied some old-fashioned photograph showing a French family taking its luncheon on the beach, the little boys in sailor suits and straw hats, as in some illustration of a scene from Proust, that the reason why this particular photograph was of particular interest was that it showed with extreme clarity the gradient of the beach at the exact point where our tanks would disembark.'[6]

The RAF was bombarded with demands for special PRU missions. At one point the Air Ministry pushed back, pointing out that to meet every outstanding request from the COHQ Intelligence Section would mean their aircraft would have to take 2,860 photographs.[7] They were 'much concerned over the question of security' and refused to comply without clearance from higher authority.

Even with saturation coverage, photographic reconnaissance could not be expected to reveal everything. The shadows cast by the cliffs obscured the western end of the promenade and entrances to the town. Neither were they going to show the gun positions in the *gobes* in the east and west headlands, nor the anti-tank guns that were rolled out only at night into the streets running down to the seafront and withdrawn in daylight.[8]

There was a dearth of supporting information to fill in the gaps. The intelligence departments and agencies were able to provide only sketchy details about the enemy units in place and how they were deployed. A German report after the operation noted that while the raiders' information about their defences had been quite accurate, 'there was a general lack of knowledge as to the location of regimental and battalion command posts'.[9]

To get this sort of fine detail the planners needed to have eyewitness reports from agents on the ground. During the planning some Combined Ops staff had 'misgivings' about the quality of the material Casa Maury was serving up, particularly 'the German arrangements for defending the beaches in front of the town'.[10] They suggested sending in an agent to investigate but were told that it would take up to six weeks to put one in place. Even then, 'the report of an agent could not be entirely depended upon and . . . a grave security risk was also involved were he to be captured.' Hughes-Hallett or one of the naval planning staff had the bright idea of tasking a Channel patrol to 'capture fishermen off Dieppe in order to get the most up-to-date information', but it came to nothing.[11] Material in the intelligence files reveals that some details were getting through from local sources. An early unattributed report gives locations for a few military posts in the town as well as other information such as the identification of a hotel-café at Puys as a brothel.[12] Another mistaken report stating that there were armoured troops in the area came via the pigeon carrier service overseen by the MI 14 department of the War Office Directorate of Military Intelligence.[13]

None of this suggested an established link between the planners and local underground networks in the Dieppe area. In fact there was a well-organised Resistance network active at this time, secretly surveying the defences to pass on to British and Free French intelligence in London and it was already well known to COHQ. The success of the Bruneval raid owed a lot to agents linked to the Bureau Central de Renseignements et d'Action (BCRA), the Free French intelligence service in London. The BCRA controlled several networks operating in occupied France including the Confrérie de Notre-Dame. This was run by Gilbert Renault, an energetic former film producer who operated as 'Colonel Rémy'.

Renault came from a large Breton family and was patriotic, right-wing and Catholic. When the war began he was thirty-five with a wife and four children to whom he was devoted. Many with his outlook accepted Pétain's claim that France had no choice but to capitulate and sign an armistice that put the government at the abject service of the Germans. Renault was appalled. He left France on 18 June 1940 with one of his brothers on a trawler bound for England. Two of his sisters, Maisie and Madeleine, who stayed behind also joined the Resistance and ended up in Ravensbrück.

In London Renault joined the embryonic court assembling around the obscure figure of Charles de Gaulle and was assigned to the BCRA, led by André de Wavrin, known as 'Colonel Passy'. The Gaullists were already working closely with MI6, and Renault was introduced to several officers including the head of the French section, Kenneth Cohen. That summer he returned to the continent and travelled around France, building a network of agents stretching the length of the western Atlantic coast who provided valuable information about German naval activity in the Battle of the Atlantic.

By 1942 the *confrérie* had extended its operations to Normandy. Some recruits with flying backgrounds were charged with finding secluded landing sites and drop zones for the RAF. Among them was a forty-five-year-old former air-force officer called Roger Hérissé, alias 'Dutertre'. On his travels in upper Normandy he noticed an unusual radio mast perched on the cliffs near Bruneval south of Cap d'Antifer, and guessed it was linked to German coastal radar monitoring RAF activity. The report was passed on to London. On 24 January Renault received a radio message from BCRA on behalf of the British with a shopping list of precise information required on the defences in the Bruneval area, right down to the state of morale and alertness of the garrison troops.[14]

He entrusted the mission to Roger Dumont, alias 'Pol', another pilot. Dumont left Paris immediately to rendezvous with a local contact, a Le Havre garage-owner called Charles Chauveau ('Charlemagne') and they set off in a borrowed Simca 5 to conduct a recce. Bruneval was a modest seaside resort and Chauveau was on good terms with the owners of Le Beauminet, the one hotel-café there. According to Renault 'after fifteen minutes they knew all the details'.[15] A month later Operation Biting was launched and succeeded brilliantly, greatly boosting the prestige of Mountbatten and Combined Operations.

COHQ should therefore have been well aware of the value of Renault and the *confrérie*. In March, Roger Hérissé visited Dieppe where he met local sympathisers. Together they spent two weeks gathering details of guns and gun positions, the location of pillboxes, anti-tank barriers and anti-tank guns, and the addresses of military HQs. There was too much material to be transmitted by wireless and the material would have to be taken to London by courier. Early on the morning of 25 March Hérissé left for Paris to hand over the dossier to Dumont at their regular weekly lunchtime rendezvous at the Farandole restaurant in the rue d'Anjou. On his way to the station he witnessed a collision between two German vehicles and was ordered to help get the injured to hospital. He missed his train and the meeting with Dumont, and had to wait another week until the next scheduled rendezvous. Dumont was arrested that morning. The dossier finally reached London in the hands of Pierre Brossolette, a key figure in the Resistance who was exfiltrated in late August. By then the material was useless.[16]

Renault laid part of the blame for the failure on the excessive caution shown by British intelligence who refused on security grounds
to give the Resistance any inkling of future plans. 'If they had let
my network know the extreme urgency of updates on the coastal
defences,' he wrote, '[they] could have organised a sea pick-up for
Dutertre's information and the raid could have been a lot less costly.'

In the third week in April the project had acquired a name. It was
Operation Rutter, a code name that had no particular meaning
beyond being the next on an approved list. Everything was being
done at high speed, creating a sense of urgency and a brisk tempo of
bureaucratic momentum. Information-gathering was coordinated by
Major Walter Skrine, a diligent and methodical officer who badgered
the service departments and intelligence organisations with ques-
tionnaires chasing up 'additional intelligence requirements' to fill in
the picture.[17] In less than three weeks the Rutter staff believed they
had gathered enough information on which to base a plan. They had
accurate descriptions of the beaches in and around the town, including their geological composition and gradients as well as the defences
and obstacles behind them and possible exit routes, all of which were
essential if tanks were to be used successfully. They had identified a
list of potential targets in and around Dieppe including military and
naval headquarters, shipping, radar stations and the airfield at Saint-
Aubin-sur-Scie. Knowledge of artillery and anti-aircraft batteries
and machine-gun and mortar posts was incomplete, but the gaps
were being filled in every day.

The details of the enemy's order of battle were also sketchy. The
main unit in the area was correctly identified as the 302nd Infantry
Division, though not the name of its commander. Force numbers
were fairly accurate as well as the strength of other units in the area
and the time it would take to reinforce Dieppe once the raid was
launched. However, there were major errors which an agent on the
ground might have corrected. The divisional headquarters was consistently placed at Arques-la-Bataille, on the southern edge of the
town, when in fact it was at Envermeu, nine miles to the south-east.

The reports tended to make casual assumptions about the calibre of the defending troops. They were marked down as 'second rate', under-equipped and in low spirits.[18] This, it was believed, applied to all German troops on the occupied coast. Some 'Notes on the Military Situation' in the occupied coastline drawn up for Home Forces claimed 'morale . . . is poor in that discipline is slack and training bad . . . Personnel, particularly officers, are generally inferior.'[19] Their low spirits were partly attributed to the success of the Combined Ops cross-Channel operations as a result of which 'there is jumpiness about raids as these usually result in casualties and dismissals.'

These snap judgements revealed an overconfidence on the part of the intelligence staffs that also appeared in crucial evaluations of the enemy's defensive infrastructure. 'The defences of Dieppe and neighbourhood are not heavy,' stated an early assessment of the aggregated intelligence. This breezy evaluation would be reaffirmed in the opening words of the outline plan.[20]

The COHQ ethos was to make light of difficulties. Even so, it was clear that the planners were concerned at the possible strength of the German artillery support. There were constant requests to all potential intelligence sources for precise information about the hardware. One dated 19 April addressed to Home Forces stressed: 'If the limits of available information merely referred to the *type* of gun *usually* found in these batteries it might have a very restricting effect on the plan in its entirety.'[21] All the supplementary information received added to, rather than subtracted from, what was known of the enemy's firepower. Yet the tone remained optimistic and almost insouciant.

There were, however, no illusions about what cross-Channel operations could hope to contribute to the overall strategic situation. The Home Forces 'Notes' cautioned that while 'British raids have caused anxiety to the German authorities and a number of measures have been taken to meet the situation . . . there are no signs that troops are being detached from Germany or the Russian front and sent to the West. In fact the reverse is the case.' The conclusion was that 'only a threat to some vital objective would cause a reversal of this policy so long as Germany is occupied in Russia'.

It was clear from the beginning that there were no vital objectives in Dieppe. No U-boat was ever seen there and it housed no important repair facilities. 'The enemy makes no great use of Dieppe,' the Home Forces report observed. 'It serves merely as a base for patrol craft and minesweepers and is likely to be of importance only in the event of a German attempt to invade England.'

It was also true that the targets on offer were of limited value and their destruction would do little to reduce Germany's warmaking capacity. High on the list was the aerodrome at Saint-Aubin-sur-Scie. However, an RAF intelligence report of 12 April revealed that it comprised only one small hangar and blast shelters to accommodate twelve Me-109 or Me-110 fighters. As such it was a minor Luftwaffe outpost with no strategic and very limited tactical worth.

But the number-one target was the forty or so invasion barges moored in the inner harbour. The intention was not to destroy them but to tow them back to England. Their value to the Allies was questionable. They were between 100–600 tons, diesel-powered and capable of lifting both men and armour. Now that a German invasion was all but inconceivable they posed no threat. As an asset they might seem fairly desirable but the risks and effort involved in a 'cutting out' operation to bring them back across the Channel were enormous, and the shipyards were now turning out landing craft for men and tanks that were designed precisely for the Allies' needs.

A host of other objectives were soon added to the list. There were various German headquarters and barracks, railways and marshalling yards, the gas and power stations, a pharmaceutical factory, oil tanks and port installations including a swing bridge across the harbour. Damage to these was unlikely to be permanent and in the case of the utilities would cause as much harm to the town's remaining population as it would to the enemy.

Some targets made more sense. The radar station on the western headland was of obvious interest and a plan was developed to repeat the success of Bruneval and seize parts of the apparatus. It was also fairly certain that searches of naval headquarters in town and ships in the harbour would yield more Enigma material, which would be of enormous help to Bletchley Park, though the need for intense secrecy meant this was not mentioned in documents.

None of this made Dieppe obviously special or substantiated

Bernard Fergusson's subsequent claim that it was 'by far the best prospect' of all the targets on the Channel coast. Nor was there anything in the preparations that lent credence to the assertion that the raid was mounted as a trial for the invasion and liberation of the continent. When the outline plan was eventually drawn up it was accompanied by a covering letter from Mountbatten with a statement pointing out 'the value of this operation in order to gain experience for future large-scale operations'.[22] But this was true of all raids. A report by the War Cabinet's Joint Planning Staff in February had stated: 'Raiding policy is intimately bound up with the problem of a return to the continent.'[23] Mountbatten went further, stating that 'apart from the military objective given in the outline plan, this operation will be of great value as training for Operation "SLEDGE-HAMMER" or any other major operation as far as the actual assault is concerned.' He went on: 'it will not, however, throw light on the maintenance problem over beaches', that is, the question of resupplying an invasion force.[24] There is no suggestion here that it is part of a much bigger design to test the myriad unknowns in what would be the greatest amphibious invasion in history. Nor do the operational orders contain anything like a systematic programme for evaluating performance and gathering data.

If Dieppe really was intended as an experiment it was a strange target for Mountbatten to approve. In the many arguments in the spring of 1942 as to where a major landing should take place he consistently opposed those who favoured the Pas de Calais, arguing that the beaches of Calvados and the Cherbourg Peninsula in Lower Normandy, though further away from Germany, would be easier to take and hold as well as to resupply. This explains his caveat about the 'maintenance problem over beaches' which would be a major consideration if his proposal was adopted.

At the outset, at least, it would seem that the Dieppe raid was neither conceived nor planned to garner vital information about how to go about launching a full-scale cross-Channel invasion. Judged on such documents as survive, it looks more like the latest and most spectacular of Mountbatten's Combined Ops productions, driven by the desire to demonstrate aggressive intent to the Germans, the

British public, the Americans and the Soviets, as well as restoring lustre to COHQ's reputation.

This was the biggest raid yet attempted by Combined Ops. It would require a scale of troops beyond the resources of the three commandos of the Special Service Brigade which numbered about 1,500 men. COHQ's official report into the raid recorded that 'though intelligence reports showed that Dieppe was not very heavily defended, a town of its size could only be successfully raided if the number of troops used was considerable.'[25] It was estimated that up to six battalions were needed. They would need armoured support so 'the use of tanks was considered very early in the planning.'

Arrangements were already in place for troops for large-scale COHQ-inspired operations to be provided by General Paget from the resources of Home Forces Command, and a procedure was agreed at the end of March that Home Forces staff officers would help prepare the plans. On 14 April a team arrived from Paget's headquarters to join the Combined Ops planning syndicate.

By then, however, the COHQ planners had already developed their own ideas as to how the attack should be launched. Despite the contention that the Dieppe defences were 'not heavy', they had quickly rejected the idea of a frontal assault on the town. Conventional military wisdom dictated that funnelling large numbers of troops into a narrow front before the defences had been effectively suppressed was a recipe for a massacre. The only justification would be if the attack stood a good chance of taking the defenders completely by surprise. It was assumed that the Germans were fully expecting some sort of major action somewhere along the Channel coast sometime soon. There was therefore no hope at all of achieving what was called 'strategic' surprise. Tactical surprise, which caught the enemy off balance, might be possible. It seemed nonetheless to Hughes-Hallett that it was more prudent to follow what was the conventional course and approach the target indirectly with attacks going in on either side of the town to envelop it from the flanks. He took the idea to Brigadier Charles Haydon, Vice Chief of Combined Ops, who 'felt there were attractive features to putting the main weight of our assault on the flanks'.[26] Mountbatten also later approved the concept.

The plan that followed was largely dictated by the topography of the coastline. There were a few gaps in the cliff wall either side where a sizeable landing was feasible. At Pourville, a holiday resort a mile and a half to the west, the heights dipped down to the flat-bottomed valley of the little River Scie. They then swooped up again for four miles before descending where the almost identical River Saâne entered the sea at Quiberville. On the eastern side, about a mile from the harbour, there was a break in the cliffs at Puys, but the beach was narrow and the valley walls leading up from it tight. After that there was no sizeable gap until Criel-sur-Mer, twelve miles from Dieppe as the crow flies and considerably more by road.

At first the team favoured landing the tanks and one infantry battalion at Quiberville who would race eastwards along the coast road, capture the west headland and seize the airfield at Saint-Aubin-sur-Scie three miles inland. Two more infantry battalions would be put ashore just to the east at Pourville, within easier reach of the town.[27]

Another two would land on the far side of Dieppe at Puys then move west to seize the eastern headland before descending into Dieppe. Two more battalions were to stay offshore on ships as a 'floating reserve'.[28] Once the town was taken, specialist engineer teams would blow up stores and infrastructure, capture prisoners and raid headquarters to snatch documents, before everyone re-embarked from the front on the second tide of the day having spent about fifteen hours ashore.

Not long after the two teams joined forces, a major difference of opinion emerged. The army staff believed that flank attacks on their own would not work. Success depended on the effective use of tanks. Quiberville was ten miles by road from Dieppe. To reach it the tanks would have to cross the Scie and possibly the Saâne and the bridges spanning the rivers might well be blown by the time they reached them.

Despite the enemy's assumed high state of readiness, they did not know where precisely the blow would fall. By striking fast just before first light it might be possible to catch the enemy on the hop and achieve an element of tactical surprise. That would be impossible with the

COHQ plan. While the tanks were trundling towards the target, or worse sitting impotently on the banks of a river, the whole of Dieppe's defences would have plenty of time to come to full readiness.

For the raid to have any chance of success it would have to confound the enemy's expectations by abandoning orthodoxy and doing what common sense and military precedent dictated you did *not* do. The army proposition was therefore that 'Dieppe should be assaulted by a frontal attack delivered against the beaches of the town itself.'[29] It would be supported by two flank attacks, one at Puys and one at Pourville. Simultaneously, or shortly before, parachute and glider-borne troops were to capture the heavy coastal defence guns menacing the Dieppe approaches at Berneval and Varengeville.

The pros and cons of the alternative plans were debated at a high-level meeting on 18 April. According to the official record it was chaired by General Haydon deputising for Mountbatten who was busy with General Marshall's visit to London to settle the great strategic issues of where and when the Allies would strike first. Leading for Home Forces was Major General Philip Gregson-Ellis, deputising for Paget. General Frederick Browning, commander of the 1st Airborne Division, was also there. At the end it was decided 'a frontal assault would have to be included in the plan.' However, this would take place only after Browning's men had successfully knocked out the coastal defence guns and the RAF had delivered a heavy air bombardment on the town. This was not enough to satisfy Hughes-Hallett who still considered that 'a frontal assault was hazardous', even though feasible from a purely naval point of view.

A second meeting of staffs was held a week later to settle the matter formally, this time chaired by Mountbatten and with Gregson-Ellis again representing Home Forces. The Home Forces team laid out in detail the arguments for their approach. Quiberville was just too far away to achieve surprise. The tanks landed there would have to cross two rivers to get to Dieppe. The bridges over them would have to be seized early to prevent the enemy demolishing them.

In a reversal of their customary roles it was now the army urging boldness and Combined Ops voicing restraint. The Home Forces representatives pointed out that the latest intelligence reports 'showed that Dieppe was lightly held by a single low-category battalion' of about 1,400 men supported by 'ten AA guns, three or four light anti-aircraft guns, one four-gun dual purpose battery and four coast defence batteries'. Furthermore the garrison would be fighting on its own for some time and it would be five hours before another 2,500 reinforcements could be pulled in with a maximum enemy strength of 6,500 after fifteen hours, just as the raiders were departing.

According to the first post-operational report drawn up by Mountbatten's team and embedded in subsequent official narratives, the COHQ naval planners were not convinced and again questioned the wisdom of a frontal assault. The army tried to reassure them with details of the proposed air attack on the town. It would go in 'just before the craft carrying the assaulting troops touched down'.[30] The bombardment would be 'of maximum intensity' with the result that the defenders 'would be too confused by it and by subsequent attacks by low-flying aircraft to be in a position to offer stout or prolonged resistance'. The army were clearly not budging. COHQ resistance ceased and 'the Plan, which included the principle of a frontal assault and preceded by bombing, was then adopted'.

Whether the debate was quite so clear cut is open to question. Walter Skrine later strayed from the Mountbatten/Hughes-Hallett line, writing to Haydon in 1958 that 'Home Forces were quite ready to take the lead from us in any plan that could be found workable. I think therefore that the military [planners] in COHQ were quite as much responsible for the idea of a frontal assault . . . as the Home Forces planners.'[31]

Certainly the vehemence of the army arguments seems out of keeping with Paget's sceptical attitude to the value of cross-Channel adventures. Under the directive given to Paget by the chiefs of staff it was his prerogative to delegate his authority for such operations to a subordinate. The man he selected was Bernard Montgomery, who since the autumn of 1941 had been chief of South Eastern Command, or as he chose to style it 'South Eastern Army'. As his area of operations covered the coastline from where the raid would have to be launched, he was the obvious choice. It is not clear when precisely Montgomery took up this responsibility, though the official account says it came shortly after Home Forces staff joined the COHQ planners on 14 April.

It makes no mention of his being present at either of the crucial planning meetings on 18 and 25 April. However, Hughes-Hallett claimed later that Montgomery was at the first discussion and led the charge to demolish the COHQ proposal. 'Coming directly to the point he opened the meeting by saying that the military part of the plan was "the work of an amateur",' wrote Hughes-Hallett. 'If it was a fact, and indeed it was a fact, that we could only allow troops to remain ashore for a maximum of fifteen hours, then it would be impossible for the flank brigades to work round and reach Dieppe from the landwards side in time. This would still be true if there were no Germans to oppose them. He pointed out that the only way the town and seaport could be captured quickly was to deliver a frontal assault by *coup de main*.'[32]

Montgomery went on to ask Hughes-Hallett for an expert view of whether it would be possible for the navy to land 'the major part of a division' on the seafront at Dieppe at the same time as putting two or three battalions at Pourville to the west and another at Puys to the east. The answer came that there would be 'insufficient sea room', meaning that the waters off the coast would be simply too crowded to get a large number of landing craft to form up in the predawn darkness without a high chance of chaos. But if the attack was staggered so that the flank attacks went in twenty minutes ahead of the frontal assault, then the landings 'would be possible from a naval point of view'. Montgomery considered this delay was 'too small to matter' and told the two staffs to work on a new plan along the lines he suggested.

Hughes-Hallett claimed that Montgomery also dominated the 25 April meeting at which Mountbatten was in the chair. Even though the chief 'made it quite clear that he and his staff preferred the original plan, nevertheless, the general insisted on the new plan . . . and that from the intelligence at our disposal there should not be any great difficulty in a frontal assault'.[33]

Whichever version is correct, Hughes-Hallett's account certainly sounds like the sort of performance people had come to expect of Bernard Montgomery. Still largely unknown outside military circles, inside them he was a controversial figure attracting scepticism and admiration in equal quantities. He came from the same sort of background as virtually every other senior officer at the time, belonging to that section of the British middle class that provided the empire with soldiers, sailors, administrators and clergymen. Bernard was born in 1887 in London, the fourth child of an eventual nine of an impoverished Anglican vicar and a cold, unloving mother. Two years later the family moved to Tasmania where his father had been appointed bishop. He took his duties seriously and was sometimes away in the bush for six months at a time. The children were left with Maud, daughter of a famous preacher, who was eighteen years younger than her husband. She handed them over to tutors imported from Britain, starved them of love and beat them regularly.

Montgomery's attempts to show affection and win some display of it in return were rebuffed and the tortured relationship ended in estrangement. He did not attend her funeral. This upbringing turned him into something of a rebel and a bully, 'a dreadful little boy' as he admitted to friends.[34] After St Paul's School in London he resisted family pressure to go into the Church and went instead to Sandhurst where he got into trouble for his violent behaviour.

He joined the Royal Warwickshire Regiment and went to France at the start of the First World War, fought at Le Cateau and the retreat from Mons and was wounded twice. Thereafter he served on various staffs finishing the war an acting lieutenant colonel. In the interwar years he attended staff college but with no real wars to fight progress was slow. At the age of around forty he discovered a life outside soldiering. In 1927 he met and married Betty Carver, whose husband had been killed in the war leaving her with two sons. She was the sister of Percy Hobart who would go to command an armoured division in the Second World War. They had a son together and the marriage was extremely happy.

The idyll ended when she contracted septicaemia from an infected insect bite, dying in his arms in 1937. Henceforth Montgomery's work was his life. At the start of the war he commanded the 3rd Infantry Division which was part of the British Expeditionary Force. In the succession of defeats following the German attack in the West, he distinguished himself by getting his men back home with minimum casualties.

The episode gave him much scope for the outspokenness that was starting to become a trademark. Monty was seen as unusually vain and egotistical in a profession where vanity and self-regard abounded. Concern for his reputation shaped his approach to truth, so that his version of the facts was concerned primarily with putting the best possible construction on his actions and judgements, making his testimony far from reliable.

For all of that, Montgomery had much to be egotistical about. His professionalism and dedication made him stand out from the ranks of the surrounding mediocrities. When the war began, there were some impressive officers advancing towards the most important command positions. Those at the very top, though, were mostly ill-equipped to lead the army into a battle against the modern world's most ruthless and efficient warriors.

The upper ranks of the army formed a club where the top jobs were decided on seniority, and incompetence and failure were treated with the indulgence that the upper classes showed to those they had grown up with. The malaise was evident in the figure of the man who served in the vital position of Chief of the Imperial General Staff in the run-up to the war and then in 1939 led the British Expeditionary Force to France. The dimness of John Vereker, 6th Viscount Gort, was legendary. 'It had never occurred to me nor, I fancy, to any of his contemporaries, to describe Gort as intelligent above the average,' wrote General Sir Edward Spears, who served with him in France.[35] His political boss, the war minister Leslie Hore-Belisha, put it more bluntly. He found him 'utterly brainless and unable to grasp the simplest problem'.[36] He was blind to the big picture but obsessed with small details, once insisting on opening an important conference at the start of the war with a discussion about whether a tin hat, when not on a soldier's head, should be carried on the left or right shoulder. By 1942 a new order was in place at the top of the army led by Brooke, the master of the big picture, who created an environment in which driven, dedicated individuals like Montgomery could flourish and their bolshiness be tolerated.

The Dieppe raid seems to have held little more interest for Montgomery than it did for his boss General Paget. The impression he gave to those close to him like his liaison officer Goronwy Rees was that it was a distraction from the more interesting work of training up his 'South Eastern Army' while waiting for some more dramatic and active command which, though he did not then know it, was about to come his way and steer him to his rendezvous with history.

Subsequently he would downplay his role in the whole affair. The outcome did not fit happily into the legend he spent so much energy constructing, often with a complete disregard for facts. Nonetheless it is clear that he approved the plan and endorsed the vital subsequent amendments that did so much to diminish the chances of success.

With the close of the 25 April meeting Rutter took a long step closer to becoming a reality. The crucial decision had been made. Dieppe was to be taken by a head-on attack launched from the sea. Work now began on an outline plan that would then be put to the chiefs of staff for their approval.

Winston Churchill would later claim that the central proposition took him by surprise. When ordering an inquiry into all aspects of the preparations in December that year, he reflected that 'at first sight it would appear to a layman very much out of accord with the accepted principles of war to attack the strongly fortified town front without first securing the cliffs on either side, and to use our tanks in frontal assault off the beaches . . . instead of landing them a few miles up the coast and entering the town from the back.'[37]

Mountbatten and his staff certainly resisted the idea. Why did they not try harder? One explanation is that Mountbatten was reluctant to oppose a scheme which was being pushed by political necessity, a dynamic he was intimately aware of due to his close involvement in a vitally important visit by the US chief of staff General Marshall which was taking place as the deliberations were going on.

Marshall arrived with Roosevelt's adviser Harry Hopkins, who held no official position but exercised more influence over the president than any other American, soldier or civilian. They were there to try to resolve the great strategic dilemma that threatened to paralyse the Anglo-American war effort. The American goals were to keep Stalin in the war and prevent his making a separate peace with Hitler, maintain and nurture the alliance with Britain and fight the Germans on the ground as soon as possible. However, the White House and the US War Department differed on how to pursue them.

Marshall and Eisenhower believed in rapid action and striking the enemy at the closest point. That meant an all-out bombing campaign followed by a full-scale invasion of Western Europe after air superiority had been achieved. As Eisenhower put it in his diary in late January: 'We've got to go to Europe and fight . . . We've got to begin slugging with air at West Europe, to be followed by a land attack as soon as possible.'[38] Churchill's enthusiasm for 'Gymnast' – the Anglo-American invasion of North Africa – they regarded as an enormous waste of time and effort that would tie up Allied troops and delay the big event of a continental invasion until 1943 or perhaps 1944.

Roosevelt and Hopkins agreed with them on the need for early action. 'I doubt if any single thing is as important as getting some sort of a front this summer,' wrote Hopkins to the President on 14 March.[39] But he was careful not to say *where* and the pair remained open to the possibility of Gymnast.

Nonetheless Roosevelt thought it wise to give Marshall his head, and with Hopkins by his side he arrived in Britain by Pan Am Clipper to begin talks on 8 April. Marshall was armed with a memorandum drawn up for him by Eisenhower laying out his proposal. It formalised his ideas for Roundup, a cross-Channel invasion by forty-eight British and American divisions in the spring of 1943.

The memorandum also promoted the cause of Sledgehammer, the emergency operation to relieve the Russians if they looked on the point of collapse or to seize the advantage in the more unlikely event of the Germans suffering a major setback that would force them to weaken their defences in France. The Americans had adopted Sledgehammer with far more enthusiasm than the British who conceived it, an irony that only added to the hosts' difficulties.

The arrival of Marshall and Hopkins put Churchill and his military chiefs in a tight corner. They had kept Washington sweet with seemingly positive noises about an early move in Europe. In fact the idea filled all of them with something like horror. They believed with justification that it was military madness. Memories of Norway, the Battle of France and Dunkirk were still red raw. They knew the paralysing pain and demoralisation of defeat in a way that the Americans could not. Marshall had experienced the First World War as a staff officer. Eisenhower, to his great chagrin, was never in action. They saw war in terms of resources, organisation and logistics which if harnessed efficiently would logically lead to victory. The British knew only too well its messiness and Lady Luck's cruel indifference when it came to bestowing her favours.

Brooke's first proper conversation with Marshall on 15 April to discuss an invasion of France was alarming. 'His strategical ability does not impress me at all!!' Brooke wrote in an exclamation-mark-studded entry in his diary that night. 'His plan does not go beyond just landing on the far coast!! Whether we are to play baccarat or chemin de fer at Le Touquet, or possibly bathe at Paris Plage is not stipulated! I asked him this afternoon – do we go east, south or west after landing? He had not begun to think about it!!'[40]

Brooke knew very well that he must never allow the visitors a glimpse of his true feelings. Like the maître d'hôtel and the staff at a de luxe establishment, he and the British war leadership had to keep their smiles in place as they danced attendance on their big-spending guests.

The essential fact was that the USA brought with it the means of victory. At the moment the relationship was presented as a partnership of equals but in time the might of the Americans' contribution would give them the upper hand. Even so, another catastrophe, squandering divisions in a doomed enterprise, was inconceivable. The British were determined to resist it, but how? The answer was a typically British combination of feigned enthusiasm for Marshall's naïve proposals, accompanied by a subtle campaign to undermine them.

The search for harmony was conducted over ten days of formal meetings interspersed with lunches, dinners and visits to Chequers. Churchill did what he did best, creating a warm symphonic swell of bonhomie, declaring with masterly vagueness after a few days that 'there was complete unanimity on the framework' of the Marshall Memorandum and committing the government to 'this great enterprise'.[41] Brooke was equally suited to sounding the discordant notes, particularly British doubts about Sledgehammer.

The visitors had plenty of opportunities to meet Mountbatten. He was now well established as Churchill's charmer-in-chief to the Americans. He had already won many conquests in his visits to the States and was about to make important new ones. Marshall had brought with him a favourite staff officer, Colonel Al Wedemeyer, a lean, blond, soldier-scholar whose intellect roamed far beyond military boundaries.

Wedemeyer was cautious in his judgements of the British brass on first meeting them but his approval of the dashing chief of Combined Operations was unqualified. 'Mountbatten was by all odds the most colorful on the British chiefs of staff level,' he wrote.[42] 'He was charming, tactful, a conscious gallant knight in shining armor.' He noticed that his relative youth told against him and 'it was obvious that the older officers did not defer readily to his views'. They were nonetheless careful to give Mountbatten 'a semblance of courteous attention', which Wedemeyer thought was at least partly explained by the fact that he was 'a cousin of the king and, no doubt about it, a great favorite of the prime minister'.

Marshall's programme included a visit to Richmond Terrace. He arrived on 10 April and liked what he saw. On his own initiative he proposed that US staff officers should join COHQ and work with them as a team. The offer gave Mountbatten the opportunity to add an international dimension to his empire which he seized eagerly. In May a nine-man team led by Brigadier Lucian K. Truscott arrived, charged with creating an American version of the commandos.

The Americans left for home on their Pan Am Clipper from Stranraer on the night of 18 April. Marshall appeared to have been satisfied by Churchill's assurances of British commitment to his memorandum. Hopkins was not so sure, and had divined that beneath the persiflage Churchill remained wedded to Gymnast and North Africa.

It was later said by General 'Pug' Ismay, Churchill's chief of staff: 'We should have come clean, much cleaner than we did.'[41] But the deception could not go on for long and sooner rather than later the British would have to make some practical demonstration of their commitment to action. Every day brought a further turn of the vice in which Churchill and his military chiefs were stuck. Domestic pressure for action to help Russia was mounting by the day. 'Public opinion is shouting for the formation of a new western front,' wrote Brooke on 16 April.[43] 'But they have no conception of the difficulties and dangers entailed! The prospects of success are small and dependent on a mass of unknowns, whilst the chances of disaster are great . . .'

It would only increase with the imminent arrival of the Soviet foreign minister Vyacheslav Molotov, due to visit both London and Washington in the coming weeks to formalise a grand alliance with Britain and renew the pressure from Stalin for the early launching of a relief operation in Europe.

There was nothing of substance that the army or COHQ could offer. Despite Mountbatten's advocacy of Cherbourg for the Sledgehammer emergency invasion he was no more enamoured of the project than anyone else who mattered. But clearly something would have to be done. In his eyes Rutter now took on a new dimension, and in the following weeks the political and diplomatic weight on its slender shoulders would grow until Mountbatten could present it as a plausible alternative to Sledgehammer. That consideration made it all the more important that it went ahead, whatever the risks and imperfections.

By 11 May an outline plan was ready to go to the chiefs of staff for their approval. The document opened on a note of high optimism with the now familiar assertion that 'Dieppe is not heavily defended'. It went on to sketch an operation of great ambition and daunting complexity. The attack would arrive from several directions and involved two air drops and three landings on tricky shores. Victory depended on every unit achieving its objectives at the precise time laid out in orders. There was little account taken of the unexpected, and the old adage that no plan survived first contact with the enemy seemed to have been forgotten or ignored.

It would take enormous skill and a great slice of luck for Rutter to have any chance of success. But the plan was now a going concern and the men who would have to carry it out had already been chosen.

7. 'You bet we want it'

After eighteen months in Britain, the men of the Royal Hamilton Light Infantry (the Rileys, as they were affectionately known) were still waiting for something to happen. Since arriving from Canada they had moved from one south-east England base to another, training endlessly and fighting mock battles, preparing to repel an enemy who never came. Sometimes these 'schemes' offered a welcome break, like Operation Malcolm in which the Canadians played the role of German paratroopers pitting themselves against the local Home Guard. 'The operation was thoroughly enjoyed by our men,' commented the regimental war diary. 'It gave them the opportunity for unlimited initiative which expressed itself in the form of tear-gas bombs in local dance halls, the disrobing and appropriation of uniforms of policemen and the changing of signals on a small railway line.'[1] Colonel Labatt, the CO, had got into the spirit, disguising himself as a vicar to observe the proceedings, only to be arrested as a suspected fifth columnist. Usually these outings were not so entertaining and the novelty of crawling over the South Downs while being bombarded with thunderflashes had long since worn off.

The Rileys were getting bored. They were all volunteers who had signed up for overseas service, driven by a mixture of motives that was often hard to disentangle. There was still a sense of duty to the motherland, and the spirit of adventure was strong in the youth of a young country. Economics also played a part. Soldiering was a job when employment was scarce and the war offered opportunity and excitement.

The Rileys belonged to the 2nd Division of the 1st Canadian Corps and, like most of the units, was a militia regiment. They belonged to a cherished tradition of volunteer citizen soldiers who according to historical tradition had rallied to save the young nation from external threats, notably from the USA. The militias had strong local identities and deep roots in the communities, both English- and French-speaking. The Rileys sprang from Hamilton, a growing port city on Lake Ontario near to Niagara Falls. They were part-time soldiers, serving at weekends and during vacations. But what the militias lacked in strict professionalism they made up for in attitude. 'They had esprit,' said William Jemmett Megill, who viewed them from the perspective of a regular force ranker who rose to become a major general, 'Their officers came from the local elites, and they threw the best parties in Canada at their armouries.'[2] For all that, there was less class distinction between officers and other ranks than in British territorial units. Family connections were strong and son often followed father into the ranks. Robert Labatt, the genial, dry-humoured young officer who took over the Rileys in March 1940, was emulating his father who commanded an earlier evolution of the regiment in the First World War.

The Canadians were 4,000 miles from home and unlikely to see their families until the war ended. Homesickness and loneliness were alleviated by the welcome they received from the local population, starting with the royal family. Shortly after the Rileys arrived a party of sixty officers and men visited the grounds of Windsor Castle. 'The king and queen and the two little princesses were driving in their car and on seeing our chaps they stopped, shook hands with our padre who was in charge of the party and engaged some of the men in conversation for some minutes,' the regimental diary recorded.[3] There were regular reminders that the notion of an imperial family was more than a propaganda conceit. 'The attitude of the British people was fantastic,' remembered Ken Curry from Stoney Creek, Ontario and who had lied about his age to join the Rileys. Customers in cafeterias would put money on the soldiers' trays so they could buy themselves a treat.[4] At this stage in the war treats were rare and 'you couldn't get a meal like you could in Canada. In most of the restaurants the waitress would tell you it was egg and chips, fish and chips, sausage and chips, beans and chips, bacon and chips.' It tasted all right though, and the English girls, one of whom Ken married, 'were exceptional'.

The officers did their best to provide diversion with sports, films and outings. However there were only so many times you could visit Windsor Great Park, walk round HMS *Victory* at Portsmouth, play cricket against ladies from the local ambulance unit (left-handed to even the odds) or board a bus to a hop at the local church hall to dance to the swing tunes of the Royal Thirteens.

By the end of 1941 there were 177,000 Canadian troops in the country. A decision had been made at the top to keep them in Britain rather than send them to North Africa, where Australian, Indian, New Zealand and South African troops were supporting the British, as Churchill was sensitive to the charge that Britain was relying on empire troops to fight its battles for it.[5] This suited the Canadian prime minister William Lyon Mackenzie King, who was concerned that the resulting casualties would accelerate the need for conscription and a rerun of the political crisis that erupted when it was introduced during the last war.

As they waited, discipline inevitably suffered. In magistrates' courts in the market towns and seaside resorts of Sussex the dock was frequently occupied by contrite soldiers up on charges of brawling, drunkenness and petty theft. At the West Sussex quarter sessions in April 1942, all but four of the forty-two defendants were Canadians. Among them were four young soldiers charged with stealing an eighteen-gallon barrel of beer from the Bracklesham Bay Hotel, loading it into an army truck and taking it to the house of a woman in East Wittering where they 'drank until they could not drink any more'.[6] The chairman of the bench was sympathetic and they got off with a fine and a warning. 'We are proud of the Canadians and the assistance they are according us,' Mr Rowland Burrows KC told them. 'But you came here to defend the country not to pillage it.'

One display of mass indiscipline would go into legend. In the summer of 1941 Mackenzie King visited Britain and on 23 August came to Aldershot to inspect the troops and attend an athletics competition between the 1st and 2nd Divisions. After watching the contestants run round a cinder track in pouring rain he mounted a stage to make a speech. The men listened for a while in silence. A boo was heard, followed by another, then his words were drowned out in a barrage of whistling and shouting.

The incident was later cited as evidence that Canadian troops were desperate to get into action. This became an established and all but unquestioned element in the Dieppe story, given credence by the official historian Colonel Stacey, who stated that 'the morale of the forces was suffering because of lack of opportunity for fighting'.[7] This was not how it seemed to one Riley veteran, Denis Whitaker, who as an RHLI platoon commander was in a position to know. 'I don't believe the morale in the Rileys was suffering, nor was it in any other units I saw or heard about in England,' he wrote. 'We believed we were fulfilling a role. Our job was to defend England from enemy invasion. There was always that possibility of a German paratroop attack.'[8]

Nor was the Aldershot demonstration quite as it was subsequently portrayed. Whitaker remembered 'a very cold, wet afternoon . . . we formed up in the open awaiting King's arrival. The prime minister was delayed by several hours and evidently did not bother to send word ahead. The guard and the bands were kept standing in the belting rain all that time, soaked and cold. This cavalier treatment was what made the men so furious. When King finally arrived, they booed. It was not from sagging morale, not from any fever-pitch for battle – it was just momentary anger at thoughtless treatment of soldiers.'

The image of soldiers actively yearning to get into the fray was a fiction promoted by newspapers, politicians and senior commanders in this war as it had been in the last. The reality, as anyone who really knew soldiers understood, was that few would want to risk death, maiming or incarceration unless they felt there was some point to the gamble they were taking with their lives. It would later be claimed that one of the reasons Dieppe was assigned to the Canadians was to provide a safety valve for their pent-up aggression. Whitaker believed fervently that 'the propaganda that the media and the government doled out to the Canadians back home in 1941 and 1942 – that *we* were the ones who wanted action . . . [was] pure nonsense.'[9]

The truth was more prosaic. Every man and woman in uniform knew that until the war was over life could not return to normal. As Colonel Labatt explained later, 'everybody was getting restless' for the simple reason that they were 'wanting to get on with the job'.[10] They were not pressing for action for its own sake, no matter what operation they were handed. The attitude of their senior commanders, however, was rather different.

The Canadian Expeditionary Force was led by lieutenant generals Andrew McNaughton and Harry Crerar, the nation's two most eminent soldiers. Their views were listened to reverently by the civilian leadership in Ottawa who tended to follow their advice on how Canadian troops should be used by the British.

Andy McNaughton was tall, lean and volatile. He was born in 1887 in the prairie settlement of Moosomin in what is now southern Saskatchewan where his parents owned a thriving hardware business. Growing up he was fascinated by engineering, conducting his own experiments which included firing projectiles from a copper tube using gunpowder from shotgun shells as a charge.[11] He was sent away to an Anglican boarding school in Quebec and then studied electrical engineering at McGill University, Montreal, staying on to take a Masters. By the time the war came he was a leading authority on the high-voltage transmission of electrical power.

He joined the army reserve in 1909, commanding a field-gun battery in Montreal. In early 1915 he went with the Canadian Corps to France, serving in the artillery. This was a gunner's war and McNaughton applied science to improving battery performance, calculating barometric pressure, ambient temperatures and wind direction to increase accuracy and using flash spotting, the analysis of sound waves and aerial photography to refine range-finding. His techniques made a significant contribution to the great Canadian victory at Vimy Ridge. He returned home with a DSO and the rank of brigadier general. In the words of General Sir Frederick Pile, who commanded Britain's anti-aircraft defences during the Second World War, 'McNaughton was probably the best and most scientific gunner in any army in the world.'[12] He stayed on in Canada's tiny and cash-starved professional army after the war, becoming Chief of the General Staff in 1929. He was later head of the primary Canadian scientific agency, the National Research Council, and therefore the country's top administrative scientist. When the Second World War came he was the natural choice to lead the Expeditionary Force to Britain.

Andy McNaughton's rangy frame and square jaw made him everyone's idea of a general. Famous in Canada, he was unknown outside it until in December 1939 his deep brooding eyes stared out of the front cover at millions of American readers of the influential *Life* magazine. He was popular with his men who appreciated his concern for their welfare and fatherly manner. James Tedlie remembered having to parade a junior officer before him on a charge of passing bad cheques: 'Andy bawled him out and said, "Remember, young man, no one ever comes before me twice." "Oh, no, Sir," replied the guilty party, "you've given me a severe reprimand before." ' McNaughton ordered Tedlie to march him out, 'barely closing the door before Andy's peals of laughter rang out'.[13] He did not stand on dignity and 'would happily get his hands dirty, sometimes scrambling under a vehicle to repair it'. But popularity with the troops was not necessarily a prerequisite of great generalship, and some of those around him wondered about his leadership qualities. According to some of his contemporaries he was 'not ruthless enough', there was 'a sense about him of refighting the Great War' and he was 'more of a scientist than a soldier'. There was no consensus. Canadian soldiers were an opinionated bunch and not shy of delivering judgement on their superiors. For every fan like Desmond Smith who thought him 'a wonderful guy, an intellect with a real brain' there was a critic like George Pangman for whom Andy McNaughton was 'a dud' who 'didn't know the capabilities of the men who had to do the fighting, had never commanded anything, and wasn't a soldier'.[14]

Views of Harry Crerar were equally divided. His bald dome and wary eyes seemed more appropriate to a judge than a warrior and he was seen as an administrator rather than an inspiring battlefield leader. 'He couldn't raise any more enthusiasm than a turnip' was the verdict of William Megill who served on the staff of the 3rd Division.[15] He was 'a first-class brain but a difficult personality'. Although not given to discussion he could 'write a beautifully organised paper . . . but he wasn't a natural commander'. Stanley Todd, who commanded the

3rd Division artillery, on the other hand thought him 'an excellent officer, 100 per cent sound'.

Crerar was born in Hamilton in 1888. His father was a lawyer who had emigrated from Scotland and his mother a public-spirited society matron. He went to the elite Upper Canada College boarding school in Toronto, going on to the Royal Military College in Kingston favoured by well-heeled anglophones 'who desired for their sons an education that included moral and physical conditioning as well as discipline and scholarly attainment'.[16] He went to France with the artillery in 1915 and fought in the Second Battle of Ypres in April and May. He did not expect to survive and was eloquent about the horrors of the experience, recording in his diary on 15 June 1915: 'War is so very truly hell and this yard by yard fighting finds it at its worst. The gains are so small when it comes to distance – it just resolves itself into a case of counting corpses, if we have fewer than they, it's a "victory".'[17] Nonetheless he enjoyed soldiering. He commanded an artillery unit before moving on to the staff, where he worked with McNaughton. He too chose to stay on in the army and his intelligence and application propelled him upwards, encouraged by his old comrade.

In April 1942 McNaughton was the senior Canadian commander in Britain overseeing the formation of the 1st Canadian Army. As yet it comprised one corps with Crerar at its head. Each knew the other's ways intimately and had boxed and coxed appointments harmoniously in the peacetime years. But Crerar was tiring of playing second fiddle and his ambition would eventually turn him against his former mentor.

Their duties carried heavy political responsibilities. McNaughton and Crerar were well acquainted with the subtleties and complexities of Anglo-Canadian relations. Both worked under British commanders on the Western Front and in the 1920s Crerar spent four years in Britain at the Staff College and War Office. As a result they had long exposure to the curious mixture of admiration tinged with condescension that marked many senior officers' dealings with their counterparts from the Dominions.

The Canadians' performance in the First World War was supposed to have altered the relationship between the nations. Canada sent 420,000 men overseas of whom 60,000 did not return. They fought at Ypres, the Somme, Vimy Ridge and Passchendaele. At Vimy in April 1917 all four divisions of the Canadian Corps went into action as one for the first time, capturing the four-mile-long ridge which overlooked the Allied lines. Six months later at Passchendaele the Canadians were brought in to take over from the mangled and exhausted British and secured what counted as a victory in one of the most appalling battles of attrition of the war.

Vimy Ridge became more than simply a victory. Though led by a British general, the battle had been largely a Canadian affair. It showed that Canadian commanders and soldiers were at least as good as their British partners.

In 1936 a tall memorial of two soaring columns of dazzling limestone arose on the battlefield. It was unveiled by King Edward VIII in front of 100,000 spectators. It commemorated sacrifice and achievement but there was more to it than that. 'There are some ideas, myths and icons that persistently carry the weight of nationhood,' wrote Canada's premier contemporary military historian Tim Cook. 'Vimy is one of them.'[18] The battle thus came to be seen as a defining moment when the country moved from adolescence to adulthood, a coming of age that had great implications for its relationship with the mother country. It seemed to signal a waning of deference as confidence mounted and a shift towards independence from the imperial centre.

In Canada as elsewhere the 1914–18 experience had left the population dreading another war. It was reflected in official policy towards the armed forces. Politicians were deeply averse to spending money on anything that suggested the possibility of another traumatic conflict. The army shrank to a vestigial force. In 1931 the permanent strength was 3,688, backed by about 50,000 in the 'non-permanent active militia', as territorial units like the Rileys were known. In the general election of 1935 all parties promised to avoid any entanglement in the fresh trouble brewing in Europe, and as late as March 1939 both government and opposition pledged that in the event of war there would be no need for Canada to send a large expeditionary force to Europe.

But when war came, politicians and public rallied somewhat resignedly to the flag. At the parliamentary debate on 7 September to approve the government's proposal to declare war on Germany, only four members spoke against it. Mackenzie King saw off an attempt by Quebecois French separatists to oppose the war by pledging not to bring in conscription. When an appeal was made in September for volunteers, Canadian men and women came forward in the same numbers as their fathers and uncles had in 1914. By the end of the month nearly 60,000 had enlisted, including many francophones.

In contrast to 1914 the mood was sombre. One report from a recruitment centre in Calgary noted the 'complete absence of jingoism or war excitement'. A visiting American journalist reported that 'Canadians are going into the current war with none of the enthusiasm they felt in the last one . . . instead the traveler finds only a profound conviction that Hitlerism is a menace that must be wiped out however distasteful the job, and a grim, calm determination to see it through.'[19]

The motives of those who came forward were a jumble of personal and abstract impulses. Someone like Cecil Merritt, a tall young Vancouver lawyer who commanded the South Saskatchewan Regiment, had military service in his blood, and his father had been killed at Ypres in 1915 when Cecil was eight years old. Nobody from the family of John Toney, born on the First Nation Neskonlith Reserve in British Columbia, had ever been a soldier. But he too felt the same compulsion to go to war, serving as a combat engineer.

Mackenzie King was a very reluctant war leader. In March 1939 he had lamented that 'the idea that every twenty years this country should feel called upon to save a continent that cannot run itself seems to many a nightmare and sheer madness'.[20] He wrote to the British prime minister Neville Chamberlain on 3 September emphasising that Canada's priority was its own defence, yet nonetheless asked for his 'appreciation of the probable theatre and character of [the] main British and allied military operations, in order that we may consider the policy to be adopted by Canada'.[21] The reply came not from Chamberlain but from Anthony Eden, the Dominions Secretary who told him Britain was for the time being more interested in food, raw materials, financial services and aircrew from Canada, though in time it was hoped that the Dominion 'would exert her full national effort as in [the] last war, even to the extent of the eventual despatch of an expeditionary force'.

Anglophone Canadians harboured fluid identities and the dual loyalties to their own country and their duty to the king were not always aligned, but the call when it came could not be resisted. Just over three months later, on 18 December 1939, the Cunard liner *Aquitania* steamed into the Clyde at the head of a flotilla of passenger ships carrying 7,448 officers and men of the 1st Canadian Division. Eden was waiting with a message of welcome from King George VI. The following day's newspapers greeted them like long-lost sons. 'Singing wartime choruses learned at the knee of their soldier fathers, Canada's manhood has arrived in Britain to serve as an active service force,' wrote a special correspondent for the *Aberdeen Press and Journal*. 'To quote the words of their commander Major General McNaughton, they came here to report to Lord Gort and say, "at your orders, sir!"' He assured the reporter: 'Canada is with the old country heart and soul.'

The command and control arrangements for Canadian military cooperation with the British were laid out in an agreement reached in 1933. The Visiting Forces (British Commonwealth) Act established that, when assigned to a British-controlled operation or larger British formation, the Canadians were under British higher command. As Colonel Stacey observed, this meant that 'in field operations . . . Canada inevitably surrendered a very large measure of operational control over her troops'.[22] The situation would create tensions between McNaughton and Crerar and the British high command.

The problems that arose were as much personal as political. The Canadians found themselves in an awkward situation that only the tortured complexities of the British social order could have created. Their service in the last war had given them every right to be treated as equals. Although they were proud Canadians, their loyalty to the empire was unquestionable. Crerar described himself as 'a British subject and a Canadian national' and throughout his career had promoted stronger ties with the imperial military establishment. He was outdoorsy, horsey and correct, and on his long stints in England had fitted easily into the military and civilian social whirl. He counted himself a friend of Alan Brooke, a fellow gunner who had joined the staff of the Canadian Corps in 1917 where he organised the colossal artillery barrages that saturated the German defences at Vimy. But even someone as well versed in the ways of the British as Crerar could mistake tolerance for acceptance. For though he might look, behave and sound not unlike an English gentleman, that did not mean he would necessarily be treated as one.

The level of respect that the British were prepared to show to their allies was largely dependent on their usefulness. Their attitude towards the brash, combative Americans was very different to the face they showed to the polite, cooperative Canadians. The Americans might often seem to be naïve and boastful but they held the keys to victory. Almost every major decision had to start with the question: 'What will the Americans think about this?' Ultimately it was power and wealth that brought respect. Whatever the top brass of the three services said about their American opposite numbers behind their backs, they flattered and accommodated them and were attentive to the point of obsequiousness.

The Canadians' contribution was appreciated but it was a tiny fraction of what the Americans brought to the party. The paternalistic habit was hard to shake off, Vimy and Passchendaele notwithstanding, and the high command's dealings with the Canadians proceeded from the assumption that they would always fall into line with their proposals. When they did push back, they were portrayed as provincials standing on their dignity. In a letter to Bernard Montgomery in early 1942 Brooke warned him of the attitude he could expect from the Canadians under his command. 'They are grand soldiers, that I realised after spending one and a half years with them in the last war,' he wrote. 'But they are very touchy and childlike in many ways. You will therefore have to watch your steps with them *far* more than you would with British troops.'[23]

Brooke had worked alongside McNaughton in France and came across him again when they were both students at the Imperial Defence College in 1927.[24] Professional differences had arisen which the Canadian felt prejudiced Brooke against him. Certainly Brooke's verdict on him was not flattering. Looking back to the summer of 1941 when the Canadians were finding their feet he recalled that 'the more I saw of the Canadian Corps at that time the more convinced I became that Andy McNaughton had not got the required qualities to make a success of commanding . . .'[25] He was 'a man of exceptional ability where scientific matters were concerned, but lacking the required qualities of command'. He decided then that at some point he would have to be sacked but accepted that this was 'not a very easy matter, as he had become somewhat of a hero in Canada'.

He thought better of Crerar, perhaps because the Canadian seems to have courted his favour, and was rewarded with regular invitations to lunch and tea, occasions which Crerar would later use to bad-mouth his chief and further undermine him in Brooke's eyes. Montgomery's retrospective judgement on both Canadians was char-acterisically brutal. McNaughton was 'a useless commander, and was really a scientist' and Crerar was 'utterly unfit to lead an army'.[26]

The Canadians tried their best but the British were hard to please. Little gratitude was shown for the obliging reception McNaughton and Crerar had given to British ideas for the employment of their men. Both stood by the Canadian government's desire to retain some semblance of autonomy over their troops but they were nonetheless open to any proposal to get Canadians into action, no matter how risky the scheme.

The pattern was established in the spring of 1940. The first Can-adian units had undergone only basic drill at home and were to complete their training after arrival in Britain under Canadian con-trol.[27] They were still raw when the British War Office approached Crerar, who was at Canadian Military HQ in London, on 16 April 1940 with a request for troops to take part in the hastily organised operation to try to reverse the German invasion of Norway. The plan involved British, French and Norwegian troops and envisaged landings at Narvik inside the Arctic Circle and in the Trondheim area on the central coast, both of which were in German hands.

The intention was to put troops ashore north of Trondheim at Namsos and south at Andalsnes who would close on the city in a

. Mountbatten meets the troops. The power of his personality could inspire even the tough and ynical.

. 'Jock' Hughes-Hallett – 'Hughes-Hitler' to his many critics.

3. The fall guy. Decent, honourable and passive, 'Ham' Roberts made the perfect scapegoat for the Jubilee disaster.

4. A Canadian icon. Andy McNaughton excelled as a soldier and a scientist.

. Monty gives a good impression of being Harry Crerar's best friend. Behind the smile, he was scathing
bout Crerar's – and McNaughton's – abilities.

6. Trafford Leigh-Mallory saw Jubilee as the chance to win glory through a great air victory. He
nonetheless warned that the plan was hugely risky.

7. Lord Lovat (*with hunting rifle*) after 4 Commando's triumph. 'Shimi' was everyone's idea of a soldier: handsome, brave and efficient. And he knew it.

8. 3 Commando's CO John Durnford-Slater (*left*) with second-in-command, Peter Young.

. Lt Col Cecil Merritt VC of he South Saskatchewans. The stounding courage of 'Cec' and nany others tinged the tragedy vith nobility.

10. Captain John Foote VC, RHLI.

11. Captain Denis Whitaker, RHLI.

12. Lt Col Dollard 'Joe' Menard, Les Fusiliers Mont-Royal.

13. Lt Col Fred Jasperson, Essex Scottish.

14. The Rileys, with CO Bob Labatt at front and centre.

15. Lt Col Hedley Basher of the Royals (*left*) with his successor, Douglas Catto.

pincer movement. Then a third attack was added. This was a bold proposal to sail a heavy naval force into Trondheim fjord and land troops to capture the aerodrome and advance from the north along the railway into the town. The entrance to the fjord was covered by heavy gun batteries. It was imperative that they be put out of action and the British wanted 800 Canadians to do the job.

Crerar immediately informed McNaughton who was at the 1st Canadian Division base at Aldershot. He rushed to London where the pair met the CIGS, General Edmund Ironside. Ironside explained that the plan was still being worked out and it could be that the Canadians were not needed for the attack on the batteries but might be used in the main landings or indeed not at all.

McNaughton accepted the mission on the spot, believing he had the authority to commit to the plan without reference back to Ottawa. He chose two of the best-trained battalions of the 1st Brigade, and on the evening of 18 April they marched to Aldershot station to the pipes of the Seaforth Highlanders of Canada and entrained for Dunfermline. The following day the chiefs of staff suddenly decided a direct amphibious assault was too risky. According to Churchill, who was then at the Admiralty, 'this change was brought about, first, by increasing realisation of the magnitude of the naval stake in hazarding so many of our finest capital ships, and also by War Office arguments that even if the Fleet got in and got out again, the opposed landing of the troops in the face of the German air power would be perilous.'[28]

In other words, a frontal assault on a defended shore was judged too costly, in both ships and soldiers' lives. Thus the Canadians were almost certainly spared the experience of a humiliating early defeat. The ramshackle Trondheim expedition soon foundered and by 3 May all Allied forces had withdrawn.

The episode demonstrated McNaughton's eagerness to get involved. Both he and Crerar were living in the shadow cast by their illustrious predecessors, and were anxious to prove themselves and their men the equals of the commanders and troops who in the Great War had made the Canadians a byword for toughness and aggression.

As Colonel Stacey noted drily: 'That the Canadian commander

was prepared to commit his force to so desperate a venture is evidence that the [subsequent] long period in which the Canadians took no part in active operations was not the result of any reluctance to embark on dangerous projects.'[29]

McNaughton's initiative was not appreciated in Ottawa. The government had not been informed about the operation until the day after McNaughton's assent and he was told that in future they were to be consulted before Canadians were committed to a big overseas action. The reprimand did nothing to dampen his willingness to respond positively to future British requests for help.

The Norway debacle was soon overshadowed by a greater potential catastrophe. On 10 May, the German onslaught in the West began and had soon breached the Allied lines, leaving them cut off in northern France with their backs to the sea. On 20 May Panzer columns reached Abbeville and prepared to swing north and east up the Channel coast, threatening to cut off Boulogne, Calais and Dunkirk. At least one of these ports would have to stay in Allied hands for there to be any chance of a fightback, or, if the worst came to the worst, to allow the BEF to evacuate. Two battalions of Guards went ashore at Boulogne on 22 May and an infantry brigade supported by tanks landed at Calais the same night.

Early on the morning of 23 May, McNaughton was rung up by the War Office and told that Canadian troops were needed in the fight to keep the BEF's supply lines open. The 1st Infantry Brigade was put on notice to move while McNaughton set off to assess the situation. That evening he took a destroyer to Calais, arriving to discover that the port was already surrounded. Nonetheless he signalled the CIGS, stressing the importance of holding Calais and recommending that the Canadian force should be sent across the Channel to 'strengthen the situation' in the town. When McNaughton returned to Dover the following afternoon the first Canadian units were arriving at the port ready to sail to France. By the time he got to London, Ironside had decided that Calais was doomed and the move was called off.

Once again McNaughton had been apparently willing to throw untrained men into a hopeless situation. Had the War Office followed his original advice the 1st Infantry Brigade would have shared the fate of the Calais garrison, which after a valiant sacrificial stand surrendered on 27 May.

This was not the end of the Canadians' involvement in the BEF debacle. As Gort fell back on Dunkirk he made a desperate appeal for fresh troops and asked the War Office to send the Canadian brigade. The units who had just been stood down were reactivated. This time McNaughton was careful to inform Ottawa. Their earlier objection to the Norway proposal it seemed had been on a matter of procedural principle rather than any reservations about the wisdom of sending Canadians early into battle, and the response was swift and supportive.

McNaughton and Crerar went to Whitehall to confer with General Sir John Dill, who had just been appointed Vice CIGS, and Major General R. H. Dewing, director of military operations at the War Office. The official history states that all four men agreed that it was useless to send more troops across the Channel. It goes on: 'McNaughton nevertheless made it clear that he was quite prepared to undertake the operation if it was decided upon, provided only that his artillery could be despatched with the rest of the force.'[30] The episode subsequently produced a revealing exchange. Writing to 'my dear Andy', Dewing restated the arguments for abandoning the mission. He said he was sure that McNaughton shared his views but that it was 'much more difficult for you to express that, because you naturally had the feeling that you might be giving the impression that you and the Canadian troops were not ready to undertake a desperate adventure'. He continued: 'I can assure you that you did not give that impression. We all know you far too well for it to be possible for any of us to entertain that suspicion for one moment . . .'

The letter brought a grateful response. 'You have clearly penetrated to the motives and considerations which governed my actions,' McNaughton wrote, 'and it is a great comfort to me to know that this is so.'

The Canadians did make it to France before the final withdrawal. Even as the Dunkirk evacuation started, Churchill was already planning to scrape together a new expeditionary force to join two formations which had so far escaped German encirclement. The 51st (Highland) Division was attached to the French army when the fighting began and stationed in front of the Maginot Line opposite the Saarland. It had then fallen back to positions along the Somme. The 1st Armoured Division was sent to France shortly after the start of the German attack but arrived too late to link up with Gort's force and was now stranded south of the Somme. The units chosen were the 52nd (Lowland) Division and, once again, the Canadian 1st Brigade.

The move was essentially political, aimed at keeping France in the war. Churchill believed that even if Paris was captured the government could retreat to a redoubt on the Brittany Peninsula where the remnants of the British and French armies, reinforced and resupplied by sea from Britain, could continue the struggle. It was a fantasy. By the time the decision was made French morale had collapsed and there was no heart left in most of its military or political leaders to carry on.

McNaughton was to lead the Canadians in the field under the overall command of Alan Brooke. On 8 June the Canadian brigade's transport set off for Falmouth for passage to Brest. The troops followed by train, to embark at Plymouth. It was the third time in fifteen days that they had gone off to war. No sooner had they got ashore than they were ordered to withdraw again. The retreat was a shambles. The Canadian units were scattered around the French countryside. The artillery, under the command of Lieutenant Colonel John Hamilton Roberts, was at Sablé-sur-Sarthe, west of Le Mans, when the evacuation order came. Arriving at Brest on the morning of 16 June they found no ships available. Loading began the following day in an atmosphere of near panic. Priority was to be given to men over equipment, and all the brigade's transport had to be left for the Germans. Roberts had a long battle with the British officer in charge of evacuation to save his guns which he eventually won but was forced to abandon limbers and ammunition. The gunners' war diary recorded that 'although there was evidently no enemy within 200 miles, the withdrawal was conducted as a rout' and the steamer which carried them back 'still had room enough to take everything that was on the docks'.[31]

There was another episode on the far side of the world which illustrated the need for caution when responding to British appeals. In

July 1940 Crerar returned to Canada where he became Chief of the General Staff. In the autumn London asked Ottawa if it would send troops to stiffen the British garrison at Hong Kong in an effort to deter the mounting threat from Japan. It was a forlorn hope but Crerar backed the move strongly. He believed, in the words of his biographer, 'Canada could not turn aside from potentially danger-ous assignments that its allies were willing to undertake' and also that 'Canadian troops needed to get into the fight.'[32] In November two battalions were despatched. On Christmas Day Hong Kong fell and all the Canadians were killed or captured. By then Crerar was back in Britain having lobbied hard to take up command of the 2nd Can-adian Division and was at a safe distance from the political storm that ensued.

The experience did nothing to blunt his enthusiasm for finding battles for the Canadians to fight. This was as much for his own benefit as to blood the troops. Through no fault of his own Crerar had never commanded anything bigger than a battery and 'wanted seasoning for his untested troops and improvement of his own knowledge of battlefield command'.[33] McNaughton was also keen and in September 1941 he met General Paget to press for the inclusion of Canadians in any raids involving Home Forces. He returned to Canada, worn out and ill, for a three-month visit at the end of Janu-ary 1942 and in his absence Crerar, who took over as acting corps commander, increased the pressure. In February he wrote to Mont-gomery pointing out the 'great stimulus' his men would receive 'if, in the near future, [the corps] succeeded in making a name for itself for its raiding activities'.[34]

This was just one move in a long campaign of persuasion during which he bent the ears of those who mattered in the bars, lobbies and restaurants of the capital where the brass gathered to do informal business: the Savoy and Ritz hotels, and clubs like the 'In and Out' (Naval and Military Club) on Piccadilly and Boodle's in St James's Street. According to Stacey, Crerar 'took advantage of being in com-mand in McNaughton's absence . . . to urge Montgomery, Sir Alan Brooke and Mountbatten to give the Canadians opportunities in raids'.[35]

By early March Brooke had come round to the idea but there was resistance from Mountbatten who wanted operations at this point to be predominantly commando affairs and resented their 'dilution' by army elements. He eventually backed down saying he 'appreciated the special position of [the] Canadian Corps and was agreeable to making an exception to policy in favour of a largely Canadian enterprise' providing General Paget agreed.

The immediate fruit of Crerar's lobbying was the inclusion of a small Canadian force in Operation Abercrombie, a raid on Hardelot, south of Boulogne led by 4 Commando to 'test the German defences' and bring back prisoners. After delays, the mission finally went ahead on the night of 21/22 April. The fifty Canadians from 1st Division got stranded and never made it ashore. They did not miss much. To Lord Lovat who led the commandos, it was 'an overrated affair which achieved limited success . . . some undeserved awards were handed out'.[36]

The much greater consequence was that the campaign put the Canadians at the top of the selectors' list when a big raid beyond the scope of the commandos arose. In the view of Colonel Stacey, Crerar's advocacy 'probably influenced the selection of Canadians to execute the raid [on Dieppe]'.[37]

That McNaughton and Crerar were thoroughly in favour of action as soon as possible is not in doubt. Their record also showed that they were likely to look positively on whatever task the British might give them. What is less clear is how the decision to use the Canadians for Rutter came about. There is little surviving paperwork to reveal the details of the process, and the subsequent accounts of the participants are often unreliable or contradictory.

At the time that their senior commanders were pressing for fighting opportunities, the men of the Canadian Corps were being put through their paces in a series of exercises that Montgomery had ordered since taking over South Eastern Command in November. Though still tasked with repelling an invasion, he was intent on replacing a defensive mentality with a spirit of aggressive counter-attack. His declared aim was to 'train all ranks up to that stage of

mental, physical and professional fitness needed to engage successfully in offensive battle against the Germans'.[38] Monty brought a
necessary new ruthlessness and application to training at all levels.
There were continuous study sessions for commanders at all levels
supplemented by field schemes on an ever mounting scale. The troops
worked with their commander's exhortations ringing in their ears.
He drove everyone very hard but inspired them too with crisp
addresses that explained his vision and gave purpose to all the effort.
He seemed to be everywhere, popping up in the middle of exercises
in what one British officer felt 'weren't visits; they were visitations'.
Staff cars would appear and 'a tough, stringy, bird-like little man
would jump out . . . Striding on ahead, with his staff stumbling
behind in the sand dunes, he'd make straight for the nearest private
soldier. "Who are you? Where do you come from? What are you
doing? Do you know what's going on? Are you in the picture? Can
you see the coast of France today? Good; that's where the enemy
is." '[39] Criticism was frequent and sometimes rough. Often it was the
performance of the Canadians that caught his bright, raptor's eye.

Nonetheless most accounts agree that when the opportunity first
came to 'engage successfully in offensive battle against the Germans'
it was to the Canadians that Monty turned. One version, apparently
supplied by Crerar himself, says that on 28 April he was summoned
to South Eastern Command headquarters. There Montgomery told
him: 'You have been wanting action for a long time. Here's your
chance.' He gave a brief sketch of the mission without revealing the
destination. He endorsed the plan which 'has a lot of possibilities',
then went on: 'The raid is yours if you want it . . . Do you want it?'
The fact that Crerar had played no part in making the plan was of no
concern, and he replied: 'You bet we want it.' Montgomery told
him: 'Then you have it,' revealing with a flourish, 'the target is
Dieppe.'[40]

It was two days before Montgomery approached McNaughton,
who as 1st Army commander had sole authority in Britain on
how Canadian troops should be used. In his official history of the
Canadian Army's war Stacey wrote that on the morning of 30 April,
five days after the outline plan had been finalised, Monty visited

McNaughton at 1st Canadian Army HQ at Headley Court, a Victor-
ian mansion near Leatherhead in Surrey, and 'broached the project'.[41]
Montgomery told him he had been 'pressed to agree' to the operation being carried out by a joint British and Canadian force under
predominantly British command. However, he disliked the idea of
mixing up units and preferred to keep the main body of troops under
a unified command. He added, flatteringly, that in his opinion the
Canadian troops 'were the best suited' and General Headquarters
(GHQ) Home Forces, under whose control he operated, had agreed.

He then revealed he had already approached Crerar who had given
his approval and even chosen the 2nd Division from his corps for the
task. McNaughton seems to have been unperturbed by this breach of
protocol. He gave his blessing, 'subject to details of the plans being
satisfactory and receiving his approval'. There was still Ottawa to
consider. McNaughton had the authority to commit Canadian troops
for minor operations, but Rutter could hardly be classed as a side-
show so he now sought approval to widen the remit to include bigger
projects, which was granted by the government's war committee.

The Canadian version with minor discrepancies is supported by
multiple other sources. Jock Hughes-Hallett wrote that the initiative
was taken by Montgomery who 'got the agreement of General Paget
[C-in-C Home Forces] and the CIGS [Brooke] for the employment
of the 2nd Canadian Division on the raid'. This too was the recollection of Goronwy Rees, one of Monty's staff officers, who remembered
being summoned to his quarters in Reigate and told that Montgomery 'had been made responsible for the operation, and he had selected
the 2nd Canadian Division, which was under his command, to carry
it out'.[42]

Montgomery later maintained that he had nothing to do with the
choice, claiming that 'somebody, I do not know who, decided that
the Canadian Army should provide the troops, and the 2nd Canadian
Division, under Major General Roberts, was detailed for the task.'[43]
He went on: 'And so it was decided to launch against a defended port
in the Atlantic Wall a Canadian division which had done no fighting,
and which was commanded by a major general who had never commanded a division in battle, not even a battalion.'

When he heard the news from Paget he protested that it was not right to use the inexperienced Canadians for the operation. Paget replied that they were 'becoming "impatient" and wanted to go fighting; if they were not allowed to, there would be trouble with . . . General McNaughton'. Montgomery then meekly acquiesced, as 'to do otherwise would have been to lower the morale of the Canadian troops'. He repeated a similar story to the Canadian Broadcasting Corporation in an interview for a documentary that aired in 1962, though he admitted that he had no documentation to back up the claim. 'I did protest verbally,' he said. 'I think I should have protested vehemently and in writing. That you mustn't do it with these troops. Well I didn't. So I suppose I must bear certain responsibilities because I didn't do it.'[44]

Montgomery's protestations are not very convincing. Humble acceptance was not his way. He was the most forceful senior officer in the British Army, famous for reacting violently to any proposal he disagreed with and for getting his own way. He could not even get his story straight. The authorised biography written by his 'quasi-godson' Nigel Hamilton gives a contradictory version that chimes with Crerar's. In this account the initiative was indeed, as Hughes-Hallett said, Montgomery's and confirms Stacey's sequencing, stating that 'he did not go first to Lieutenant General McNaughton . . . but made arrangements first with his own subordinate Corps Commander Crerar – even selecting which division would participate . . .'[45] The choice was presented as 'an honour, and there is little doubt that Bernard intended it to appear as such – a gesture of appeasement to the oversensitive charges who seemed to find his "driving" too fierce and his criticism of Canadian commanders after exercises too humiliating'.

Montgomery's motive for distancing himself from the decision to use the Canadians can easily be guessed. The thought that his name might be closely linked with a major debacle was an affront to his vanity. The truth was that even though he took little interest in the development of the Dieppe raid he presided over the meeting where the frontal-assault plan was adopted and was present for a later crucial discussion which helped to seal the Canadians' fate. Even if he did not personally choose the Canadians for the main force, he did nothing to block their selection.

Using the Canadians seemed to jar with several major considerations, both military and political, currently crowding the minds of Churchill and the chiefs. Rutter had taken on a significance which went far beyond that of a mere raid. The pressure from Moscow and Washington gave it a political dimension which meant much more was at stake than simple success or failure. The raid on Dieppe would provide the first major demonstration since Dunkirk of Britain's ability to wage war on the continent. The eyes of the Americans and the Russians were upon it. If things went wrong, the Germans and their Axis partners would make a propaganda feast of the failure. At home, morale was sagging. The government and armed forces simply could not afford another debacle. With so much riding on the venture it would perhaps have made more sense and carried a greater symbolic charge if British units were used.

Mountbatten always maintained that he proposed a joint force of commandos and marines for the assault but had been overruled by a 'high-level political decision'.[46] On the other hand, the Canadians were as well trained as the British 12 Corps troops in South Eastern Command, who were equally untested as neither of the two divisions had fought in France. In the end the Canadians' – and in particular Crerar's – eagerness for their men to see action seems to have been the decisive factor.

Immediately after the 30 April meeting with Montgomery, McNaughton ordered Crerar to make an infantry division, a tank battalion and ancillary units from his corps available for Operation Rutter. The reasons for his choosing the 2nd Division over the 1st Division which arrived in Britain earlier are unclear but it may have been that it had performed particularly well in recent exercises. To provide security cover, all Canadian units were told to prepare for amphibious training. This, it was hoped, would dampen speculation when the 2nd Division went off to get ready for the real thing.

Meanwhile 2nd Division's commander Major General John Hamilton Roberts was summoned to see Crerar in London with the excuse that 'we haven't had a chance for an undisturbed chat for a long time'.[47] His exploit saving his guns in France had boosted his reputation and he was regarded as a good trainer of troops. When he arrived at Canadian Military Headquarters in Cockspur Street, just next to Canada House on Trafalgar Square, he discovered the real reason for the meeting. There was little that Crerar could tell him at this point beyond the broadest outlines of the attack and the fact that it was aimed at Dieppe.

Everything about Rutter was swathed in secrecy. The security arrangements the War Office made for Roberts assigned him a curiously passive role in the undertaking ahead. He was checked into the Mayfair Hotel to be on hand if needed by Home Forces or Mountbatten, with instructions to stay in his room as much as possible to avoid the risk of being followed and to keep outgoing telephone calls to a minimum for fear of spies.

Meanwhile the British were also making it clear to McNaughton his place in the proceedings. On 5 and 7 May, the Home Forces chief of staff Lieutenant General John Swayne wrote to him on behalf of Paget. The letters established Montgomery's position as the 'General Officer Commanding selected by the commander-in-chief [Paget] to prepare the outline plan' and the military commander responsible for Rutter. Citing the need for secrecy Swayne said details of the operation would be tightly restricted and proposed 'to send information to you from time to time personally', adding that 'if you desire any amplification of specific points at any time the planning staff at GHQ will be at your disposal'.

The message was that the British were directing the show with a Canadian cast and that his role in the production would be watching from the wings. McNaughton resisted. His counter-proposal was for a chain of command that ran from Paget at GHQ Home Forces to Montgomery at South Eastern Command to Crerar at 1st Canadian Corps HQ to Roberts at 2nd Division. He also wanted his chief of staff Lieutenant Colonel G. P. Henderson to act as a formal liaison officer between himself and Home Forces, COHQ and Crerar. This still left him outside the executive machinery but at least kept him in the bureaucratic loop. It was a meek enough request and the matter was settled – though the command structure would cause problems further down the line.

On 8 May Roberts was called to the War Office for a meeting with Montgomery where he at last got a detailed briefing on the outline plan. When Roberts returned to his division, his senior staff officer Brigadier Clarence Churchill Mann stayed behind in London as his representative leading the Canadian team which now joined the COHQ and army planners. Mann was thirty-eight, tall and good-looking, from a wealthy family who had emigrated from New York to Canada. 'Church' Mann charmed everybody including even Montgomery who confided to Goronwy Rees 'he's a card, that fellow'. Rees was a Welsh minister's son from the Valleys who had shaken off his provincial background at Oxford and before the war moved in a well-connected left-wing journalistic milieu in London. He was similarly impressed with the Canadian's 'sleek black hair and the long legs of a cavalryman'.[48] He was also 'a brilliant staff officer, but what was more exceptional was that his mind had a wild and incalculable originality, and his contempt for normal military codes and conventions was extreme'. With this attitude he would fit right in with the cool, assured types at Richmond Terrace with their disdain for difficulties and boyish delight in dreaming up warlike schemes.

It was Mann's job to make the first appraisal of the outline plan. It was a heavy responsibility. The Canadians were coming blind to Rutter having played no part in its genesis or development and it therefore took no account of their concerns. Here was the first, and likely the most effective opportunity to register doubts and objections. Mann approached the task in a positive spirit. In his report to Roberts he made light of the obvious difficulties and accentuated the benefits of boldness. Much of it dwelt on the question of where to land the tanks which he identified as 'the outstanding feature of the plan'. Mann agreed with the army that the problem of the rivers made putting armour ashore at Quiberville impracticable, though the beach at Pourville might be used to deliver later flights. The main landing would therefore have to go in on the town beaches. It was, he acknowledged 'on the face of it . . . almost a fantastical conception of the place most suited to land a strong force of AVFs [armoured fighting vehicles]'. It was nonetheless 'well worth evaluating with an unbiased mind'.[49]

The direct approach, he felt, 'had the advantage of simplicity'. If successful it put the tanks 'in easy striking distance of the most appropriate objectives for their employment'. It would deliver surprise, resulting in 'a terrific moral effect on both the Germans and the French'. There were disadvantages in 'attacking the enemy frontally . . . at a point where penetration was obstructed and engineer effort was required' to maintain progress. The rubble resulting from the proposed preliminary bombing raid meant there was a 'danger of failure to penetrate through Dieppe'. However a similar attack on an English coastal town – something the Canadians had studied in their endless counter-invasion exercises – would have a good chance of succeeding, providing the engineers dealt with obstacles. As for the opposition, the strength of the Dieppe garrison was 'only two companies of infantry not of the best quality, plus some divisional troops'.

For all its risks, the project seemed to offer 'a reasonable prospect of success'. In a judgement that was immediately endorsed by Roberts, Mann concluded: 'I am in favour of adopting the outline plan.'

8. Simmerforce

On 16 May the Isle of Wight began to fill up with Canadian soldiers. As far as they knew, they were there to undergo yet more training and no one apart from those at the very top were aware they were preparing for a real operation. The new regime marked a departure from their usual drills. According to Major Forbes West of the Royal Regiment of Canada, these had been 'largely endurance propositions' designed to build up stamina. What they got now was 'commando-type training. They really ground it into us and life was really very difficult.'[1]

The Isle of Wight was the perfect place to prepare for the task ahead. It had cliffs, coves, and rolling downland just like the coastline around Dieppe. It also met another vital criterion: it could easily be sealed off from the outside world, and the intense secrecy surrounding Rutter could, it was hoped, be maintained. Once on the island, the troops were stuck there and every letter was scrutinised by army censors.

Roberts set up his divisional HQ at Osborne Court, a 1930s mansion block close by the navy's much grander HQ in the Royal Yacht Squadron clubhouse. Within a week, 5,000 men had arrived. From the 2nd Division's 4th Infantry Brigade came the Rileys, the Royal Regiment of Canada and the Essex Scottish Regiment. The 6th Brigade provided Les Fusiliers Mont-Royal, the Queen's Own Cameron Highlanders of Canada and the South Saskatchewan Regiment. The 14th Army Tank Regiment, known as the Calgary Regiment, supplied the all-important armour. The specialised jobs of blasting through obstacles to get the armour off the beaches, then carrying out the numerous demolition tasks, were in the hands of the Royal Canadian Engineers.

The trials of two years spent far from their homes and their loved ones had reinforced each unit's sense of identity. The battalions were about 800 men strong including soldiers and support staff, small enough for everyone to know everyone else and for the character of the commanding officer to count for a lot, shaping the morale and efficiency of his men. In some cases they also acted as father figures to soldiers who were often little more than boys. 'I knew almost everyone very well indeed,' said Lieutenant Colonel Dollard Ménard of the Fusiliers Mont-Royal.[2] 'They were almost all French Canadians like me and they would show me photos of their wife, their children their mother or their fiancée, with smiles on their faces but tears in their eyes.'

Each battalion had its own ethos and identity. The 'Royals' were a new formation, an amalgamation of other militia units including the Toronto Regiment. Before the war recruiting policy was informal and, according to West, 'the CO invited people that he thought suitable to hold a commission to join'. If after two years they had proved acceptable, they became lieutenants. Their current commander was Lieutenant Colonel Hedley Basher who had fought in the last war and took them on their first assignment on garrison duty in Iceland before moving to England in November 1940. He would soon be promoted and his place taken by his deputy, Major Douglas Catto, a former Toronto architect.

The Essex Scottish came from south-west Ontario and were commanded by Fred Jasperson, in civilian life an easy-going lawyer from Windsor who wrote stories for Canadian magazines in his spare time. The Fusiliers Mont-Royal would represent French-speaking Canada in the Rutter force. Their commander Colonel Ménard was always known as 'Joe' and had a rather more colourful background than most COs. After graduating from the Royal Military College (RMC) he turned his back on peacetime soldiering and joined the British Army, took a commission with a Sikh regiment and spent two years guarding the Khyber Pass. When war broke out he offered his services to his native country only to be rejected. By luck, charm and persistence he made his way back to Ottawa and after a spell at staff college was given command of the Montreal-based Fusiliers.

The Camerons of Canada were drawn from Winnipeg, where their commander, Alfred Gostling, had in peacetime once been a radio repair man. The South Saskatchewans were led by Cecil Merritt, an athletic twenty-nine-year-old and the youngest of the battalion commanders. He went to school in Vancouver and Victoria then graduated from the RMC and trained as a lawyer. He was called to the Bar in 1929 practising in Vancouver and joining the militia.

Most of the men in the Calgary Tanks came from small farming towns in Alberta where they grew up around heavy machinery. Their CO Johnny Andrews was another RMC graduate who joined the tiny Permanent Force where he specialised in the neglected area of armoured warfare.

Apart from Andrews and Ménard all the battalion commanders were pre-war part-timers, but they strove to be just as rigorous in their preparations for action as their professional counterparts and their British Army colleagues. Many of their subordinates were cut from the same cloth as themselves. Among them were men who had proved themselves in the civilian world as farmers, tradesmen and small businessmen and the social gap between officers and other ranks was relatively narrow. In pre-war British regiments officers and men were treated as different species and an unscaleable social barrier stood between the leaders and the led. The Canadians did things differently. The headquarters of 4th Brigade directed that 'parties among all ranks should be encouraged', something that would never have occurred to a British brigade at this stage of the war.[3]

Although Canadian commanders tended to come from the same sort of middle-class, professional backgrounds and most had passed through the RMC, they nonetheless had behind them a broader social hinterland and wider life experience than their British counterparts. Even the two brigade commanders were not career soldiers but products of the militia with distinguished civilian careers behind them. The 4th Brigade's Sherwood Lett was a former Rhodes Scholar and partner in a prominent Vancouver law firm, while Bill Southam of the 6th Brigade was a publisher.

The man at the head of the division seemed at first sight to be made of slightly duller metal. John Hamilton Roberts was opaque, reserved and spoke quietly in an Anglicised accent, the result of two years between the ages of fourteen and sixteen spent at Epsom College, an English boarding school south of London.

He was born in the south-western Manitoba village of Pipestone in 1891 the son of a Vancouver estate agent. After the family returned home from a spell in Britain, he went to Upper Canada College then on to the RMC where he was best known as a sportsman, excelling at football, tennis, shooting and cricket. In 1914 he was commissioned into the Royal Canadian Horse Artillery and went to France with the Expeditionary Force. According to Robert Rothschild, who served in his battery, he was 'a gentleman who looked after his men'.[4] He won an MC at the Somme and two years later was wounded badly enough to have to see out the rest of the war in England. He stayed on with the Permanent Force serving as a gunnery instructor.

Roberts started the war a lieutenant colonel. He was tall and thick-set and his jowly, expressionless features made him hard to read. According to William Anderson, who served under him as a young artillery officer before the war, he 'didn't hang around the mess', however 'the men adored him because he could sing "Old Man River" better than Paul Robeson.'[5] He was regarded as able but not particularly hard-working. He did not attend staff college and had never commanded infantry before he took over 2nd Division. Views differed as to his intelligence. Rothschild generously judged him 'as bright as Harry Crerar'. Bob Bennett, who was among the officers gathered for Roberts's first address to the division, took a different view. He 'had no brains. When he took over . . . he shuffled his feet and looked at the floor, telling the officers that he'd forgotten what he was going to say.'[6]

He soon revealed a streak of ruthlessness, weeding out superannuated commanders and replacing them with younger, fitter and more motivated men. The high standard of fitness they had reached by the time they arrived on the Isle of Wight was largely due to his hard driving. Roberts's problem was that he saved his assertiveness for his Canadian comrades. When it came to dealing with the British, he was inevitably overawed by Monty's blazing self-confidence and the aura of God-given superiority that shimmered around Mountbatten. What doubts he had he expressed softly and did not make a fuss when they were ignored.

★

The units gathered on the island were now designated 'Simmerforce'. The Canadians regarded the move as a welcome change from their old routines. The Rileys found their new quarters a great improvement on the dismal camp they left behind in Sussex. After finishing Beaver III, the last exercise inflicted on them by Monty, they were sent to Billingshurst where, the unit diary noted, 'roads were very poor, buildings only half completed [and] wet weather and mud made it an unpleasant site'.[7] The companies were divided between Billingham Manor, the former home of the novelist J. B. Priestley, now a prolific broadcaster doing his bit to buoy public morale, and Northcourt, a Jacobean mansion once owned by Lord Byron, both in the centre of the island and altogether 'most extensive and picturesque'.

The beauty of the surroundings was some compensation for the brutality of the new regime. All the battalions regarded themselves as fit and competent. As well as being physically toughened up they had all received solid battle-drill training which grounded them in infantry war fighting. '[It] taught all ranks to appreciate a battle situation quickly, to issue brief orders and then swing immediately into an attack,' wrote Denis Whitaker.[8] 'Everything was done at top speed in open country. Each section was divided into two groups: a Bren-gun group of two men and a rifle group of five. The section commander would give an order: "Enemy machine gun, line of my arm (pointing) 200 yards – Bren give covering fire – GO!"' The rifle group then raced to attack the enemy position while the Bren poured down fire until it was captured. This routine was 'the guts of any infantry attack at any level' and it was repeated until everybody had it down.

On the Isle of Wight the training moved into a different realm. 'This began where battle drill left off,' remembered Colonel Bob Labatt.[9]

> We swam with and without our uniforms, with and without Mae Wests. We climbed slopes, hills, 250-foot chalk cliffs, sheer and over-hanging, complete with weapons. The same with rock quarries. We learned all about house-to-house fighting in bombed-out sections of Cowes. We learned to shoot from the hip and to reload quickly by slipping in a full loaded magazine in place of the empty one, instead

of charging it from clips. Every rifleman carried five magazines. All our movements were in battle order, carrying all weapons and ammunition. And all training was carried out with and under the fire of live ammunition – Brens et cetera – [firing] just overhead and to a flank.

Their weapons were now a part of them, as familiar as a limb. The rifle was an improved version of the standard Lee Enfield .303 as carried by their fathers in the previous war. There were two types of sub-machine gun, the American .45-inch Thompson and the Sten which had just been introduced. It was light, simple and cheap to make and initially very unpopular. The bullets – 9 mm calibre so captured enemy ammunition could be used – had a tendency to jam and the firing mechanism was temperamental requiring patient filing to fix. There would be several stories of soldiers throwing away their Stens after they jammed in the heat of action on the Dieppe beaches. The Bren light machine gun on the other hand was the essence of reliability, not as quick-firing or long-ranged as the German equivalent but steady and dependable.

For mortars they had a two-inch which fired a 2.5-pound bomb. The three-inch could lob a ten-pound bomb about a mile but was much heavier and needed a wheeled dolly when employed in an amphibious landing.

Reveille was at 05.30 and everyone was on parade at 07.00. The Rileys' first day of training, 22 May, took place in the Royals' area near Freshwater on the west coast. The morning was spent 'going through a very tough and difficult obstacle course. This consisted of scaling a cliff, through barbed wire at the top, climbing scaffolding and crawling through culverts, through muddy trenches, over water-filled ditches by swinging from ropes and hand-over-hand, jumping more ditches and finally clambering down to the beach again.'[10] This was all done 'at the double and all ranks such as clerks, drivers, mechanics, pioneers etc. went through the course'. So too did the padre. The Reverend John Weir Foote was good-natured, tolerant and very popular with the regiment. He was ordained a Presbyterian minister in 1934 and after the war broke out enlisted as an army chaplain. Foote knew there was only so much formal religion the soldiers could take. 'I didn't preach all the time,' he remembered. 'I only preached ten minutes on Sunday. If I preached fifteen, I'd have been shot and never been in the war at all.'[11] He saw his duty as being alongside the troops at all times, doing what they did, no matter how arduous or dangerous. On the Isle of Wight he marched with them every step of the way, though at thirty-eight years old 'I felt my age.'

In the fields and woods of the island, safety was pushed to the limits to bring the troops as close as possible to feeling the reality of combat. Lucien Dumais was a short, tough thirty-eight-year-old sergeant with the Fusiliers Mont-Royal who had joined as a territorial in 1934. He was in the middle of the Achnacarry commando course with other battalion NCOs when they were ordered to the Isle of Wight to oversee training. They applied the lessons they had learned in the Highlands with the zeal of the newly converted. 'Physical and psychological resistance had to be brought to a peak,' he wrote.[12] 'To this end we drove our men more and more ruthlessly. We were asking for more than they could give – and we got it – and then we asked for still more.' There was 'no question of using blanks for training; when firing around or over our troops we used regular service ammunition'. One afternoon the men were made to crawl along a ditch while the instructors fired a Bren above their heads. 'One soldier refused to get dirty and we could see his kit moving above the top of the trench. Using my very accurate rifle I put a bullet right through his haversack less than two inches from his skin'. The round pierced his water bottle and 'as the tepid water ran down his back he subsided quickly in the mud, convinced he had been hit'.

On 6 June Roberts recorded in his war diary that 'the condition of the men has improved and better results have been secured from speed marches', though there was not enough time to get his men to the standard he wanted before the operation was due.[13] This seemed an overly cautious assessment. The training had been linked closely to the targets each unit would be assaulting, and the landing exercises were carried out by the same craft and crews that would carry the men to the beaches. The men were fit and hardened by cold, wet and exhaustion, and as habituated to the crack and whine of bullets and the flash and thud of incoming mortars as they would ever be without experiencing the real thing.

The tight focus of the training fuelled speculation that this was the prelude to a major operation, perhaps even the invasion of Europe. The boat drills were one giveaway. On 30 May the Rileys travelled to Cowes to board assault landing craft (LCA) and mechanised landing craft (LCM) which took them to Thorness Bay and Osborne Bay where they landed and re-embarked under a smokescreen. Two days later they went on board the landing ship *Princess Beatrix* at Yarmouth to practise loading onto the landing craft prior to being lowered into the sea and then heading for Osborne Beach where they waded ashore under a smokescreen. Then on 3 June they progressed to a full battalion mock beach landing. One company acted the part of the enemy manning machine-gun posts and a four-gun field battery, while three others made the assault with one company in reserve.

There was another glaring indication that something big was in the offing. One morning the Rileys' officers were summoned to Osborne Beach for a demonstration laid on by the Calgary Tanks. They watched Churchill tanks fire their two-pounders, machine guns and smoke projectors before loading and unloading from the new tank landing craft (LCT).

The Churchill was designed to support dismounted infantry by suppressing strongpoints and machine-gun posts and had yet to go into action. It had been conceived in a hurry to replace the equipment left behind in France, and its history was one of serial reworkings to overcome flaws in its design. It was heavy, weighing forty-three tons with a long chassis and multiple bogies, but the Bedford 350-horsepower engine lacked power and was unreliable and difficult to access. The tracks were unable to sustain a direct hit and the noise they generated tended to drown out radio conversations. Against these shortcomings, the weight of the armour offered good protection to the crew. When German experts examined the remains of the Churchills that got ashore at Dieppe they judged them inferior both to their own tanks and to the Soviet T34s. Their conclusion was that the best tank the British could then put into the field: 'in its present form, is easy to combat'.[14]

By the middle of 1942 three versions had been produced. The Mark I mounted a feeble two-pounder (40 mm) in the turret as its main armament alongside a coaxial Besa medium machine gun, plus a three-inch howitzer in the hull for use against infantry. The Mark II replaced the howitzer with another machine gun and the Mark III upgraded the main gun to a six-pounder (57 mm). The Calgarys' sixty Churchills included all three types as well as a few equipped with flamethrowers.

Johnny Andrews and his men had been chosen for the raid because of their outstanding performance in the Beaver III exercise. They were delighted to get their hands on the Churchill after years of making do with antiquated relics from the First World War. A technique for waterproofing them up to a depth of six feet had been worked out using rubber balloon fabric and extending exhaust pipes vertically to raise them well above the waves when they drove off the LCTs.

The next obstacle was the steep beach. Pre-war research had established that pebbles could pose fatal problems for tracked vehicles. The Royal Tank Regiment conducted experiments on the shingle beach at Lydd in Kent which proved that 'movement on shingle was not possible unless tanks were prepared to move straight and on the level'.[15] Establishing the precise geological composition of the beaches at Dieppe and Pourville was clearly of vital importance. The flat, rounded *galets* of Dieppe were known as 'chert stones' in English. After the war Stan Kanik, a geological engineer who had been a trooper with 'A' Squadron of the Calgary Tanks, made a technical study of where he had gone ashore. 'The entire beach is composed of chert stones, boulders and rubble,' he wrote, which the action of the tides pushed into an 'angle of repose' of fifteen to twenty degrees.[16] The layers were deep, meaning that vehicles could not dig down to a solid rock base for traction. The result was that 'when a tracked or wheeled vehicle tries to climb up this slope, it immediately digs itself down; when the tracks are turned to either side the stones roll in between the drive sprocket and track and the object that first gives way is the pins holding the track links.'

The German defenders had already come to the conclusion that the beach was impassable to tanks and did not bother siting anti-tank guns or anti-tank mines on the beach in front of the town. The Canadians would find this out the hard way. It would have been a relatively easy task to send a small commando team at night to bring back samples of the pebbles. They could then be matched to an equivalent British chert beach – such as Dover – and the Churchills tested in something like real-life conditions. But no such reconnaissance was ordered. Instead they carried out their landing tests on the firm, sandy beaches of the Isle of Wight and the small-pebbled beaches of Dorset.

The problem posed by chert was only recognised after the event in a report to Mountbatten by the War Office intelligence department on 1 November 1942, which casually acknowledged: 'That tank tracks should tend to sink in or spin round without taking hold is to be expected particularly in well-rounded shingle which may act as a pile of ball bearings.'[17]

The preparations did address the problem of the sea wall which ran for nearly a mile along the promenade. Its height varied according to the level of the pebbles pushed up against it by the tide. Major Bert Sucharov of the Royal Canadian Engineers came up with a device mounted on the hull which unrolled a carpet of wooden 'chespalings' in front for the tank tracks to climb. However these were 'only fitted to a very few tanks one or two days before the raid'. The report finished with the recommendation that 'in view of our Dieppe experiences we suggest that exhaustive studies and experiments be put in hand now so that in future combined operations we can be confident of what tanks can and cannot do on selected beaches.'

Given that Rutter was to be the first occasion on which tanks were to be used in an amphibious attack, it was astonishing that someone had not come to this conclusion before it was launched. The Churchill's bulk was not suited to the narrow streets of Dieppe, and Trooper Stan Edwards, a loader/wireless operator who sat next to the driver in the upper tier of the tank, found them 'very big and cumbersome' and 'hard to handle'.[18] Sight was restricted to a couple of periscopes and a narrow triplex vision port, and a commander opening the lid to get a better view was liable to get a sniper's bullet through the head.[19]

Yet nonetheless they could provide much-needed firepower for the raiders. As long as they could get off the beach.

The COHQ reflex when confronted with difficulties was to make light of them. It was on display in 'Imperator' which was being developed in parallel with Rutter. Of all the schemes under consideration in the early summer of 1942, this was the most reckless. The idea that an armoured column could be landed on the coast of northern France, race to Paris, shoot up various military headquarters then retreat to a captured port and sail home to England appears to have originated with Hughes-Hallett. When the plan was revealed to the RAF, who would have to protect the raiding force, it was met with near incredulity. The chief of Fighter Command's 11 Group, Air Vice Marshal Leigh-Mallory, pointed out that Paris was beyond the range of his squadrons which meant 'the Force will be operating outside the area in which air cover can be provided for two to three days'.[20] He went on: 'If I were the German air-force commander I would concentrate my attacks on the motor transport carrying fuel with cannon fighters. If such an attack were carried out with determination, I think that the inevitable result would be the loss of the entire Armoured Force through lack of petrol to get it out of the country again.'

The prospect of annihilation in detail did not deter Colonel Antony Head, military adviser to Mountbatten, who wrote back: 'I do not accept this opinion for the following reasons: 1. The march of the Armoured Raiding Force on Paris . . . is likely to take the Germans by surprise . . . 2. The raiding force will not move concentrated on one road but will be dispersed over a wide front. 3. The majority of the roads in France are lined with trees and in August a good deal of concealment should be possible.' Fortunately the idea that raiders should put their faith in surprise and the plane trees along the *routes nationales* was never put to the test and Imperator was eventually dropped, though not on the grounds of its inherent craziness.

The impulse to emphasise the positive was sharpened by the arrival of Americans on the Combined Ops staff, following the arrangement agreed between Mountbatten and Marshall in April. Here was an opportunity for Richmond Terrace to enhance its prestige with its powerful allies and the Brits were eager to impress. Nine US officers led by Brigadier Lucian Truscott joined COHQ on 20 May.[21] On day one Truscott was taken by the vice chief General Haydon to a meeting at Home Forces headquarters, across St James's Park at 20 Queen Anne's Gate, presided over by Paget's deputy Gregson-Ellis to discuss the outlines of 'operations in North-West Europe in 1943' – in other words, Roundup. At first he found he had difficulty following the discussions as the British 'spoke with astonishing rapidity, practically through closed teeth and with little action of the lips'. In time he came to appreciate their way of doing business and the 'unfailing courtesy of British officers towards each other as well as toward ourselves'.

That did not mean that there were not real animosities and passions swirling below the surface civility. Truscott quickly picked up on the frustration and resentment felt by many at COHQ that their approach and efforts were unappreciated. They were being held back by the 'defensive and defeatist attitude' of Paget and the Home Forces team and by the indifference shown to their projects by the RAF's Bomber and Fighter Commands who were 'interested only in the air war'.

The Combined Ops team believed they deserved a privileged place in the organisation of the war effort. The aspiration came from the top. Mountbatten was as angry as anyone at what he saw as the hostility shown towards COHQ schemes, complaining to the senior Conservative Leo Amery of the 'incredible mass of obstruction' he had to overcome.[22] He believed, reasonably enough, that the organisation should be given its head on raids. But his ambition went much further than that. As Truscott soon discovered, Mountbatten interpreted the original brief given to him by Churchill in the broadest possible terms and claimed ownership of the great invasion enterprise for COHQ with himself, naturally, at the head. 'Admiral Mountbatten,' he wrote, 'believed that COHQ was the organisation most eminently qualified by training and experience for planning the assault, conducting training for it, and actually controlling it when it should take place.'[23]

This grand conception greatly magnified the dimensions of Rutter in the minds of COHQ. It would test the claims which they made for themselves and, if it succeeded, bolster their candidacy to lead the effort to reconquer north-west Europe.

At the same time, the political dimension of Rutter was expanding at a rate that greatly increased the pressure for it to go ahead. The distaste at the top for Sledgehammer was now strong. There seemed to be no plausible circumstances in which Churchill and the chiefs could justify a decision to launch it. At the Chiefs of Staff (CoS) Committee meeting of 5 May, Mountbatten warned that landing-craft shortages meant the operation could not go ahead until the middle of August. Brooke already doubted that it would achieve anything anyway, predicting that 'no effort that we could make this year would be likely to draw off land forces from the Russian front.'[24] In the circumstances, Mountbatten suggested, it 'would be advisable to have something on a smaller scale ready by say 15 July', and reminded them that Rutter was scheduled for the end of June.

At the CoS Committee meeting of 1 June aversion to Sledgehammer had deepened further. Mountbatten pointed out that persisting with it would tie up all available landing craft and therefore push back preparations for Roundup. It would also mean stopping all amphibious training and would disrupt arrangements for Imperator. He therefore 'reluctantly felt obliged to recommend . . . that we should not attempt to mount [Sledgehammer or Roundup] this year'.[25]

This was not at all what the Americans or the Russians wanted to hear. Another round in the Anglo-American wrestling match over the time and place of the Allied offensive was about to begin. Churchill was due to visit Washington later that month to try to lower American enthusiasm for an early landing in France and push his alternative of an Anglo-American invasion of North Africa. Mountbatten, accompanied by Hughes-Hallett, was about to board a flying boat to take him to the States on an advance diplomatic mission to soften the Americans up.

If Sledgehammer was to be killed off, something had to be offered in its place to dull the blow and offer proof of aggressive intent. Such a decision, he told the chiefs, 'made it all the more important to do one more big raid'. He pointed to Rutter, due to take place at the end of June when conditions were suitable, with the start of the flood tide coinciding roughly with daybreak and a moon phase during passage that offered sufficient but not too much light. There was 'every chance therefore of this operation coming off'. If, however, the weather did not oblige he proposed that 'the operation should be remounted a month later'.

No one had suggested the Dieppe plan was a substitute for Sledgehammer. A one-day hit-and-run raid would do nothing to divert German troops from Russia. However, it might achieve another much-discussed objective – to drag the Luftwaffe into an attritional showdown that might conceivably force the Germans to switch air assets from the East. 'Peter' Portal, the steely, cerebral Chief of the Air Staff, offered support, recommending that 'our military operations should be confined to a series of minor raids with only one larger-scale operation, calculated to bring on a big air battle'.

Everything was now pointing in the same direction. Brooke ordered a report to be drawn up recommending that policy for the continent that year 'should be confined to a series of small raids, together with one larger-scale raid which would be Operation RUTTER in June, or a similar operation staged in July'. In its short life the Dieppe plan had thus assumed an importance far in excess of its military significance. On its back rested the prestige of COHQ and the reputation of Britain as a reliable ally whose promises of action were sincere. It would now take a remarkable change of circumstances to prevent it going ahead.

On the same day as the chiefs' momentous meeting, the Rutter senior commanders gathered at Richmond Terrace. There was a new face at the table. Rear Admiral Tom Baillie-Grohman had been appointed the naval force commander for the operation when the chiefs gave their approval for the outline plan two weeks before, but illness had prevented him from starting work until now.

Baillie-Grohman had come directly from Cairo where he was head of the Combined Operations Directorate for the Middle East.[26] In many respects he was a typical British naval officer, institutionalised since adolescence, who knew only the ways of the senior service and had fierce opinions about the way things should and should not be done. He had done wartime service on the Dover Patrol and peacetime duties in China and the Mediterranean, where as commander of the 1st Destroyer Flotilla one of his junior captains had been Lord Louis Mountbatten.

Baillie-Grohman worried that Mountbatten and Edwina would set a standard of extravagant living that his humble shipmates would ruin themselves trying to emulate. He took the pair aside 'for a private word', he recalled, 'with the result that they always lived modestly'.[27] Baillie-Grohman grew to like Mountbatten and when he joined Rutter regarded them as being 'on terms of intimate friendship'.[28] However the reversal of roles did not incline him to any great deference towards his new boss, the Combined Ops acolytes or the Rutter plan.

For the first time, the proposal was subjected to the stern scrutiny of a man who had played no part in its inception and was not conditioned by any considerations other than its merits as an operation of war. Unlike many of those he was working with he had direct experience of mounting large amphibious operations. At Middle East HQ in Cairo he had planned an operation, subsequently abandoned, to capture the island of Rhodes. Baillie-Grohman made free with his opinions, peppering Mountbatten with criticisms of staff arrangements and weak intelligence as well as his vitriolic opinions of some of the COHQ officers. Mountbatten's responses were always civil and wherever possible accommodating. Despite his blasé manner he respected the traditions and protocols of the navy which had shaped him since boyhood. Baillie-Grohman with his total lack of sophistication and mistrust of smart foreigners was far from being Mountbatten's usual cup of tea. Yet the rear admiral had earned the rings on his sleeve and the chief showed him a marked respect, listening patiently to his numerous complaints and criticisms.

Baillie-Grohman was now charged with delivering the crucial part of the plan. Without the navy there would be no landing and he had just three weeks to devise a way to get hundreds of craft across a hostile sea and arrive exactly where they were supposed to be at exactly the right moment. In Rutter the timings were calculated in minutes not hours, and even a small delay could make the difference between success and catastrophe. At least enough landing ships and landing craft for both men and tanks were now available to do the job. Training crews to sail them was another matter. Landing craft were flat-bottomed and hard to handle and there were few who had experience of their ways. The British and Canadian officers detailed to command them were mostly young and green reservists. They were now required to learn in short order how to form up in columns, manoeuvre in the dark without lights and ground on beaches at the right point for men and machines to get safely ashore and not drown or sink. An added complication was that the training craft could not all be assembled in the main anchorage at Cowes for fear of being spotted by German reconnaissance flights, so many of them had to be dispersed at ports around the island.[29]

Baillie-Grohman learned the size of the task ahead of him at the 1 June meeting. Also present were generals Paget and Montgomery and Air Vice Marshal Leigh-Mallory whose squadrons were providing the air cover for Rutter and had been nominated air-force commander. Baillie-Grohman listened as the plan was rolled out and then raised two questions. He asked if there was any prospect of increasing the strength of the naval gunfire support available in order to better suppress the Dieppe defences. He also wanted to know where he could obtain further intelligence on enemy dispositions.

The provision – or lack thereof – of heavy-calibre naval gunfire had been a sore point from the start. The only naval artillery mentioned in the plan was that of the flotilla escort of eight Hunt-class destroyers whose main armament was four 102 mm (four-inch) guns. These would have little impact on the blockhouses and pillboxes shielding the enemy guns. It would take the shells from the fourteen-inch guns of a battleship or the eight-inch guns of a heavy cruiser to do real damage. The principle of naval fire support in Combined Ops raids had been established five months earlier when the salvos from HMS *Kenya*'s six-inch armament on the German garrison at Vaagso had helped make Mountbatten's debut as chief of COHQ such a success. Vaagso was much more lightly defended than Dieppe. Yet

Baillie-Grohman was told that the Admiralty was not willing to risk anything bigger than a destroyer for the raid.

In their eyes, sending a capital ship into the narrow waters of the Channel with German airbases all around was asking for disaster. The sinking of the battleship *Prince of Wales* and the cruiser *Repulse* by Japanese bombers off the coast of Malaya in December 1941 was still fresh in everyone's mind. The story was told that when Mountbatten had bearded the First Sea Lord Dudley Pound to ask for a big ship, he was told: 'Battleships by daylight off the French coast? You must be mad Dickie!'[30]

Baillie-Grohman thought the Admiralty's attitude 'pretty feeble'.[31] He had taken part in several combined-operations exercises at both the army and navy staff colleges and elsewhere 'and always heavy gun support had been presumed'.[32] He was partially reassured by Leigh-Mallory that a heavy air bombardment before the raid would have the same effect. The promise of a primary high-level attack by as many as 300 bombers had earlier soothed the COHQ planners' fears about the dangers of a frontal assault. Nonetheless he later pressed Admiral Sir William James, the Portsmouth naval commander who would have control of Rutter while the flotilla was at sea, for a capital ship, only to get another firm negative.[33] So it was, he recalled later, that the 'only gun support for the troops attacking would be from the little four-inch guns from a few destroyers wallowing about in the sea'.[34]

On the Isle of Wight the Canadians went about their training ignorant of these fateful decisions. As the days passed the 5,000 Canadians were joined by another 4,000 sailors, airmen, airborne troops and motley Allied units. They included Free French commandos and men from the US Rangers, a new specialist unit established by Truscott, fresh from the Achnacarry course. The hard training and the tight security put a charge of expectancy in the island air. The censors combing the mail noted a high level of cheerfulness, professional satisfaction and readiness for whatever lay ahead. 'You wouldn't recognise the regiment now,' wrote a soldier of the Royals. 'All dead wood weeded out and we're now the trimmest and fightingest little unit you ever did see.' Another from the Camerons of Canada reported that 'the battalion is in good shape and ready for anything, getting the good old offensive spirit.' A survey of the mail judged that 'the troops are generally satisfied with conditions and life . . . on the whole they are keen for action.'[35]

Security was a constant concern. To drive the message home, every unit was taken to watch a newly released film called *Next of Kin*. It was an expensive production using well-known actors and told the story of the efforts of a security officer to maintain secrecy during the preparations for an amphibious operation on the coast of northern France that bore an uncanny resemblance to Rutter. During the training, complete with cliff-climbing and boat drills, he tries to drum into officers and men the need to keep their mouths shut. Even so, careless talk soon reaches the ears of Nazi agents and the force goes ashore to be massacred by the waiting Germans.

The Rutter field security team were satisfied that the men of Simmerforce had got the message. Everyone was 'very aware of the importance to themselves of not giving away any information'.[36] However the main danger now facing the Canadians was not German spies, but the decisions of their own commanders.

9. Surprise

On Friday 5 June, the Rutter force commanders gathered at Richmond Terrace to review progress. Mountbatten was in Washington smoothing the path before Churchill's visit and Montgomery was in the chair. However, it was Air Vice Marshal Leigh-Mallory who dominated the discussion.

He was large and pink-faced with sleek hair and a neat moustache, the very picture of a military grandee. He was also ambitious and frustrated. Fate had denied him a starring role in the Battle of Britain. Since it ended, Fighter Command had been engaged in a costly and largely pointless campaign of attrition with the Luftwaffe over the French Channel coast. Dieppe would give his fighters the opportunity for a massive showdown with the German air force and himself the chance of a victory as glorious as that of the summer of 1940. Today, however, the subject at hand concerned not fighters but bombers.

The minutes recorded: 'Air Vice Marshal Leigh-Mallory proposed and the meeting agreed that air bombing of the port itself during the night of the assault would not be the most profitable way of using the bombers, as a raid which was not overpowering might only result in putting everyone on the alert.'[1] The bland wording disguised the shock of the thunderbolt Leigh-Mallory had delivered. Even the Home Forces proponents of a frontal assault accepted that it was potentially a very bloody affair. The plan was adopted on the understanding that the risk could be significantly reduced by a heavy bombardment by sea and air. It was these elements that made it acceptable, if only just, and even then the naval officers involved had retained severe doubts.

First, the sea bombardment had been stripped out, victim of the Admiralty's refusal to put a precious capital ship at the mercy of the Luftwaffe. Now the aerial bombardment was being taken away and the Canadians would be wading into the teeth of German defences untouched by heavy shell or bomb. Instead they would have to put their faith in 'tactical surprise', the intangible and unmeasurable supposition that German amazement at the audacity of a frontal attack would at least temporarily slow their reactions.

This was an alarming development but equally startling was the apparent ease with which Montgomery and the force commanders accepted it. Leigh-Mallory had offered an alternative bombing proposal by way of compensation in the form of a diversionary raid by seventy aircraft on Boulogne and further attacks on Crécy and Abbeville aerodromes, timed between 02.30 and 04.00. The latter two would 'tend to occupy the RDF [radar] organisation at DIEPPE and might put out of action, at least for some hours, two aerodromes which the enemy would wish to use during the day of the operation'.

The force commanders knew there were political and practical problems with bombing French towns.

Bomber Command raids on the German naval bases in French Atlantic ports like Brest, Lorient and La Pallice had killed many civilians. This had led to a War Cabinet directive inspired by Churchill banning attacks on targets in Occupied France unless 'weather conditions are such that accurate attack can be expected'.[2] This rule was resented at COHQ who blamed it for depriving the Saint-Nazaire raiders of a preliminary bombardment during Operation Chariot. When presenting the outline plan to the chiefs on 13 May, Mountbatten had reminded them of the difficulty and they agreed to 'seek Cabinet approval for the air bombardment of the town should the force commanders decide that this was desirable'.[3] Churchill relented and ruled that though 'still against the indiscriminate bombing of French towns at night . . . an exception would be made in the case of a coastal raid'.[4]

There remained the problem of accuracy. Bomb aiming was primitive and aircraft attacking a small port town huddled in a cleft in a wall of cliffs would be incapable of discerning between friend and foe. If their bombs hit a machine-gun post rather than a school it would be through luck rather than judgement. Leigh-Mallory fixed on this truth to soften the bad news. The fear was, he said, that collapsed buildings would block the streets of the town making it impossible for the Calgary Tanks to get through to the aerodrome at Saint-Aubin-sur-Scie several miles to the south. This was an argument that Roberts would later accept though no mention is made of his reaction in the minutes of the meeting.

The main reason put forward by Leigh-Mallory for the cancellation of the bombing was more contentious. The claim that an air raid would 'only result in putting everyone on the alert' was unconvincing. Dieppe had often been bombed, albeit not heavily. There had been five attacks since the beginning of May and it was bombed again on the very night of the meeting. The lesson that the Germans might be expected to draw from this was that an air raid was just another event, not the precursor to an amphibious attack. The flank attacks timed to go in half an hour before the main assault were much more likely to put the Dieppe garrison on the qui vive. The elevation of the Saint-Aubin-sur-Scie aerodrome to the status of a major objective was puzzling. If it was so important, why not just bomb it, which for all the problems of accuracy facing the RAF still stood a better chance of success than a convoluted armour and infantry attack and had already been proposed in the 25 April version of the plan? Why, if Rutter was, as subsequently claimed, a 'dress rehearsal' for a full-scale amphibious landing, was it necessary for the tanks to push through the town to Saint-Aubin-sur-Scie at all? In the contemporaneous documentation and the subsequent testimony of some of those present there is no mention of these questions being raised, let alone answered.

Whether an air raid by heavy bombers would have done much to improve the chances of a frontal attack succeeding is doubtful. The 25 April plan talks of the bombers targeting 'the town and the aerodrome'. In the revised version circulated on 13 May the scope has been reduced to simply 'the dock area'. The bomb sight on the four-engine Halifaxes and Lancasters now arriving at Bomber Command squadrons was not capable of pinpoint attacks on batteries, strongpoints and the like, and any reduction of Dieppe's defences would have been achieved by the bludgeon not the rapier. All this was well known. When killing off Operation Blazing, the raid on Alderney which was supposed to be preceded by an air raid, Brooke declared he was 'strongly of the opinion that indiscriminate air bombardment would not succeed in neutralising well-sited coast defences particularly on undulating and open ground', which well described the terrain overlooking Dieppe.[5] The best the heavies could do to help the Canadians was create general mayhem that might keep the defenders' heads down, at least for a while.

Given Bomber Command's current preoccupations, it was not certain that even this help would materialise. When revealing the change of plan, Leigh-Mallory failed to mention a major factor in the decision. Some time before he had approached Bomber Command's newly appointed chief, Arthur Harris, to ask him to allocate 300 bombers for the raid. This meant diverting a large part of his force from their current mission and he was unlikely to be amenable. Since his takeover in February, Bomber Command's war had entered a new phase. The arrival of four-engine bombers and improved navigational aids gave him the means to start a war on German cities, euphemistically termed 'area bombing' and designed to destroy civilian morale as much as damage war production. The results were devastating. Five nights before the meeting Harris had scraped together every available aircraft to launch the first 1,000-bomber raid against Cologne, destroying more than 3,000 buildings and killing nearly 500 people.

The raids generated huge publicity and were thoroughly approved of by a population eager for revenge for the Blitz. As a demonstration of British resolve and aggression they were valuable to Churchill as he struggled to maintain the confidence of his Soviet and American partners. If Harris said yes to Leigh-Mallory's request it would mean diverting his precious squadrons from what he regarded as the vital business of the war. According to one account of the meeting, Harris told him: 'I have neither planes nor crews to spare for useless sideshows.'[6]

Harris could afford to be obstinate knowing that he would not be overruled by either Portal his chief, who was a fervent supporter of area bombing, or Churchill who was uncharacteristically wary in his dealings with Harris. Leigh-Mallory left the meeting accepting that 'if Rutter depended on the air bombardment, it would probably never take place'.

The contribution that Bomber Command could make to Rutter was probably psychological as much as practical. A heavy bombing raid just before the troops went in would hearten them and give the impression that as much as possible was being done to support them. As such it was still valuable, though not as much use as a heavy naval bombardment which could deliver much greater accuracy. With both now gone, a prudent commander might have concluded that the plan was unsound and that to proceed with it risked large-scale casualties and – not the least important consideration – severe damage to the reputations of those whose names were attached to it. There were some murmured caveats and expressions of concern. But no one was prepared to deliver a forthright rejection of the plan as it now stood and thereby in all likelihood scupper its chances of ever being mounted.

Each of the force commanders had his own reasons to go along with the new arrangements. Due to his passive temperament and lack of seniority, Roberts was the least likely to dig in his heels. This was Canada's chance get into the war in the European theatre. Putting the brakes on just as the project was gaining seemingly unstoppable momentum risked annoying the British. To object forcibly to the change he would need the backing of McNaughton and Crerar, both of whom had been eagerly pushing for action for months. It was a daunting prospect for an unassertive man who would also be throwing away the sort of chance that came rarely in a military career. A story later circulated that Roberts had felt obliged to pass on some criticisms of the plan voiced by the brigade commanders Lett and Southam to Crerar, who assumed that Roberts shared their views. Crerar told him: 'If you don't want to do it, I'll find someone else who will.'[7]

Baillie-Grohman, like Hughes-Hallett, already had doubts about the wisdom of a frontal assault which the new developments reinforced. However he was only five days into the job and anyway his task was to get the troops across the Channel and back. It was not his place to put a spoke in the wheel of the whole enterprise. It was a decision he would regret. 'I feel I should have taken a stronger line on this point than I did,' he wrote later. 'I should have done more . . .'[8]

For Leigh-Mallory, the landing was not his main concern. His mind was focussed on a much bigger conception that had little to do with the arguments about the form of the main attack. The disparity in goals was noted by Montgomery's liaison officer at COHQ, Goronwy Rees, who remarked later that from the air-force commander's point of view 'it hardly mattered whether Rutter succeeded or failed as a purely military operation. For it appeared to the RAF its principal objective was to force the Luftwaffe into the air and to give battle over the Channel.'[9] He went on: 'We were assured that a landing in France on the scale of Rutter would compel the Luftwaffe to react violently; if it did so, the RAF was confident of winning a decisive victory in the air.' To his eyes it seemed that 'the military forces . . . were also bait. What did it matter if the bait was devoured whole, as long as the fish, or rather the Luftwaffe, was properly hooked?'

This was a cynical interpretation. On the day the air force would do an outstanding job protecting the troops and the fleet. It was true that Leigh-Mallory saw the raid as the climax of the offensive he and his chief, the head of Fighter Command Sholto Douglas, had been waging since early 1941, but in planning meetings he had shown more sympathy than anyone to Roberts's efforts to beef up naval gun support.

Montgomery was the one with the least to lose by pulling the plug on Rutter. It was not really his show. He had not been there at its birth and was given custody of it by Home Forces only because it would be mounted by troops from his command. His lack of engagement was noted by Rees who wrote that Montgomery implied to him that this was 'an operation which had been decided on by the chiefs of staff, not by himself, and for reasons with which he was not concerned . . . the planning of the operation had not been in his hands; its execution equally was not in his hands but in those of the military, naval and air-force commanders. There was nothing he could do to affect the result, and it would therefore have been a waste of time and effort for him to worry about it.'[10]

If true this was a remarkable display of cold-bloodedness, and Rees admitted he was 'surprised . . . that the army commander should be so little perturbed about the risks of the operation'. Montgomery's own wartime experiences taught that a frontal attack with no heavy bomb or gun support was a recipe for a massacre. At this stage intelligence was reporting the presence of numerous machine-gun posts the length of the promenade facing the beach where the main body of troops would go in. Anyone who had served on the Western Front in 1914–18 knew what that meant. As Ballie-Grohman reflected later, he 'must have seen what devastation a small nest of machine guns and barbed wire could cause to attacking troops'. At Dieppe the results were likely to be more devastating still as 'the troops would be more concentrated in their landing craft and when emerging from them and thus an easier target than would be the case on land. And all this without a comparable preliminary bombardment.'[11]

Monty never gave a satisfactory answer. In his memoirs and elsewhere he claimed to have disagreed with the decision to cancel bombing. Yet it was he who had chaired the meeting which eliminated it. Had he spoken up Rutter would have been killed stone dead. Why didn't he? His failure to answer the question honestly leaves only speculation. Perhaps he believed that, left alone, Rutter would die a natural death, a reasonable expectation given the current mortality rate of projected COHQ operations. He might have wished to keep a hand in the enterprise, calculating that if it succeeded he could claim the credit for the success and if it failed the blame would fall on Mountbatten.

It was lucky for the chief that he was in Washington when the aerial bombardment decision was taken. He wrote afterwards that he had been 'surprised' to learn of it.[12] In a long memo four months after the raid, written in response to the prime minister's demand for answers to criticisms of Mountbatten's conduct, he stated that he regarded it as 'a very important alteration indeed'. He had 'taken up the point [with the force commanders] several times and again on 17 August [two days before the raid finally went ahead] but was unable to alter their opinion'.[13] This suggests a passivity on Mountbatten's part that was at odds with the enthusiasm he consistently showed for Dieppe even when, as later on, other considerations intervened to make dropping the whole thing the sensible option.

On the Isle of Wight from dawn to dusk and beyond, the soldiers marched up and down hills and climbed in and out of boats, oblivious to the developments in London. By now it was impossible to maintain the pretence that their exertions were unconnected to forthcoming action. Cowes was inundated with important visitors and inquisitive officers who managed to wangle themselves a security pass to see what was going on. Their presence was unwelcome to Baillie-Grohman who had only three weeks to train and rehearse mostly inexperienced landing-craft crews for the most complex amphibious operation yet undertaken. He was infuriated by the arrival from COHQ of a Royal Marines officer, Robert Neville, a polo-playing friend of the chief who had apparently been despatched to prepare a confidential report on preparations. 'It appears that you are unaware of how this officer is disliked by the navy in general for very good reasons,' he fumed in a letter to Mountbatten.[14] 'I must ask you quite firmly to see that Col Neville is not sent down to any forces under my command in future.'

Among the observers was a senior figure taking a worm's eye view of the preparations. Jock Hughes-Hallett's part in the planning was over and on returning from Washington he got himself ready for a very different role. He decided that he wanted to witness the raid himself as an ordinary soldier with the Camerons of Canada. 'This was not merely idle curiosity,' he wrote. 'The truth was that I had always been a little uneasy about planning hazardous operations backed by no personal experience and no sharing of the risks.'[15] Mountbatten approved and General Roberts gave his blessing providing Hughes-Hallett joined the troops for training. It was decided he would go disguised as 'Private Hallett', a clerical worker from COHQ who was being sent off for infantry training. After being briefed by a security service major on how other ranks addressed NCOs and behaved in the presence of an officer, he set off in his scratchy battledress down Victoria Street to catch the train to the Isle of Wight, 'praying inwardly that I should not come face to face with any friend or colleague'. He had never worn army hobnail boots and after only a few paces skidded on the pavement and fell heavily, to be helped to his feet by a kindly old lady.

Life in the Camerons camp near Wootton Creek was 'rather an eye-opener' for a man used to the cocooned existence of a naval officer. He lived in a tent with eight men from his platoon. 'Most of the men came from the Winnipeg area and a number of them earned their living as hunters and trappers [and] were aged by their tough life,' he remembered. 'They were naturally very fit and displayed a complete indifference to all outward forms of discipline. The days were long and hard starting at 6 a.m. and finishing at 9 p.m. with a meal which normally consisted of one or two chickens stolen from a local farm and boiled in milk.' After that 'we went to bed and slept the sleep of the just'. 'Private Hallett' stayed with the Canadians for much of the next four weeks. The 'outstanding impression' they left on him was 'a friendly acceptance of strangers like myself . . . coupled with a total lack of curiosity'. The ordinary soldiers and sailors surrounding him were not quite as unobservant as Hughes-Hallett imagined. When he turned up at the start of the operation someone reported him as a suspected German spy. The result, as Baillie-Grohman pointed out forcefully to Mountbatten, was 'my security officer and his limited staff spent many wasted hours through shadowing and watching him.'[16]

Rutter provided an opportunity for others who were keen to get a taste of action. Lucian Truscott had arranged for American Rangers to undergo the Achnacarry course and he persuaded Mountbatten to allow fifty commando-trained men to be spread through the units. Several were assigned to the Rileys and Labatt remembered that they were 'terrifically keen about it'.[17] They came armed with the new M1 Garand semi-automatic rifle, and were 'very excited to be the first ones to take [it] in against the Germans'. However, they would have to ditch their steel helmets as 'in the half dark and the hurly-burly our people might have mistaken [them] for German helmets.'

The Special Operations Executive (SOE) also sought an invitation

to the 'party'. They offered the service of six men described as Sude-
ten Germans who could make themselves useful acting as interpreters
as well as 'shouting instructions calculated to mislead and confuse the
enemy'.[18] The request was approved and the six, now serving as
privates Bates, Harvey, Smith, Platt, Rice and Latimer, were ordered
to report to Cowes. A six-man French team from SOE were at one
point also assigned to raid the Dieppe prison and rescue French
Resistance members and bring them back to England.[19]

On 10 June the battalion commanders were called to Roberts's headquarters and finally told what they had long suspected. 'We were shown
a model,' remembered Bob Labatt, 'but not told that it was Dieppe
though some of us recognised the place.'[20] Mann told each of them the
objective they had been allotted. They were then instructed to 'get on
with training each individual part of our regiment [in] the tasks that it
would have to perform without letting them know it was going to be
an operation of war'. Labatt had no qualms about the plan as Mann had
laid it out. For him and many others, they would come later.

Each of the units had been assigned a colour-coded beach. From east
to west, the Royals were to attack Blue Beach, the narrow strand at
Puys just east of Dieppe harbour. The Essex Scottish and Royal
Hamilton Light Infantry would land at Red and White Beaches
respectively, which lay directly in front of the town, at the same time
as the Calgary Tanks. The South Sasketchewans would go ashore at
Green Beach (Pourville). The Camerons would join them once the
objective was secured while the Fusiliers Mont-Royal were to float
offshore, landing on the main beaches to secure the town for the
withdrawal.

Putting each force ashore at the precise times and places laid out in
the plan was crucial to its success. After nearly a month on the island,
the navy's ability to do so was tested in a large-scale exercise called
'Yukon', a simulated landing at West Bay just south of the Dorset
town of Bridport which had similarities with the Dieppe coast. It was
also the same sea distance as the passage across the Channel, though
the tidal conditions were trickier than would be faced at Dieppe.

On the morning of Thursday 11 June the docksides at Cowes were crowded with Canadians boarding their landing ships. The Rileys were onboard the *Glengyle*. An hour before dawn on the 12th, 'boat stations' were called and the troops climbed into the flat-bottomed LCAs to be winched onto the water six miles from the shore. The sea 'was quite rough and many were seasick', the war diary recorded. 'Several times searchlights found us but no ill effects resulted.' From then on all went well. The boats touched down at exactly the right place at exactly the right time. They were 'held up momentarily by heavy wire entanglements which had to be cut'. However 'all Coys [Companies] got through . . . and were on their way to objectives with exception of A Coy.' In the next hours 'many prisoners [were] taken and numerous vehicles' which were 'used to good advantage evacuating casualties'. By 15.00 they were all back on *Glengyle*. For them and the Essex Scottish on neighbouring Red Beach, the exercise had gone rather well. There was one ominous note, however. The diary reported: 'We saw no LCTs arrive on the beaches.'

The LCT carrying the Calgary Regiment Churchills appeared only an hour and a half later having got lost in the dark. The Rileys and Essex Scottish were the exceptions. Thanks to the difficult tide conditions and the crews' inexperience, almost every other unit arrived late or in the wrong place and the plan's minute-by-minute timetable lay in ruins. The South Saskatchewans were put ashore a mile from Green Beach and the Royals two miles from Blue Beach. To landlubber eyes, nautical twilight was not much better than total darkness. Major Walter Skrine of the COHQ staff took part in the exercise and went ashore with the South Saskatchewans at what was designated 'Pourville'. He remembered embarking the landing ship *Princess Beatrix* and boarding the landing craft 'in the *dark*. We were almost onto the beach before we could pick up the coastline and I found to my *horror* that there were some houses just inshore [where] there should have been cliffs! We could do nothing about it . . . I remember stopping the men from going into a minefield which had not been cleared . . . the point is that you couldn't see more than a hundred yards.'[21]

Goronwy Rees also witnessed the shambles. 'The division on landing fell into an indescribable confusion, which was in itself sufficient to throw doubt on the feasibility of the operation,' he recalled, 'even though there was no enemy present to turn confusion into bloodshed and slaughter.'[22]

Given the navy's performance Rutter could not possibly go ahead as planned. The question was whether to postpone it until competence improved or cancel it all together. General Paget's limited patience was spent and he was all for folding. The Canadians, from McNaughton downwards, were as eager as ever to proceed. Roberts believed, with reason, that the Canadians had performed well enough in Yukon. It was the navy who were the problem.

Mountbatten arrived back from Washington too late to witness the exercise but he also refused to be daunted. Too much time and too many resources had been invested in Rutter and the imperatives for action had not changed. Baillie-Grohman's reputation stood to suffer if Rutter was cancelled and he moved to salvage the operation proposing a fourteen-day postponement 'in order to improve the very inadequate training of the whole force'.[23]

At a meeting at Richmond Terrace on 15 June of Mountbatten, Montgomery and the force commanders it was decided to postpone the raid until a date between 4 and 9 July inclusive, when the tides and moon phase would again be favourable. In the meantime there would be another rehearsal, Yukon II, scheduled for 22/23 June. Paget did not object and Rutter staggered on.

Yukon II turned out better than its predecessor, but not by much. Once again the troops landed at dawn on the same stretch of coast and once again there were delays and diversions. This time the Rileys and Essex Scottish were the victims. 'Royal Navy took us six miles or more WEST of our beach,' the war diary recorded. They finally landed forty-five minutes late. However once ashore A Company 'did a particularly good piece of work in capturing a Div[isional] HQ and returning with prisoners and important papers'.

Despite these setbacks, at a meeting with his staff at his Royal Yacht Squadron HQ in Cowes the morning after, Baillie-Grohman announced that 'on the whole everything was satisfactory'. Roberts was not so sure. He would continue to fret about the navy's navigational abilities and the amount of smoke available to cover the landing, a factor which had taken on great significance in the absence of any serious bombardment. Paget and McNaughton shared his concern and Montgomery and COHQ were ordered to put things right. With that, the Rutter juggernaut jolted forward again.

The meteorological reports forecast fair weather on 4 and 5 July. A week before, all Canadian officers were finally let in on the secret and about 300 of them gathered at HQ. Below the dais stood an irregularly shaped object, about ten feet long and six feet wide, covered by a cloth. The expectant hubbub subsided as a phalanx of staff officers strode in with 'Ham' Roberts at the head. As he mounted the stage, the cover was removed, revealing a relief model of an unidentified port town and the neighbouring coastline. Roberts was not much of an orator but he tried to rise to the occasion, declaring: 'Gentlemen, we have waited over two years to go into battle against the Germans. The time has now come for a party.'[24] He then delivered the outline of what the 'party' entailed.

Without revealing the name of the objective he rapped out the essentials that must govern the action and the most crucial were speed and momentum. 'You must get in and secure the beaches fast,' he told them. 'Any hesitation will only result in senseless casualties. When you are over the beaches, run over the Boche defences just as fast as you can. You may see men fall. But if you stop once it will be much worse.' The raid was not just a chance to get into action. Roberts made it clear that success could make a real contribution to final victory. This was not, though, in the form of a 'dress rehearsal' that would iron out problems before the real invasion. 'Important things are at stake,' he declared. 'Certain pieces of equipment are needed for examination by our boys.' They included 'a new four-barrelled flak gun'. But beyond that, 'overall, the information we get back may have an important bearing on the outcome of the war.'[25]

The sense of drama was reinforced by strict warnings to maintain secrecy. There must be no hint to the men that they were going to Dieppe and they would not be told the truth until they were sealed on the landing ships.

Roberts urged them to study the model and the maps and photographs in the detailed 'confidential book' prepared by the COHQ

Intelligence Department. Roberts knew the necessity of displaying confidence and boosting the illusion that mortal combat was an experience to be looked forward to and enjoyed. The term 'party' said it all. It wasn't Roberts's invention. It was a commonplace of the vocabulary of the war, heard on the lips of fighter pilots and commandos. Later some at the briefing claimed that he had told them that the operation would be 'a piece of cake'. It was not the sort of thing that Ham Roberts would say and he always denied saying it. The story though reflected the bitterness subsequently felt at the gap between what the Canadians were asked to do, and their chances of actually achieving it.

As they crowded round the model, some felt a chill of apprehension. The Canadians had spent the last two years training to repel an enemy invasion. If the Germans had attacked a similar British Channel port the Canadians would have been utterly confident in smashing them back into the sea.

'We doubted the words of wisdom that were being fed to us,' remembered Lieutenant John Edmondson, who commanded D Company of the South Saskatchewan Regiment.[26] On garrison defence duty, 'when the tide was right and the moon was right we doubled everything. The Germans couldn't possibly gain surprise. So we said, the Germans are just as smart as we are. How do you think *we* can gain surprise?' To this vital question 'there was no answer'. When Lieutenant Art Hueston of the Essex Scottish saw the model he was reminded of one of the first tactical lessons he had been given, which was 'you never go into a defile, which is a valley. So the first thing we are doing is we are going into a defile if I ever saw one and I thought this is crazy.'[27] Denis Whitaker wondered at the long list of tasks assigned to each regiment. 'They had company objectives that you wouldn't give to a battalion,' he remembered.[28] These feats were expected to be completed in times that would have been difficult to achieve on an exercise, let alone in battle. Mann's orders read like a military symphony in which everyone had to come in exactly on time and play their part perfectly.

As the operational window approached, Paget asked Montgomery to make one last review of the preparations. On 30 June he visited

Cowes to talk to Mountbatten and the force commanders. Roberts was still concerned about the navy's navigational abilities and worried about the enemy gun emplacements on the east and west headlands. In the plan they were to be engaged from the rear by the parachute troops then overrun by the Royals and South Saskatchewans advancing from east and west respectively. That would take time. He asked if destroyers could be tasked with bombarding the headlands until the beaches were secure. Baillie-Grohman was discouraging. The destroyers' four-inch guns were incapable of knocking out reinforced gun positions. They would be much better used in supporting the frontal assault by concentrating on the machine-gun posts fronting the beach where they could make a difference.

Roberts was unconvinced but did not press the point. More reassuring was the news that navigation risks would be reduced by the presence of a 'mark' ship stationed in the Channel to direct the fleet on a straight course for Dieppe.

Montgomery left believing all outstanding difficulties had been cleared, and on 1 July he assured Paget that in his opinion everything was now ready to go ahead.

'I went over to the Isle of Wight yesterday and spent the whole day there, checking over the whole operation with Roberts, and with the naval and RAF force commanders,' he wrote.

> I am satisfied that the operation as planned is a possible one and has good prospects of success, given: –
> (a) Favourable weather.
> (b) Average luck.
> (c) That the navy put us ashore roughly in the right places and at the right times.

In a jaunty PS he added: 'The Canadians are 1st Class chaps; if anyone can pull it off, they will.'[29]

The hammer was now cocked on the Dieppe operation. The prime minister regarded it with mixed feelings. It was an uneasy time for Churchill. The trip to America had gone well. As always he had been sparing with the truth of Britain's real intentions. He continued to make encouraging noises about an early initiative on the continent, but was silent about the de facto decision taken by himself and the chiefs on 1 June that Sledgehammer would never happen. When he left for home on the 25th there were signs that the president was leaning towards Churchill's cherished proposal for an Anglo-American invasion of North Africa later that year, though the American generals were still far from convinced. The visit was marred by another shocking blow to British pride and morale.

On 21 June, during a meeting with Roosevelt, a messenger arrived with an urgent telegram for the president. Without a word Roosevelt handed it to Churchill. The news was so bad that at first he did not believe it. Tobruk had surrendered to Rommel's forces and 33,000 men had been taken prisoner. 'This was one of the heaviest blows I can recall during the war,' he wrote.[30] 'Not only were its military effects grievous, but it had affected the reputation of the British armies.' It was a national and personal humiliation. 'Defeat is one thing,' he reflected; 'disgrace is another.'

Churchill felt vulnerable. He was 'politically at my weakest and without a gleam of military success'. The Germans were once again pressing forward on the Eastern Front, Rommel seemed poised to enter Egypt, the Japanese threatened India, and in the Atlantic U-boats were sending hundreds of thousands of tons of ships to the bottom every month. At home his prestige was faltering and he was bracing for a no-confidence vote in the Commons on the issue of the government's handling of the war. The last thing he needed was another catastrophe.

On the eve of the parliamentary debate, 30 June, Churchill summoned Mountbatten, Brooke and two of his senior military advisers to an informal conference at Downing Street. According to Hughes-Hallett who was also present, the prime minister wanted 'one final review of the outlook for the Dieppe raid [to] decide whether in the prevailing circumstances it was prudent to go on with it'.[31]

They met at 15.00 in the Cabinet Room and while they talked, Clementine Churchill arranged flowers in the background. The prime minister wanted reassurance. He asked whether Mountbatten could guarantee that the raid would be a success. It was an absurd question and the fact that Churchill asked it was a measure of how low his spirits had sunk. In Hughes-Hallett's account Churchill was answered by Brooke who told him that if success could be guaranteed 'there would indeed be no object in doing the operation'. It was 'just because no one had the slightest idea what the outcome would be that the operation is necessary'.[32]

Churchill replied tartly that 'this was not a moment at which he wanted to be taught by adversity. "In that case," said Alanbrooke [as Brooke later became when raised to the peerage], "you must abandon the idea of invading France because no responsible general will be associated with any planning for invasion until we have an operation at least of the size of the Dieppe raid behind us to study and base our plans upon."' This argument carried the day and 'Mr Churchill at once agreed that if that were Alanbrooke's considered view, we must go forward. He would ask Mr Attlee to inform the War Office and he would inform the king.'

This encounter became a keystone in the narrative constructed by Mountbatten and his team later. It was a very useful story. It transformed Dieppe from a raid that went horribly wrong to a calculated gamble, which if it came off would pay huge war-winning dividends. It also spread the responsibility wider to include Churchill and Brooke. However with no other record of the meeting we have only Hughes-Hallett's account, written long afterwards, to go on. Brooke barely mentions it in his diary ('meeting with PM and Mountbatten to discuss the large raid which is to be carried out next Saturday . . .'). He felt no need to expand on this when in the years 1951–6 he went through his journals adding copious notes and comments. If Brooke's intervention had been as significant as Hughes-Hallett suggests, it would surely have merited more than a few words. His unsupported account is so favourable to the COHQ version of events that it must be treated with caution. It also raises questions. Having persuaded the prime minister and the CIGS of the necessity for the raid, why did Mountbatten not press his advantage and demand the heavy ship support that he knew was so important to its success?

The last barriers were falling. Protocol required the Canadian high command to give their formal approval. McNaughton and Crerar had played only a tangential part in the project and Montgomery seemed determined to keep it that way. His letter approving the operation was directed to Paget, and the Canadians were merely copied in. McNaughton felt compelled to insist that Crerar deliver an opinion on the troops' preparedness. He arrived on the Isle of Wight on 2 July to meet Roberts, Mann and the brigade commanders Southam and Lett. Roberts took the opportunity to press once again for a naval bombardment of the headlands but the visit was a formality. Despite their prickliness on matters of protocol he and McNaughton were determined not to miss this chance. The following day Crerar reported to his chief that Roberts 'and his brigadiers expressed full confidence in being able to carry out their tasks – given a break in luck'. In his view 'the plan is sound, and most carefully worked out.' Indeed, he would 'have no hesitation in tackling it, if in Roberts' place'.[33]

On 1 July in the ports of the Isle of Wight, Canadian soldiers marched up the gangplanks of their infantry landing ships in the belief that they were sailing off on yet another exercise, this one called 'Klondike I'. Cowes Roads, Yarmouth Roads and Southampton Water and the small Sussex port of Newhaven were now crowded with nearly 200 vessels of all shapes and sizes: destroyers, gunboats, motor torpedo boats and radar ships. By breakfast time on 3 July, everyone was aboard and the ships were sealed. The Rileys were aboard several vessels and Bob Labatt had to visit them by launch to tell them they were embarking on the real thing. All ranks were told they were off on 'a large-scale raid on the German-occupied coast . . . one of the largest yet attempted' and that preparations have been so well considered that 'success is assured'. The diary recorded that 'great enthusiasm was shown by the troops', and as the commanders spread the word to other battalions, the sound of cheering swelled over the anchorages.

That afternoon Roberts toured the landing ships to give a final pep talk, telling them: 'At last you are going to meet the enemy. Shortly after midnight you sail for France. The target is the port of Dieppe. This is the operation you have been trained for, so at dawn tomorrow come off those boats running and don't stop until you have reached your objectives.'[34]

Mountbatten planned to watch the operation from Fighter Command's 11 Group Headquarters at Uxbridge, alongside Leigh-Mallory, Montgomery and Crerar who, after being initially told he could not be present as there was no room, had finally been allowed to attend. That afternoon he arrived on the Isle of Wight to wish the troops Godspeed, together with General Eisenhower who was there to do the same for the US Rangers. Rousing speeches that mixed chumminess and noble sentiment were a speciality, and as dusk fell the force had been tuned to a fine pitch of emotional readiness for what lay ahead.

Midnight passed. The Canadians listened in vain for the rattle of anchor chains to announce the adventure had begun. As the ships came to life on the morning of the 4th the news spread through the cramped decks that the operation was off for at least twenty-four hours. The delay was caused by the unseen element in the attacking force – the paratroops. The previous evening General Browning who commanded the 1st Airborne Division had received a met report forecasting strengthening south-westerly winds during the night. Glider operations were cancelled and by morning an accurate parachute drop was deemed impossible. He recommended postponement. Mountbatten pressed Paget to urge a special effort from the Airborne but was overruled. The following day the forecast was still negative and the launch was put back again. The outlook was more promising for the 8th – the last day that tides and moon were favourable.

Then came news that darkened the picture. Intelligence reports, accurate as it turned out, stated that the 10th German Panzer Division, a unit which the British had learned to fear during the Battle of France, had moved to Amiens. That put them within eight hours of Dieppe. On the current two-tide timetable which allowed fifteen hours ashore, the tanks could arrive well before disembarkation. Given the other factors, this might have seemed enough to deliver the *coup de grâce* to Rutter. Instead the staffs of the army and navy force commanders worked frantically to redraft the orders and strike out some of the demolition tasks. The operation was now compressed into the span of a single tide, so that all troops would be re-embarked by 11.00.

The new plan was agreed by Mountbatten and Montgomery and zero hour set for dawn on the 8th. A very noticeable flotilla had been sitting in the anchorages of the Isle of Wight since the beginning of the month. It was inconceivable that the daily Luftwaffe reconnaissance flight had not spotted them. At 06.15 on 7 July four Focke-Wulf 190 fighters each carrying a 500 lb bomb appeared over the Yarmouth Roads to the west of the island and attacked the landing ships *Princess Astrid* and *Princess Josephine Charlotte*, loaded with men of the Royals. The bombs smashed through the decks without exploding and only four men were injured. One of the ships was at risk of sinking and the troops were put ashore. The setback was surmountable. The weather was not. The naval experts were now saying that the outlook for the 8th was bad. By mid-morning there had been a unanimous decision to cancel and the troops returned to dry land. That afternoon, sitting again in the billets they had left six weeks before, the men of 2nd Division heard a message from their commander: 'It is with the deepest regret that I have to announce that our party is off . . . the Gods were against us and the weather conditions and tide have defeated our attempt.' He appealed to them 'to say nothing about this operation . . . because if you do not there is always the possibility that we may be able to do it at a later date'.[35] That Dieppe could remain a secret or that it should ever be a target again seemed highly improbable. Montgomery's immediate recommendation to Paget that 'the operation be off for all time' seemed no more than common sense.

10. Resurrection

The Isle of Wight emptied and the Canadians returned to their camps in Sussex to unwind and take off on overdue leave. In canteens and pubs, dance halls and cinema queues, the story of the raid that never was rippled across south-east England like wind through a field of barley. The army censors struggled to prevent its spreading further. Combing through the letters home they noted 'a continuity of censorable matter', which they put down to 'the mistaken idea that it would be permissible to write once the expected operation did not take place . . .'[1]

The outline plan had allowed the possibility of the raid being remounted if weather conditions forced cancellation. With security in tatters, that option had surely vanished. Rutter was yet another might-have-been and Montgomery, for one, was 'delighted' to see the back of it.[2]

For COHQ the death of Rutter was a calamity. The evening after the cancellation, Mountbatten met the staff for what Hughes-Hallett called 'a long inquest on the Dieppe operation'.[3] In fact it was the start of an effort to bring the corpse back to life. Roberts and Leigh-Mallory were also present, but not Baillie-Grohman. His services had been requested by Admiral Bertram Ramsay, commander-in-chief designate of Churchill's cherished North African landing. The vacancy as naval force commander was now filled by Hughes-Hallett. A sceptic had been replaced by an enthusiast, and whereas Baillie-Grohman could always be expected to highlight an obstacle on the path ahead, Hughes-Hallett's impulse was to steer round it.

The organisation's pride was dented. As Hughes-Hallett wrote later, the cancellation was 'rightly felt to be tantamount to defeat. That is why so much importance was attached to remounting and carrying out the Dieppe raid after all.'[4] Combined Ops had enjoyed no major success since Saint-Nazaire in March and was already feeling under pressure to perform when Rutter was conceived. Pride, ambition and a genuine desire to get to grips with the enemy compelled them to do something with all the training, planning, organisation and emotional energy that Rutter had generated. There was nothing in the pipeline that could serve as a substitute. A huge amount of effort stood to be wasted. Six thousand men were honed for action and a painful process of trial and error had at last produced workable arrangements for getting them across the Channel. Was all this to be thrown away? Someone at the meeting – the record does not say who – reached for the simplest but boldest solution. Before they left that night, all had resolved that one way or another, the Dieppe raid should be resurrected.

For Leigh-Mallory the revival presented no particular problems. Trying to get the Luftwaffe to come up and fight was what his squadrons did every day. For Roberts the question was more difficult. He was well aware of the plan's flaws but if Dieppe was to be resuscitated it would have to be more or less in its original form. Abandoning the frontal assault and returning to the initial idea of flank attacks would mean a complete rethink and much extra training. With the summer half over there was no time to remount a substantially revised operation before autumn made it unfeasible.

The decision was not his to make. Crerar had made clear to Roberts that his views were irrelevant. Both he and McNaughton were still anxious to get the Canadians into action. They decided that, despite the risks, the 2nd Division would again be available. On 11 July Roberts phoned Hughes-Hallett at COHQ to pass on the news that the Canadians were in. That evening he met Mountbatten and Leigh-Mallory, and according to Hughes-Hallett it was 'virtually decided to remount the Dieppe raid with only slight modifications . . . and carry it out on or about August 18'.

The push was all coming from Mountbatten and his team and he never subsequently tried to play down his central role in the rush to remount. Long afterwards he described how he 'talked the situation over with the chiefs of staff and the prime minister. All were agreed that unless we could carry out an actual raid before the end of the "raiding season" our return to the continent would be delayed, while awaiting the necessary operational experience in 1943.' However there was one huge concern that had to be addressed. 'Mr Churchill and the chiefs of staff remained understandably worried about security.'[5] Here, what Mountbatten called a 'brainwave, so unusual and so daring that I decided that nothing should be put on paper', came to the rescue. When he put the idea to the chiefs of staff, 'for the first time, nothing whatever was recorded in writing'.[6] So once again there is no documentation to illuminate a contentious turn in the story.

According to Mountbatten's version, he seized on a reverse-logic argument to allay the fears at the top. It was of course sensible to assume that the Germans knew about the raid or would soon. Air reconnaissance alone would tell them something big had been planned. But could that not be used to the raiders' advantage? When the German air force attacked the invasion fleet on 7 July 'there was no suggestion that they knew what the actual mission of the force was'. If 'by some unexpected chance they had stumbled on Dieppe as our target, they would never for a moment think that we should be so idiotic as to remount the operation on the same target'.

This was classic Combined Ops thinking. Mountbatten and his men were risk-takers and needed to be if they were to do their job. Even so, some of his own staff were startled by this argument. Walter Skrine, who had helped plan the original raid, was 'horrified to hear that the thing was on' again.[7] As Baillie-Grohman later pointed out, 'any commander, German or British, who once got the news that there had been a plan to raid his port, whether it had been cancelled or not, would most certainly look again, not once but twice or thrice, at his defences, and they would be strengthened.'[8]

That was true even if the precise objective of the operation was not known. In order to justify their initiative, Mountbatten and Hughes-Hallett would later cite German documents discovered after the war to support the claim that the enemy had no special knowledge about Rutter. There was no way of knowing that at the time. Their decision to press for a revival was based on a hunch and amounted to a gamble. Their willingness to take it could be explained by an anxiety, bordering on desperation, to pull off another coup and restore the fortunes of COHQ. The official historian of British intelligence in the war, Sir Harry Hinsley, believed that the suggestion that 'pressure for the revival came from COHQ whose *amour propre* had suffered from the cancellation' was 'consistent' with Mountbatten's previous behaviour in the story.[9]

The secrecy imposed on the proposal means there is no record of what objections, if any, were raised by the Churchill or the chiefs when Mountbatten made his case. If resistance was offered, it was overcome, for on 14 July Mountbatten issued a directive to the force commanders and his senior COHQ staff informing them that 'the chiefs of staff have directed that if possible an emergency operation is to be carried out during August to fill the gap caused by the cancellation of Rutter'. The resurrected plan was code-named 'Jubilee'. Like its predecessor the code name was chosen from a pre-written list. It had several meanings, from the contemporary one of a celebration to the biblical one of a time of remission and liberation. They all carried a festive ring that would later seem to echo the hubris in which the whole enterprise had been conceived.

The cancellation came at a time when the utility of raids was coming under attack from a distinguished quarter. Admiral Bertram Ramsay was greatly respected for his handling of the Dunkirk evacuation. He had been closely engaged in Roundup and was now involved in naval preparations for the proposed invasion of North Africa. In late July he delivered a crystalline memo to the chiefs which seemed to demolish the case for any further cross-Channel operations. They might provide training for the troops involved but they were also 'training the enemy'. Indeed it seemed likely that 'the Germans welcome these raids for nothing shows up weakness in the defence more than an attack with a very limited objective. Every time we find a weak spot on the enemy's coast we point out his weakness, and there is ample evidence that he has taken and is taking full advantage of this information to increase the strength of his defences both at sea and on land.' He concluded: 'As it is our present intention at some future date to make an attack in force upon the enemy's coast, we are now doing our best to make that attack less likely to achieve success.'[10]

Ramsay's implied indictment of Jubilee had no effect on Churchill and the chiefs. Once again there were bigger considerations in play than the simple military value of the operation. When Mountbatten presented the 'brainwave', another round in the delicate dialogue to settle Allied strategy was approaching. On 8 July Churchill had broken the news to Roosevelt that despite the belligerent noises made during the recent trip to Washington the Cabinet had now decided to drop Sledgehammer in its current form. If Anglo-American troops were to go into action in 1942, North Africa was the only feasible option. He flatteringly presented the scheme as at least partly inspired by the president. 'This has all along been in harmony with your ideas,' he wrote. 'In fact it is your commanding idea. Here is the true second front of 1942 . . . Here is the safest and most fruitful stroke that can be delivered this autumn.'[11]

Roosevelt and his *éminence grise* Harry Hopkins were anyway coming round to the British position and the idea of 'Torch', as the operation would be known. General Marshall was still unconvinced and his scepticism was shared by the Secretary of War Henry Stimson and the chief of the Army Air Forces, General Henry Arnold. Together they composed a robust memo to the president demanding the British be given an ultimatum. Either they commit themselves unambiguously to a 'concentrated effort against Germany' or America would reverse the fundamental strategic decision taken at the start of the Anglo-American alliance and turn its main effort to the destruction of the Japanese in the Pacific.[12]

Marshall and his supporters were on shaky ground. The US Navy's great victory at Midway on 4–7 June had turned the tide in the Pacific. The Japanese advance westwards had been stopped and there was now no possibility of the Axis powers joining up in the Middle East. As Roosevelt explained to Marshall, turning to the Pacific left the Germans with a free hand against the Russians, greatly increasing the risk of a Soviet collapse. Nonetheless the havering had to stop. He was therefore sending Marshall, the Chief of Naval Operations Admiral King and Harry Hopkins to London to urge the British 'with the utmost vigor' for a cross-Channel invasion, but if they could not be persuaded then they must 'determine upon another place for US troops to fight in 1942'.[13] That, as everyone now knew, could only mean North Africa.

The American team arrived at Prestwick, near Glasgow, on 18 July, with a presidential instruction to reach agreement within a week. Marshall was not prepared to abandon Sledgehammer without a fight. Together with Eisenhower, who had moved to London at the end of June to take command of European Theater operations, he expanded the original plan to a wholesale and permanent occupation of the Cherbourg Peninsula.

A slogging match with Brooke ensued that lasted two days. Nothing Marshall said, observed Hopkins, 'appeared to make the slightest impression on General Brooke's settled convictions . . . He kept looking into the distance.' The view of the CIGS was unrelievedly pessimistic. The RAF did not have the range to cover the invasion force. The six divisions the British could muster would be outnumbered, soon besieged and almost certainly lost to the war for ever. When Roosevelt cabled the US team saying that if the British would not agree to Sledgehammer then his choice for a 1942 battleground was for North Africa, Marshall was forced to give ground. He and his staff devised a new formula which accepted Torch but attempted to lock the British into committing to a cross-Channel invasion the following year. On 24 July Churchill and the War Cabinet happily agreed to it. 'We have just got what we wanted out of the US chiefs,' Brooke wrote in his diary that night. There would be no more talk of Sledgehammer and the Cherbourg Peninsula. Their eyes were now jointly fixed on Torch. An exhausting tussle that had tested the alliance was over. 'I cannot help feeling that the past week represented a turning point of the whole war and that we are now on our way shoulder to shoulder,' Roosevelt wrote to Churchill after his team had returned.

The fearful prospect of a premature invasion had vanished and Churchill had got his way. This did nothing to relieve the pressure for action. Public clamour for a second front was now deafening, led by the Canadian press baron Max Aitken. His elevation to the British peerage as Lord Beaverbrook and his close friendship with Churchill did nothing to curb his troublemaking instincts. Before the war Bea-verbrook had been an appeaser, a supporter of Munich and an enemy of Bolshevism. By 1942 he was an ardent militarist and an admirer of the Soviet Union, at least for the time being. On 26 June tens of thousands of men and women, many of them in uniform, gathered outside Birmingham Town Hall before a stage decked with the ham-mer and sickle and Union Jack to hear the short, bald multimillionaire proclaim to thunderous applause: 'We believe in Stalin's leadership! Yes! In Stalin's leadership! We believe in Stalin's leadership and this is the day to proclaim our faith! We must carry the battle on, the Battle of the Second Front!' A few days earlier the ideological opposite of 'the Beaver', Stafford Cripps, delivered an identical message to an-other large crowd at the Empress Hall in London.

The US too seemed to have fallen in love with Russia. Before the war, apart from the leftward fringe of the trade union movement, the Soviets were regarded with fear, suspicion and hostility. Within days of Pearl Harbor, Russia was America's best friend. American correspond-ents in Moscow felt the same awe at the determination and willingness to self-sacrifice of ordinary people that Cripps had publicised on his return to Britain. 'Heroic' was a communist word. The capitalist press now lavished it on their allies with the profligacy of a *Pravda* hack.

Ralph Parker of *The New York Times* extolled the proletariat's achievements and believed it 'would need a Tolstoy to describe the heroic endurance of the men and women who have made these things possible'.[14] General Douglas MacArthur, the essence of American martial manhood, praised the Russian fightback on the Eastern Front as 'one of the greatest military feats in history'. Hollywood, which had never made a film about the Soviet Union before the war, had at least nine under consideration by July 1942 of which five got made: *Mission to Moscow*, *Song of Russia*, *North Star*, *Days of Glory* and *Three Russian Girls*. Pro-Russian rallies attracted the same big crowds as those in Britain. During Churchill's June visit to Washington Harry Hopkins had addressed a large Russian War Relief rally at Madison Square Garden in New York, bringing the audience to its feet with a somewhat disingenuous promise of 'a Second Front . . . Yes, and if necessary a Third and Fourth Front!'

The decision to go ahead with Torch might go some way to satis-fying the perceived desire among the British and American publics for action. But Roosevelt and Churchill understood it would do nothing to relieve the Red Army, who whatever MacArthur said were in a perilous situation on the Eastern Front. Stalin would not be fooled. In his eyes the move was further evidence that his democratic allies were content for the time being to leave the communists and the fascists to exhaust themselves in a death grapple costing millions of lives before they committed their armies to the opening of a front in Western Europe. In a few weeks' time Churchill would have to face the man directly. In August he was due to visit Moscow for the first time and was braced for a rough reception.

The Dieppe operation was already regarded by the government as a valuable asset in its diplomatic dealings with the Russians. On the eve of Rutter, Mountbatten passed on to senior officers a request from the Ministry of Information who were 'anxious to promote good relations between Great Britain and Russia'.[15] It requested that 'messages be sent from force commanders on their return . . . to their opposite numbers on whichever part of the Russian front is then prominent in the news' which would produce 'beneficial results in the cause of Anglo-Soviet good relations'. In the circumstances anything that demonstrated Britain's positive intentions was welcome. Jubilee nevertheless fell far short of what Stalin was demanding.

Mountbatten and the force commanders and their teams now had five weeks before the new launch date. The preparations were haunted by the need for absolute secrecy. Hughes-Hallett came up with a way of disguising the naval preliminaries. Even if the Germans remained ignorant of the original plan, reconnaissance flights were bound to spot any concentrations of shipping and transport or large-scale prac-tice drills conducted in home waters that would tell them something new was afoot. Preparations, he decided, had to be kept to a min-imum. Fortunately most of the assault flotilla vessels were still in the area. So too were the troops. Units could go straight to the embark-ation phase without the need for further training. Roberts agreed. The troops were as ready as they would ever be. All that was needed was to issue last-minute orders to get them back into the starting blocks with no movements of ships and craft needed until dusk on the evening before the landings.

Following the approval of Churchill and the chiefs, the force commanders got together to re-examine the plan. Though there was no time to alter the basic concept, one major change could be made without fuss. This time the 1st Airborne Division would not be involved. There had been some resentment of their insistence on perfect conditions of wind, moon and cloud before committing to action. The longer nights of late summer would create more problems as the paras would have to land in darkness. A much better option was to use commandos who could arrive by boat like everyone else. They could take care of the big batteries at Berneval and Varengeville and one area of uncertainty was diminished. The commanders also confirmed that Jubilee would be a one-tide operation. The reported presence of the 10th Panzer Division at Amiens which had forced the truncation of Rutter dictated that.

Jubilee would go forward under a revised command structure. The new plan gave McNaughton and Crerar the chance to press Mountbatten and Paget for a change in the arrangements. During Rutter they had been consigned to the sidelines with Montgomery the 'responsible military authority'. McNaughton now moved to assert Canadian control demanding a chain of command that bypassed Montgomery and descended from Paget to McNaughton to Crerar to Roberts. Crerar thus had military responsibility for Jubilee. Monty raised no objection. He had never been fully engaged in the Dieppe project which, according to his biographer, had been 'a peripheral if not actually distracting operation', and by his unequivocal recommendation that it be cancelled for all time he willingly disqualified himself from further involvement.[16] He would anyway in a few weeks be off the scene, on his way to his appointment with destiny in the desert. Canadian hands were henceforth firmly on the military planning, led by Mann, recently promoted to brigadier.

Everyone now shaping Jubilee had a heavy personal investment in its success and were keen to press the pace. Qualms were to some extent allayed by thoughts of the kudos that would accrue to all concerned if it came off. This would likely be the biggest operation launched from Britain before the actual invasion and it had widened into a multinational event with participants from every corner of the empire as well as the US. Several countries that had felt the stamp of the Nazi jackboot would be represented including Free French commandos, Belgian and Czech pilots and the Polish navy, whose ship *Slazak*, formerly the Hunt-class destroyer *Bedale*, was part of the naval force.

But the risk of serious reputational damage for all directing the enterprise was also high. Jubilee would provide a demonstration of the British military's capabilities at a delicate stage of the war, and their competence to bring off a complex and tightly coordinated land, sea and air operation. Everyone would be watching; the German enemy of course but also the American and Russian allies, as well as the world at large.

There was one concern about the plan that would not go away. At a meeting of the commanders on 16 July Roberts again raised the question of a preliminary heavy bombing raid. Leigh-Mallory had to tell him that nothing had changed. Accurate bombing of the houses on the seafront where German strongpoints had been identified 'could not possibly be guaranteed'. Any raid would have to go in at the last possible moment, just before the troops hit the beaches. This was doubly dangerous, both for the bomber crews who would be operating at the break of dawn, and for the Canadians who had as much to fear at that point from friendly bombs as they did from the Germans.

The decision to dispense with a raid was confirmed and the units storming the Dieppe beach would have to rely on the success of the flank attacks and the destroyers' four-inch guns to suppress enemy fire at the crucial hour. Ham Roberts accepted the decision stoically. If the raids had to take place in darkness, he explained later, then 'inaccuracy rather than accuracy was guaranteed'. The enemy would be alerted and the streets of Dieppe choked with impassable rubble. The matter was not settled there. Roberts's disquiet over the inadequate air and sea support persisted. Just two days before the raid he raised the question for the last time at a meeting with Mountbatten and the other force commanders at the Tangmere aerodrome on the south coast, only to receive the same answer.

Bomber Command would be helping the operation in another important way, however. In the time between the raid being stood down and remounted, the Germans had relaid a minefield in mid-Channel, right across the line of passage that the Jubilee armada would have to take.

Sweeping a wide corridor and laying marker buoys would be a long job, requiring minesweepers to operate in daylight. Hughes-Hallett reckoned two narrow flotillas of sweepers could clear two passages each a quarter of a mile wide, under the cover of darkness. The nine assault ships carrying the bulk of the troops and the eight destroyers would follow immediately behind.

Hughes-Hallett had recommended that if any one of the landing ships was sunk on passage, then the whole operation should be called off. Once in the minefield there was 'no margin of time, or indeed of sea room', Hughes-Hallett wrote. 'The guiding ship of each group of assault ships must, therefore, hit off the north-westerly end of the narrow swept channels with dead accuracy, and the question was how?'[17] Since March, Bomber Command had been using a radar navigation device called 'Gee' to guide them to their targets. The results had transformed their target-finding capability. COHQ pressed the Admiralty to secure some sets for fitting to key vessels in the armada which would receive signals from the Gee shore stations to keep the fleet on track.

All this was done 'with astonishing speed' and by the end of July the hardware was ready. For it to work, however, the navy needed the active cooperation of Bomber Command. The system used two chains of transmitters, only one of which was switched on at a time, depending on whether that night's bombing raid was directed at targets in central or eastern Germany or in the Rhineland and France. Clearly the southern chain would have to be working on the night of the raid. There was only one person who could make sure that it was. Leigh-Mallory advised Hughes-Hallett that there was nothing for it but to approach Arthur Harris directly. This was not an encounter to look forward to but Hughes-Hallett caught him on a good day. 'The air chief marshal proved more than friendly and helpful,' he remembered. The sets were trialled at sea on several nights in early August and 'the results gave us every confidence in the new navigational aid'.

By 11 August the force commanders had agreed all the details of the plan and Crerar wrote to McNaughton with his assessment. For security reasons he spoke of the raid as a practice rather than the real thing. He was 'satisfied that the revisions made in respect to the previous exercise plans add rather than detract to the soundness of the plan as a whole'. Given 'an even break in luck and good navigation, the demonstration should prove successful'.[18] Three days later, after going over the whole plan again with Crerar and Roberts, McNaughton exercised the authority he had demanded from the British and pressed the Canadian seal of approval to Operation Jubilee.

For such a short operation, Jubilee involved an enormous amount of activity over a wide spread of locations. There were to be five attacks launched on a front of roughly thirteen miles stretching from Berneval in the east to Quiberville in the west. Four were aimed at the inner and outer flanks of Dieppe. The landing craft for these attacks would hit the beaches at 04.50 British Summer Time (GMT plus 1). This was 'nautical twilight' when, at sea, the first faint glow of dawn smudged the horizon. To the German sentries posted on the clifftops it would still feel like night, with the moon in its first quarter and a mere gleam in the sky. The hope was that they would realise what was happening only when the attackers opened fire. Half an hour later, the landing craft carrying the main body would scrape the shore directly in front of the town.

Holiday beaches and villages were now colour-coded targets on the raiders' maps. Places that once evoked sunny summer days would soon be swept with bullets and the shingle stained with blood. The beach below and slightly east of the village of Berneval-le-Grand and another a mile to the west near Belleville-sur-Mer were designated Yellow 1 and Yellow 2. This was where one commando group would land to deal with the heavy battery code-named 'Goebbels'. The short foreshore at Puys, just round the eastern headland overlooking the town, was Blue Beach. This was the landfall of the Royal Regiment of Canada who would then head up the steep wooded slope behind, through the half-timbered holiday villas, to take out the guns which commanded the port and the beaches in front of the town.

In Dieppe, the seafront below the mile-long promenade was divided into two. Red Beach was next to the western edge of the harbour breakwater. This was to be attacked by the Essex Scottish who would penetrate the town and harbour then move onto the eastern headland to join up with the Royals arriving from Puys. Next to it was White Beach, where the Royal Hamilton Light Infantry would fight their way into the town and then advance to the western headland. The first flight of Churchills were due to land with them, followed by successive waves accompanied by engineer teams tasked with blasting through obstacles.

Pourville, about two miles to the west, was Green Beach where the South Saskatchewan Regiment would go ashore. Once they had overcome the opposition they were to head south and east to take the strongpoint at Quatre Vents farm and meet up with the Rileys. Half an hour later the Queen's Own Cameron Highlanders of Canada would land and pass through them and join up with the tanks which would by then have cleared Dieppe and be hurrying towards the aerodrome at Saint-Aubin. If time allowed, the battalion would move on to Arques-la-Bataille to capture the divisional headquarters which COHQ's intelligence service claimed was sited there, and seize 'secret documents'.

The other commando attack would go in at Orange 1, just below the village of Varengeville and Orange 2, a mile to the west near Quiberville. They would then move half a mile inland to take out the 'Hess' battery. Meanwhile, waiting offshore, were Roberts's 'floating reserve', the men of Les Fusiliers Mont-Royal. Once the town was taken they would go ashore and take up positions on a perimeter inside the town to hold off the Germans as the main force returned to the ships. According to the immaculate timings of the plan, within two and a half hours of the assault beginning Dieppe would have fallen and the raiders would control a perimeter around the town about four or five miles deep.

With the town in their hands, the stated object of the raid could begin. Royal Canadian Engineer demolition parties were to fan out through the town blowing up infrastructure and enemy assets. Even in its amended form to take account of the reduction of time on shore, the array of targets was vast. It included railways, marshalling yards, tunnels, bridges and locks, a pharmaceutical factory, food stores and petrol dumps. The gasworks, power station and main telephone exchange were also listed, though the destruction of these would cause as much grief to the inhabitants as they would to the Germans.

The 'cutting out' operation to capture the forty-odd invasion barges in the Bassin Duquesne and Bassin de Paris, deep in the inner harbour, was in the hands of Commander Ryder, who having won a VC at Saint-Nazaire was now in the thick of another desperately hazardous show. Once the enemy artillery was silenced he would take the heavily armed, flat-bottomed river gunboat HMS *Locust* into the harbour followed by seven Free French submarine-chaser 'Chasseurs'. About 200 Royal Marines split into specialised parties would open the locks and bridges to the *arrière port*. Landing craft would then sail in and ferry the barges to the Chasseurs in the *avant port* to tow to an assembly point offshore.

The force was also assigned more sensitive tasks. The last objective listed in the military orders was to 'capture certain material'.[19] This was a cryptic reference to a mission to seize Enigma machines and code books from naval headquarters in the town, part of the Naval Intelligence Division's ongoing campaign in the cipher war. The raid provided a vehicle for another specially commissioned task. An RAF NCO radar expert was attached to the Saskatchewans to investigate the radar installation above Pourville.

The cutting-out plan typified the extraordinary complexity of Jubilee and the optimistic assumptions that it rested upon. Timings were almost ludicrously precise. The move of the *Locust* to the harbour was dependent on the suppression of the overlooking artillery which the orders 'hoped . . . will be silenced by 05.45'. Anyone who had first-hand experience of battle knew that timetables were liable to evaporate once the shooting started. Mann had never been in combat, and his orders followed a minute-by-minute sequence of interdependent events.

They were setting off, as Hughes-Hallett declared in his last order before sailing, on 'an unusually complex and hazardous operation'. From the beginning, Dieppe had been conceived as not one big mission but a conglomeration of small ones with many disparate objectives and no single aim. The action was spread over several locations using numerous units all of whom were attacking separately and who would meet up only if everything went well. It was impossible for a single military maestro to orchestrate events. As Hughes-Hallett admitted, success ashore was 'likely to depend far more on the action of individual commanding officers than anything I shall be able to do from the command ship'.

Once they had landed, the troops were essentially on their own. On board their HQ ship, the destroyer *Calpe*, Roberts and Hughes-Hallett might get a rough idea of what was going on ashore, though given the limited signals capacity this was far from certain. The only person who could affect the course of events was Leigh-Mallory, who would be sitting at Fighter Command HQ at Uxbridge, in West London. Even then the difference air power could make was limited. All the aircraft at his disposal were already committed to the plan and there were no reserves to call in. Furthermore it would be difficult to respond swiftly and effectively to a particular circumstance on the ground. There was an unavoidable time lapse between a request for air support being made and a mission being ordered, so that by the time it arrived, the situation was very likely to have changed.

The plan was a delicate instrument. As the report prepared at COHQ afterwards stated: 'It will be seen at once that its success depended upon a number of factors of which, perhaps, the most important was the correct and accurate timing of the successive phases of the operation by all services taking part in it. Synchronisation was, in fact, its keynote.'[20]

The commandos were spared entanglement in the central plan. They were coming late to the show and their missions were clear-cut and free-standing. They also had the luxury of being allowed to come up with their own schemes. John Durnford-Slater, commanding officer of 3 Commando, first heard of Jubilee when summoned to London by Brigadier Bob Laycock of the Special Service Brigade. There he learned there was 'a big operation on against Dieppe'.[21] His force was assigned the Goebbels battery at Berneval. No. 3 Commando had seen no action since Vaagso and Durnford-Slater was delighted to be asked. Laycock told him: 'You can see that it will be absolutely impossible for the ships to lie off Dieppe while your battery is in action. Can you guarantee to do the job?' He replied that 'given a proper landing you can be quite sure that our battery won't fire on the shipping.'

The men moved from their base in Largs to Seaford in Sussex, near Newhaven, and began cliff-climbing and day-and-night landing drills at Gurnard Bay on the Isle of Wight. Sledgehammer came in handy as a cover story. They were told that they were training for an invasion of the Cherbourg Peninsula. Meanwhile Durnford-Slater made his plan. Intelligence reports said there were up to 350 enemy troops in the Berneval area 'so it was evident that we had quite a battle on hand'. He had done a photo interpretation course and could make his own analysis of recce images. Two narrow gullies on either side of the battery site provided a way up from the sea. However, both were blocked by thick wire and the more easterly one, directly above Yellow 1, was covered by machine guns. Nonetheless he was 'entirely confident that our battle-trained officers and men would overcome all these obstacles'. Once on the heights they would overrun the battery, kill the garrison and then plant charges to blow up the battery's three 170 mm and four 105 mm guns.

He was less sure about the arrangements for getting his men across the Channel. They would be carried directly to Yellow 1 and 2 aboard twenty-three small American-designed unarmoured LCP (L) personnel craft, also known as R-boats, with the headquarters in a river gunboat.[22] Durnford-Slater was 'not happy about the prospect of a sixty-seven-mile passage in small boats'. An abortive raid on Guernsey had demonstrated the unreliability of landing craft on long journeys. What if some of the craft broke down and only a depleted commando force made it ashore? In that case, the orders made clear, the tactics were to keep the crews from serving the guns by constant harassing sniper fire.

If Durnford-Slater was sanguine about 3 Commando's chances he was less sure about the prospects for the main force. At the end of July he was at a force commanders' meeting with Mountbatten presiding when the air-bombardment issue surfaced. Once again it fell to Leigh-Mallory to explain why a heavy air raid was unfeasible. But the airman did not hide his disquiet with a decision that was beyond his control and told the meeting: 'I don't like this . . . I think these Canadians are going to have a bad time in the centre.' Durnford-Slater agreed. 'After our recent tough battle at Vaagso, against comparatively minor defences, I was most doubtful of the Canadians' success,' he wrote. He was surprised at the attitude of the commander whose men were most affected. 'General Roberts did almost no talking . . . he made no adverse comment at all.'

The task of knocking out the 'Hess' battery at Varengeville was given to 4 Commando led by Lieutenant Colonel the Lord Lovat. Known to his friends as 'Shimi' from the Gaelic version of his first name, Simon, Lovat radiated a feudal glamour. He was chieftain of the Fraser warrior clan and had a castle and vast estate near Inverness. As well as being rich and aristocratic he was intelligent and good-looking. Men wanted to be like him and women wanted to be with him. He had his detractors. Evelyn Waugh, who passed an ignominious spell in the commandos, sneered at his perceived vanity. Shimi gave as good as he got, later demolishing the pudgy social climber as 'a greedy little man – a eunuch in appearance – who seemed desperately anxious to "get in" with the right people'. Lovat was certainly pleased with himself but nobody could deny his abilities. Under his leadership 4 Commando had been thoroughly rehearsed for battle and was bound together by a tight *esprit de corps*.

In July 1942 they were eager to show what they could do. To Lovat's annoyance they had not been chosen for Saint-Nazaire, though if they had, the likelihood was that most of them would now be dead or behind the wire in some Stalag. Their most recent exploit raiding Hardelot on the coast near Boulogne in April had been a damp squib. Officers and men felt 'it was time to prove something'.[23]

In late July Bob Laycock appeared during a live-firing exercise in the ruins of Dundonald Castle in south Ayrshire to tell Lovat that 4 Commando were about to get their chance. Lovat headed for London to start planning and the men followed forty-eight hours later to begin training near Weymouth. Fortunately for them they would be carried most of the way in the former Belgian cross-Channel ferry the *Prince Albert*. Then they would climb into eight assault landing craft (LCA) for the run in to Orange Beaches 1 and 2. The LCAs were powered by two Ford V8 engines and were each forty-one feet long with a ten-feet beam and drew only 2.5 feet of water. They were cold and wet in a running sea but, unlike the wooden-hulled R-boats or 'Eurekas', were bulletproof until the bow door went down.

Lovat had plenty of resources to make his plan. As well as aerial photographs there was a scale model of the terrain and they got to learn every fold and feature of the ground between the landing beaches and the battery. By the end 4 Commando were as ready as they would ever be. 'The demolition squad could blow gun breeches in their sleep. Wireless communications were tested and counter-tested. Every weapon was fired over measured marks . . . The 2-inch mortar men became so accurate they could drop eighteen out of twenty shots into a 25-foot square at 200 yards.'[24]

As the launch date approached, RAF reconnaissance flights recorded the changing face of Dieppe and the surroundings. Every sortie brought evidence of new defences springing up. Photos taken on 5 August revealed 'a four-gun battery position is under construction at 184650 . . . three medium or heavy guns have appeared in the open close to the battery already reported at 308720. Two circular emplacements are under construction close by . . .'[25] By August every inch of the Dieppe seafront was covered by guns of various calibres, skilfully sited to give layer upon layer of fire from multiple angles. Almost every position was sheathed in thick concrete impervious to all but a direct hit from a large shell, and the beach and promenade hedged with barbed wire. Every road from the seafront into the town was blocked by a wall and gun position.

A fair number of the defenders were not German. There was a

constant seepage of garrison troops eastwards to replace losses on the Russian front. Their places were taken by conscripts and recruits from newly conquered territories. In the spring the 571st Infantry Regiment, which held the Dieppe sector, was badly under strength. Its numbers were topped up in March by a draft of 160 men followed by another of about 500 at the beginning of August. Four-fifths of them were Poles who had been granted the status of naturalised Germans. They were undernourished and some of them in such bad physical shape they had previously been rejected by the Polish army. But as the German army doctor who examined them remarked, 'for cannon fodder, all are good.'[26]

The Jubilee team were under the impression that the enemy formation facing them had changed. From the start, intelligence had correctly reported that the 302nd Division held the area. On 6 August Home Forces issued a new enemy order of battle saying they had been relieved by 110th Division, 'although this cannot be regarded as absolutely certain'.[27] It soon became treated as fact and the final orders stated that they now held the area. They had 'recently seen service on the Russian front' with a 'good fighting record' and were therefore more formidable than the 'second rate' soldiers they replaced. The report may have been misinformation fed to an agent who had been turned. The mistake changed nothing. The 302nd Division had not moved and although untested were primed to a high pitch of readiness and fully expecting action at any time.

Even without any specific intelligence warnings, the Germans had no doubt an attack somewhere along the Channel coast was imminent. Throughout July and early August warnings blared from Berlin and Paris. The timing was easy to predict. All that was needed was a glance at the moon and tide tables. On 7 July, the commander-in-chief in the West, Gerd von Rundstedt, ordered a general alert along the Channel coast because 'it is the most favourable period for Allied landings'. He thought it unlikely that the blow would fall on Dieppe, as it was too small to use as an invasion base.[28] Hitler thought otherwise. A directive dated 9 July pointed out the suspicious build-up of craft across the Channel and warned: 'The areas particularly threatened are, in the first place, the Channel coast . . . between Dieppe and

Le Havre and Normandy since these sectors can be reached by enemy planes and also because they lie within range of a large portion of the ferrying vehicles.'

On 10 August, nine days before the raid, the divisional commander General Haase issued an excitable order of the day:

> The information in our hands makes it clear that the Anglo-Americans will be forced in spite of themselves by the wretched predicament of the Russians to undertake some operation in the West in the near future . . . I have repeatedly brought this to the attention of the troops and I ask that my orders on this matter be kept constantly before them so that the idea sinks in thoroughly . . . The troops must grasp the fact that when it happens, it will be a very sticky business.
>
> Bombing and strafing from the air, shelling from the sea, commandos and assault boats, parachutists and air landing troops, hostile civilians, sabotage and murder – all these they will have to face with steady nerves if they are not to go under. On no account must the troops let themselves get rattled. Fear is not to be thought of. When the muck begins to fly the troops must wipe their eyes and ears, grip their weapons more tightly and fight as they have never fought before. THEM OR US. That must be the watchword for each man.[29]

The exhortation came as Rundstedt ordered the 302nd Division to the 'Threatening Danger' level of alert for ten days from 10 August as 'lunar and tidal conditions are such in this time span that they could be favourable for an Allied landing'.[30] On Friday the 14th, Haase raised the garrison to 'Stufe 2', meaning all action stations were fully manned and everyone slept in their battledress and boots, weapons to hand. Whatever surprise the attackers achieved would not last long.

It was not until 1 August that the brigade commanders learned that the Dieppe raid was on again. Bill Southam and Sherwood Lett were summoned along with the Calgary Tanks CO Johnny Andrews to a meeting with Roberts and Mann at 2nd Division HQ to discuss a new operation. There was consternation when Mann unveiled a model with which they were already very familiar. Lett had originally thought that 'if tactical surprise could be attained [Dieppe] had a chance of success.'[31] The exercises on the Isle of Wight had made him realise that even with good luck, casualties would be extremely heavy. Now, as the fact that the operation was on again sank in, 'I knew at once that we were for it.'

Three days later it was the turn of the battalion and commando COs. As Bob Labatt recounted it later, 'General Crerar was there and he was the one who told us that the party was on again and we said "Fine, whereabouts?" And he said "The same place." That shook us just a little bit.'[32] Labatt had to keep his concerns to himself. Secrecy was more crucial than ever and it would be another ten days before company commanders were briefed.

Under various pretexts, the specialist soldiers, airmen and sailors who had been assembled for Rutter were now summoned again. Few were fooled. Something big was on and they felt once more the fluttering of excitement mixed with apprehension that precedes action. Captain Derek Turner, a young gunner attached as bombardment liaison officer to the destroyer HMS *Garth*, was told to report to Eastbridge House in Crondall, Hampshire. Turner was an upper-class Scot with a friendly, open nature. In his diary he described with unusual frankness his conflicting emotions as the moment of truth approached.

Like everyone, Turner found the countdown to battle hard to endure and the war-film cliché that 'it's the waiting I can't stand' was no more than the truth. During this time the sense of collectivity, of mutual interdependence, was overpowering and solidarity demanded that fear was internalised. But inside every head the same tussle was going on and the same opposing emotions clicked backwards and forwards with the regularity of a metronome. The *tick* of excitement at the prospect of finding out at last what battle really meant and whether your courage was a match for it was followed by the *tock* of fear: of death, maiming or, worst of all, some hideous loss of control and the lifetime stigma of cowardice. In between there was no comforting equilibrium. It was *tick* or *tock* and the only relief was to throw yourself into your work and take shelter in the hubbub of banter and horseplay raised by your comrades as they too struggled to still the ominous beat pulsing inside them.

Laughter, no matter how strained, was almost as good as whisky, cigarettes or hot sweet tea when it came to calming nerves. The tension hanging over the briefing room where Turner and his fellow gunners were studying their orders evaporated when 'Jimmy James, a small man who wore thick glasses and a silly, bristly moustache suddenly leapt from his chair and shot up in the air hitting himself all over with his hands and then went one further than any of us expected and took off his trousers . . . out flew a large wasp'. This 'put us all in excellent humour and I decided to read no more orders'.[33]

To everyone's relief they found the navy was operating an onshore wardroom and Turner and a good friend Captain Denis Woolley, who was the bombardment liaison officer on HMS *Berkeley*, grabbed a drink and settled down in armchairs looking out on the sunlit lawns of the house. Melancholy soon cast a shadow. Turner watched the old lady who owned the place walking towards a flower bed with a basket over her arm. He 'couldn't help feeling how strange it all was for us to be sitting there looking at a Hampshire garden on a beautiful August day and at the same time tomorrow we'd be looking at France. I thought how nice it would be if all the world were as peaceful as it seemed to be for that old lady and her flower basket and we were all going to France for a holiday.'

At 14.15 the transport officer began calling them in groups to board the buses taking them to Southampton and their ships. Denis was one of the first to leave and he 'collected all his junk and went out as if he was going out to a tennis party'. Derek did not see him off. 'I knew that I must have no feelings towards my friends and we all behaved as if we'd hardly ever met each other before.'

Then it was his turn. As they drove round the docks looking for *Garth* he felt 'a horrible sinking feeling in the pit of my stomach'. It was quickly replaced by panic when it turned out that the destroyer had left without him. He boarded HMS *Bleasdale* which laid on a whaler to row him over to *Garth*, lying at anchor in the Solent awaiting the final departure. His mood was lifted by the crew of the whaler as they pulled away. They were all 'such hearty fellows'. It fell again as the destroyer grew closer. He 'couldn't help thinking how very small and frail she looked . . .' But then he was on deck and the sailors he knew from training were greeting him with the amiably derisive nickname they reserved for all soldiers ('Good old Pongo!') and the captain, Lieutenant Commander Scatchard, was leading him below for a large brandy and ginger ale. He was 'relieved beyond belief to find everyone in such high spirits'.

Roberts and Hughes-Hallett oversaw the last preparations from Fort Southwick, an underground headquarters buried in Portsdown Hill overlooking the Portsmouth naval base. On Sunday 16 August, the force commanders decided to postpone for twenty-four hours due to an adverse meteorological report. On Tuesday morning, even though the weather situation was still uncertain, all agreed they could wait no longer and the fleet would sail that night. A cover story had been constructed to explain the troop movements to get the units to the assault ships, and various landing craft lying at Southampton, Portsmouth, Gosport, Newhaven and Shoreham. The units were told they were taking part in a movement exercise. Throughout Tuesday 18 August at battalion bases strung along the south coast troops boarded buses that carried them along country roads through villages and seaside towns to the embarkation ports and the waiting ships. By early evening they were all aboard and everyone was told they were bound again for Dieppe.

The Royals embarked on the *Princess Astrid* and *Queen Emma* at Portsmouth. The British war correspondent Alexander Austin was on board when the CO Doug Catto addressed the men from the head of the troop-deck stairs. 'The sergeants quieted the buzz of talk round the hammocks and the weapon racks and the trestle tables,' he wrote. 'Dixies of meat, potatoes and vegetables were being carried in. The men stood quiet in their khaki shirtsleeves, gaze fixed on the stairhead . . . some with towels in their hands, hair wet and faces freshly scrubbed . . . When the CO began to speak, the only sound you could hear was the drip of water from a tap.'[34]

By Austin's account Catto's promise that 'we are not going to land in England again until we have met the Boche' was met with 'a great explosion of human sound forced from them by the impact of news they had been waiting months to hear'. The regiment's battle adjutant

Forbes West remembered it differently, seeing little of the enthusiasm for action the men had shown seven weeks previously. 'The first time they were pretty hopped up,' he recalled.[35] 'The second time it was more "ho-hum". I think we thought it wasn't really going to happen.' Denis Whitaker noted the same subdued reaction among the Rileys. 'We did our best to prepare them, but the feeling of optimism many of us had shared before Rutter was now being replaced by apprehension,' he wrote.[36] Before they sailed Mountbatten toured the ships giving one of his pep talks, just as he had before Rutter. The men of 4 Commando embarked on *Prince Albert* cheered dutifully. 'It was a very nice talk,' remembered Private George Cook. 'He said he wished he was coming with us . . . Two hundred blokes thought, well, we wish you were going instead of us.'[37]

An assortment of military spectators and pressmen were also taking their places for the show. Mountbatten's predilection for publicity ensured there was room for plenty of journalists. Thirteen civilian reporters and cameramen accompanied the troops, assisted by numerous army, navy and air-force press officers. The Canadian and American media were well represented. A place for the unspecified operation had been offered to a London-based Soviet correspondent but he decided he did not want to assist in what he assumed was a propaganda stunt designed to take the place of a real second front, and turned it down.

The lavish coverage arrangements reflected the optimism among the Canadian brass and at COHQ. Despite the risks, there was a feeling that the gamble would work. Alexander Austin was impressed by the brisk confidence of Mann who Roberts charged with meeting the press party and 'putting them in the picture' before they boarded their ships. He was 'slight, thirtyish, with a humorous face and a quick, dry wit, he perched himself on a shelf above the relief plan of Dieppe and, using a splinter from a packing case as a pointer, began to talk to us at midnight . . . He talked without flagging for two hours, marshalling his points lucidly, choosing his phrases with care and yet with a sense of fun.'[38]

As for the object, it was to 'test the German defences; to take prisoners and bring back military papers and every possible kind of information which the Germans would wish to keep to themselves; to rehearse, under fighting conditions, the movement and timing of a large force across the Channel, and its landing on enemy beaches'.

It was from this point that the idea of Dieppe as an experiment and a 'rehearsal' started to gain a strong footing in the subsequent narrative. Bob Bowman, the Canadian Broadcasting Corporation reporter who was accompanying the Calgary Tanks, would tell listeners on his return: 'We've learned a most valuable lesson which may enable us to free the continent of Europe and end the war . . . That was the purpose of the raid as set out officially and told to us before we set sail.' Although there was nothing in the orders to reflect it, this now became the official justification for the events that followed.

At 19.30 Hughes-Hallett left Fort Southwick and was driven to the docks to join Roberts on their headquarters ship. At 20.00 they sailed. 'It was a beautiful night and the *Calpe* stopped at the gate through the Spithead anti-submarine boom and watched as the whole force passed through, eastward-bound, in perfect formation and dead on time.'

PART THREE

Passage

The moon hung in half-silhouette over the Channel, picking out the shapes of the armada coalescing below. Any German pilot passing over would see instantly what was happening. Ears and eyes strained for the sound and sight of a reconnaissance plane, but none came. The luck on which so much depended was holding.

The day had been warm but the night air was cool. Lucian Truscott stood at the rails of the destroyer *Fernie*, the back-up command ship should *Calpe* be put out of action and watched the

> low, flat tank landing craft crawling along like great dark water beetles with white waves now and again splashing against their tall, snout-like ramps. We passed the infantry assault ships gliding along like dark grey ghosts with moonlight reflecting like jewels in the trailing wakes. In the distance, dim shapes of other destroyers and gunboats were barely visible now and again through the slight surface haze. No lights. No noise. All was dark and still.[1]

As the English coast dwindled behind them, the raiders carried on with last-hour preparations against the background throb of engines and the swish of bow waves. There was a lot to do. There were weapons to distribute, as well as demolition charges, Bangalore torpedoes and smoke bombs. There were maps and photographs to be studied and orders gone over again and again until they were driven so deeply in the memory that the shock and cacophony of battle could not dislodge them.

The men were on board before they were issued with Sten guns. They were brand new and came still packed in grease and in the below-decks gloom it took hours to strip, clean and reassemble them, giving the Canadians another reason to hate the gimcrack 'plumber's nightmare'. Screwing detonators into No. 35 Mills Bombs was a delicate business, and even before departure one had gone off on board the *Duke of Wellington*, killing two and injuring eighteen more.

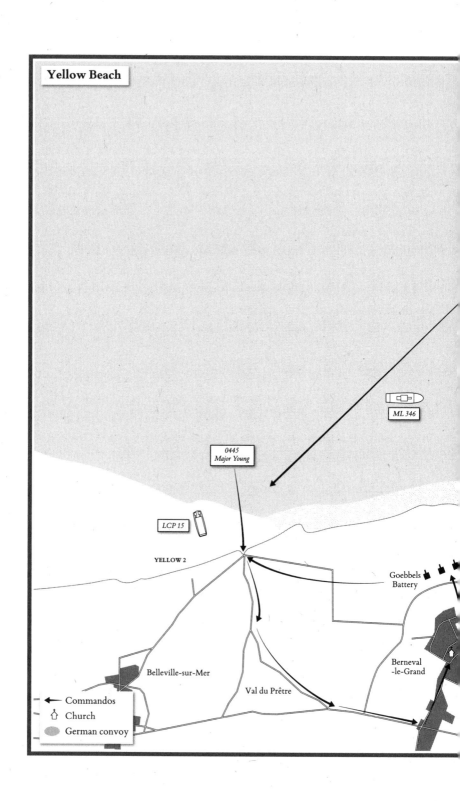

Yellow Beach

ML 346

0445
Major Young

LCP 15

YELLOW 2

Goebbels
Battery

Belleville-sur-Mer

Val du Prêtre

Berneval
-le-Grand

Commandos
Church
German convoy

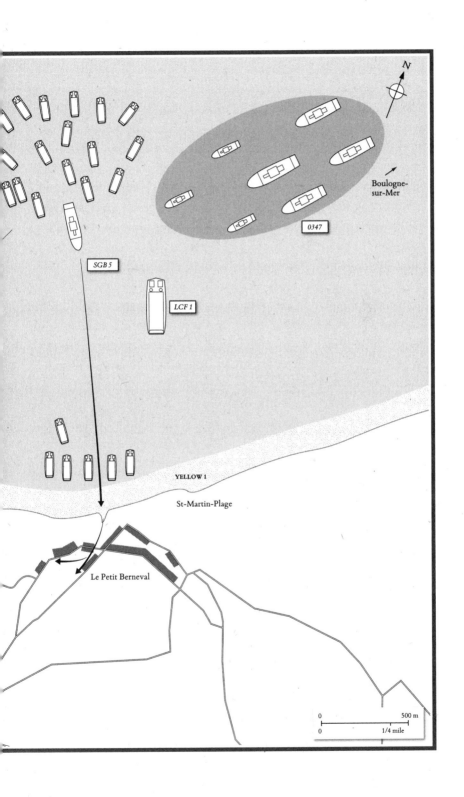

N

Boulogne-
sur-Mer

0347

SGB 5

LCF 1

YELLOW 1

St-Martin-Plage

Le Petit Berneval

0		500 m
0	1/4 mile	

From the bridge of *Calpe* Hughes-Hallett and his deputy David Luce surveyed the assembled armada. There were 'hundreds of ships and craft as far as the eye could see wherever we looked and knowing that all were under our command and committed to the greatest amphibious operation since Gallipoli had a certain dreamlike quality'.[2] There were 237 vessels of one type or another arranged in thirteen groups. They included nine assorted infantry landing ships, eight destroyers, a sloop, twenty-four tank landing craft (LCT) transporting the Churchills of the Calgary Regiment, six anti-aircraft flak landing craft (LCF), seven French Chasseurs, four steam gun boats (SGBs) and twelve motor gun boats (MGBs) as well as the many landing craft that would ferry the 6,088 troops ashore.

Between the fleet and the French coast lay a minefield, laid by the Germans in mid-Channel while the raid was being hatched. Just before the armada set sail, two flotillas of minesweepers cleared two paths each a quarter of mile wide through it. They marked the way with a corridor of buoys fitted with green flags and lanterns which showed up only feebly in the dim and intermittent moonlight. This was the first big test of the operation and *Calpe* led the way, nosing into the swept channel at 01.10. The American journalist Quentin Reynolds watched from the deck. 'We ploughed along at rather a brisk pace and looking over the rail I could see the water churning to a white froth as we cut through it,' he wrote.[3] He turned to Sub Lieutenant Ranald Boyle, who had been assigned to look after him and asked nervously: 'Couldn't we take it easy through this minefield?' Boyle laughed and told him: 'If you hit a mine going at twelve knots it has the same effect as if you hit one travelling at two knots.'

By 01.45 the last green light slid past and they were through to clear water. *Calpe* was not much more than thirty feet in the beam and 280 feet in length. A large infantry ship like *Glengyle* weighed five times as much and was twice as long and broad. It would take only one landing ship to trigger a mine for the whole enterprise to have ended there. But one by one, large and small, every craft in the armada emerged intact and took up its station ready for the next phase of the voyage.

The enemy were less than thirty miles away. The men on the infantry ships braced for the fight ahead. Most of them had never been in action and this would be their first real test as soldiers. On board *Glengyle* Bob Labatt had managed a few hours' sleep in the captain's cabin and was woken by a steward telling him breakfast was on its way. He decided to make the most of the handsome facilities and bathed and shaved in the tiled bathroom, then put on fresh socks, underwear and shirt, remembering that clean garments would reduce the risk of infection if he was wounded. He sat down to porridge, bacon, eggs and kidneys, the last civilised meal he would eat for years to come.

Then he climbed into his battle kit: webbing, Colt .45 pistol with two extra magazines, water bottle, prismatic compass, maps in oiled silk and field message book in left leg pocket. Pencils, pen, torch, cigarettes, chocolate, wallet and escape kit in breast pockets. In his haversack were a packet of sandwiches given him by the steward to take ashore, message pads, Sten mags, two grenades and a smoke canister. With his binoculars round his neck and his Mae West life jacket, Sten gun in hand, 'there [I] stood, the 1942 amphibious soldier'.[4]

Once again he reviewed the orders stamped in his memory. Every commander was doing the same. The plan had a balletic symmetry that looked beautiful on paper. Very soon zero hour would strike – 04.50 British Summer Time. This was calculated as the beginning of nautical twilight when at sea the first faint light of dawn touched the eastern horizon. At that time four simultaneous attacks would go in on the inner and outer flanks of Dieppe.

The Rileys' moment would come half an hour later when they stormed ashore at White Beach on the western half of the Dieppe front. The Essex Scottish would go in alongside them, attacking Red Beach on their left. Then, supported by the Calgary Tanks they would together take the town, knocking out the strongpoints and pillboxes and sniper nests one by one until Dieppe was in their hands and the specialist teams could go about their work demolishing infrastructure and stores, raiding headquarters, capturing prisoners and seizing the invasion barges. Meanwhile some companies would break off to move up onto the western headland and join hands with the South Saskatchewans who had gone ashore at Pourville. The Essex Scottish would do the same on the eastern cliff, meeting the Royals advancing from Puys.

Labatt had felt a jolt of unease when first told by Roberts and Mann that Dieppe was on again. With a few hours to go before the curtain went up, he still believed that the plan 'looked good'. However, 'its success depended largely on surprise'.

Without surprise the finely balanced mechanism of Jubilee would spring irreparably apart. It was the essential component in the flank attacks, which had to succeed if the main assault was not to become a bloodbath. Unless the Goebbels and Hess batteries at Berneval and Varengeville were captured or silenced, the expedition could founder in a shower of heavy shells long before the landing craft reached the shore. The air attacks scheduled to go in on the town defences a few minutes before the main landing might distract the garrison, but they would not significantly suppress the guns. The Saskatchewans and Royals had only half an hour to engage the all-important headlands before the Rileys and Essex Scottish went in. If they failed, their comrades would be walking into a killing zone. The fate of Jubilee thus rested to a large degree on good fortune plus a level of coordination rarely seen in the distilled chaos of battle.

The commandos had been allowed to make their own plans and once ashore would be operating more or less independently. No. 3 Commando were touching down at two gullies in the cliffs, codenamed Yellow 1 and Yellow 2, either side of the battery at Berneval. Durnford-Slater had decided on a simple scheme to land two parties of equal strength on each beach. The gullies provided 'excellent cover and the needed approaches inland'.[5] Each group would work their way towards the guns which sat in the middle of a clifftop, then attack together. That way 'if one landing failed, the other should be able to neutralise the battery by keeping it under fire so that it could not harm our shipping'.

Lovat had taken a similar approach. One party led by Derek Mills-Roberts would land at Orange 1 and move up a gully through the hamlet of Vasterival to attack Hess from the seaward side and keep the defenders busy. The other party under Lovat would go ashore a mile to the west at Quiberville and work their way round behind the battery. The first group would start their attack at 06.15. While the defenders were distracted Lovat would launch the real assault from the rear fifteen minutes later.

Aboard the *Prince Albert* there was an issue of rum along with the supper of beef stew to lift spirits. Then everyone filed to their boat stations and lined up to board their LCA. As they waited Lovat appeared and called for silence. He was dressed in his own idiosyncratic style in corduroys with a pullover showing under his tunic. His preferred weapon was a Winchester hunting rifle. He told his men: 'This is not the hour for a speech. None of us feel very strong at this hour of the morning. But I'd like to say this is the toughest job we've had, and I expect every man to contribute something special . . . I know you'll come back in a blaze of glory. Remember that you represent the flower of the British Army.'[6] Then the lights went out and the files shuffled up the ladders and on to deck.

The commandos' objectives were straightforward. The inner-flank attacks presented greater problems. The approaches were better defended and once ashore each unit had been given a multitude of tasks. The shore at Puys (Blue Beach) where the Royals were to land was narrow and lay at the end of a steep valley whose slopes were known to house machine-gun posts that could cover every seaward angle. Once ashore they were expected to race off to capture the guns on top of the eastern headland.

The South Saskatchewans, followed by the Camerons should have an easier time at Pourville (Green Beach) where the beach was broader and the exit from it wide open. There were still plenty of machine-gun posts to contend with which they would have to silence quickly if they were to attack Quatre Vents farm and distract the defences on the western headland as the main attack went in. The Camerons of Canada should then just be touching down at Pourville, prior to moving south to attack the airfield at Saint-Aubin-sur-Scie and capture the German divisional HQ thought to be at Arques.

★

It was 03.00. There was no turning back now. At some point in the crossing, everyone wrestled with the same thought. Sergeant Marcel Swank, one of three US Rangers attached to the Camerons, had to endure the voyage crouched in the belly of a landing craft as there was not enough room in the landing ship. Swank had passed through Achnacarry and done everything possible to put himself in harm's way but now that danger beckoned he wondered whether he could face what was coming. He sat in the dark, hearing the slap of spray on the hull 'with my hands folded over the muzzle of my rifle, with my chin on my hands, hoping very much that I wouldn't be a coward, hoping very much that I wouldn't be killed'.[7] It was the opinion of others that worried him most. He was an American among Brits and he 'didn't want to disgrace my uniform and my organisation . . . I just wanted very much to be strong.'

The naval officer commanding the flotilla was troubled by another thought. 'The hours passed . . . every minute nearer to the bash on the front door,' wrote Lieutenant Michael Bateson in an account written shortly after his return. 'One had only to reverse in one's imagination what would happen had Jerry raided Dover or Newhaven in force – and the consequences to that force – to know what we are tackling . . .' That consideration, though, 'was never even discussed during the work up to the raid'.[8]

Once through the minefield the troop ships had dispersed to their lowering positions opposite their designated beaches. Destroyers and motor gun boats fanned out along the flanks to guard against attack from fast enemy E-boats, but none came. As the infantry ships hove to twelve or so miles from shore the men filed to their boat stations and climbed onto the landing craft swaying from the davits. Then the quiet was filled with the rattle of chains as they descended jerkily to the water.

On the eastern flank of the armada the men of 3 Commando were approaching the end of an uncomfortable crossing in twenty-three R-boats. With the commandos were forty men of the United States 1st Ranger Battalion, from the fifty Truscott had assigned to the raid.

The force was designated Group 5 of the expedition. It was led by

SGB 5, a fast and heavily armed steam gun boat which carried the naval leader Commander Derek Wyburd and Durnford-Slater. Alongside were LCF 1, a flak boat mounted with dual purpose anti-aircraft guns, and ML 346, a small submarine-chaser carrying a three-pounder cannon and twin machine guns. The flotilla was protected by two destroyers, HMS *Brocklesby* and the Free Polish navy's *Slazak*, which creamed along on the flanks ready to deal with any E-boats.

The departure from Newhaven had been delayed by an air-raid warning. Wyburd had increased speed to make up the lost time and four R-boats had developed engine trouble trying to keep up and been forced to turn back. That did not seem to matter overmuch. Durnford-Slater still had more than 300 men. At 03.40 the destroyers swept reassuringly from starboard to port across the bows of Group 5. It was seventy minutes to zero hour and all seemed well.

Seven minutes later the darkness was ripped away. Sub Lieutenant David Lewis was in LCP 15 bound for Yellow 2. They were hard behind SGB 5 when 'a star shell went up on the starboard hand and lit the whole fleet in a horrible, quivering semi-daylight'.[9] His craft was leading the starboard column and was 'immediately enveloped in the hottest tracer fire I have ever seen. The air was filled with the whine of ricochets and the bangs of exploding shells'. There was nowhere to hide from the bullets. Lewis saw a burst kill a Canadian naval officer, Sub Lieutenant Clifford Wallace aboard LCP 42 'instantly', while 'a shot through the windscreen killed the coxswain.'

In the initial chaos it seemed the incoming fire might be from *Slazak* and *Brocklesby* mistaking the flotilla for the enemy, but the destroyers were now patrolling four miles away to the north oblivious to the danger to their charges.

The convoy was in fact under attack from the escorts of a small German convoy en route from Boulogne to Dieppe. Hughes-Hallett's orders to the senior officers of each group were to make smoke and run for it if they encountered enemy shipping. Wyburd, however, had determined that if Group 5 hit trouble they would try to fight their way through. Instead of fleeing, SGB 5 headed straight for the muzzle flashes stabbing the darkness.

Lewis noted that very soon 'the SGB's thin armour was riddled and the shells exploding inside filled her boiler room with steam. She lost way. The fleet was stopped.' Durnford-Slater had just arrived on deck after taking a nap when the star shells 'made day out of night'.[10] He saw tracer pouring straight towards him and was peppered with fragments from the 40 mm shells. A voice shouted to him to take cover behind the armour plating of the bridge. When he got there it was 'piled up with dead and wounded like a collapsed rugger scrum. There must have been ten casualties there, all hit when looking over the top of the armour plating.'

Once lit up, the R-boats were easy meat for the Germans. The commandos on LCP 87 'saw an E-boat circle round and open fire on us'.[11] The first shell 'went across the bows and the second entered the cabin, exploded, killed three naval ratings, severely wounded the naval officer in charge and mortally wounded our own officer Mr Kenward. He knew he was done for but with his last words he shouted for Sergeant Collins to come forward and take the wheel of the boat.' He was given a compass bearing for England by the naval officer before he 'became delirious and unable to take any further part'.

The fight went on for ten or fifteen minutes. The flak ship and motor launch did their gallant best to fight off the attackers. LCF 1 managed to range its guns on one of them, not an E-boat but an armed merchantman or trawler. It caught fire then exploded. SGB 5 was by now 'holed like a sieve, particularly in the engine room', wrote Durnford-Slater. 'Steam hissed like a thousand snakes out of the pipes.' The engines gave out and she lay there wallowing help-lessly, her guns all knocked out. The expected *coup de grâce* never came. The German convoy moved away leaving Durnford-Slater to survey the battered remains of Group 5. Four R-boats were too badly damaged to go on and could only try to limp back to England. Five more clustered around SGB 5, full of dead and wounded. The rest had disappeared and there was no sign of his second in command, Peter Young. Durnford-Slater was to lead the assault on Yellow 1. 'There was no chance of landing until well after daylight and very little chance of finding the beaches,' he reported afterwards.[12] The landing was 'not considered practicable'. Wyburd ordered some of

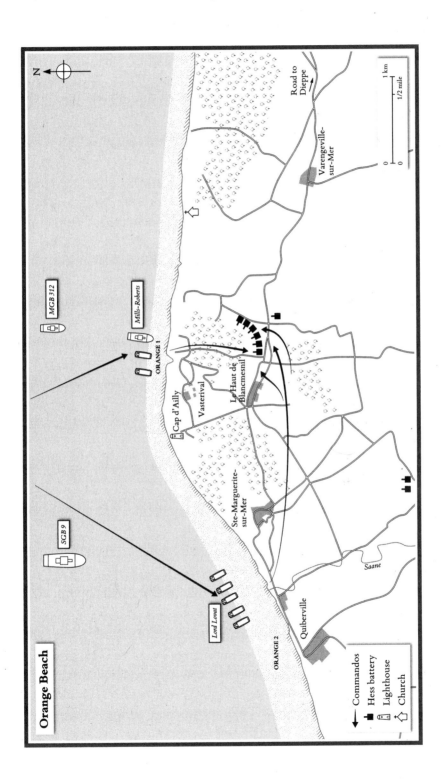

Orange Beach

N

MGB 312

SGB 9

Mills-Roberts

Lord Lovat

ORANGE 1

ORANGE 2

Cap d'Ailly

Vasterival

Le Haut de Blancmesnil

Ste-Marguerite-sur-Mer

Quiberville

Saane

Varengeville-sur-Mer

Road to Dieppe

1 km

1/2 mile

0

0

Commandos

Hess battery

Lighthouse

Church

the LCPs to tow the SGB back to Newhaven. There was no way of communicating the disaster to Hughes-Hallett as the radio was dead. He and Durnford-Slater boarded an R-boat and set off to find *Calpe*. It took LCP 87 five hours to limp back across the Channel. Before arriving at Newhaven the survivors 'laid our dead on the deck, all but two who were too mangled to be taken from the cabin'.[13]

Almost everyone in the armada had seen the pyrotechnics in the eastern sky. There was no way of knowing what had caused them but to many it seemed the moment when their luck changed. There was still another hour until touchdown. Truscott noted the 'grave faces on board the *Fernie*. Now that surprise was lost, the enemy would be waiting at his guns to greet the landing troops.'[14]

None of the ships in the expedition had seen the German convoy on their radar. Its passage had nonetheless been picked up by radar stations along the coast of south-east England. The Portsmouth station logged three plots at 00.40, 01.20 and 02.26 and alerted Admiral James. He sent a signal to the command ships at 02.44 which warned: 'Two craft, 302 degrees, Treport, 10 miles, course 190 degrees, 13 knots at 02.26.' Le Tréport was twenty miles north-east of Dieppe. The enemy ships were therefore sailing straight into the path of the armada. No action was taken. Hughes-Hallett did not mention any alert in his memoirs though James's warning was recorded in *Fernie*'s log.[15]

The signal arrived at an awkward moment in the operation. At 03.00 the fleet was twelve miles offshore and all the troop carriers were immobile as they lowered landing craft crammed with men into the Channel. They were at their most vulnerable from enemy attack and escorts could not be spared to dash off to investigate.

Protecting Group 5 was anyway the job of *Slazak* and *Brocklesby*. The ships were maintaining radio silence but given the near certainty of a clash it would seem worth breaking. As it was, the two destroyers maintained their patrol oblivious to the plight of the group, a performance that caused much bitterness afterwards. According to Durnford-Slater they had 'found travelling with us at a slow ten knots too dull, and had dashed off friskily into the night'. Even when the shooting began the captain of the *Slazak* thought it was coming from the shore and did not change course to investigate.

Scores of landing craft were now butting towards the enemy coast. Even if Hughes-Hallett had wanted to call them back it was too late. He later claimed that he was not unduly worried by the fracas at sea for he 'thought it unlikely that the Germans would have associated what must have looked to them like a coastal force skirmish with a major combined operation'.[16]

He wrote this years after the war in the knowledge that this was precisely how the Germans did initially react. Shortly after the clash Naval HQ West reported the 'opinion of the Naval Command that it has been one of the usual attacks on the convoys'.[17] The response was to alert the radar stations and the Goebbels and Hess batteries whose primary role was to shoot at hostile ships rather than repel an invasion. However at 05.00 another signal informed Army HQ in Paris that 'troops have intensified their lookout. Air and navy authorities have been advised.'

It was one of many such alarms and initially the defenders reacted calmly. The favourable tide and moon conditions meant they were already on a heightened level of alert. The sector between the harbour and Puys was commanded by Hauptmann Richard Schnösenberg of the 3rd Battalion of the 571st Infantry Regiment. 'The navy had given us times which were especially favourable for a landing and one of these included the 19th of August,' he remembered. 'We did not know about an attack but we had . . . an increased level of vigilance.'[18] He had spent much of the night visiting positions, making sure his men were wide awake and even shifted a mobile gun to a new site.

He was in Puys when he heard firing out to sea. He was not particularly concerned as 'the English speedboats were continually shooting it up with our patrol vessels'. On returning to his command post on the heights above the port he checked with the naval signal station next door and was told 'don't get yourself worked up, it means nothing at all'. A convoy had clashed with some enemy 'speedboats' but would shortly be arriving at Dieppe. He was about to climb into bed when his adjutant came in to tell him that there had been a renewed warning following the sea skirmish.

He was clearly going to get no sleep that night. He decided to make the best of it by calling an 'early morning alarm drill' for the garrison and surrounding batteries. Further to the west all was serene. The lighthouse on the Cap d'Ailly, the headland between Quiberville and Pourville, continued to flash and the harbour lights still shone in Dieppe.

Seven R-boats from Group 5 had emerged from the convoy battle unscathed. Despite having lost all their support craft the commanders decided to press on. One was LCP 15, captained by a reservist, Lieutenant Tom Buckee, who had on board Lieutenant Lewis, the beachmaster for Yellow 2, charged with overseeing the landing and departure. In the middle of the mayhem Buckee had followed Wyburd's instructions unquestioningly. 'Orders were to land the troops at all costs or the operation would be a bloody failure,' recorded Lewis in his after-action report. 'At full speed we tore away from the lashing beams of flak.' Another star shell went off but it was too far away to reveal them. Still unhit except by shrapnel they 'belted all alone for the French coast'.[19] Amazingly they were still on time. They could see no sign of the other four boats assigned to Yellow 2. At ten minutes to zero hour . . . 'the white cliffs of Berneval loomed up. We could see our objective and the coast was quiet.'

Among those on board LCP 15 was Captain Peter Young, commander of the Yellow 2 party. It now consisted of twenty men, a tenth of the original force. They mustered between them one Bren gun, six Thompson machine guns, ten rifles and two mortars. Young said later that 'it wasn't as bad as it sounds.'[20] During the planning they had come to the conclusion that 'one or two men who mean business in the back of the enemy's position can make themselves felt whereas a whole mob milling around might be absolutely useless . . . we realised that [the situation] was fairly serious, but we weren't unduly depressed'.

Buckee had put them down at exactly the right point and five minutes ahead of schedule. The sailors volunteered to join the raiders but

Young 'discouraged this idea. I wanted to get home and I thought if
they didn't stay in the craft and keep it near the shore this was not
going to be very likely.' All was quiet. The gully stood out a black
gash in the chalky marl of the cliff face. Either the defenders hadn't
seen them or they were holding their fire.

The crack in the cliff was V-shaped and blocked with head-high
barbed wire. There were no wire cutters or Bangalore torpedoes in
the boat. They would have to climb up and around it. Young led the
way but twice slithered down the clammy gully walls. Then he
noticed that the Germans had driven pegs into the chalk on which to
hang the wire and, using them as footholds, he worked his way to the
top. A sign there told him he had just passed through a minefield.
After twenty minutes everyone had got through unharmed, though
the three-inch mortar tube and bombs were too much to carry and
had to be left on the beach.

From the clifftop Young looked out to sea. It was now broad daylight and to the east he saw six landing craft heading for Yellow 1.
That 'meant 120 men, and so I realised that I must now push on and
get to the rendezvous which was the church at the back of the battery
and no doubt I would meet these people there and we would then fall
on the battery from behind'. There was still no sign of the Germans.

Since early morning at aerodromes all over south-east England pilots
and air crews had been arriving by lorry, bicycle and foot at dispersal
areas to board their aircraft. The fighter force was the biggest ac-
cumulation of fighter power ever assembled, and more squadrons
would be in action that day than even during the most crowded hours
of the Battle of Britain. There were forty-eight Spitfire squadrons on
hand and eight Hurricane units, two of them equipped with 'Hurribombers', each carrying two 250 lb bombs for use against strongpoints
and machine-gun posts. Leigh-Mallory also had the loan of three
squadrons of Bostons from Bomber Command to lay smoke and
bombard the batteries. Army Cooperation Command was contributing two squadrons of Blenheim bombers as well as squadrons of
Mustang fighters to scout the approaches behind Dieppe and report
any German troop movements.

The men leading the formations were mostly veterans. Fifty squadron leaders and flight commanders had flown in the Battle of Britain. Many had also survived the long and very hazardous campaign of provocative cross-Channel raiding that had followed under the leadership of Douglas and Leigh-Mallory. So far the Luftwaffe had reacted cautiously, calculating the risks, husbanding their resources and only accepting the challenge to fight when they calculated that the odds were favourable. Today would be different. The German air force could not look away from the threat posed by an amphibious attack on this scale. The day promised an epic clash in the heavens.

The vital importance of air power had been painfully demonstrated at every stage of the war to date, in Norway, the Battle of France, Singapore and Crete. The necessity to control the skies above the battlefield had been demonstrated defensively at Dunkirk. Now, if Britain's first big return to the continent was to succeed, the RAF would have to dominate the narrow airspace beneath which the ships and troops would operate. At RAF Manston, Wing Commander David Scott-Malden spelled out the importance of the task to the British and Norwegian pilots he led. 'We were to maintain air superiority throughout the operation and regardless of opposition or cost to ourselves,' remembered Wilhelm Mohr, commander of 332 Norwegian Squadron. He told them they were to 'fight it out, even if you are to remain there alone to the end'.[21]

The Spitfires' job was to open a robust air umbrella above the fleet and troops at the two most vulnerable stages of the operation – the assault and the withdrawal – and to try to control the skies all the time the force was ashore. The light bombers and Hurribombers were there to blast the known gun positions and smother the approaches with smoke to hide the attackers' movements at sea and over the beaches.

The Germans were outnumbered in the air. The Luftwaffe had two fighter groups within easy striking distance with about 320 serviceable aircraft. Many of them were Focke-Wulf 190s, in most respects superior to the standard Spitfire Vs flown by most of the squadrons. The British fighter force totalled nearly 650. As Fighter

Command well knew, this did not add up to guaranteed victory. The old Battle of Britain roles were now reversed. The RAF would be fighting at distance. Each sortie meant a considerable journey back and forth to the battle zone with a limited time over target. The Germans were playing at home. They could make two sorties for every one carried out by the enemy.

The Luftwaffe mustered more than a hundred bombers. Most of them were twin-engine Dornier 217s supplemented by Junkers 88s and Heinkel 111s, the machines that had fought the Battle of Britain and delivered the Blitz. If the RAF failed to do its job, they were capable of doing catastrophic damage to the expedition. The air operation was overseen by Leigh-Mallory, alongside Mountbatten and Crerar, from his underground command post at Uxbridge, west of London. Uxbridge was a long way from the action but he had a direct link to his representative with the fleet, Air Commodore Adrian Cole who was on board *Calpe*. Two more officers charged with controlling the close-support squadrons and the fighter-cover squadrons were on *Berkeley*.

At 04.47 Flying Officer Harry Jones and Sergeant R. L. Reeves of 129 Squadron took off in their Spitfires from Thorney Island and set course across the Channel. Their target was the lighthouse at Cap d'Ailly which served as an observation post for the Hess battery. It lay between Orange Beaches 1 and 2 and was protected by a flak tower. The pair crossed the coast four miles to the west then swung round and went in low, shooting up the lantern room. Jones was hit with flak and went down in the sea, the first pilot to lose his life that day. Reeves carried on the attack, turning away when the beam was extinguished.

From the assault landing craft the men of 4 Commando looked up and saw the Spitfires flashing above and the fountains of flak rising to meet them. The flotilla had just split, carrying one party of seventy-two to the beach below Vasterival for the diversionary action and a larger force to Quiberville for the main attack. Derek Mills-Roberts was in charge of the smaller group. The sight of the fighters was welcome but he feared that 'surprise might have been lost and haste was now essential'.[22] They headed for the cover of the cliff then turned left searching for the buttress which marked two gullies that appeared to offer a way up.

It was a perfect landing. The armoured bow doors of the LCAs went down and they stepped ashore without getting their feet wet. The commandos were fighting light. They wore thin denims and woollen cap comforters instead of cumbersome helmets and many preferred rubber-soled gym shoes to boots. The weight-saving meant they could boost their firepower by carrying more ammunition for the Brens and bombs for the mortars.

The left-hand gully looked the best bet as recce photos revealed no defences at the exit. They found it choked with barbed wire and fallen lumps of chalk so they tried the other. It too was wired in. The dark was fading fast and someone heard noises at the top of the cliff.

There was no time for subtlety now. The Bangalore torpedo was simple but effective – an explosive-packed tube that came in handy eighteen-inch lengths and could blow a ten-foot path through an obstacle. Lieutenant David Styles laid one on the first bank of wire, lit the fuse and ducked for cover. The breach was narrow but after a second explosion they were through to the gulley and making their way single file along the sides, taking great care not to step on the track which it was assumed was sown with mines.

It was dark inside the gulley and the air was filled with the scent of damp earth and dew-soaked ferns. The sky was showing through the overhanging trees and the birds were starting their dawn chorus.

The gully opened onto a path leading up to the Hôtel de la Terrasse, where in normal times the bourgeois clientele would be slumbering before another day of tennis, swimming and sunbathing. Among the surrounding villas was La Lézardière where eleven-year-old Gérard Cadot and his family had just been woken up by the sound of low-flying planes and anti-aircraft fire. Together with his father Gaston and mother Simone, they dressed and crossed the lane to La Maisonnette to take shelter in a storeroom beneath the *pigeonnier*. The ground was littered with cartridge cases from the aircraft and Gérard burnt his fingers picking one up. From the windows he saw fire and smoke to the east. Then there was the sound of movement outside.

16. With the successful Commando raid on Vaagso in December 1941, Mountbatten set the tone for his reign at Combined Ops HQ.

17. This was to be the first outing of Churchill tanks in battle.

18. None of the armour landed made it back home.

19. Training for Dieppe. Whatever the weaknesses of the plan, preparations were rigorous.

20. South Saskatchewans taking a break from Simmerforce, the combined operations training on the island.

21. A gun emplacement on one of the streets leading from the promenade. Every likely line of attack was covered by German fire.

2. On passage. Some troops made the crossing in peacetime Channel ferries, others in thirty-six-foot R-Boats.

3. 4 Commando running in at Vasterival, prior to the attack on the Hess battery.

24. RAF reconnaissance photo of Dieppe at the time of the raid.

25. Dieppe was a frequent target of air attacks, this one a daylight raid on shipping in the harbour.

26. The dragon's mouth: artillery fire flails the waves as the landing craft go in.

27. The crowded sea off the main beaches.

Gaston was as inquisitive as his son and the pair went outside to investigate. They saw 'four soldiers in khaki come up the slope out of the darkness . . . they had black paint on their faces and woollen caps on their heads and they carried rifles and machine guns'.[23] They tried talking to them but none spoke French and the soldiers moved stealthily on, taking the path that led off to the lighthouse.

Mills-Roberts checked the time. It was 05.40 and they were well ahead of schedule. The battery was only half a mile up the lane. They were due to be in position to open fire on it at 06.15. Lovat's assault would go in a quarter of an hour later, preceded two minutes beforehand by a low-level cannon fighter attack.

Just then 'the silence was broken by a shattering noise'. Hess was opening up. The first 5.9 inch shells roared over their heads towards the fleet, now well within range off Dieppe. It would be fifty minutes before Lovat's party arrived. Six more salvoes swished over in quick succession. The timetable was forgotten. They had to engage the battery immediately. Stealth was abandoned and 'we crashed ahead like a herd of elephants'.

Lovat's group of 152 on four LCAs were twenty minutes out from Orange 2 to the right of the lighthouse when white star shells blossomed over the sea ahead. Lovat ordered full speed and as they charged towards the beach fighter-bombers streaked above. The dark hump of land lit up with flak and tracer unmasking the locations of the enemy guns. First ashore were a party from A Troop. They were led by Lieutenant Arthur 'Fairy' Veasey, a very popular officer who claimed to hold the title of pork-pie-eating champion of England. Their job was to knock out two pillboxes on the higher ground at the east end of the beach. The first was unoccupied. The second was silenced and all the crew killed. Trooper Tom Finney shinned up a telegraph pole and with bullets thudding into the post cut the wires connecting Quiberville to Sainte-Marguerite.

The craft of the second flight now scraped over the *galets*, the ramp doors went down and the men plunged waist-deep into the water and struggled for the beach. They were met with a shower of mortars, fired on what seemed like fixed trajectories, which sent bomb splinters scything through the air.

The first 'wiped out' a subsection of B Troop.[24] The commander, Captain Gordon Webb, was hit in the shoulder but 'one thing we'd learned about landings was you get off the beach fast' and he stumbled on.[25] The exit was blocked by a thicket of barbed wire. The drill was simple but effective. Designated soldiers threw rolls of rabbit netting over the top while others in thick leather jerkins trampled it down and cut a clearing.

The recce party led the way through. The commandos ran doubled over ducking a stream of fire from a machine-gun post on the right. Lovat had often claimed that 'the German soldier is not at his best at night' and that the enemy marksmanship would be poor. He seemed determined to test his theory, not deigning to make a smaller target of himself. As Private George Cook of F Troop cleared the wire he heard his CO remark casually: 'Oh, they're firing too high.'[26] He thought 'Lord Lovat is about six foot, I'm five foot four . . . If they're firing over his head there's no danger they're going to touch me.'

Ahead lay the muddy shoulders of the River Saâne and they ducked gratefully into the lee of the east bank and caught their breath. They had got off reasonably lightly but not unscathed. The beach they left behind was dotted with fallen men. Moving among them were Joe and Jimmy Pasquale, brothers from Liverpool who joined the commandos from the Royal Army Medical Corps. 'A few had been hit and a couple were dead on the wire,' recalled Jimmy. 'The numbers one and two on the mortar were kneeling ready to fire and had been killed in that position. There was a man named Mercer with his eye hanging out and of course he was in a terrible state so I stayed with him.'[27] Jimmy did what he could for the wounded until he was captured. Joe had two walking wounded killed alongside him by friendly naval fire as he escorted them along the coast to the evacuation beach at Orange 1. Jimmy spent the rest of the war in a prison camp. It was only after his release that he learned that Joe had been killed on D-Day.

The commandos were seeing the sights of war that they could not show you at Achnacarry. Lieutenant Donald Gilchrist, the former bank clerk from Paisley, saw his first German killed when a soldier broke cover just as a fighter was making a low pass. 'Like an ungainly, grey-uniformed grouse, [he] ran across a field. He wasn't fast enough . . . A burst of cannon fire lifted him off his feet, hurling him for several yards before he tumbled head over heels and lay still.'[28] Sergeant Alex Szima, a US Ranger advancing on the battery from the other side, came across a dead German whose 'potato masher' stick grenade had exploded before he could throw it. In the cool morning air 'steam was rising from his intestines'.[29]

The Lovat group worked their way up the riverbank. The second meander marked the spot where they had to move up the east slope of the valley to the wooded plateau on which the battery sat. This meant crossing a mile of fields before they reached the cover of lanes, orchards and hedges. To Lovat's amazement no one shot at them. They could hear firing just to the north as Mills-Roberts's men opened up on the battery from the front. Then at zero plus forty 'the heavy crump of a [two-inch] mortar added a pleasant note to the barrage and shortly afterwards a roar of sound supplemented by sheets of flame that rose high into the air increased our confidence that all was going well.'[30]

The first group had managed to get close enough to the battery to be able to hear orders being shouted without being detected. They were now concealed in an empty barn-like house 170 yards from the three right-hand gun pits. Another group was scattered among the trees on the west of the battery. The hundred or so Germans inside the wire still seemed unaware of the imminent danger. As the crews reloaded to fire another salvo Mills-Roberts selected a target for one of the riflemen, a tall German who was shouting orders to the gun servers. The sniper took his time. Then 'at last the rifle cracked; it was a bull's eye and one of the Master Race took a toss into a gun pit'.[31] The rest of the commandos now joined in with Brens, rifles and a Boys anti-tank rifle whose half-inch thick bullets ripped through the armour plating protecting the gunners in a revolving flak tower that stood on stilts over the battery.

Two mortar teams had come up. The two-inch mortar was directed by Troop Sergeant Major Jimmy Dunning assisted by privates Dale and Horne. They set up in a wood near the house. It was simple weapon, just a twenty-one-inch steel tube mounted on a baseplate and a hinged elevator. One man held the barrel at the agreed angle and pulled the trigger when the other dropped in the bomb.

The first round whirred off to land harmlessly. Dunning corrected the team's aim and a second flew towards the guns. Accounts vary as to whether it was this round or the next that produced the dramatic result that followed. What is certain is that one of the missiles, weighing a mere two pounds two ounces, plunged into a stack of cordite standing unprotected next to the battery's No. 1 gun. The war correspondent Alexander Austin who had gone ashore with the commandos at Orange 1 was lugging mortar shells up from the beach when 'an explosion in front of us, louder and longer than anything we had heard that morning, made us crouch suddenly. It seemed to be the father and mother of all explosions, far louder than the biggest bomb I had heard in the London Blitz.'[32]

Mills-Roberts emerged from the woods, grinning with pleasure. 'We've got their ammunition dump,' he explained. 'Mortar shell bang on top of it. Bloody fools! They'd got their ammunition all in one lot.' Jimmy Dunning never claimed that any great skill was involved in the mortar-men's coup. It was, he would say afterwards, 'the biggest stroke of luck I think in World War Two'.[33] But with one shot he and his men had accomplished 4 Commando's mission. The Hess battery fired no more.

Lovat had more than 200 men at his disposal. Peter Young had nineteen. Having scaled the gully at Yellow 2 he led the party down a cart track towards Berneval-le-Grand. The Goebbels battery lay in the middle of a field of standing corn just north of the village facing out to sea. The plan had been for Young's party to attack it from behind while the first group approached from Yellow 1. The five R-boats they had seen heading for the beach ought to have been in place by now. Private Sayers had lugged his No. 18 radio set up the cliff intact and Young now tried to raise the other group. There was no reply. He decided that if the battery started firing they would attack, with or without their support.

A boy appeared on a bicycle. He was 'obviously very frightened' but told them that there were about 200 Germans in the battery.[34] He was so relieved to be sent on his way that he kissed Young on both cheeks, to everyone's great amusement. As they approached the village six Spitfires flew over spraying cannon fire at the battery. The consequences of the raid for the local population were already clear. They saw three men 'running inland with a woman on a handcart'. They said she had been wounded in an air raid. A fireman in an old-fashioned brass helmet hurried past to deal with a house burning in the distance.

Entering the village they came under fire for the first time from a light-machine-gun post. They took cover behind the church. Young had the idea of putting snipers in the tower to shoot up the battery but there was no ladder to the belfry. He 'then determined to get into the cornfield . . . and engage the battery from there'.

They worked their way round to the west side of the battery and prepared to make a dash for the cover of the crops. Young assured his men that 'nine feet of corn would stop a bullet.' This 'went down quite well'. They 'set off gallantly into the field galloping as fast as their legs would carry them and we formed up about 200 yards from the left-hand gun in two lines in very widely extended order'.

Both files kept up a steady fire at the gun flashes coming from the battery interspersed with rounds from the two-inch mortar. The Germans replied with small arms but apparently lost patience because 'they turned round the left-hand gun and suddenly there was a great cloud of smoke and black and orange flame and a large shell wobbled over our heads'. It was a mark of frustration for the barrel could not be depressed to a low enough angle to hit them. They nonetheless kept on firing. Young's 'only thought was well if they're firing at us they can't be firing at the ships'. He looked out to sea and was reassured to see that the fleet was covered in protective smoke so he 'rather doubted whether the Germans could see what they were doing'.

The thought of charging the battery crossed his mind but was quickly dismissed. That 'would be playing into their hands. It was bound to end in our losing say half our strength and then falling back in disorder and that would be the best thing that could happen from the German commander's point of view.' As it was he and his tiny band were doing what they were supposed to do. 'The object of the mission was to prevent the battery causing casualties to the ships . . . we were attaining our objective.'

This end had to be weighed against another consideration. So far there had been no counter-attack from the garrison. It seemed clear now that the Yellow 1 party were not coming or would arrive too late. That meant he and his men were outnumbered by ten to one. He feared that any minute tanks would appear and scythe through the corn towards them. Young 'felt I owed it to my soldiers to give them a chance of survival'. It became a 'question of timing my withdrawal', finding the right moment between 'going away too soon and seeming too windy for words or staying too long and getting overrun'.

Before they could fall back they had to be sure that the landing craft was still waiting to take them off. He sent a party off to investigate. Soon after, three white flares appeared above the clifftop telling him the faithful Buckee was still at his post.

They dropped back to the gully. On the way a fire fight broke out with the battery's observation post perched above the sea. The Germans at last emerged from cover and peppered the main party as they scrambled down the ravine. A mine went off injuring Lance Corporal Bill White but he was able to get to the shore where he was fit enough to fire some rounds from the abandoned three-inch mortar back up the cliff. Young and Lieutenant Anthony Ruxton held the Germans off while the navy hustled the others into the boat.

There were moments of near panic as they struggled to get away. The craft stuck on the rock shelf at the foot of the beach and equipment was thrown overboard to lighten the load. By now the Germans were on the clifftop firing down. Having covered the retreat Young, Ruxton and Private Herbert Abbott waded out to get aboard but the boat seemed always out of reach. It was, said Young later, like a 'nightmare when you're trying to run but nothing happens'. Finally the three were thrown lifelines and towed out to sea. Buckee hove to 300 yards out and they were hauled onboard. As they headed for home the sounds of battle drifted over from Yellow 1.

★

The little flotilla of landing craft Young's group had seen from the cliff had come through the sea battle unharmed, though they were well behind schedule and the darkness had made way for a summer morning. Still, they saw no reason not to carry on and regrouped around motor launch ML 346 commanded by Lieutenant Alexander Fear which stood back to cover their approach to Yellow 1. Lieutenant Commander Charles Corke, the most senior officer present, took command of the naval party. The Germans on the cliffs could see them clearly as they approached. The only element of surprise that remained was that with all the advantages on the side of the defenders, the raiders were persisting with their attack.

What happened next is obscure. Only a few of those who landed were taken off again. The rest were either killed or taken prisoner. There are no immediate after-action reports to go on so accurate details are sparse. The five R-boats touched down sometime after 05.10 and were met with gunfire from the cliffs. A sixth arrived a little later. At some point Corke was hit and mortally wounded and his coxswain killed moments later. Most of the soldiers on board made it ashore. The precise number is unknown but about 120 commandos landed together with six US Rangers and a small number of Free French commandos.

The beach lay in a dip in the cliffs which stretch like gull wings on either side of a valley. Behind lay Saint-Martin, a genteel resort in peacetime dotted with holiday villas and the hotel where Oscar Wilde stayed briefly after release from Reading gaol. In these seaside lanes and overgrown gardens a ragged battle ensued that lasted for four hours as the Germans gradually whittled away the hopelessly outgunned and outnumbered raiders.

The garrison was soon reinforced with a battalion-strength force despatched from Dieppe. The commandos and their comrades must have known from the beginning that the attack was doomed but they pressed on gamely. Leaving a naval party on the beach they tried to move up a valley on the right which led to the clifftop and the battery. It was hopeless. The Germans took their time, chopping away at the attackers whenever they showed themselves. After ninety minutes the raiders accepted the inevitable and tried to retrace the track to the beach. Fighting their way back was just as difficult as fighting their way in. Some battered R-boats had been summoned by flares to attempt an evacuation. They sailed in through a storm of machine-gun and mortar fire but found no troops waiting. One boat embarked the naval beach party but got stuck on the rocks on departure. A second went to the rescue and also grounded, and the two hung there while fire rained down from the cliff. The officer in charge of the landing craft, Lieutenant Dennis Stephens, finally decided the commandos were not coming and put to sea. The troops who eventually made it back to the beach found only the blazing and submerged carcases of three R-boats waiting. They clung on in the lee of the cliff, still hoping to be rescued. Elsewhere scattered groups tried to hold off the encroaching Germans. At 10.30, with ammunition running low the survivors made the choice to live. As the Germans closed in they threw down their weapons and raised their arms.

Of the men who landed on Yellow 1 thirty-six or thirty-seven died then or subsequently – the figures are not exact. Eighty-two were taken prisoner. Most of those who die in war are known only to those who grieve for them. Two names stand out from the dead of Berneval by reason of their novelty. As far as it can be determined US Ranger Lieutenant Edward Loustalot was killed somewhere on the journey back to the beach, cut down by machine-gun fire.[35] Loustalot was a good-looking twenty-three-year-old from Franklin, Louisiana. He was keen and hard-working but also quiet and popular with his men and according to Peter Young 'a charming young man who got on very well with the troop he was attached to'.[36] If not for the war he could have been anything. Instead he will have a certain sort of immortality as the first American to be killed by Germans on land in Europe in the Second World War.

Serge Moutaillier died trying to cross the little bridge over the ravine connecting Saint-Martin to Berneval. His body was never found. He too was twenty-three, a Parisian who joined the navy at fifteen and volunteered to join the Free French Fusiliers Marins commando force when it was formed in July 1941. He was remembered as the first French commando to be killed in action on his native soil, and all his distinctions would be posthumous.

The crushing defeat at Yellow 1 was balanced by the triumph at Varengeville. With the battery silenced by the lucky mortar strike, 4 Commando moved in for the kill. The action was described in savage detail by Lovat in his after-action report. By 06.10 B and F Troops had taken up their attacking positions at the rear of the enclosure and everything was in place. Two minutes before the attack Spitfires appeared on cue to shoot up the battery. Lovat fired a flare pistol to signal the charge and the commandos 'attacked with the bayonet'.

'It was a tremendous charge which went in, in many cases over open ground swept by machine-gun fire through a barbed-wire entanglement overrunning strongpoints and finally ending up on the gun sites themselves where the enemy were bombed and bayoneted into submission,' wrote Lovat. 'F Troop, who behaved magnificently, suffered heavy casualties. All their officers [Captain Roger Pettiward and Lieutenant John Macdonald] were killed leading the charge. Captain [Pat] Porteous took over and was wounded twice but continued until he fell, shot through the legs on top of a gun position. The company sergeant major had his foot blown away by a stick grenade but continued to engage the enemy in a sitting position.'[37]

The mopping up was pitiless. 'Considerable numbers of Germans who had hidden in underground tunnels containing stores and ammunition, in the battery office, under tables in the cookhouse and the outbuildings were either bayoneted or shot at close range by submachine guns. Two officers including the military commander were also killed after a rousing chase from one house to another.'

The firing faded to a few desultory shots. Lovat moved forward to inspect the gun pits which were 'in a remarkable state [with] burnt and mangled bodies . . . piled high . . . the last survivors had fought it out with F Troop during their successful attack with the bayonet. Other bodies which had been sniped by Major Mills-Roberts and C Troop lay in heaps all around . . . many Germans had been badly burnt when the cordite had been set alight . . .'

The demolition men prepared the charges to blow the guns.

Captain Pat Porteous, who later won the VC for his exploits that day, watched them load a shell into the breech and place a wodge of plastic explosive behind. It took two minutes for the fuse to burn down then the explosion 'opened up the guns like banana peel'.[38] Before leaving the commandos laid out their dead and ran up a Union Jack over the wreckage of the battery. The wounded were loaded onto stretchers and salvaged doors. Four Germans lucky enough to be taken prisoner were ordered to act as stretcher-bearers. The two carrying Porteous were 'scared stiff. They thought they were going to have their throats cut or something.'

Their departure went as smoothly as every other phase of this part of the operation. The 4 Commando action had conformed to Lovat's plan almost to the minute and achieved total success. It was a small compensation for what was happening elsewhere.

Blue and Green

I

Blue Beach was the objective that mattered most. The attack had to succeed for the rest of the plan to work. According to Hughes-Hallett, 'it had always been realised that unless the east headland . . . was captured the frontal assault on the town on which the whole operation chiefly depended would probably fail.'[1] The outcome balanced on a single factor. The orders made clear that 'surprise is the element on which reliance is placed for the success of the landing.'[2]

The landing craft had to arrive in darkness if there was to be any hope of catching the garrison off guard. That depended on accurate timing which as the Yukon exercises had demonstrated was hard to achieve. It was likely that the timetable of one or other of the landings would go awry. Fate decreed that it unravelled on the beach on which the whole operation hinged. The blunder came as the 554 men of the Royal Regiment of Canada boarded their landing craft. The resulting carnage was in its way as shocking as any of the great Canadian sacrifices of the First World War.

The Royals were to go ashore in three waves, with A, B and C Companies and an advance HQ group landing first followed by D Company and the rest of the headquarters including the CO, Colonel Catto. A third force made up of three platoons from the Black Watch of Canada, plus an artillery and an anti-aircraft detachment would go in when signalled. Once they had overcome the Puys defences the Royals were expected to capture the machine-gun posts, flak batteries and four-gun Rommel battery just to the south, then 'go into reserve' leaving one company to descend into the town to protect the demolition party when they blew up the gasworks and power plant. The gunners would take over the captured guns and turn them on the enemy. They were also tasked with bringing back a new German gunsight that was of great interest to the War Office.

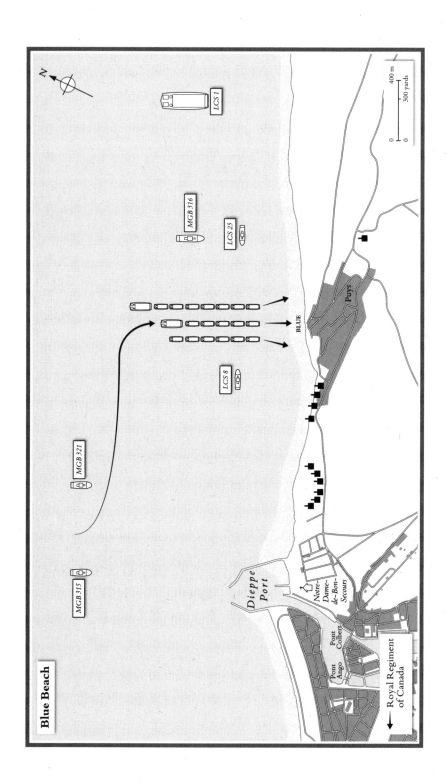

Blue Beach

LCS 1

MGB 316

LCS 25

BLUE

Puys

LCS 8

MGB 321

MGB 315

Dieppe Port

Notre-Dame-de-Bon-Secours

Pont Colbert

Pont Ango

Royal Regiment of Canada

400 m

300 yards

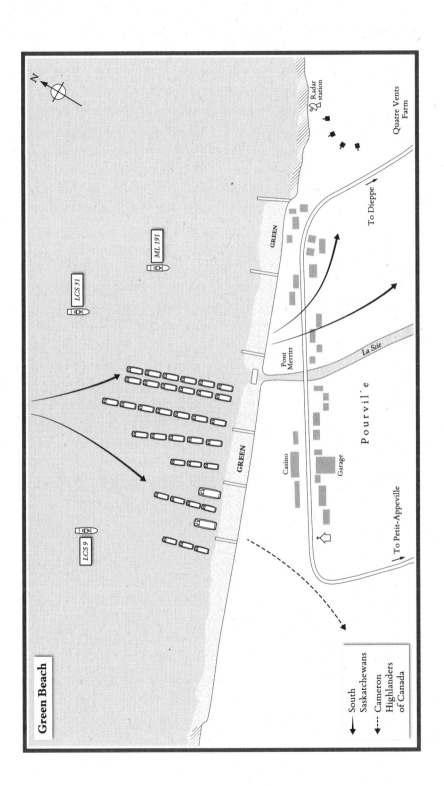

Green Beach

N

LCS 31

ML 191

LCS 9

GREEN

GREEN

Radar station

Quatre Vents Farm

To Dieppe

Pont Merritt

La Scie

Pourvil·e

Casino

Garage

To Petit-Appeville

South Saskatchewans

Cameron Highlanders of Canada

The Royals sailed on the *Queen Emma* and the *Princess Astrid* with the Black Watch on the *Duke of Wellington*. They were going ashore in eighteen assault landing craft and two mechanised landing craft.

The LCAs were flat-bottomed and looked like barges. Unlike the R-boats, the bow door and sides were armoured, as was the narrow deck that ran around the inside of the hull. A Bren gun mounted on the prow provided a minimal defence. They could carry about a platoon's worth of troops, thirty-six men, who sat astride narrow benches on the run in. The LCMs could carry a hundred men apiece or one tank.

Things began to go wrong just after 02.30 when the landing craft were lowered into the water for the final approach. Major Forbes West, whom Catto had chosen as his 'battle adjutant' to stay at his side and liaise with the units during the fighting, was in an LCM when he detected 'a great deal of what appeared to be confusion'.[3]

Each group was assigned a motor gun boat to lead it in. One MGB had strayed from its station and the craft from *Princess Astrid* mistakenly lined up behind it. By the time the muddle was sorted they were fifteen minutes behind schedule. The naval commander overseeing the landings, Lieutenant Commander Harold Goulding, had already decided on an indirect approach to shore. Blue Beach, a mere crack in the cliffs, would be very hard to pick out in the dark. He reckoned that the safest course was to head for the lights of Dieppe harbour which were still gleaming out of the darkness, presumably to guide the German convoy that had just clashed with Group 5 into port. He would then turn north and steer at right angles to the shore looking for the first break in the chalk walls. The dog-leg meant a longer journey and Goulding increased speed to try to make up the minutes. The LCMs were slower than the LCAs and fell behind. One developed engine trouble and had to stop to make repairs. A 'huge white flare' rose from the shore as they passed the port and searchlights probed the darkness.

As West's craft approached Blue Beach 'it was coming on daylight and there was a great burst of firing and then it petered out to almost nothing'. The first wave were going in. Later he remembered saying to the CO, 'Well, they must have got through.' Catto replied: 'No they didn't. They're all dead.'

Exactly how late the navy were in putting the Canadians ashore would become a matter of dispute. The flotilla officer for *Princess Astrid*, Lieutenant Howitt, said they landed at 05.07, a delay of only seventeen minutes.[4] Surviving officers conducting a bitter post-mortem in a German prisoner-of-war camp three weeks after the disaster remembered things differently. Their recollection was that the first fragmented companies landed thirty-five minutes after zero hour with the second wave arriving one hour late. 'Effect of darkness and smokescreen entirely lost,' they noted. Whatever the precise delay it was clear the mission was no longer viable. Even before West's craft grounded 'it was quite obvious . . . that none of the plans that had been so carefully laid down in such detail could possibly work . . .'[5] But even had they landed in pitch darkness, the Royals' chance of success was slim.

The Germans were confident of the impregnability of the Puys defences. The beach and rear areas were manned by a single unit, the 12th Field Company of the 3rd Battalion of the 571st Regiment, totalling 115 men. They looked out to sea over the barrels of 75 mm cannon and MG34 machine guns concealed in pillboxes and case-mates or poking from the reinforced and heavily sandbagged windows of villas perched on the slopes of the valley. All the guns were trained on the small patch of shoreline where the Royals would have to land. The beach was bounded by a stone sea wall, ten to twelve feet high, topped by dense rolls of barbed wire, which had not shown up in the photo-reconnaissance images. Behind it lay a long low building, a casino in peacetime, transformed into a strongpoint, which commanded the beach in front of the sea wall. Anyone reaching the wall would be out of its arc of fire. However, they were exposed to enfilade fire from the left. Looking straight down on them and covering every inch of the beach was a small concrete bunker, sitting incongruously in the garden of a four-square brick villa on the eastward slope next to the sea. The machine gun inside would probably account for more Canadian dead than any single other German weapon that day.

The defenders were already on the alert following the clash at sea an hour earlier, and the sector commander Hauptmann Richard Schnösenberg was scouring the lightening skyline with his binoculars when he saw 'a big shadow looming out to sea in the mist'.[6] At first he thought it was the Dieppe-bound convoy. Then he saw the Union Jack fluttering from a mast. 'I said, "It's the English! Fire!"' he recalled later. The vague images came into focus. There, 'swimming along like little ducks' were 'hundreds of landing ships'.

Official reports stressed the calmness of the troops as they sailed into the mouth of the dragon. The Canadian Forward Observation Officer Captain George Browne, who was to coordinate naval gunfire from the destroyer *Garth*, reported that 'the Royals in my LCA appeared cool and steady. It was their first experience under fire and although I watched them closely they gave no sign of alarm, although first light was broadening into dawn and the interior of the LCA was illuminated by the many flares from the beach and the flash of the Bostons' bombs.'[7] As they readied for touchdown 'small-arms fire was striking' and there was 'a not unnatural hesitation in the bow in leaping onto the beach. But only a split second [later] . . . the troops got out and onto the beach as fast as they could and got across the beach to the wall and under the cliff.'[8]

The first rounds clanged against the sides of the LCAs when they were a hundred yards from shore. Some went straight through the armour and men started to fall. Then the troops in the first nine LCAs felt the scrape of pebbles under the hull and the bow doors went down. The German gunners now had a perfectly framed target before them and fire poured into the tightly packed ranks. Men clambered over the bodies of the dead and wounded in the rush to get out. Some hauled themselves over the sides and tumbled into the sea. Those at the front had no choice but to charge ahead. Private Tom Hunter 'was in the very front rank when the door went down. I jumped into the water which came right up to my chest'.[9] Holding his rifle above his head he floundered to the shore then slithered over the treacherous pebbles running for the sea wall which was the only cover in sight. He had 'no time to look around and I only wanted to get there as fast as possible'. Ten feet from the wall's meagre shelter shell splinters smacked into his forehead. He dived flat and pressed his head into the unyielding pebbles. 'There was nothing we could do. I didn't even have the chance to shoot back.'

Private J. E. Creer made it to the wall unharmed. He heard a Bren gunner, Private John Stevenson, shouting that he had been hit. 'He was lying behind his gun, right in the open. He had no protection around him at all. He kept shouting: "Fight! Keep fighting!" Then he was hit again and he died right there on the beach . . .'[10]

Catto's second in command Major George Scholfield was killed leading the first wave. Catto arrived with the second wave about twenty minutes later. Ross Munro, a Canadian correspondent aboard an LCM, described how 'vicious bursts of yellow tracers made a veritable curtain' around the craft as bullets whanged off the armour.[11] 'As soon as the ramp at the bow of our boat fell, fifteen Royals rushed the beach and sprinted up the slope, taking cover along the cliff side. Machine-gun fire held back the rest . . .' The cliff was at the western end of the beach and its lee provided some protection from the guns.

At the last moment the commander of Munro's LCM baulked at landing and reversed away with many of the troops still on board. Onshore, officers were shouting at their men to retreat to the second-wave boats if they could. Some managed to scramble aboard but just as the LCAs fell back, six more were arriving. They carried the Black Watch contingent led by Captain Edward Hicks. They were supposed to wait until summoned, but seeing what was happening Hicks and the flotilla commander Lieutenant Leslie Breach had taken their own decision to go to the aid of the Royals. Most of the landing-craft crews were Canadian and it was surely the intense emotion of seeing comrades in distress more than any simple military calculation that drove them on into the furnace. Hicks asked for the force to be put ashore to the west of the sea wall. They landed relatively unscathed then rushed for the cliff base where the second-wave survivors had been joined by some from the first.

Among them was Forbes West. He had stumbled ashore alongside

Catto to see 'people lying there . . . within two or three paces of where they must have left their own landing craft'. Catto was shouting instructions when West was 'hit by a machine gun which was fifty yards away on the top of the cliff . . . my left leg was completely useless'. That was the last he saw of Catto and he assumed he had been killed until he met him months later in a prisoner-of-war camp.

He lay there helpless until a fellow officer Bob Stuart, himself shot through the knee, managed to get him onto a stretcher. He lay there 'just inside the tide and there was this fellow up at the top of the cliff [who] kept throwing down stick bombs which fortunately for me landed just outside the tide mark . . . he seemed to have an endless supply'. The machine-gunner who had wounded him was determined to finish him off. 'I was in a little bit of a hollow and he could hit behind my head and he could hit in front of my feet but he couldn't hit me . . . the angle of the depression of the gun was such that he just couldn't quite make it . . .'

In the space of about twenty minutes the Royals had been reduced from a disciplined, coherent force to a remnant of dazed and powerless men, curling up to make as small a target as possible behind whatever scrap of cover they could find. There was a recess where two stone staircases led up from the sea wall which gave the illusion of a sanctuary but nowhere was really safe. 'We just had to stay close to the wall,' Sergeant John Legate told an officer conducting the first post-operational report from his hospital bed a few days afterwards.[12] 'The crossfire coming at us made it impossible to move two feet from the wall or you got it. There was nobody around to look after the wounded and if there was it was impossible to get near them.' There was no protection against the mortar bombs which 'were dropping all around us . . . it was impossible to give orders to try and do anything and it turned out to be every man for himself.'

Training had drummed home the most basic lesson of amphibious landings. To stay alive you had to get off the beach. Yet to step out of cover and charge the enemy was to invite instant death.

The unwounded officers in the first wave organised several efforts to cross the sea wall. That meant clearing a way through dense rolls of concertina wire choking the landward side. These had not been visible in the recce photographs but Colonel Catto had nonetheless ordered Bangalore torpedoes to be brought along. At least two attempts were made to blast through the barrier. Captain William Patterson 'tried to join his Bangalore torpedoes together but could not do so because stones had jammed in the locking device'.[13] He grabbed the section with the fuse in it and heaved it onto the wall 'but was hit and his equipment broke into flames'. He 'smothered the flame, went back to the wall, came up and was not seen again'.

The commander of A Company Captain Gus Sinclair was sheltering with the remnants of his group in the steps on the right of the sea wall. He and Corporal Leslie Ellis flung a Bangalore across the wire and detonated it. Ellis managed to scramble through the gap but Sinclair was killed when he tried to follow, leading a small party of men.

The shock of combat was deepened by an awful sense of powerlessness. Death came out of nowhere. Ellis spent more than an hour onshore and never saw a single German soldier.[14] They were present only in the stuttering flame of muzzle flashes, the lash of bullets and the constant din of explosions and spatter of shells and bombs. Most of the German officers and NCOs had taken part in the French campaign but a third of the defenders had not yet completed their training. Yet, as their commander Hauptmann Schnösenberg remembered proudly later, they 'shot from their dugouts, exactly according to plan . . .'

'Snipers were everywhere,' remembered Private Jack Poolton. 'One hit the rim of my helmet . . . fellows were trying to throw hand grenades . . . they'd get hit just as soon as they pulled the pin.'[15] He took cover in the recess in the wall and wondered what to do next. He was 'waiting for orders' just as he had been told to do for the last two years but no orders came. He had no idea where his platoon was and the twelve two-inch mortar bombs in the haversack on his back were much more of a danger to him than they were to the enemy for 'there was no way you could fire a two-inch mortar. You couldn't see these guys and you might hit your own men.'

Desperation drove some to self-sacrificing acts of supreme courage. Lieutenant William Wedd landed with a platoon in the first flight, only a third of whom reached the sea wall. According to survivors 'he there found he was still being fired upon by a pillbox'.[16] He broke cover 'and sprinted the short distance directly to the pillbox with an M36 grenade'. Then 'with complete disregard for his own safety and displaying great skill he flung the grenade through the fire slit . . . killing all its occupants and putting the gun out of action'. Wedd too was killed, his body 'riddled with bullets'.

The mortar teams were dead or scattered and their equipment strewn everywhere in the chaos. But when an offshore smokescreen drifted briefly over the beach Sergeant Ewart Peaks seized the chance to get a tube into action. According to Private M. Hamilton of C Company he 'got the mortar set up. I couldn't make out who helped him on account of the smoke but there were three others. They didn't get many more than three bombs [off] when Heinie found them with his machine gun and they were cut to pieces.'[17]

This was not just a figure of speech. A picture taken by the Germans immediately afterwards shows a bare-chested man lying serenely on his side on the *galets* as if he has fallen asleep while sunbathing. The bottom half of him is entirely missing.

The Germans recorded everything. It is their photographs that have printed the horror of Blue Beach for ever on the memory of anyone who wants to look at them. The most poignant is the sight of once virile young men, now inert and still as only dead bodies can be, stretched out in a crumpled row below the fatal wall.

The tight confines of the beach gave the killing a horrible intimacy that the Canadians' fathers and uncles would have known from the trenches. A man was lying next to you, cursing monotonously, his eyes wild and his breath laboured. Then a sound, indescribable but unforgettable, as metal hit flesh and life vanished. A comrade was now a corpse. It was an experience that defied description and accounts of death were strikingly detached.

'I was right behind Jack Colson when he got his,' wrote Lieutenant Mark Mather of the Black Watch from captivity a few days after the event. 'A burst of machine gun [fire] right through the eyes and head . . . except for poor Jack the BW didn't lose a man!' The nonchalance provided emotional insulation, at least temporarily.

It did no good to think about it. Nor was it possible to forget: the mingled smells of cordite and seaweed, the crack and whine of rounds and the thud of mortar bombs splintering the *galets* and the sight of humped bodies, face down and arms outstretched, seemingly at rest, swaying in the tide at the edge of a sea that was tinged with red.

At the west end of the beach beyond the wall Gunner H. J. Howe, one of the anti-aircraft detachment who landed with the Black Watch, started to climb the cliff above alongside a captain, a corporal and a few others. He was wounded before he had got a few feet and three men around him were killed. 'All of the party were knocked out and the captain alone got halfway up the cliff before his body came rolling down.'[18]

Only one group made it off the beach. Shortly after 06.00, thirty-five minutes after getting ashore, Colonel Catto took the lead in cutting a hole through a barbed-wire entanglement blocking a route up the cliff at the western end of the sea wall. A party of twenty followed him up a path leading past the Villa Les Falaises to the gardens of a house built seventy years before by the Marquess of Salisbury. Beyond it lay the road along the clifftop to Dieppe. On the way they cleared two large houses, 'resistance being met in one only'.[19] When the Germans saw what had happened they sighted a machine gun on the gap in the wire, cutting the CO off from the rest of his men. The party set off to the west hoping to join up with the Essex Scottish who by then should have left Red Beach. The enemy was all around and they were twenty men armed with rifles and Sten guns. They spent the next hours concealed in a wood behind the six-gun 88 mm anti-aircraft battery on the clifftop, watching impotently the disaster unfolding below.

Any ship daring to approach shore was at the mercy of the gunners who, though the smokescreens laid by aircraft and ships made their job more difficult, could still calculate accurately where destroyers and gunboats would have to manoeuvre to fire, and focus on the patches of sea where they were likely to emerge.

Captain Derek Turner of the Royal Artillery was directing the guns of HMS *Garth* and supposed to be liaising via wireless with George Browne onshore. His first attempts to raise him failed. In the meantime *Garth* carried on shelling targets on the eastern headland though it was clear that the effects were slight. They were engaged in a duel in which the enemy had the advantage. 'Their rate of fire was just a little higher than ours – round about ten to twelve rounds per gun per minute' he recorded in his diary.[20] 'Every time they flashed we all ducked down behind the hopelessly thin 'armour plating' around the bridge . . . there was an infernal whine of muck flying around . . . our high-velocity guns had little chance of scoring a hit on the Germans' "hull-down" positions on the clifftops.'

Garth's captain, Lieutenant Commander John Scatchard, reported later that '[enemy] fire was extremely accurate and it was impossible to go in and carry out a steady bombardment.'[21] It was 'a matter of going in through the smoke till close, squaring off and then retiring, then circling round and repeating the manoeuvre. On each occasion we were straddled and it seems extraordinary that more ships were not hit.'

When Turner at last received a message from Browne it was clear that he was in no position to help. It read: 'Landed. Sea wall too high to cross. Can you send boats to take off casualties.' Turner sent an acknowledgement and then passed on Browne's plea to the HQ ship *Calpe* by Aldis lamp.

This, like other crucial signals, was never received, or if it was, no action was taken. Browne's appeal did somehow get through to Lieutenant Noel Ramsay on LCA 209 who took the enormous risk of responding to it. Together with a support landing craft, LCS 8, commanded by Lieutenant Francis Keep, he steered towards the smoke and flames.

Keep gave what covering fire his 40 mm cannon and four machine guns could provide as Ramsay headed full tilt for the shore, grounding the craft on the beach. 'There was a terrible scramble and nearly everyone still alive made for the small ramp doors,' Private Edward Simpson of the Royals reported later. 'The slaughter was awful. The boat had to be pushed off the beach. It was so full of holes it began to sink'. Simpson reckoned at least fifty men were aboard. 'Bullets were still pouring in and a bomb landed alongside.' The bow door was so thick with bodies that it jammed when they tried to raise it. Corporal

Ellis who had made his way back to the beach saw 'a naval rating hitting the hands of men who were trying to climb aboard'.[22]

Holed and hopelessly overloaded, LCA 209 capsized but stayed afloat. A few men swam away while others, including Simpson, 'clung to the still-floating craft. We were only a few hundred yards from the shore and were still being blasted by enemy fire.' The sharpshooters scanning the shoreline added the boat to their list of targets. A post-operational report told the story of Gunner Rowe from the Light Anti-Aircraft detachment who was also clinging to the LCA's hull: 'If anybody onshore or where he was, a hundred yards offshore, moved the slightest bit the move was rewarded with a sniper's bullet. The chap clinging next to him was hit three times immediately after moving from the pain of his wounds.'

Ellis had decided to swim for it. Dread of capture outweighed the terrible risk and 'taking off his boots and equipment [he] plunged into the sea. While he was doing the crawl a sniper fired at him and a bullet came within a few inches of his nose. He pretended to be hit . . .'[23] He pulled off his life jacket and all his clothes and swam for the next two hours. He salvaged another Mae West from a corpse with a neat bullet hole through his forehead, the victim he assumed of a sniper. Just before he passed out from exhaustion he was picked up by survivors from Ramsay's LCA who had climbed aboard an abandoned dinghy.

Ramsay paid for his gallantry with his life. After that no more boats came. The men on the beach were on their own. They huddled in the lee of the cliffs. The noise of firing gradually faded. Now there was just the occasional crack of a sniper rifle or the thud of a mortar or stick grenade tossed from above. More than 200 men were dead or mortally wounded and very few were untouched by bullet or shrapnel.[24]

Around 08.00, the Germans began to show themselves. Forbes West was lying immobilised from his useless leg when 'the Germans came along the beach and allowed our people who were sound to start gathering up the wounded.'[25] He had just been hoisted onto the sea wall on a stretcher when an RAF attack came in. 'There wasn't anything we could do to stop it . . . we couldn't say, boys, it's all over and you're killing us not the Germans. So the bombs came down and then the Germans made all the people who had been helping pick up the wounded get off the beach. And then the tide came in and unquestionably some people who might have been picked up went out with the tide because they were too badly wounded to help themselves.'

At the water's edge the stretcher-bearers saw a nightmarish sight. 'It was unbelievable,' remembered Jack Poolton.[26] 'There were boots with feet in them, there were legs. There were bits of flesh. There were guts. There were heads. This was my regiment. These were the guys I had lived with for the last two and a half years.'

The third casualty he helped carry back was a heavily built man who had been shot through the groin. 'We got him up . . . and I don't know how we did it. It just seemed as though you had superhuman strength or energy . . . it was something that must be done.'

After three trips the Germans ordered them to stop. An officer walked the beach, 'shooting the worst of the wounded Canadians in the forehead'. Poolton felt physically sick but had 'nothing in there to puke . . . I thought, God almighty, is there no end to this slaughter?' He told himself that perhaps it was 'an act of mercy' on the Germans' part, 'but I didn't quite buy it'. What he saw on the beach would never leave him: 'Guys had their guts out . . . you could see these intestines and they were trying to stuff them back in. The men were still alive. Not crying, not screaming, not moaning, not saying anything.'

On board *Calpe* Ham Roberts looked out at the smoke-shrouded shore, ignorant of the true situation on Blue Beach. Contact with the men on land was almost non-existent and the messages that did get through were contradictory. Roberts's stolid features had never given much away. The American war correspondent Quentin Reynolds who was by his side noticed him once 'shifting uneasily in his chair' but nothing he said betrayed his feelings and it was impossible to tell whether his impassiveness was a sign of stoicism or a mask for panic and despair.[27]

What small sway he had over events was now crippled by a breakdown in communications with the fighting units. The signals arrangements devised for Jubilee were as complicated as the operation itself. The plan sought to keep all the disparate elements on land, sea and air in touch with each other and required numerous overlapping networks and frequencies.

The signals instructions were tinged with the same delusional quality that permeated many of Mann's orders, taking little account of the actions of the enemy or the reality of battle. One instructed signals teams to run telephone lines between the two brigade HQs ashore which were 'to be checked at repeated intervals and any faults or breaks will be repaired immediately'.[28]

The attention to detail was faultless. There was even provision for thwarting enemy attempts to break into the networks to pass bogus orders. Suspect callers were to be challenged by asking them to supply a code word for a given number. There were twelve of them, all beginning with 'V', ranging from 'Varnish' to 'Volume'. The arrangement conjured up the blackly farcical image of a signaller yelling 'Vomit' to a disbelieving colleague across the net as the battle raged all around.

The signals plan failed to address a likelier scenario: the wholesale loss of equipment and operators due to enemy action. On Blue Beach, the landing craft carrying the beachmaster and his signals team was driven back by enemy fire and unable to land.[29] The battalion HQ No. 18 wireless set linking it to *Calpe* was soaked and useless and the signallers anyway almost all dead or incapacitated. One radio that did survive was the set with Captain Browne. Via his signaller Browne managed to get several messages to *Garth* between 05.41 and 07.47, all of which made clear the desperation of the situation. However neither they, nor the Aldis lamp signal that Turner reported sending after his first contact with Browne, was noted in the *Calpe* intelligence log. The signals they did receive gave entirely the wrong picture of what was happening. The first, timed at 06.20 reported: 'R. Regt C. not landed.'[30]

Roberts's response to this was inexplicable. The failure of the Royals to land meant that the eastern headland was in all likelihood still in enemy hands, in which case the frontal assault by the Essex Scottish on Red Beach was almost certainly going to end in disaster.

Nevertheless, twenty minutes after receiving the report, Roberts ordered the Royals to Red Beach to support the Essex Scottish. Had the report been true, this command would have resulted in the Royals' likely annihilation.

It was not until sometime after 07.00, when the senior Blue Beach naval officer, Lieutenant Commander Goulding visited *Calpe*, that Roberts learned the truth. The news was followed by a plaintive message passed on by *Garth*: 'From Blue Beach: Is there any possible chance of getting us off?' Roberts did then order an evacuation attempt but it was far too late. The Royals, and the Black Watch and gunners with them, were already finished.

II

For all the shortcomings of the plan, the events on Green Beach showed that, given an element of surprise, determined troops and outstanding leadership, some degree of success was possible. Pourville was an easier proposition than Puys. The beach was long and the valley of the Scie behind was wide. The heights on either side were strongly defended but the landscape provided scope for both cover and positions from which to launch attacks.

The South Saskatchewans landed in one wave and on time at 04.50. Their first task was to establish a bridgehead. The Camerons of Canada were to land half an hour later and pass through them on their way to attack the aerodrome at Saint-Aubin and, if time allowed, the divisional HQ believed to be at Arques.

The Saskatchewans' A Company was to push east of Pourville, capturing the guns on the cliff as well as the radar station. The company was supposed to link up with the Rileys advancing from Dieppe. Then, supported by a troop of the Calgary Tanks they would reinforce D Company's effort to overrun the defences around Quatre Vents farm south of the headland and just under a mile from the beach. Meanwhile C Company would clear positions on the high ground to the east before consolidating with the others around Quatre Vents. Mission completed they would fall back on the Dieppe beaches for re-embarkation.

As they neared the shore there was no sign of the enemy. It was only when the last craft touched down on the extreme right of the beach that gunfire was heard and the first men were hit. Officers commanding men in action for the first time were learning the necessity of leading by example. When Lieutenant John Edmondson arrived at the head of D Company at the sea wall and the barbed-wire barrier that ran along it, he called for a Bangalore torpedo only to be told there were none. Then he ordered wire cutters and scaling ladders to be brought up. He remembered saying, ' "We need the wires cut" and the tracer going *tat tat tat* over the top. And they look at you and you look at them and it's painfully obvious that this is a question of who goes first, the officer or the man.' He ended up 'crawling up the ladder and cutting the thing myself as the tracer whistled over . . .'[31]

Once across they were dismayed to find that like most of the troops they had been put ashore at the wrong place. The landing had been planned so each company grounded at the point nearest its objective, with those attacking to the east touching down left of the River Scie and those to the west to the right. As they regrouped in Pourville's main street it was clear that instead of the landing being made astride the river, the bulk of the force were stuck to the west of it. To get to the eastern headland meant crossing the river, which was spanned by a narrow bridge which was covered by the numerous gun positions on the eastern heights.

What slight edge of surprise the raiders had gained by a timely arrival under cover of darkness was now lost. The error thus determined that few of the day's objectives would be achieved.

Nonetheless the morning started well. Pourville was essentially a single street lined with villas and hotels. A battalion HQ was set up in a garage while the village was cleared. Shells and mortar bombs were landing in the streets now. Despite the raised alert level ordered by the divisional commander, many of the defenders were still in bed and many had joined the fight still in their underwear. The Canadians cleared the town with sub-machine-gun fire and grenades. One large seafront hotel was found to be full of foreign workers from the Todt organisation whose bunker-building programme had been in full swing for weeks. A platoon from A Company killed or captured the guards and then moved on to take positions around a white house referred to in intelligence reports as the 'Maison Blanche'.

The action that followed showed what the Canadians could do if the odds were not, as they had been on Blue Beach, devastatingly stacked against them. At the crest of the first rise they came under fire and there were several casualties including Sergeant Harry Long who was leading them. Lance Corporal Guy Berthelot and Private William Haggard stepped forward to take the initiative. The fire was coming from slit trenches around the house, held by about fifty Germans equipped with four machine guns. Haggard told two sections to stay where they were and attack when they heard the volume of firing increase. He then took the third section and they worked their way round the trenches to attack the defenders in the rear. In the rush that followed, Berthelot was wounded as he ran across the open ground, firing his Bren from the hip. The fight was brief. Twelve prisoners were taken and the rest killed.

A small portion of the battalion was landed to the east of the river or had waded across it, unmolested, at the mouth. This was the Special Platoon tasked with taking out a wired strongpoint under the eastern cliff which could fire straight down on the road leading to the headland and Quatre Vents farm. They stepped ashore apparently unobserved but after a hundred yards came under fire from a roadblock lying on a bend where the route leading east out of Pourville turned south past Quatre Vents. Lieutenant Leslie England and several others were wounded and Sergeant Ralph Neil took command. As they pushed forward they met heavy machine-gun fire. With only light weapons it would be impossible – or suicidal – to attempt to take the strongpoint.

Meanwhile A and D Companies had to cross the short span over the Scie to approach their objectives. The bridge was about a hundred feet long and just over twenty feet wide. It was obvious to the Germans the line of attack an amphibious force would have to take. Barbed-wire barriers created a funnel at either end and machine guns and mortars were ranged to cover every yard. Captain Murray Osten of A Company led his men across while D Company gave covering fire. Others found a way round the wire, slithered down the bank and waded across.

Sergeant Basil Smith and his section were right behind Osten and ran straight into 'very heavy machine-gun fire'. Once across 'the fire was very heavy from two pillboxes situated one on top of the other on the forward slope of the hill'. In addition 'there were snipers and riflemen firing from the slope along the road leading up the hill. The machine guns appeared to be firing on fixed arcs and were very accurate and all were mutually supporting covering nearly all dead ground.'[32]

Despite losses, a group from A Company made it across and gathered around Osten in the shelter of a roadblock where the road swept inland. They were joined by the remnants of the Special Platoon. The path to the radar station lay straight ahead but a pillbox sited on the bend blocked the way. For half an hour they were pinned back by its fire until Private Charles Sawden announced that he was willing to 'take out the bastard'. With a grenade in each hand he moved out of cover. Private Victor Story was one of those watching in horrified admiration as he 'strolled nonchalantly up the hill to the pillbox, lobbed the two grenades through the gun slits and wiped it out killing four Jerries'.[33]

The A Company men now swung inland and began to climb the slope. Within their ranks was an RAF electronics expert charged with one of several secret operations bolted onto Rutter during its conception. Flight Sergeant Jack Nissenthall worked before the war under Robert Watson-Watt at the experimental radar station at Bawdsey Manor in Suffolk. He had agreed to go with the Canadians to try to bring back equipment and documents which would help British scientists understand how the new Freya 28 apparatus worked.

He was briefed by Bobby de Casa Maury who told him that, given his expert knowledge, it was imperative that he was not captured and if he was wounded his escorts were ordered to shoot him rather than leave him behind.[34] Now, led by Osten, they were 'zigzagging uphill, crawling in the drainage ditch alongside the gravelly, flinty road'. Intense machine-gun and sniper fire poured from positions further up the hill. It was supplemented by uncannily accurate mortar fire and it seemed to Nissenthall that the Germans had worked out precisely where attacking troops would have to advance and where they would look for cover. They managed to clear a battery on the clifftop, but as they moved on to the radar station, hugging every ditch and hollow in the hillside, casualties mounted. Long before they reached the perimeter, of the ten-man escort, three were dead and three were walking wounded.

By now the Camerons were running in to shore. They were arriving a little late, fifteen minutes after their scheduled time of 05.20 as their CO Colonel Alfred Gostling had decided on a short delay to give the Saskatchewans more time to pacify Pourville and suppress the beach defences. Hunched in his R-boat Sergeant Marcel Swank of the US Rangers watched 'tracers streaming into our flotilla. They seemed to just float in . . . I could see mortars landing on the water's edge.' However he was soon distracted by something else. 'With all the noise; the roar of the motors, the sound of gunfire off the beach, the mortars exploding, the destroyers firing back at the shore batteries, I heard this sound. At first I couldn't understand what it was . . . I turned to my right and there, braced against the cabin of the craft next to me stood a piper with a Highland bonnet on, streamers flying from his bonnet, pipes under his arm, playing the "Hundred Pipers".' It was the B Company piper, Alex Graham, and Swank felt that 'never in my life before had I been so emotionally stirred'.[35]

Gostling seemed supremely confident. He was 'very cool and collected', reported a young Canadian naval sub lieutenant Johnny O'Rourke afterwards. As the din of battle rolled over the water he called out to his men 'different explanations of the different types of fire under which they found themselves – for example "Listen to that – that's the mobile artillery."'[36]

They landed in full view of the strongpoint on the left of the beach. Gostling was killed almost as soon as he stepped ashore, going down in a squall of bullets. The Camerons stumbled over pebbles 'the size of eggs and terrible to cross' to the shelter of the sea wall which they scrambled across in a shower of mortar fire.

They had planned to reach Saint-Aubin-sur-Scie and Arques-la-Bataille via the road that ran south along the east side of the Scie valley where they would meet up with the Calgary Tanks advancing from Dieppe. Major Andrew Law who had taken over command now judged this to be impossible. There was an alternative route south along the road that ran up the west bank of the Scie. Law radioed the change of plan to the companies, leaving one to help out the Saskatchewans.

A substantial part of the Saskatchewans was still stuck at the eastern end of Pourville, bottled up behind the terrible chicane of the bridge. The village was being reduced to rubble around them and they were taking casualties from mortars, machine guns and a four-gun 105 mm battery south of the town.

The Saskatchewans' medical officer Captain Francis Hayter set up the Regimental Aid Post in two locations: one, a double garage in a house on the main street where the battalion had established its first HQ, the other a shed on the seaward side of the road near the beach. The equipment he and his team had to work with was minimal, just basic surgical instruments, antibacterial sulphanilamide powder, morphine and lots of shell dressings.

The first patients were the victims of a single mortar bomb which killed several German prisoners and some Canadians and wounded others. After that, Hayter reported, 'casualties were brought in quite rapidly for some time and I would go first to the garage then to the shed and the field, attending to the wounded in each place and then repeating the circuit.'[37] After treatment the wounded were stretchered or walked to a collecting point by an abandoned machine-gun post on the promenade and lowered onto the beach along the foot of the sea wall which offered some protection from enemy fire. An attempt was made to bring a landing craft in to take off the wounded but it was forced back by machine-gun and mortar fire from the cliffs.

The Germans had been steadily militarising the seaside village in the weeks before the attack, blowing up some houses and turning the others into strongpoints, but there were still civilians living in Pourville and the surrounding villages and hamlets. The soldiers were astonished by their insouciance as they emerged from their homes to see what was going on.

Mountbatten had given precise instructions on how to deal with

French civilians. Troops were issued with leaflets announcing 'this is a raid and not the invasion' and advising the locals 'not to get involved in any way that could result in enemy reprisals'. It finished: 'When the time comes we will let you know and it is then we will take action side by side for our common victory and your freedom!'[38] No civilians were to be evacuated except for 'certain individuals to be selected by representatives of SOE' who had invited themselves along in yet another bolt-on mission.[39] However, commanders were allowed to 'permit the last-minute evacuation of such individuals as cannot reasonably be left on humanitarian grounds'. An exception was also made for 'fisherfolk who have their own craft' who would be allowed to sail to England under Allied protection.

Despite the devastation being done to their village, an unnamed intelligence officer attached to the Camerons (probably Captain E. D. Magnus) reported later that the inhabitants were 'undoubtedly glad to see us' and 'helped us on many occasions . . . their complete disregard of personal danger was most remarkable'.[40] In one house young women fed wine and cakes to snipers firing from upper-storey windows. Some were eager to leave with the Canadians including a sixteen-year-old boy who 'came from the hills to join our forces. He displayed marks on his wrists where he had been slashed by the Germans for allegedly not working hard enough.'[41] The story may have had a tragic ending. Local French official Roger Lefebvre recorded in his diary how a young man who had been dissuaded from going back with the Canadians was nonetheless trying to get into a boat to join the departing flotilla when German machine-gun fire 'hit him right in the heart while he was still on the *galets*'.[42]

Taking captives was one of the raid objectives and Green Beach produced a big haul. It seemed to some that guarding prisoners while you were fighting for your life was a waste of manpower. Later a few admitted shooting their charges out of hand.[43] Most prisoners briefly interrogated by the Camerons' intelligence officer who was unimpressed by the quality of the enemy. Beforehand they were disabled by having their thumbs tied together with cord, a practice taught to the units during training on the Isle of Wight.[44] Roberts had objected to this when it appeared in the Jubilee orders, only to be overruled by Mountbatten.

The twenty-five taken by the Saskatchewans in Pourville were 'of extremely poor calibre, thoroughly frightened and badly chewed up by small-arms fire. There were about four Polish conscripts in the lot who could not speak German. In fact they could barely understand it . . . The NCO in charge was, however, a higher type of soldier, a competent-looking Rhinelander, evidently a stiffening element. They were all anxious to talk . . .'

As the raiders were learning all along the front, their superior fighting qualities counted for little when faced with a mass of well-protected positions manned by troops who only needed to stay at their posts and keep firing their weapons to turn back even the most determined attack.

Without effective naval gunfire and bomber and fighter support there was no chance of taking the headland and high ground to the east. The Saskatchewans had gone ashore with a Canadian gunner, Captain Harvey Carswell, whose job was to coordinate with the guns of HMS *Albrighton*. Colonel Merritt ordered him to work his way forward to a position where he could call down fire and observe the fall of shells on the headland. He got as far as the bridge where enemy fire made crossing impossible, so he asked for mortars to be brought up but they did not have the range to hit the hillside positions. Next he radioed *Albrighton* and called in a bombardment but the shells fell over or under, and the fire mission was called off for fear of hitting A Company and Special Platoon men in the area. Carswell was soon convinced that the Germans were using radio detection and 'had our set located as every time we endeavoured to signal [the] ship, houses and vicinity were shelled'.[45]

The force was now cut in half. A Company and most of D Company had got across the bridge but their advance was stalled. A portion of D Company and most of B Company were still stranded on the west side of the bridge. Another rush produced another crop of casualties. Private J. Krohn of D Company told later how 'Chiltern, Evenden, Pickford, [Private] Carswell and myself were fired upon when we reached halfway across . . . Carswell was wounded together with two other boys beside me.' He 'flattened out, rolled myself over the side into the canal [*sic*] at the same time dragging one of the boys with me'.[46]

Colonel Merritt had been trying to direct the battle from his HQ, which had now shifted from the garage to the abandoned casino on the seaward side of the main street. Messages arrived by radio and runner reporting the crisis at the bridge. He now decided to lead from the front in the most literal manner possible, setting an example of icy courage that those who witnessed it would never forget.

It was a cardinal – though often violated – principle of military leadership that you did not ask your men to do anything that you were not prepared to do yourself. Merritt now honoured that rule, not once but over and over again.

On the approach to the bridge, men from D and B Companies were crouched in cover, eyes fixed on the short stretch of tarmac littered with the dead and wounded. Lieutenant Edmondson and some of his D Company HQ team were preparing to stretch a toggle-rope line underneath the bridge to help them get across the river when Colonel Merritt arrived. He immediately took charge telling Edmondson this would take too long. He then took off his helmet, wiped the sweat from his eyes and swinging the tin hat by its strap walked calmly into the middle of the span and with bullets kicking around him, shouted to the men to come across. Lieutenant Nesbitt got to his feet and he and the men of 17 Platoon followed their commander. 'He led the way and we crossed OK and I do not think we had any casualties,' he recalled. [47]

Once over they ran for cover while Merritt returned to lead another group of forty, mostly from B Company. Captain R. M. Campbell watched Merritt 'continually exposing himself. On many occasions he crossed over the bridge, urging his men forward and calling, "See, there is no danger here!"' The men 'followed him splendidly but were shot down time after time'. By the end, according to Lieutenant Edmondson, 'the dead were piled up two deep for about fifty feet along the bridge.' [48]

Merritt made at least four crossings to break the impasse. Those who had made it regrouped in a large grey house a hundred yards beyond the bridge. There was yet another peril to overcome before they could advance on the heights.

The men who had gone before them had noticed that even when

they put a pillbox out of action it did not stay silent for long and enemy soldiers sometimes slipped forward to reoccupy it. A machine gun dead ahead and covering the road appeared to be in action once more. All eyes were fixed on the CO as everybody steeled themselves to rush into its field of fire.

Merritt ordered a discarded mortar to be collected and smoke rounds to be fired at the pillbox. Then, according to Private Leslie Thrussel, he 'stepped out into the road and loped up to the pillbox and blew it up'.

Merritt was determined to keep the attack moving. 'There was heavy fire coming down on the road and I joined a group of men who were held up,' remembered Sergeant Barney McBride. 'I heard the colonel speak and he said, "We must get ahead lads. We need more men up front as quick as possible. Who's coming with me?" I replied, "We're all going with you." He said, "Good lads. Let's go." We ran up the road with Colonel Merritt leading. Disregarding all danger he led us straight up the road and after forty yards he stopped. Soon the colonel said, "Are you ready again?" We answered. "OK sir", and away we went again . . .'[49]

At last D Company reached the slopes below Quatre Vents farm. They had been joined by a squad of Camerons, among them Marcel Swank. In an attempt to give some coherence, descriptions of battles invariably impose a sequence and order on events that give the combat a shape that is not apparent at the time to those fighting it. Swank's experience gave some taste of the disjointed reality, a hallucinatory mixture of chaos and sudden devastating violence interspersed with surreal interludes of calm.

He went ashore with another Ranger, Sergeant Lloyd Church. A Cameron sergeant had been assigned to escort them but as they entered Pourville a mortar bomb burst nearby blowing Swank to the ground. When he looked up the sergeant was dead and Church had disappeared. He was on his own. He walked up the street, hugging the wall of 'what looked like a large white hotel' until he realised a sniper was shooting at him and 'slid into a wine cellar which made beautiful cover'. Inside were 'a Frenchman and about three Frenchwomen'. They 'talked for a while as best we could'. Then they were joined by a Canadian soldier. Swank could have stayed there all day but 'personal pride' drove him to ask the new arrival for directions to the nearest command post.[50]

He left his sanctuary and found the Saskatchewans' garage HQ. No one took any notice of him. There were bodies lying around and prisoners were being interrogated, the first Germans he had seen. He felt a sense of uselessness. He had been shot at a lot but not fired a single round himself. He was there to gain battle experience and represent his country, yet as he wryly recalled thus far he had 'not done one thing for the honour or glory of the United States Army'.

He returned to the main street and the mortars. They were crashing on the roofs, blasting shards of slate that were just as deadly as shrapnel in all directions. He headed east to where he knew the main attack was aimed and somewhere along the way ran into gaggle of Saskatchewans and Camerons forming a scratch platoon. He joined them and they moved off, eventually joining the D Company attack on Quatre Vents farm. They 'did the best [we] could [but we] just weren't able to get through the wire and the automatic-weapons fire that covered it to get to the mortars and what have you that were plastering the town'. After throwing smoke canisters they eventually fell back, leaving 'five or six dead on the hillside' and 'most of the balance of the platoon wounded'.

Guts alone could not overcome the defenders' advantages. Without proper artillery support and with most of the mortar teams now out of action they were merely sacrificing themselves in a useless venture. After falling back, Merritt ordered a party off to help A Company at the radar station. The situation there was no better. Jack Nissenthall managed to cut the telephone wires meaning the radar operators had to revert to insecure radio communication which could be intercepted in England and might provide some useful data. But the Freya compound and the equipment inside, 'with its barbed-wire fence, its machine-gun nests . . . was simply impregnable to our small force'.[51]

The Camerons' advance up the west bank of the Scie was also caught in the same web of interlocking fire that ensnared the whole gallant effort. The only event that could change the situation was the arrival of the Calgary Tanks over the headland. After three hours ashore it was clear that they would not be coming. All they could do now was hold on for the order to withdraw. This would not now be through Dieppe as the plan had so optimistically ordained, but from the same beach they had arrived on, and with the Germans falling on them with every backward step they took.

Red and White

As the craft carrying the Essex Scottish and the Rileys neared Red and White Beaches for the main assault it was still possible for Ham Roberts to believe that things were going well. The landing craft were on time, touching down at 05.20 or a few minutes after. The destroyers were banging away at the shore defences.

Meanwhile light-bomber squadrons were scheduled to attack the east and west headlands and batteries behind the town ten minutes before the landings. Others would lay smoke to mask the landing craft as they closed the beaches.

At 05.09 ten twin-engine Bostons from 226 Squadron arrived over the east headland and 100 lb smoke canisters tumbled from the bomb bays. According to Squadron Leader G. R. 'Digger' Magill the bombs were 'simple enough being largish "biscuit tins" filled with a phosphorus compound which simply ignited and made masses of smoke when exposed to the air'. It was, as he wryly observed, 'a handy load to have in the bomb bay when there was a lot of flak about . . .'[1]

As he came in, his aircraft shook with the impact of a flak shell – not from the German 88s, he believed, but from the Oerlikon cannons of the British fleet – and 'we found ourselves with a fine old fire going on underneath until we dumped our load as near as we could to the battery . . . just over the clifftop.' Then it was the turn of the enemy anti-aircraft guns and nine aircraft were hit. The gun crews knew their job, as bomb-aimer Flight Lieutenant Jock Cairns of 88 Squadron learned when he began his bombing run, still in semi-darkness, on the Rommel battery just south of Blue Beach. '[The] searchlights came into operation at the same time as the [AA] batteries opened fire,' he remembered. 'When we were about ten seconds from dropping point we were picked up by . . . what we assumed was the master searchlight – possibly radar-controlled as it just came straight up at us and held us without any searching, and then we were coned by several others . . .'

For all the perils, the crews had no wish to change places with the tiny figures in the landing craft. The upturned faces watching them go over reminded James Pelly-Fry, the 88 Squadron CO, 'for some reason of a *Daily Express* Giles cartoon – little men with snub noses and round faces. I was thankful to be an airman.'

Five Hurricane squadrons were also in the air over the main beaches. The first to arrive was a wing of thirty-four fighters led by Squadron Leader Daniel le Roy du Vivier of 43 Squadron, who flew with the Belgian air force before escaping to England and joining the RAF. They took off in darkness from Tangmere near Chichester at the foot of the Downs at 04.25 arriving exactly on time at 05.10. The Hurricanes were armed with four 20 mm cannon. They approached in line abreast delivering one attack then peeling off to return for a second run. It was still too dark to pick out individual gun positions and they soaked the seafront and headlands with fire which even if inaccurate cheered the Canadians as their craft closed the beaches. The German gunners were uncowed. A Canadian, Flight Sergeant Hank Wik of 43 Squadron, was the first pilot to die when his Hurricane was caught by flak and went down in flames in a field behind the town. Pilot Officer A. E. Snell, also of 43 Squadron was forced to bail out but was picked up by an LCT and spent the rest of the day on board manning a machine gun.

That day, the Royal Air Force and the Luftwaffe fought their greatest battle. In the sixteen hours that it lasted, the RAF threw the largest array of aircraft it had ever assembled in the war to date, flying 3,000 sorties against the Germans' 945. From first light, Leigh-Mallory intended to open an umbrella over the sea approaches and beaches to protect the fleet and the troops from attack and to fend off the enemy fighters swarming to shield their bombers which throughout the day pressed home attacks on the armada with grim determination. The result was an epic that distracted the men on the ground from their own intense experience and moved them to awed admiration.

★

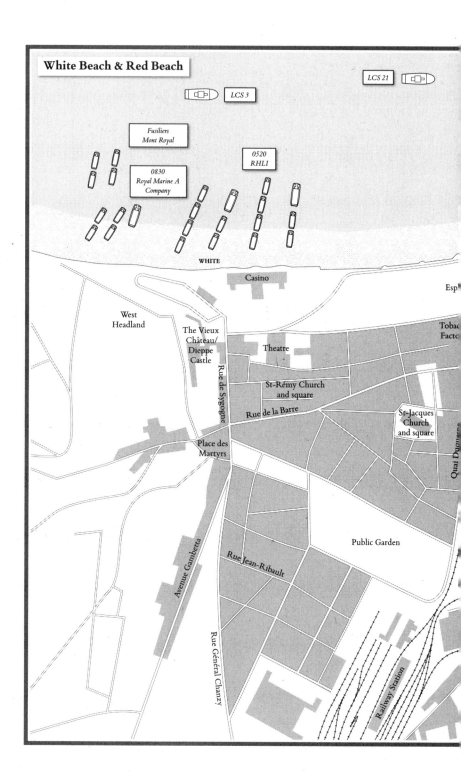

White Beach & Red Beach

LCS 21

LCS 3

Fusiliers
Mont Royal

0520
RHLI

0830
Royal Marine A
Company

WHITE

Casino

Esp

West
Headland

The Vieux
Château/
Dieppe
Castle

Theatre

Toba
Fact

St-Rémy Church
and square

Rue de la Barre

St-Jacques
Church
and square

Rue de Sygogne

Place des
Martyrs

Quai Duquesne

Public Garden

Avenue Gambetta

Rue Jean-Ribault

Rue Général Chanzy

Railway Station

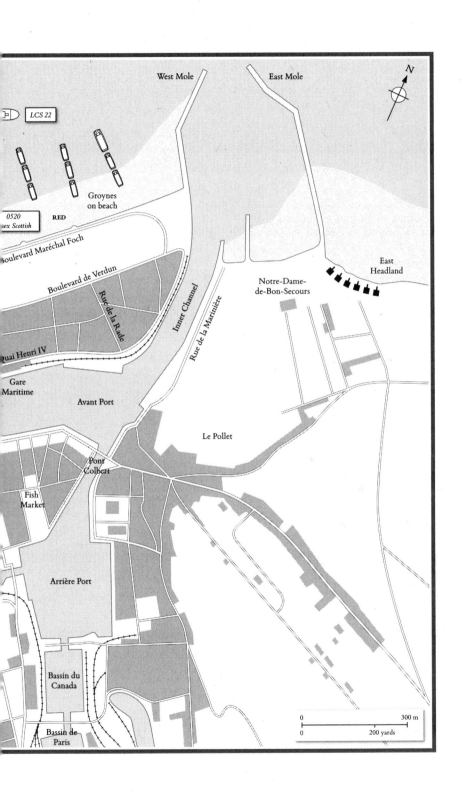

West Mole

East Mole

N

LCS 22

Groynes
on beach

0520
sex Scottish

RED

Boulevard Maréchal Foch

Boulevard de Verdun

Rue de la Rade

Quai Henri IV

Gare
Maritime

Avant Port

Inner Channel

Rue de la Martinière

East
Headland

Notre-Dame-
de-Bon-Secours

Le Pollet

Pont
Colbert

Fish
Market

Arrière Port

Bassin du
Canada

Bassin de
Paris

0		300 m
0		200 yards

While the German gunners were firing at the attacking bombers and fighters they were distracted from shooting at the approaching craft. They were also having to contend with the barrage raised by the destroyers *Berkeley*, *Bleasdale*, *Garth* and *Albrighton* which, as the air assault opened, laid smoke then joined in the general bombardment, setting three buildings on the front ablaze. On board *Garth*, Goronwy Rees, Montgomery's liaison officer who had got himself attached to the force as an observer, described Lieutenant Commander Scatchard's technique with anxious respect. 'Calm and unmoved on the bridge [he] continued to issue his series of rapid, precise, thin-lipped orders,' he wrote.

> *Garth*'s tactics were simple. We dashed along the shore and when opposite the gun position fired broadside with all our guns. At the same time the gun on the cliff replied, bracketing us with one shot over us, one short of us and one accurately on the target. At that moment *Garth* dived behind the blanket of smoke which she had raised as soon as her salvo had been fired; then we raced behind our protective smokescreen to reappear again and release our broadside at the gun position . . . [2]

Watching from the deck of *Calpe*, Hughes-Hallett's personal assistant Sub Lieutenant Ranald Boyle scrawled the progress of the attack in a reporter's notebook, as ordered by his boss. Everything seemed to be going to plan.

> 05.12 Smokescreen being laid. Extremely effective. Large amount of fire now and planes flying very low inshore.
>
> 05.15 Destroyers start smoke barrage. Terrific fire from coast guns now. Planes all round.
>
> 05.20 Spitfires [*sic*] attacking coastal batteries. 4 LCTs approaching beach. Terrific fire . . .
>
> 05.38 Terrific fire all round. Some shells passing overhead, others at side. Bullets also. Smokescreen still most effective. LCTs going in firing all round under smoke. Wind is offshore so smoke slowly drifting this way. Other ships coming round firing. All most effective. [3]

The LCTs were carrying the first flight of the Calgary tanks. Despite Boyle's optimism, things were already going wrong. For the

Essex Scottish and the Rileys to get across the beach and into the town it was vital that the defences were suppressed or at least distracted by a continuous bombardment. The naval and air attacks were due to cease just before the Canadians hit the beach. Fire support would then be in the hands of the tanks, the first of which were timed to touch down alongside the LCAs and open up on pillboxes, strongpoints and batteries while the infantry scrambled across the bleak expanse of bullet-swept pebbles and mounted the promenade. Once the seafront was secure the engineer parties on board the LCTs could blow the obstacles blocking the tanks' path into town.

The transition from one barrage to the other had to be all but seamless. As soon as the navy and RAF overture stopped the German gunners would be unmolested and could start to chop down the platoons as soon as the bow doors opened. If there was not to be a massacre, the LCTs could not be a minute late.

The first three LCTs and their nine tanks were due to touch down at 05.20. They arrived at about 05.35. The missing minutes would later be blamed for almost everything that went wrong on Red and White Beaches. The LCT flotilla was under the command of Lieutenant Commander Earl Beatty, son of the famous First World War admiral. Hughes-Hallett's subsequent despatch said they 'approached too far from the westward and were about ten to fifteen minutes late in touching down'.[4] Subsequent inquiries never established the cause for the delay which was vaguely ascribed in the Admiralty's report as due to 'navigational difficulties'.[5] It is unlikely that punctuality would have changed anything. The tanks could not on their own neutralise the enfilade fire pouring down from the headlands or the guns pumping out from the promenade. At best, their presence at the crucial moment might have lightened the casualties but they would never have swung the balance from defeat to victory.

Half an hour before landing the 350-horsepower engines of the Churchills coughed into life filling the LCTs with exhaust fumes. Crouched claustrophobically in each was a crew of five: commander, gunner, loader/radio operator, driver and a co-driver cum hull-gunner. There was a mixture of types from the Mark I which carried a 40 mm 'two-pounder' and a .303 machine gun in the turret and a three-inch howitzer in the hull, to the Mark III which mounted a 57 mm 'six-pounder' as its main armament. Their view of the battlefield was restricted to the small patches of vision offered by an armoured glass slit and two periscopes.

They were facing a huge test and without the benefit of prior experience. Never before had tanks been landed on a hostile shore to do battle. The choice of Dieppe as the first place to attempt it was, as Mann had acknowledged, 'almost a fantastical conception'. Nonetheless with characteristic optimism, he judged that the appearance of the tanks would create a shock that 'could have a terrific moral effect on . . . Germans'. The next few minutes would show whether or not he was right.

The first two flights of six LCTs landed within ten minutes of each other, carrying eighteen tanks. It was clear that the effect of the air and sea bombardment had been only temporary. Sergeant John Marsh, commanding a Black Watch detachment, was on LCT 2 which arrived at the east end of Red Beach, next to the harbour breakwater. His post-action report gave a taste of the drama that ensued. 'Letting the ramp down seemed to be a signal for all hell to let loose,' he told the preliminary post-operation inquiry.[6] It was a phrase that would be heard many times in the survivors' accounts.

'Enemy mortar and shellfire seemed to hit us on all sides and tracer and explosive bullets were sweeping the decks and coming in around us. It seemed ages until the ramp was finally lowered onto the beach.' Marsh had a 'clear view of the tanks as they left the craft'. The first 'was hit three or four times but kept going', bounding over concertina rolls of barbed wire which seemed to spring back into shape once the tank passed over it. It was hit again by rounds from the French tank turret concreted into the east end of the promenade. The shots had little effect for the tank fired back and 'must have scored a direct hit as the French tank seemed to explode into the air'.[7]

Meanwhile a second tank was off and immediately engaged a pillbox on the left. Those inside ran for it but were cut down. The third tank on board now tried to make its exit. It was towing a wireless-equipped scout car. Halfway down the ramp both got stuck and the LCT captain reversed in an effort to shake them free. Just then 'a shell burst on the ramp and broke both winch cables', releasing the tank which 'rapidly pulled the scout car through the wire and also tore through the [sea] wall'. The last Marsh saw of the scout car 'it was tearing like hell up Foch boulevard.'

The craft was listing and drifting but the captain was not done yet. There were still engineer and mortar teams on board to put ashore and once again he went full ahead to attempt to beach. It was impossible. The ramp had folded under the hull and he was forced to reverse away. As he did so, 'four or five shells seemed to hit us at once and we began to take water rapidly'. The last salvo had killed both crews manning the craft's two two-pounder Bofors guns and Marsh and his men stepped in to replace them. By then he reckoned they had suffered 'about twenty casualties . . .' They limped out to the offshore boat pool where, after delivering their cargoes, landing craft were to congregate to await further orders, dazed, shocked but alive.

The LCTs were 160 feet long with armour only on the wheelhouse and gun shields and made an easy target. Of the first flight, LCT 1 got its tanks ashore but sank in shallow water near the west breakwater. The first tank to leave LCT 3 went off the ramp too soon and sank. The other two made it onto the beach but not to the promenade. The craft was crippled in the effort and unable to pull away. The next flight managed to land their Churchills but one LCT sank off the beach, another never got off it and only one got away.

The Calgary's CO Colonel Johnny Andrews was with his regimental headquarters in the third flight. It arrived on time at 06.05. Andrews was in LCT 8. The first tank off dug itself in the shingle, blocking the ramp. The craft pulled back for another approach but was hit by shellfire which snapped the chains and the ramp flopped down, preventing the craft from touching down. In the confusion Andrews' tank nonetheless drove off and plunged into eight feet of water. The Churchills were proofed to a depth of six feet and the sea closed over the top of the turret so that only the commander's pennant was showing. Andrews announced 'I am baling out', and the crew swam for it. According to one report he boarded a small craft but was killed almost immediately. Corporal Thomas Carnie, who was in the CO's tank, after returning from a prisoner-of-war camp in Germany maintained that all the crew got out safely and he 'saw Lieutenant Col Andrews waist-deep in water approaching the shore'. A sergeant from the same tank told him that he later saw Andrews's body 'washing about in the shallows at the edge of the beach'.

The first three flights succeeded in getting twenty-seven of their thirty tanks on to dry land, a remarkable achievement in the face of the fire pouring down on the crews of the LCTs as they attempted what was in any circumstances a difficult manoeuvre. One huge problem had been overcome but there were daunting obstacles ahead in the shape of the sea wall and the roadblocks barring the way into town. It was essential that the tanks kept moving, creating a momentum that would suck the infantry along in their wake.

To do that they needed the beach assault party commanded by Major Bert Sucharov of the Royal Canadian Engineers. It was made up of four officers and eighty-four men, supported by two infantry platoons. The force was broken down into teams and distributed through the first six LCTs.

Their job was to get the armour across the beaches and onto the promenade, clearing minefields and obstacles. As well as the four bulldozers on board they carried an enormous amount of equipment: timber, 'chespalings', railway sleepers, wall charges, twelve-foot vehicle bridge ramps, Bangalore torpedoes, mine detectors and bulk explosives.

The plan was for four-man squads to run ahead of the first tanks to carpet the *galets* with chespaling, twenty-five-foot-long rolls of chestnut slats, linked like a fence, for the armour and scout cars to run over. The timber was to build ramps, which in training teams had managed to build in five minutes flat to help the tanks over the sea wall. Intelligence reports said it was up to six feet high. It turned out that in places it was only two feet high due to the action of the sea which piled the pebbles against it. Another mercy was that thanks to the Germans' belief that the beach was impassable to tracked vehicles, there were no mines to clear.

Had there been ramps to build or minefields to negotiate, there was no one on Red or White Beach to do so. Within a few minutes, those engineers who got ashore were either dead, wounded or flattening themselves into what dips and hollows they could find in the pebbles to shelter from the awful squall of fire. Sucharov himself was unable to get ashore before the captain of his LCT withdrew. Only half the 350 engineers making up the beach party and the demolition teams were put ashore, and of those up to 90 per cent became casualties.[8]

The twenty-seven tanks that made it ashore had to flail towards the promenade unaided. Remarkably, fifteen of them got over the sea wall. Of the rest, two sank leaving their LCTs and the rest stayed stranded on the beach. Four had their tracks shattered by shellfire. At least four, and perhaps as many as seven were immobilised by the *galets* which worked their way into the tracks and bogies bringing progress to a literal, grinding halt.

Trooper Archie Anderson came in on LCT 7 on the third flight. All the tanks had code names and he was the loader/wireless operator on 'Bellicose'. The commander, Lieutenant Edwin Bennett, had been badly burned when a shell hit the craft just as they landed. Nonetheless, he saw what was happening to the other tanks and 'by staying close to the water we escaped the rolling-stone effect of loose shingle'.[9]

They climbed onto the promenade near the casino but with the roadblocks barring the way into town still intact, like the rest of the tanks they were limited to moving back and forth, guns blazing as they sought to do the best they could for the infantry. Anderson served the tank's six-pounder main gun, which had a range of about a mile, burning his hands on the red-hot casings as he reloaded. Bennett 'had to hold one eye open with his fingers to see but he managed to pick up a target' a battery on the east headland. They fired at it repeatedly but 'didn't know how much damage we did to it, if any'.

The first thing the Essex Scottish saw when the bow doors lowered was a hill of stones. It rose before them in undulating waves that ended at the sea wall – the first bit of real cover. Each man was laden with the maximum load they could carry, toting extra mags and bombs for the Brens and mortars as well as their own equipment. Hobnailed boots wedged ankle-deep in pebbles that slithered underfoot. Rolls of concertina wire snaked across their path. The first men went at them with the cutters while the rest crouched behind, as mortar-bomb splinters mixed with shards of pulverised *galets* sliced the air. Private Tom McDermott decided it was taking too long and threw himself on top of it to make a bridge for the others.[10]

In these opening minutes – which in the memory of the survivors felt like hours, each second magnified by the hyper-reality created by massive, eardrum-bursting violence – the guts were torn out of the Essex Scottish.

The A Company commander Captain Dennis Guest reckoned he had lost all but thirty-five of his 108 men by the time they reached the sea wall. Another captain, Donald MacCrae estimated that 40 per cent of the regiment had been killed or wounded within twenty minutes of landing.

The sections, platoons and companies that had taken the place of families for the last few years were shredded, and the NCOs and officers whose word had ordered their lives were no longer in command of anything. Both brigade commanders were to land on the main beaches and set up their headquarters in town. The 4th Brigade CO Sherwood Lett was wounded on the run in and did not make it ashore. Bill Southam commanding 6th Brigade arrived on LCT 9 but soon found he was incapable of exerting any control on the battle. With him was Lance Corporal Leo Lecky, who was in charge of the brigadier's map case. They came ashore separately and Lecky was shaken by the utter chaos he saw as the ramp descended. The memory was still raw when he recalled it more than thirty years later: 'I was scared . . . I didn't know what to do. There was an officer . . . he was sitting on the beach and one arm was completely torn off. . . he was holding his stump and he said "Get off the beach . . . it's murderous. Try to get to the sea wall." '

The shingle slope ahead was barred by a concertina wire barrier. A gap had been blown in it and he remembered the advice his First World War veteran uncle had given him: when crossing an obstacle, never hesitate. It just gives the snipers time to zero in. 'I thought, oh boy, here goes, so I ran and tumbled through and crept up to the sea wall.' He found Southam next to a radio-equipped scout car belonging to the Calgary Tanks. The brigadier's set linking him to *Calpe* had been destroyed, and over the objections of the two NCOs manning the car he commandeered their comms and began trying to gather information and issue orders. 'There was stuff flying all around but he tried to maintain communications,' Lecky remembered. 'He was standing alongside [the car] with the microphone in his hand. There was no room for him inside because the two chaps weren't getting out and I don't blame them.' Lecky marked on the maps 'the little bit of information we were getting'.[11]

The Essex CO Fred Jasperson was no more bulletproof than anyone else and was immediately forced into cover, incapable of observing more than the ten yards of beach around him. He and his staff huddled in three hollows in the *galets* below the sea wall, unable to communicate with either the companies or *Calpe* as most of the signallers were dead or wounded or their radios out of action. In a letter from captivity he gave a glimpse of his plight. 'Mortars and shell splinters were whistling all around me, some as close as eight feet but none got me.' A man next to him had a limb blown off by a mortar shell, showering him with blood. 'The experience was quite harrowing and how I was missed God only knows . . . it all will be imprinted on my mind forever.'[12]

It seemed obvious now that there could be no salvation. If the attack on Blue Beach had succeeded then the Royals would have been on the clifftop now and the guns there turned against the enemy. Instead, the batteries pumped fire down on them freely, supplemented by the machine guns flickering from numerous points in the chalky grey rampart below the church of Notre-Dame-de-Bonsecours. This was a horror they had not reckoned with. The intelligence reports had pointed out the caves in the cliff face. They did not mention that they might be an ideal place to site guns. Instead it was claimed they were used as storehouses, in particular for 2,300 torpedoes, a precise number which gave an entirely false impression of omniscience.

The guns could play on the cowering troops on the beach all day with almost complete impunity as no fighter attack or destroyer's four-inch shell was ever likely to dislodge them. To survive, the attackers had to get off the beach and into the town.

Constant training and endless repetition had conditioned every soldier to do his part, to follow drills and obey orders with robotic obedience. Many of those who reached the sea wall chose not to anchor themselves in its slight but immensely welcome shelter, and stepped out into the maelstrom to try to keep some momentum going. Below the wall stretched a barbed-wire barrier pegged out on metal posts. Once through that there was another thicket of wire, this one much broader and as much as fifteen feet deep.

The first men to try to penetrate it died in seconds. Soon the wire was festooned with bodies. Those who were not already dead soon died as the German fire played on any sign of movement. Exposure for more than a moment or two invited instant death. Lieutenant Percy Lee scrambled onto the wall to try to see a way through the sea of wire and was killed by a mortar explosion. The Canadian mortar teams made sacrificial efforts to support their comrades. A three-inch mortar crew scrambled to set up their weapon and were all wiped out by a single shell. The German mortars were the biggest killer. An analysis of wounds in the 'Combined Report on the Dieppe Raid', produced in October, estimated that at least 31 per cent were caused by mortar bombs. Another 19.5 per cent were the result of 'splinters of unknown origin' – very likely shards of blasted pebbles. Of the rest, 20 per cent were caused by machine-gun bullets, nearly 11 per cent from sniper fire and 2.6 per cent from hand grenades.

The Essex Scottish attack died on the wire. For most of those who survived the beach crossing, the next hours were spent crouched in the lee of the sea wall, frozen in the knowledge that movement probably meant injury or death.

Until leaving the *Glengyle*, the Rileys' CO Bob Labatt had been too busy to think about his feelings. He had been taken aback by the news that Dieppe was on again. Yet now, heading ashore in the LCA with his battalion headquarters he found 'any misgivings I may have had regarding the plan had completely disappeared.' They were 'launched upon a daring expedition, undoubtedly the most hazardous operation undertaken by Canadian troops. I was elated to think that we had been amongst those chosen to carry it out.' The eyes of his 520 men would be on him, watching for signs of fear. He was 'pleased to realise that I was not scared and none of the physical reactions of this emotion manifested themselves'.[13]

As the sky lightened the horizon came slowly into focus and Labatt started to pick out the prominent features of the waterfront which he recognised from hours of studying the recce and intelligence photographs: the tall, flat-fronted hotels on the promenade, the chimneys of the tobacco factory and there, on the right below the chateau was their aiming point – the neoclassical pleasure dome of the casino.

The casino was the Rileys' first objective. It had to be taken fast for the rest of their tasks to be completed. As ever the list was absurdly ambitious. After clearing the casino, B Company led by Major Bud Matchett was to maraud through the town capturing enemy headquarters and offices. Major Richard Bowery's D Company were expected to scale the cliff, capture the chateau, knock out the clifftop batteries and then hook up with the South Saskatchewans advancing from Pourville. Each mission would have tested a battalion, shored up with full artillery and air support. In the delusional military plan they had become company tasks.

Heads turned upwards now as Hurricanes flashed above them and 'flashes of flame ran up and down the esplanade as the bursts exploded'. Labatt saw three bombs strike the eastern headland followed by clouds of white phosphorus smoke. Then 'all too quickly it was over'. The men who had stood up to identify landmarks and watch the show 'were disappointed. "Is that all?" they asked.'

Captain Denis Whitaker was in the same landing craft as the CO. His platoon's job was guarding the battalion and brigade HQ once it was set up in the church of Saint-Rémy just behind the promenade. 'We looked at one another,' he remembered. 'Something was terribly wrong. Everything was intact! We expected a town shattered by the RAF's saturation bombing . . . We thought we would see a lot of damage to the seafront buildings from the shelling. There was no sign of bombing. The window panes were glittering, unbroken, in the reflections of the sun's first rays.'[14]

With 400 yards to go Labatt heard a 'sharp staccato note' rap out from the shore and machine-gun rounds thumped into the armour.

They were followed by mortars and shells from anti-tank and field pieces that crashed around the craft, now spread out in line abreast, so that 'the surface of the water was hidden by spray'. They appeared to be crossing a belt of pre-aimed fire, for a hundred yards from the beach the racket subsided. Already two landing craft on the right of the flotilla were sinking and the two platoons on board likely dead or lost to the fight. As they closed the beach they could see the muzzle flashes from the upper windows and ground floor of the casino.

The ramp dropped. Whitaker led the thirty-odd men inside in a charge about twenty-five yards up the beach. 'We fanned out and flopped down just short of a huge wire obstacle,' he wrote. 'Bullets flew everywhere . . . mortar bombs started to crash down. Around me, men were being hit and bodies were piling up, one on top of the other. It was terrifying.'

Nearby, Corporal John Williamson was regretting the enormous weight he was carrying. 'We had loaded ourselves down with so much ammunition we could hardly walk,' he remembered. Besides ammunition for his Thompson he had 'a couple of hand grenades and two mortar bombs. When the craft hit the beach, I stepped off and fell flat on my face in the bloody water. I struggled to get up, but with all this ammunition, as well as my battledress and heavy, hobnailed boots, I was weighted down.'

Labatt managed to get a signal off telling HQ he was ashore. He had landed in the middle of his companies. The one on the right was 'having a bad time'. Twenty yards ahead the centre company was cutting through the first roll of wire. The lead section were pouring fire into a pillbox on the leftward side of the casino. He ran forward at a crouch to cross the wire and get a better look. Halfway through he got stuck and lay there for a few seconds with 'the strands above me thrumming like banjo strings as they were hit'.

The section was in a hollow fifteen yards from the pillbox. Labatt watched a 'lone man worming his way through the jungle of wire surrounding the emplacement. He reached it, then having pulled the pin from a grenade, he stood up and shoved it through a loophole.'

The capture of the casino had begun and the entire effort of the battalion would be exhausted in achieving it. Labatt's 'right-hand

company had been practically annihilated before reaching the wire'
and 'the left company . . . got through to the esplanade there to be
practically wiped out'.

The casino finally fell at about 07.00 after an hour of fighting.
Assisting the Rileys was a demolition party of engineers led by Lance
Sergeant George Hickson who were charged with cracking the safe
in the Dieppe post office and blowing up the torpedoes cached in the
eastern headland. Hickson and his men moved through the halls and
salons dealing with snipers holed up in seaward-facing rooms by the
simple means of blowing down the walls. Many decided to come out
with their hands up and twenty-three prisoners were taken.

Labatt remained on the beach below the casino where he felt he
stood a better chance of making some sense of the surrounding chaos.
He was in intermittent contact with 4th Brigade headquarters who
first informed him that Brigadier Lett was about to join him, then
told him that Lett had been wounded and he was now in charge. Labatt tried contacting the other brigade battalions but there was silence
from the Royals on Blue Beach and the message from the Essex was
that they were pinned down and bereft of any cover.

The Rileys were luckier. The casino offered a sort of protective
corridor into the boulevard de Verdun and the adjoining streets. Labatt
decided to 'siphon everyone I could through the casino into the town'
and then work left via the buildings on the front to assist the Essex.

Another engineer party under Lieutenant William Ewener used the
casino as a launch pad to try to blow up a roadblock at the top of the
rue de Sygogne, which ran below the chateau ramparts into town, but
were beaten back by heavy fire. At least two groups did make it out of
the casino and into town. The first was led by Captain Tony Hill who
had taken over the remnants of B Company after Major Matchett was
killed in front of the casino. He and about a dozen men dashed across
the boulevard from the rear entrance, and finding the rue de Sygogne
impassable, worked left ending up in a cinema theatre. Its rear entrance
took them onto the street leading to the church of Saint-Rémy which
in the plan had been assigned as the main headquarters. They spent the
next hour and a half in the streets around the church, running into
groups of the enemy and sparking ragged firefights before falling back

to the casino. Sergeant Hickson and his group also penetrated the town as far as the rue de la Barre, a main street running parallel with the boulevard de Verdun. Here there was 'much activity by enemy snipers'. They killed one with a Boys anti-tank rifle. Coming under fire from a house they cleared it and 'the party of German infantry holding it [was] destroyed. There was hand-to-hand fighting . . .' Having all but exhausted their ammunition and seeing no other friendly units with which to join forces they retreated to the casino, cutting telephone cables on the way.

Despite the sniper fire the Hickson party reported seeing 'civilians, or at any rate persons in civilian clothes . . . moving freely about the streets and making no attempt to take cover'. They decided the 'civilians' were giving away their position to snipers and 'therefore cleared the streets with Bren-gun fire'.

This seems to have been an example of the scrambled perceptions that afflict men on battlefields making any scenario possible. The likelihood is that they were simply curious Dieppois displaying the same remarkable disregard for safety that the raiders found almost everywhere they went ashore. Pierre Delvallée was woken in his third-floor apartment opposite the church of Saint-Rémy on the rue de la Barre that morning by the sound of shooting out to sea. He thought nothing of it as convoy clashes 'were pretty routine around Dieppe'.[15] Half an hour later he was woken again, this time by aircraft flying low overhead. RAF raids were another habitual occurrence but when the noise persisted he turned on the wireless and heard the six o'clock news on Radio Paris announce 'an attempted English landing at Dieppe'. He went downstairs and peered out of the front door. German soldiers, weapons in hand, were filtering into the rue des Bains and the rue de la Martinière which formed two sides of the church square.

A lorry with a gun on the back, camouflaged with branches, trundled past, firing skywards at British aircraft. The streets were empty of civilians. Then he saw a boy, 'about ten years old, milk can in hand' saunter across to the dairy on the corner. It was closed and the pavement in front carpeted with shattered glass. The boy walked away again at the same leisurely pace. Then a girl of the same age appeared, also heading calmly for the dairy. Delvallée yelled at her to go home. Then he found a balcony with a good view and settled down to watch the show.

A mile to the north and against all odds, men of the Essex Scottish also managed to cross the promenade and get into the streets around the port. Company Sergeant Major Cornelius 'Tommy' Stapleton was in charge of a section of cooks and drivers who had been trained up to provide a security detail to protect battalion headquarters. They were not in the first wave to land and were put down in the centre of the beach opposite the tobacco factory on the boundary with the Rileys. This stretch of beach was empty and Stapleton assumed that the rest of the regiment was inside the town. They awaited a lull in the firing and mortaring before launching 'one mad dash' across the bare space of the promenade to the boulevard de Verdun. They broke into a hotel, killing two Germans inside and exited from the back and into the harbour area. On the odyssey that followed they failed to find any of their comrades. This did not stop them shooting up every German they saw, including a truckload of troops they took on with their two Brens, one Thompson and three or four rifles.

News of the Stapleton party's exploits somehow filtered back to *Calpe*. In transmission its importance became greatly and disastrously magnified. By the time it reached the headquarters ship it had been inflated to signify that the Essex were now across the beach and into town and one major aspect of Jubilee was being executed as planned.

Hughes-Hallett claimed later that one glance at the shore was enough to tell him the situation was dire. *Calpe* was less than three miles from shore and had a 'grandstand view'. Although the smoke-screens and fires made it impossible to see anything in detail he 'felt sure that things were going badly, partly through the sight of so many damaged landing craft limping back . . . and partly because the reports being received by General Roberts in his improvised Operations Room below the bridge were chaotic and uninformative'.[16]

Hughes-Hallett's assessment of the state of communications was correct. The surviving log of messages received reads like gibberish and it must have been impossible to discern any clear narrative about events on the beaches from the mangled phrases arriving over the net. To confuse things further, the timings attached to them are often much later than the events they describe.

As he studied the garbled scraps of intelligence Ham Roberts seemed determined to find a positive interpretation. Bad tidings were marked as 'believed phoney' or 'may be bogus', and dismissed as disinformation planted by the Germans who it was believed had somehow broken into the networks.[17] The few wisps of intelligence lightening the picture were clung to gratefully even though they contradicted the evidence of his eyes.

The battalion and brigade commanders had been allotted code names that matched their first names so 'Fred' was Colonel Jasperson and 'Bob' was Colonel Labatt. A signal at 05.28 stated 'Fred in houses. Bob landed.'[18] Another at 05.44 reported 'No news from Doug [Catto] yet.' There was no information coming in from the Yellow, Orange and Green Beaches attacks but the absence of shells from the coastal batteries at Berneval and Varengeville gave grounds for cautious optimism. At 06.20 began a stream of signals suggesting that events at Puys and on one of the main beaches were going into reverse. The first stated: 'Blue Beach landing has failed.' Five minutes later came 'Impossible to land Blue Beach.' It was followed at 06.31 by a desperate-sounding signal from Red Beach: 'Fred – we have to get off beach.' Fifteen minutes later came another to Lett: 'Fred to Sherwood – we have to get off beach. Coy [Company] held on beach.'

Those around Roberts searched his stolid face for some reaction. In vain. When he spoke his tone was positive and Lieutenant Dan Doheny, a 2nd Division liaison officer on *Calpe*, 'gathered from [him] it was proceeding satisfactorily and it was just a matter of time before the town was in our hands'.[19]

Behind his monumental impassiveness Roberts was wrestling with a fateful decision, the responsibility for which was his alone. The only resource he controlled that could affect the outcome was his 'floating reserve', the main body of which was the men of the Fusiliers Mont-Royal. They were his to throw into the battle at the time and place where he judged they would make the most difference.

Around 06.40 he decided the moment had come to send them in.

At that point, as far as he knew, the Royals had not got ashore. Imagining them to be holding somewhere offshore he now ordered their landing craft to divert to Red Beach and help the Essex. At the same time he ordered Lieutenant Colonel Ménard, the Fusiliers' CO who had come aboard *Calpe* half an hour earlier, 'to land and moving to the west, establish themselves on White Beach'.[20]

In his post-operational report Roberts justified the move by stating that 'about one hour after touchdown information received indicated that Red Beach was sufficiently cleared to permit the landing of the floating reserve'. That 'information' seems to have been the signal reporting that the Essex had penetrated the town. Later there were various versions of what was originally transmitted and how it was subsequently misinterpreted.

Sergeant Dave Hart, a 4th Brigade signaller who survived the Red Beach landing along with his set, remembered reporting that 'one man in the Essex Scottish has penetrated the town'.[21] Colonel Stacey, the Canadian official historian, traces the decision to a signal from the Essex to the Rileys stating 'twelve of our men in the buildings', an accurate enough summary of the Stapleton foray. This was picked up at 06.10 on *Fernie* as 'Essex Scots across the beaches and in houses' and transmitted on to *Calpe*.

By 07.00 the Fusiliers were on their way. Twelve minutes later came another signal that seemed to suggest their mission was worthwhile: 'Casino taken – Bob.' That, by then, was true, but it did not alter the truth that the French Canadians were sailing into disaster.

By the time Roberts made his choice there was evidence to hand to contradict the dim picture painted by the signals. Hughes-Hallett claimed later that he learned of the catastrophe at Blue Beach at about 06.30 from Lieutenant Commander Colin McMullen who had led in some of the landing craft carrying the Royals and then come on board *Calpe* to give a verbal report. Hughes-Hallett was shaken. His first thought was for the Royal Marines' 'cutting out' party, crammed into French Chasseurs and led by HMS *Locust*, who were due to sail into the harbour at 07.00 to capture the German landing craft. With the eastern headland still in enemy hands they would come under fire at point-blank range and every ship would probably be lost.

He 'reluctantly . . . with General Roberts's full permission . . . cancelled the *Locust*'s mission' and had the marines transferred to LCAs.[22] Roberts understood, as did everyone, that Dieppe could not be captured as long as the guns on the east cliff were firing. Yet not only did he launch the Fusiliers on a futile charge, he then ordered the marines to follow them. Roberts never made any serious attempt to justify or explain these decisions. In the absence of his testimony they will always remain incomprehensible. There was nothing apart from a few words over the radio to suggest that the battle had reached a tipping point and that one more push would bring victory. All the evidence suggested that a disaster was in the making and a responsible commander's thoughts should have focussed on saving what lives and equipment he could. Instead Roberts violated a cardinal military principle so commonplace and obvious that it was widely known to civilians. He was reinforcing failure and he was doing it twice.

Lieutenant Colonel 'Joe' Ménard led his men in on a motor launch. At 200 yards out, fire started to smack into the R-boats behind. Ménard's throat was 'dry and burning. I was desperate to do something instead of being nailed down in the bloody boat.'[23] On touching down he ran through a gap in the wire cut by the sappers and towards the sea wall. He had not gone three yards before he was hit for the first time. As he explained later, the word 'hit' was a euphemism. It was 'like being stunned with a blacksmith's hammer. There's no sudden pain. What really shakes you is that you don't know where you have been struck or by what.' Even so, he waved his men on telling them 'It's nothing.'

He felt for damage and found he was bleeding heavily from his right shoulder. He fumbled in his hip pocket for a field dressing but found it impossible to apply with his left hand. He 'lost all sense of the outside world'. Then the 'fog lifted'. He stumbled forward across the beach shouting an order to spread out. Shell splinters slashed open his cheek. A soldier dropped in front of him. It was an officer he was particularly fond of. The man was clutching his stomach with both hands and struggling to breathe. Ménard groped in his first-aid kit and found a morphine tablet. 'My friend never took his eyes off me but he didn't say a word. He pushed out his tongue a little. I placed the pill on it and he swallowed it. He knew very well that there was nothing else I could do for him.'

Until now his body had responded to the disciplines drummed into him by many years of training but the sight of his stricken friend threw him into 'a blind rage and I had only one idea in my head: to shoot, to get even with these pigs'. The madness passed and an analgesic numbness set in. He reached the sea wall and was crossing it when a bullet struck him above the wrist. He hardly felt it and reaching the cover of a bombed-out pillbox directed his men as best he could for the next hour until he was hit yet again, this time in the leg. Before he finally passed out his eyes wandered over the battlefield. 'Not even a cat could move on the beach or promenade. Anyone who tried was immediately immobilised by a gust of machine-gun fire or a sniper's bullet, not to mention mortar bombs and artillery shells. They were even firing at the corpses, as if they wanted to kill them twice . . .'

The sacrifice of the Fusiliers had changed nothing. Roberts meanwhile had added another sacrificial offering to the pyre. Shortly after 08.00 he issued an order to the Royal Marines. Its ambition revealed how far Roberts was now removed from reality. They were to go in and 'support the Essex Scottish through White Beach . . . the idea being to pass through the beach to the town and there reform and report to the colonel of the Essex Scottish, the object . . . being to pass around the west and south of the town and attack the batteries on the eastern cliff from the south'.[24] After the first three flights, no more of the twenty-seven tanks still afloat had gone ashore, yet some of them were now detailed to land alongside the marines. Ten minutes later the order was rescinded and the remaining LCTs turned for home.

Roberts may have been prompted to send in the marines by a string of encouraging-sounding signals from the main beaches. At 08.10 *Calpe* received 'Elements of Johnny [the Calgary Tanks] have made progress now in front of Tobacco Factory.'[25] It was followed at 08.17 by 'have control of White Beach'. This did not amount to evidence that a breakthrough was imminent. The timetable had long since ceased to have any meaning, and the idea that any of the main objectives were attainable was a fantasy.

The marines went ashore in two LCMs and five LCAs led by Lieutenant Colonel Joseph Picton Phillipps. It was now getting on for 08.30. They were shielded on either side by an escort of Chasseurs. The senior officer Lieutenant Malcolm Buist wrote in his after-action report that 'it was not long before I realised that this landing was to be a sea parallel of the Charge of the Light Brigade . . . shells started to burst all round the group of landing craft which we endeavoured to screen by smoke . . . I shouted to Colonel Phillipps to ask what he thought about going on but I doubt whether he heard me. Anyway he merely waved his arms and grinned to show that he meant to land at all costs . . .'[26]

Buist's Chasseur was then hit and he pulled away to inspect the damage. When he resumed position 'the landing was all over. Five of the seven craft had reached the beach and been shot to pieces.' The other two had been saved thanks to Phillipps. At the last second he stood up on the deck and waved frantically for them to turn back into the cover of the smokescreen. Then he fell, mortally wounded. Two officers spared by his gesture reported that 'the beach was a shambles with bodies of the soldiers lying in arrowhead formation as they had advanced from the landing craft'.

Above the carnage the Germans looked down in awe. Hauptmann H. H. Ditz, commanding a battery on the west headland, saw a 'picture which . . . could teach any man what fear means'.[27] The beach 'was strewn with infantry equipment: machine guns, packs, grenade throwers, munitions'. The Canadians were 'clinging tightly against the concrete wall, seeking protection'. On the broad lawn that ran the length of the promenade 'tanks were twisting and turning . . . trying to get through into the town'. It seemed to Ditz that 'they could try forever' and it would make no difference.

Vanquish

By 09.00 it was clear that Roberts's gamble had failed. Even Mann despaired. He turned to the American observer aboard *Fernie*, Lucian Truscott, and admitted: 'General, I am afraid that this operation will go down as one of the great failures in history.'[1] The only option left to the force commanders was to get the surviving troops off as quickly as possible, yet Roberts still seemed reluctant to accept the inevitable. In the end it was Hughes-Hallett who pressed for the withdrawal order to be brought forward. He suggested that re-embarkation begin at 10.30 or earlier. Roberts held out for 11.00 which the senior air officer on *Calpe*, Air Commodore Cole, told him would give the RAF time to maximise air cover.

All Canadian units were supposed to be evacuated from the Dieppe beaches. The re-embarkation schedule was just as elaborate as every other part of the plan. The South Saskatchewans, for example, were expected to fall back in ten precisely timed phases, although the orders did admit that 'the tactical situation during re-embarkation cannot accurately be forecast' and 'large deviations from this plan must be expected'.[2] Reality now dictated that the Green Beach units would have to leave from Pourville. As for Blue Beach, there was no one left to take off.

The evacuation would be a desperate business, more testing even than Dunkirk. Human life was the priority and the tanks would have to be left behind. The code word for withdrawal was 'Vanquish'. Somehow it filtered through the airwaves, reaching the headquarters of 4th Brigade, still afloat on an LCT at 09.40, who then passed it by their sole remaining set to the Essex and the Rileys. Whatever relief was felt at the news was crushed by the knowledge that the retreat would be as traumatic as the attack. All the efforts of the RAF had failed to reduce the Germans' firepower. In the hours since the landing it had actually increased as General Haase ordered more artillery and troops into the area. The Germans could afford to bide their time. 'Enemy along headlands, waiting for Vanquish,' ran a fatalistic message from the main beaches as they prepared from their next ordeal.[3]

The man left commanding the Camerons, Major Andrew Law, had already decided to fall back to Green Beach when the news reached him. The battalion penetrated further inland than any other unit but were still far short of the Saint-Aubin-sur-Scie airfield. They had made painful progress up the west side of the Scie and stopped on high ground near Petit-Appeville on the main road leading east into Dieppe. Law had intended there to cross the river and swing north to attack Quatre Vents farm from behind. From his vantage point he could see this was now impossible. Horses were hauling guns up to the hill overlooking the bridge. He ordered the men to fall back to Pourville, just as his radio operator picked up a signal from 6th Brigade to the Saskatchewans telling them to rendezvous on the beach and prepare to be taken off.

The Saskatchewans were still fighting on the east bank of the Scie but soon after 10.00 everyone had made it back to Pourville. As they retreated the enemy moved in to fill the vacuum. Rearguard parties took up positions in the shattered houses of the village to cover their comrades hurrying for the shore.

When Sergeant Marcel Swank of the US Rangers arrived at the eastern end of Pourville he was ordered to hold the perimeter and settled behind a hedge with his M1 Garand rifle trained on the road ahead. A Canadian Bren-gunner dropped down beside him and began loosing off bursts at unseen enemies. The Germans fired back and 'laid a streak of fire over our heads through the hedge and little leaves began to float down on us'.[4] The Canadian took off and Swank was on his own. For the first time since going ashore he felt really frightened. Long afterwards he remembered 'pulling my rifle back through the hedge, laying my head on the stock and praying. I wanted to live so badly.' Swank was a Roman Catholic and said an act of contrition in readiness for death, then 'rolled over on my back and looked at the sky . . . It was a beautiful day, little puffy clouds floating over. I was nineteen years old and I just didn't want to die.'

He heard a voice behind asking: 'Are you frightened, Yank?' He turned to see a Canadian major and told him, 'I'm scared to death.' 'Don't worry about it,' the major told him. I've been in stickier places than this and got out.' Swank gave up thoughts of dying and followed the major's orders to get down to the beach to help evacuate casualties.

By the time the first wave of LCAs arrived at 11.04 the Germans were already on the high ground at either end of the beach.[5] Gunboats and destroyers fired shells and smoke at their positions throughout the evacuation but with little effect.

The tide had gone out. To reach the boats meant a 200-yard dash through a heavy crossfire of mortars, machine guns and artillery. The wounded went first and German prisoners, at least two dozen of whom had been taken during the day, were ordered to carry stretchers. The enemy guns did not spare their comrades. Only one captive made it back to England.

Swank teamed up with a fellow Ranger, Sergeant Lloyd Church. He had landed with him but not seen him since. Together they moved men to an abandoned pillbox on the promenade where stretcherbearers carried them to the boats. On the shore men were steeling themselves for the fateful dash. He saw them 'run across the beach, get hit then roll as they were hit . . . you could tell where a boat had loaded because there were bodies rolling in the sand at that point.'

He and Church dropped to the beach and ran. Halfway across Swank realised he was alone. Church was down. He turned back and dragged his buddy back to the sea wall. He had a head wound but was conscious. He asked him, 'Do you think you can make it?' Church said 'No.' Swank thought hard. He could 'stay with this man and be captured, possibly killed, or I could make my break across the beach and back to England'. He made his decision – one that Church subsequently 'had no complaints about' – and ran for the nearest LCA. It had come in fast and got stuck. 'Men were all about the boat, some up front pushing, some along the side dragging on ropes some at the rear pulling and the motors were racing and all around there was mortar fire and automatic weapons playing into this group.'

As he waded out, semi-submerged corpses bumped against his legs. He was clinging to the side of the boat when a young Canadian started to haul himself over the side. He had 'just got his head and shoulders above the level of the deck . . . when I heard this "slam!", just like someone had rammed his fist into a piece of raw meat and the kid came tumbling back down on me and knocked me down into the water. I picked him up by the front of his battle jacket. Most of his face was gone and I just laid him back in the water.'

The craft was still stuck. He saw another boat pulling away and decided to try to reach it. He pushed through the water, clutching his rifle. 'The butt was up and the muzzle was down and I felt something tugging. I couldn't understand what it was. I turned around . . . my [rifle's] front sight had caught in the clothing of a body and I was dragging it out to sea with me as I walked.' He broke down his Garand and scattered the pieces, dumped his steel helmet and ammunition and struck out for the landing craft as machine-gun bullets and sniper rounds smacked around him. Someone on the boat saw him and it stopped to pick him up. Then his hands closed around a rope and he pulled himself aboard. He heard the whine of a ricochet and a bullet struck his arm. It was the first injury he had received all day and it was a flesh wound.

About a dozen LCAs made it in to Green Beach. Some of them had been ordered to Red Beach but, confused by the smoke that drifted everywhere, had landed at Pourville. Only eight made it out again. Nonetheless, the majority of the waiting Saskatchewans and Camerons got off. Colonel Merritt led the party covering the withdrawal. 'Throughout the day his actions had been almost incredibly gallant,' declared Captain John Runcie of the Camerons in his after-action report.[6] There was one more act of selfless heroism before the end. Incredibly, Merritt had got through the day without injury but had just been wounded by a sniper. Nonetheless he now 'crossed the wide beach through . . . extremely heavy fire and carried to shelter under the wall a wounded soldier who was lying at the water's edge'.

The landing craft withdrew leaving about 250 men on the beach. They knew the rescuers would probably not be returning. The enemy fire slackened. It was replaced with the roar of Merlin engines, and six Spitfires, believing the figures below to be Germans, swept in and machine-gunned the beach, causing further casualties.

The dozen or so officers held a 'confab'. They had little ammunition left. Runcie recalled later how they argued whether they should 'fight to the last man and the last round or . . . surrender in order to prevent further loss of life'. There was little hope of inflicting further damage on the enemy. They decided unanimously to surrender. There were still men firing from a scaffolding frame shoring up the sea wall. They were ordered to climb down and 'we chucked our weapons down and called it a day.' The Germans were already on the beach.

For the men on Red and White the signalling of 'Vanquish' marked the start of another appalling ordeal. The battle was lost. The struggle now was to stay alive and in one piece until the boats got in. Those on the beach who had not made it to the casino clung to the sea wall or flattened themselves on the *galets*. Few were unwounded. A sort of exalted fatalism gripped some, inspiring unforgettable displays of courage. Captain the Reverend John Foote, the Rileys' burly Presbyterian military chaplain was one of four padres who went ashore. On landing he attached himself to the makeshift Regimental Aid Post (RAP) sited in a dip in the beach which gave just enough cover if you were stretched out flat. Later when the tide retreated they shifted to the shelter of a stranded LCT. Over and over again, Foote darted out to carry back casualties then helped to dress their wounds. The LCT was hit by shellfire which set off the ammunition on board. There were 'bullets flying back and forth and ricocheting all over the place and it eventually got red hot and we had to take the men out', he remembered.[7] They moved the casualties into the lee of the LCT but several of their charges were dead. Throughout it all he stayed calm and even cheerful and ever afterwards made light of his actions, as if ministering to his flock in the middle of a battle was normal behaviour: 'Everybody did the same thing. They carried their wounded, they bound them up and they did what they could.'

Bob Labatt was beside the casino where he had set up his dual headquarters as CO of the Rileys and acting 4th Brigade commander. If they were to hold out before the evacuation began at 11.00 it was 'essential to keep pressing . . . and to plaster West Cliff and the buildings across the esplanade with everything available'.[8] Over the one barely functioning radio he made repeated requests for aircraft to lay smoke and bombard the positions.

The Calgary Tanks were doing their utmost to support their comrades. Most of those which reached the promenade had returned to the beach, reckoning it was safer and offered better scope for spotting and hitting targets. As long as they had shells left they would fire them. The Churchills' tracks may have been vulnerable but their armour was not and artillery and anti-tank rounds seemed to bounce off. Trooper Elmer Cole's Mark I 'only had a two-pounder gun on it and it didn't have much firepower but we were pretty safe in it'.[9]

The sight of them cheered the 130 or so troops, most of them Rileys, sheltering in the casino. Wounded and prisoners were collected on the ground floor on the north-eastern side and at least some of the latter had their thumbs bound. It was impossible to get the casualties across the beach to the RAP and the uninjured applied what first aid they could to friend and foe alike. They were sharing the same hell and it brought them together. Sapper W. Price, one of the engineer party which had earlier entered the town, spoke German. He got into conversation with a prisoner wearing a metal badge awarded for athletic prowess. The prisoner told him he was a 100-metre sprint champion and had represented Germany at the 1936 Olympics. He also confirmed 'that the enemy knew we were coming but didn't know when'.[10] That was now believed by everybody, with a minority convinced that the defenders also knew the time and place.

The Germans showed no signs of counter-attacking. The tanks on the beach were a deterrent but for the moment there was no need to take risks. Labatt was alerted to an astonishing sight by Company Sergeant Major Harris who handed him his field glasses. He looked towards the west headland to see 'a large group of German officers, some in white summer tunics . . . these people were standing right in the open obviously out to see the fun. Some were smoking cigars.' He ordered two Brens to open fire and they disappeared 'in split seconds'.

Shortly before 11.00 he sent runners out to tell the men to start moving to the water. It was a sunny day, the visibility perfect. Just as they prepared to run two aircraft swooped in trailing smoke that magically cloaked the beach from one end to the other. All enemy guns turned on the aircraft and the soldiers took their chance, rushing gratefully into the fog.

The withdrawal was taking place as the air battle reached a new height of intensity. The Luftwaffe was slow to act at first but by 10.00 was launching continuous bombing raids on the fleet. As Leigh-Mallory had calculated, the enemy would have to throw every asset into repelling the attack, and by the end of the day all units within reach had been in action. The fighter air umbrella shielded the troops from the added trauma of air attacks, and of the many horrors recorded in their accounts, strafing and bombing are hardly mentioned.

It was at sea that the danger felt closest. On board *Garth* Goronwy Rees watched the German bombs falling 'slowly downwards, turning in the air like beer bottles, so slowly that it seemed impossible that they should not hit [us]'.[11] He was on the bridge when bomb splinters 'ricocheted madly [a]round'. Standing beside him was 'a tall, fair-haired young artillery officer . . . He turned to me with a look of surprise on his young serious face, a look so intense that at first I could not understand what had so profoundly startled him. Then slowly he tumbled to the deck . . .'

The man was Derek Turner, the bombardment liaison officer for Blue Beach. 'I felt an extraordinary numb bang on my fingers on my left hand and heard the loudest noise I've ever heard – a short sharp scream of metal,' he wrote in his diary. 'I looked at my fingers. My index finger was hanging nearly off and I felt no pain. I then felt the back of my left leg with my right hand and felt nothing but hot rawness but again, no pain.' He lay down. To his surprise he was not frightened. Instead 'the shock made me feel very collected and natural.' His gaze fixed on the side of the bridge. 'It was splattered with blood and there was a piece of meat about the size of a large mouthful sticking to some woodwork and sliding down. I looked around to see if anyone else had been hit – they hadn't and that meat was a bit of *me*![12]

Thanks to the fighters none of the larger ships were sunk in the first hours of attacks, though the sheer weight of the bomber assault suggested that the Luftwaffe's luck was bound to change. The withdrawal would stretch the RAF's abilities and resources to the maximum. The squadrons would have to simultaneously shake up the defences with bombs and cannon attacks and blind them with smoke, while all the time fending off the bombers and engaging the fighters sent to protect them.

The precision smoke-laying on the Dieppe beach that so impressed Labatt was one of numerous coordinated sorties being flown at that minute. The airmen were an international motley, drawn from America, Canada, Norway, France, Belgium and every corner of the British Empire. The assault on the headlands was opened by several squadrons flying Hurricane Mark II 'Hurribombers'. No. 174 Squadron hit the east headland while 32 Squadron attacked the west cliff. After they dropped their 500 lb bombs two more squadrons, 3 and 43, delivered cannon attacks. This operation cost 174 Squadron three aircraft. Turning over the town, Pilot Officer Raymond Van Wymeersch of the Free French was hit by flak and wounded but survived to be taken prisoner. An Australian, Flight Sergeant C. B. Watson, was shot down into Dieppe harbour and was rescued by the Germans. Sergeant Charles James did not survive.

The Hurricanes were followed by smoke-laying runs on the headlands by Bostons from 226 Squadron. It was two aircraft from 226 which trailed the carpet of smoke from fifty feet for a mile along the beach. All were braving German fire that was as lethally effective as ever. They were also frequently at the mercy of the fleet gunners whose poor ability to identify their own aircraft was painfully revealed that day.

Their long experience of raiding over the French coast had taught the fighter squadrons to fear the Focke-Wulf 190s and respect the skill of their pilots. As they twisted in the tight airspace over the battle-field, searching for that instant of advantage that decided a dogfight, they found that weight of numbers alone did not tip the balance in their favour.

Wing Commander Myles Duke-Woolley was leading 232 Squadron who were 'new to the scene' on a patrol over the fleet when 'one German fighter dived out of the sun from a great height, attacked us head-on, and I did not see him until he was maybe 600 yards away and firing. Our . . . closing speed was probably around 800 mph, say 400 yards a second, and I failed to react in the second or second-and-a-half at my disposal.'[13] The F W 190 shot down two Spitfires, killing both pilots, but 'the squadron most commendably did not waver.'

Duke-Woolley was enormously experienced. So too was Wing Commander James 'Johnnie' Johnson, a superb air fighter and consummate tactician. In an early dogfight over the town he had some desperate minutes shaking off an F W 190 which got on his tail and he counted himself lucky to survive. The day proved to him the 'all-round superiority of the Focke-Wulfs over our Spitfire Vs' and he judged later that 'the Luftwaffe bested us in the air fighting'.[14] In general, the episode demonstrated how much the Allies had to learn about the tactical use of aircraft to support forces in close-locked combat.

The presence of controllers on *Calpe* made no difference to Johnson for he 'could never establish communications with it on the four times we flew that day . . . we never heard a thing from them'.[15] There was little to show for all the RAF's enormous efforts. The imperviousness of the batteries to air attack was witnessed by an expert, George Browne, the forward artillery observer on Blue Beach who, having climbed the cliff with Colonel Catto's party, spent hours watching the anti-aircraft battery on top of the east headland in action. The team manning it 'served its guns magnificently', he reported later.[16] Between 10.00 and 16.00 'it was low-level bombed at least four times and machine-gunned oftener by our fighters with us as witnesses and each time the guns were back in action within a matter of a few seconds, firing upon the departing aircraft.'

★

The evacuations called for another great effort of will from the crews of the landing craft. They had sailed into the hecatomb once and were being asked to do so again. The original idea had been to take most of the troops off in LCTs but they had proved to be too big and too vulnerable and the LCAs would have to do the job. Their chances of success were tiny. The operation required mustering the available landing craft grouped in the boat pool and somehow directing them to the right beaches. The wireless networks were in tatters and ships had now to resort to signal lamps and loudhailers to communicate with one another. The Luftwaffe roared overhead, their bombs flinging up great geysers of spray and disrupting and discouraging all movement except flight. The smoke that from time to time masked the boats from the guns and planes also brought confusion and disorientation, greatly increasing the risk of putting ashore in the wrong place. Finally there was the question of courage. It was a finite commodity. Every boat commander knew what the order to close the shore entailed. They would have to reach deep inside themselves to find the resolve needed to go forward again as death advanced towards them, bony hands outstretched.

The boat-pool officers rounded up what craft they could and the roughly assembled force moved towards the smoke- and flame-wreathed shore. Five destroyers fell in behind them, belching smoke and pumping shells: *Slazak*, *Brocklesby*, *Berkeley*, *Fernie* and *Calpe* herself. The onshore wind pushed the smokescreen before them, providing relief from the guns but the Luftwaffe and the artillerymen knew that anything they landed in the murk was likely to hit something.

As the beach approached, the barrage thickened making landing an all but suicidal prospect, and the decision not to press on was an act of sober sanity rather than cowardice. The officer in charge of the boat pool, Commander H. V. P. McClintock, was frank about his reactions as he closed the eastern limit of Red Beach in a motor launch. 'I got as far as abreast the end of Dieppe breakwater when a bombing and cannon attack developed and I rather think that we were also under fire from the shore but am not sure,' he told the post-operational inquiry. 'At any rate I retired very hurriedly to seaward, followed by quite a few landing craft.'[17]

Only half of the thirty-six or so craft available attempted to touch down on the main beaches.[18] The Canadians were waiting, crouched beside beached and burned-out landing craft. They looked out to sea, urging onwards the craft that were their only way home. Captain McGregor of the Essex was crouched alongside the principal military landing officer Major Brian McCool, squinting through the haze at the approaching LCAs: 'A Stuka bomber would dive on them and a great spray of water would go up. When it went down there would be no landing craft.'[19] The few that arrived were overwhelmed and the boats sagged under the weight of desperate men. One flotilla officer who reached the shore described how 'the boats . . . were literally swamped by sheer weight of numbers of troops trying to embark. Sub Lieutenant Lonnon's boat was hit by heavy gun fire whilst on the beach and capsized. The remaining three boats of the 10th flotilla succeeded in getting off with approximately seventy troops each on board and only by going full astern.'[20]

The sanctuary offered by the craft was illusory. Private Provencal of the Fusiliers Mont-Royal was hit by shrapnel as he scrambled aboard an LCA. It began to sink and after baling for a while with their steel helmets everyone on board slipped back into the sea.

Only eight landing craft arrived at the Essex Scottish end of the beach, and six of those were sunk. Some cruised parallel to the shore rather than facing almost certain annihilation if they touched down, trailing ropes over the side for the men to wade out to.

Bob Labatt managed to get aboard a 'frightfully crowded' LCA with a group of his men. He was surprised to see that 'only ten to twelve . . . had come in and none on the Essex beach' as far as he could see. He was 'no sooner aboard than the smoke cleared completely', catching 'most of the LCAs either backing away or in the act of turning. Every German weapon turned upon them and all hell let loose.' What they had experienced before 'was nothing to this furious hurricane of fire. In no time the sea was littered with the wreckage of shattered LCAs and dotted with heads and waving arms. A shell burst inside the crowded boat next to us with ghastly results.'[21]

He could feel the boat being hit but 'was not conscious of anything amiss until I saw the naval crew jump overboard and found that I was

standing in water up to my knees'. He ordered his men to inflate their
Mae Wests and swim out to meet incoming boats or head back to shore.
He struck out in the direction of an LCT half a mile distant. 'Hundreds of men were swimming around, some out, some towards shore.
I tried to keep clear of groups as they presented tempting targets and
the sea about them was lashed into foam by machine guns, mortars and
artillery.' As he neared the LCT he saw that it had been hit and was
settling by the stern. He kept on swimming, 'however when there was
nothing left to be seen but the bows sticking vertically out of the water,
I realised that she wasn't in very good shape.' Neither was he. He was
tired and very cold and now 'turned reluctantly back towards the
shore'. By 12.20 the flotilla had withdrawn, battered and listing and
crammed with dead and wounded. Behind, the hundreds who had not
made it watched them go, wondering if they would ever return.

The naval effort was not quite exhausted. The craft that McClintock
had turned back were still intact. He had decided that any further
effort was impossible. After leaving some wounded men on *Alresford*
he came across several landing craft returning from a bid to evacuate
Blue Beach. News that the Royals had in fact landed had finally
reached *Calpe* and Hughes-Hallett gave orders to the man who had
organised their landing, Lieutenant Commander Goulding, to try
to get troops off. When Goulding approached Blue Beach he chose
not to proceed. The report he sent to *Calpe*, logged at 11.45, stated:
'Could not see [the position of] Blue Beach owing to fog and heavy
fires from cliff . . .'[22] Some craft did attempt to get in, including LCP
159 commanded by Michael Bateson. 'What a sight!' he wrote in a
personal account a few days later. 'Overturned craft, half-submerged
craft, floating craft with apparently no living thing aboard and at the
foot of the cliff a fairly large number of Canadians with Jerry at the
top of the cliff quite visible.'[23] The Germans seemed so close that Bateson started shooting at them with his revolver while the crew engaged
with Lewis guns, but 'the stuff coming back at us was nobody's business, everything but the kitchen stove! Jerry was *not* going to let us get
in and the Canadians waved a white flag to us and they were shooing us
away . . .' They were 'pleased to get the hell out'.

Bateson's craft would appear to be one of those that McClintock crossed coming from Blue Beach. Hearing their news he 'came to the conclusion . . . that it was not possible to evacuate from Blue, White or Red Beaches'. He 'told such landing craft as had followed me to form up on a course for home'.

He now set off for *Calpe* to seek instructions from Hughes-Hallett but was unable to find her in the smoke. By McClintock's account he then sent a radio message to Hughes-Hallett's deputy David Luce, asking what to do. Luce replied saying, 'if no further evacuation possible, withdraw to four miles from shore'. Somehow this was received as 'no further evacuation possible, withdraw'. This McClintock did at about 12.30 but 'foolishly . . . made no reply to this signal so left the force commander in the dark as to what I was doing . . .'

According to Hughes-Hallett the signal from *Calpe* originated from himself in response to a request from Ham Roberts who had asked 'that a further effort be made'.[24] Though he feared that this would only result in more losses he thought it right to leave the choice to McClintock – hence the conditional wording of the message. Even if it had arrived ungarbled the decision was McClintock's and he had long since made up his mind.

At about 12.50 Hughes-Hallett decided to make a last approach in *Calpe* for 'a final personal view'. Until now her four-inch guns had stayed silent for fear of disrupting the communications kit on board, but now as she headed for the eastern end of Red Beach she opened fire 'from the foremost guns at the breakwaters on which machine-gun posts were reported to be preventing the troops . . . reaching the water. When about two cables from the beach [roughly a quarter of a mile] *Calpe* came under heavy fire and no sign of troops or landing craft, other than derelicts, could be seen on the beach.' The destroyer sought cover in smoke and Hughes-Hallett now 'felt convinced that any further attempt to take off troops would be unlikely to succeed'.

The decision to abandon the brave men onshore clashed with every instinct. Before taking it, he set off to find the gunboat *Locust* whose shallow draught allowed it to get closer in and whose commander Robert Ryder might have a better appreciation of the situation. As he did so Roberts informed him of a signal from Bill Southam's 6th Brigade headquarters on the shore. Messages were still getting through and they told with tragic brevity the story of the final minutes:

13.05 Give us quick support. Enemy closing in on beach. Hurry it up please.

13.07 We are evacuating.

13.08 There seems to be a mass surrender of our troops to the Germans on the beach. Our people here have surrendered.[25]

There was nothing more to be done. Withdrawal was ordered and as the fleet turned for home the shield Fighter Command had raised above them finally cracked. The destroyers were ordered to make smoke and regroup around *Calpe* four miles offshore. At the rendezvous, three Dorniers dodged in and scattered bombs through the fog. At 13.18 two hit the *Berkeley*, on the starboard side just forward of the bridge, breaking her back. The order was given to abandon ship and a gunboat went alongside to take off all the crew. Then a torpedo from HMS *Albrighton* sent her to the bottom.

As they turned away the Luftwaffe closed in. Messerschmitt fighters swooped in a cannon attack on *Calpe*'s bridge injuring several and severely wounding Air Commodore Cole. It did not deter her from leaving the cover of the air umbrella to pick up a fighter pilot who was spotted in the sea.

The smoke-fringed shore dwindled behind them and the cacophony of battle faded until it was just a ringing in the ears. Occasionally a German aircraft would appear but was soon chased off by the RAF. The destroyers had become hospital ships. The decks were covered with wounded and the cliché of scuppers running with blood became a reality. The medics worked with the same quiet intensity they had shown all day. When a man died they pulled his shirt over his head to save others wasting time when there was nothing more to be done.

Goronwy Rees had studied the eager faces of the Canadians before they went ashore that morning. He studied them again as landing craft unloaded survivors on *Garth*. They 'were not the same men', he wrote. They 'looked as if they had learned some terrible lesson that was still too vivid for them to express it clearly either to themselves or to anyone else.' Many were badly wounded and all shocked and exhausted. 'They had the grey, lifeless faces of men whose vitality had been drained out of them; each of them could have modelled a death mask.' As they came aboard he heard 'the oaths and blasphemies, the cursings and revilings, with which men speak of leaders by whom they feel that they have been betrayed and deceived. I thought that this is what a beaten army looks like . . .'

Rough men schooled to hide emotion showed an unexpected softness. The navy crew treated them with 'tenderness and gentleness . . . soothing the hysterical with words like women's, comforting the exhausted with cups of hot sweet tea'.[26]

Was Rees right to see defeat in those faces? The big picture was the concern of generals and politicians. For the men who had survived the battle the outcome turned first on a simple consideration. As Marcel Swank sat in a gangway, sipping a mug of rum-laced tea, he began to believe at last that the ordeal was over. The terrors and dangers of a lifetime had been distilled into the space of a few hours, and as he started to examine what he had been through the bigger significance of it all was the last thing on his mind. 'You're not really interested in the success or failure of something,' he reflected later. 'I was just happy to be alive.'[27]

But there was a scale on which every man weighed their experience. They first asked themselves: did I let myself and my comrades down? It was the actions of you and your section, your platoon, your company and your battalion that mattered and what happened beyond that was so remote as to be barely relevant. What concerned Swank and his comrades was their small corner of the battlefield. It was in that space that 'whether you won or lost [was] important. Most of the men I talked to felt they had won their fight. This to them was the important thing. This to the rifleman is the important thing . . .'

There was a nobility in defeat that in its way was as profound as the glory of victory. For Jack Poolton, the stoicism of the Royals on Blue Beach was a source of great pride. 'We took our licks,' he said long afterwards. 'We didn't ask for any quarter . . . We didn't beg. We didn't crab. We didn't bellyache. We knew we'd been licked and we knew the Germans had licked us and we were going to take it like men, like soldiers.'[28]

If the venture failed it was not their fault. The task they had been given was immense and unrealisable but they gave everything they had in trying to make the impossible happen with so many acts of courage that they could never properly be counted. It came in many forms.

There were the moments when men abandoned all thoughts of safety in their zeal to get to the enemy, the cases of individuals running into streams of fire to silence machine guns, usually dying in the process. When Colonel Ménard of the Fusiliers tried to analyse this kind of heroism he decided it was formed of many impulses, among them 'a blind anger, a violent thirst for revenge and also a certain fatalism, when you tell yourself "oh what the hell . . ."'[29] But there were other sorts of heroism on display that had nothing to do with fighting spirit, those times when compassion overwhelmed self-preservation and led men to step out of cover and into spaces filled with red-hot flying metal to drag back casualties. Then there was the indomitable spirit shown by those who refused to accept the crushing logic of their situation and stripped off their uniforms and plunged into the waves, ready to risk death by drowning rather than to raise their hands and be marched off to prison.

There were many others whose courage was of a quieter sort. Quentin Reynolds noted the discreet heroism of Joe Crowther, a Yorkshireman and the wardroom steward on *Calpe* who through unquenchable cheeriness and endless cups of tea and tots of brandy kept dread at bay among the wounded stuck below decks as the ship was shaken by explosions. 'Occasionally a bomb fell fairly close, and down below the waterline we were never sure whether we had received a direct hit or not,' he wrote. 'We'd hear an explosion and the ship would creak and list a bit, and we'd be quiet and then Joe Crowther would laugh and say, "Hell, that was half a mile away."'[30]

Of the 6,000 soldiers who set off, just over half were returning. Of those left behind, 980 were dead or would die of their wounds. In the end the landing craft evacuated 975 men – 601 off Green Beach, 368 off Red and White and a mere six from Blue Beach.[31] Over the afternoon the 2,010 left behind became prisoners.

Surrender was a yearned-for relief for some, a bitter acceptance of failure for others. After swimming back to shore Bob Labatt had arrived just before all resistance ceased. He came across Bill Southam, limping from a wound in the leg, gathering Bren-gunners and riflemen to try to suppress the snipers, still preying on the pathetic, defeated figures scattered below them.

Labatt had lost all his equipment and half his clothes in the swim and now kitted himself out in 'a poor dead tank chap's socks, boots and overalls and an ex-naval rating's duffel coat'. He organised a party to carry casualties into a derelict LCT and with an NCO started to pull casualties back from the waterline. He saw a man run out from cover waving a white flag only to be shot dead, 'whether by our people or the enemy I do not know', but 'probably by both for he had not orders to do it and a stranded tank was in action not twenty yards from him'.[32]

The tankers had made their decision to stay and fight until their ammunition was exhausted, even if it meant inevitable capture. Enemy fighters were flying over at a hundred feet now not even bothering to bomb or machine-gun. Labatt believed he had to have orders from above to surrender but he had no way of communicating with Southam or anyone else. As acting 4th Brigade commander it was in his hands. Whatever the protocols, individuals were anyway making their own decisions. Another white flag was flying from the LCT medical post, apparently on the instructions of the medical officer.[33] At just before 15.00 he 'made the most unpleasant decision of my life'. The Rileys had captured a downed German airman and he was now sent forward waving a white towel. 'Firing died down, mortar shells ceased to fall.' Thirty or forty Germans had advanced across the promenade and they 'leaped up on the sea wall and covered us with tommy guns, light machine guns and rifles'. To his disgust some stick grenades were thrown but then it was over. The Canadians came forward with their hands behind their heads, and were searched and their remaining weapons and steel helmets removed.

They filed through the barbed wire and onto the promenade to join the many other prisoners already there.

This was the first time the Germans had seen their enemy up close. The fight had been an impersonal affair with the raiders catching only rare glimpses of those trying to kill them, and the defenders operating at distances that gave the slaughter a clinical remoteness. Lieutenant Titzman who commanded a battery on the west headland descended to inspect the carnage to which his guns had contributed. 'It was a terrible sight,' he said. 'I remember the driver of an armoured car who had made it on to the beach. He was killed and he sat in his car, burned to a skeleton.'[34]

The beach was a vision from a nightmare. After getting the order to abandon his tank, and leading Lieutenant Bennett who was now completely blind to the promenade to surrender, Archie Anderson managed to slip away and resume retrieving some of the many wounded scattered along the water's edge. 'It was almost impossible to step between all the bodies they were so crowded in the water,' he remembered. 'Their arms would float on the waves and flop around in such a way as to wrap around the legs of anyone who came close to them.' One man had lost both legs. He told Anderson, ' "There's no point in taking me. Leave me here." But I said my mother always told me, where there's life there's hope so we've got to try. I took one arm over each shoulder and carried him that way. I was amazed that a man . . . could be so light.'[35]

The only Canadians still at large were the band of twenty led by Colonel Catto who were sheltering in the woods behind the east headland. They were surrounded on all sides, with no effective means of fighting and the men he had left on the beach were dead or captured. Those who felt fit enough slipped away, armed with the escape kits with which everyone had been issued. At 16.20 Catto came forward to make his formal surrender. It was taken by the local commander, Hauptmann Schnösenberg. They shook hands and the German led him off to his command post. Later the division would leave France for the Eastern Front. Schnösenberg would remember this day as 'the last knightly encounter with the enemy on the field of battle'.[36]

★

In the streets of Dieppe, civilians emerged from their houses to inspect the shattered streets. Georges Guibon, the former hotelier and meticulous diarist of the occupation, paused at the corner of the rue Pasteur to watch a column of prisoners, guarded by a handful of Germans with machine guns. 'They were very close to me and as each one passed I murmured "Thank you! Thank you!",' he wrote that night. 'They looked at me and smiled. Some of them wore overalls. Others were just left with a shirt or a pair of pants. One was naked. Some had wrapped sacking tied up with string around their feet to protect them. There were 200 or 300 of them. It was appalling and desperately sad.'[37]

Pierre Delvallé left his flat in the rue de la Barre and went down to the promenade. The ground behind the casino was littered with cartridge belts, bayonets, rifles and empty ration tins. Propped up against the low wall around the garden were five wounded French Canadians.[38] They begged him for water and he collected some from a broken pipe flowing into the gutter. They drank it gratefully. One gave him a letter addressed to someone in Le Havre, covered in blood.

As the ships neared England those on board savoured the sight of home. 'Shall I ever forget Beachy Head and the Seven Sisters showing through the evening haze? No,' wrote Michael Bateson as he nursed LCP 159 towards Newhaven.[39] At the docks tea wagons waited and YMCA volunteers handed out mugs by the hundred to the ragged, dirty and exhausted arrivals. They were the lucky ones, capable of walking. There were more than 600 wounded scattered through the fleet. The original plan had been for casualties to be landed at Newhaven but to get them to hospital quicker Hughes-Hallett diverted the destroyers carrying most of the serious cases to Portsmouth.

To preserve security, the medical services were not told of the operation until 05.30 that morning. That left only a few hours to improvise arrangements in the five military hospitals in the area, and the numbers arriving far outstripped the optimistic predictions on which plans had been based.

The wait at the quayside for an ambulance was agonisingly long for Derek Turner whose leg and hand had been shattered when *Garth* was bombed. The one that eventually picked him up 'bumped roughly along – then stopped. What ages it took!' When he reached a dressing station there were 'nurses, doctors, padres – hundreds of 'em – and bodies and corpses sprawling everywhere'. He was placed on a stretcher, 'face downwards gazing at the drain which ran around the room, full of Jeyes Fluid'. He felt a 'great relief' that he would soon be treated. Such was the pressure of more urgent cases that it was not until three days later that he was operated on.[40]

Later that evening the staff in the COHQ cafeteria at Richmond Terrace were surprised to see their chief at one of the tables, interrogating officers who had clearly come straight from the battlefield. Among them was Peter Young of 3 Commando who after getting back to Newhaven from Yellow 2 had headed straight to London to make his report. 'I was received by Mountbatten himself,' he remembered. He was taken off to the staff mess where he was served a sandwich and 'they all sat round the table while I was eating – Mountbatten, Robert Henriques, General Haydon and all the top brass, all peppering me with questions.'[41] The operation was over but a pressing new task had arrived, one that had great public and personal implications. Since eight o'clock that morning the news had been carrying reports of the operation presenting it as a major success. That fiction could not be maintained for long. But on no account could the world be allowed to believe that the Dieppe raid had been a bloody and pointless failure.

28. The sky over Dieppe was the scene of what would be described as the greatest air battle of the war to date. Aircrew from many nations flew for the Allies. These pilots are American.

29. A Boston bomber from the RAF's 88 Squadron over the battlefield.

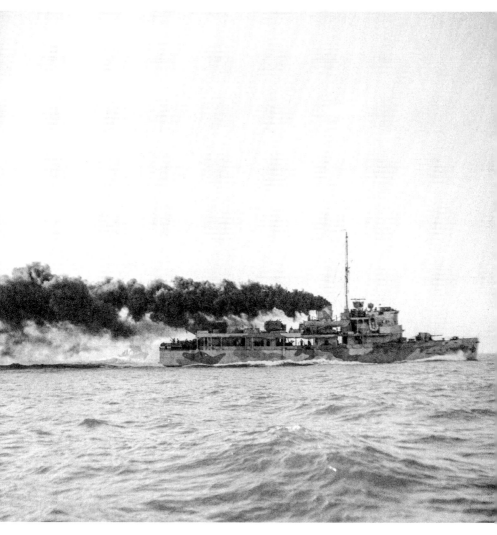

30. Destroyer making smoke. In the absence of heavy naval gunfire support, smokescreens offered some slight protection from the onshore batteries.

31. The Churchills were meant to sweep through the town to attack targets inland. This one got further than most.

32. The wall of death: the slaughter at Blue Beach.

33. Aftermath of defeat.

34. Comradeship: The debacle forged a bond between the survivors that would last until death.

35. Marching into captivity.

36. As adrenaline ebbs, exhaustion sets in.

37. Victors and defeated mingle on the smoking beaches. The Germans could afford to be magnanimous.

38. Devastation: a destroyed bunker at the beach, with the ruins of the casino in the background.

39. Germans inspect a stricken tank landing craft. Images like this reinforced propaganda claims that the attack had been repelled with ease.

40. Smiles and V-signs as survivors return. For a few hours Jubilee was presented as a victory. The truth could not be hidden for long.

PART FOUR

Aftermath

'Big Hun Losses in 9-hr Dieppe Battle' was the headline in the *Daily Mirror* the next morning. Across the Atlantic the front page of the *Toronto Star* announced: 'Canadians Spearhead Battle at Dieppe . . . Help Smash Nazi Opposition'. Details in the first reports were sparse, mostly repeating the communiqués issued by COHQ.

The official account told few outright lies. Nor did it bear much resemblance to the truth. The confident tone seemed at odds with the few facts on offer. There was an admission that 'casualties are likely to have been heavy on both sides' but there did not appear to be much to show for the losses. The list of successes amounted to the destruction of 'a radio location station and flak battery as well as a six-gun battery and ammunition dump', and the lame-sounding boast that the forces 're-embarked only six minutes late'. Even these modest achievements were an overestimation, for the radar station on the eastern headland was still intact.

Nor did the figures claimed for the air battle – eighty-two enemy aircraft destroyed and more than a hundred probably destroyed or damaged against ninety-five definite RAF losses – look like a great victory. It did not need unusual military acumen to guess that there was something not quite right with the picture. Nonetheless, the first foray into selling Dieppe seemed to have worked. Editors fell into line and readers and listeners took away the feeling that the raid had been a considerable success.

Jubilee's architects now had the problem of how to explain what had happened to Churchill and the military hierarchy. First, they had to agree a version among themselves. On Thursday morning Mountbatten, McNaughton and Crerar, the force commanders and members of their various staffs gathered in Room 21 at Montagu House on the Embankment. The reports that followed revealed a stunned reluctance to accept the scale of the failure. Hughes-Hallett talked up the naval achievement. The assembly and naval passage had gone according to plan. The clash with the German convoy had disrupted the attack on Yellow Beach but it 'had not prejudiced tactical surprise' for the other flank attacks 'since the lighthouse near Dieppe continued to function . . . even after the first landings took place'.[1]

The discussion revealed how little they yet knew about what had actually happened onshore. The difficulty was that the battalion commanders who would have been in the best position to tell them were either dead or captured, and the one surviving CO, Joe Ménard, was in hospital with severe wounds. Instead they made do with the optimistic conjectures of naval officers. Hughes-Hallett claimed that the Royals had landed at Blue Beach 'without much difficulty'. Lieutenant Commander Goulding, in charge of the naval party, also stated that they 'crossed the beach without many casualties'. As for Red and White Beaches, according to Hughes-Hallett, 'the arrangements for fighter support appeared to work well.'

This was not the time to start pointing fingers. When Ham Roberts questioned whether tactical surprise had in fact been achieved, pointing out that the 'German gun crews appeared to be standing by when the first flight arrived and that all defence posts were manned', Mountbatten stepped in to put him right, stating firmly that 'this state of alert was normal at dawn and that the condition of weather and tide might have increased the state of alert'. The message was clear and Roberts folded. The minutes recorded that 'the meeting and General Roberts accepted the evidence . . . of tactical surprise'.

It was essential for all concerned that this point became an accepted part of the narrative. Jubilee hinged on surprise and everyone involved at the top had gambled that it was possible to catch the enemy with his guard down. For all their sakes it was vital to show that their faith had been justified. Roberts's intention was not so much to challenge the soundness of that judgement as to raise the suspicion that the Germans knew they were coming. This too had implications for reputations. Following the cancellation of Rutter, security had undoubtedly been compromised but in their rush to remount the raid Mountbatten and Co. had constructed ingenious arguments to suppress their colleagues' concerns. The question of a leak became a major theme of the examinations that followed, and Mountbatten directed his friend Colonel Neville, the Combined Operations Royal Marines adviser, to begin an investigation.

Mountbatten cabled a preliminary report of the meeting to the prime minister who was in Cairo recovering from a bruising summit with Stalin in Moscow. Despite subsequent claims of a lapse of memory, Churchill knew the raid was on, having been told: 'Weather good. Jubilee has started' in a cable sent just after the fleet sailed.[2] He was sent a brief and guarded progress report at mid-afternoon on the 19th. The absence of detail seems to have warned him to expect the worst, for that evening he had a message relayed to COHQ instructing them to describe the operation as 'a reconnaissance in force', a slippery term that allowed a broad interpretation of what constituted success and which duly entered the official vocabulary.

Mountbatten's updated account was evasive and polished up the very few bright points in the story, claiming that 'tactical surprise was achieved' and that 'the synchronisation of each part of the assault was perfect' and highlighting the 4 Commando triumph at Varengeville.[3]

He also claimed 'the Germans must have been rattled as they have been plugging two entirely contradictory lines: 1. that this was an invasion which it has taken us ten months to prepare and 2. that this raid bears all the signs of having been hastily conceived in four or five days as a result of instructions received from you after visiting Russia.'

Churchill had left Moscow on the 16th after fifty-seven hours of gruelling talks and vodka-fuelled banquets. If news of the raid was intended as a *douceur* to sweeten the discussions it did not work. Stalin was his usual cynical and mistrustful self and Brooke, who accompanied the prime minister, looked at the dictator's 'unpleasantly cold, crafty, dead face' with fascinated horror. In the first meeting 'the discussion ranged mainly round our inability to establish a second front, and the fact that they cannot understand why we cannot do so.'[4]

Churchill, though, had something more substantial than Jubilee to lay before his host. Now that the Americans had agreed to Torch, another front would indeed be opened in 1942, albeit in North Africa rather than Europe. Churchill left believing that his host was 'entirely convinced of the great advantages of TORCH'.[5] In all, the British delegation thought they had got the main message across. General Archie Wavell expressed his satisfaction in a verse penned on the flight to Teheran: 'Prince of the Kremlin, here's a fond farewell; / I've had to deal with many worse than you. / You took it though you hated it like hell; / No Second Front in 1942.'[6]

The skeletal account laid out in the Dieppe communiqués was not going to satisfy press, public or politicians for long. In the days following the raid the COHQ and government propaganda teams got busy fleshing out the story with correspondents' despatches and combatants' accounts, all carefully censored. At the same time they began spreading an interpretation of what had happened that invested what seemed at first sight a rather perplexing event with value and meaning.

The reporters' accounts rightly stressed the extraordinary bravery and fortitude of the soldiers, sailors and airmen. The primary role of the Canadians was initially underplayed and the impression given that this was a largely commando show with significant American support, an exaggeration which was amplified in the US and which was viewed indulgently by British propaganda chiefs. However, their rightful place was soon recognised. Frederick Griffin of the *Toronto Star* stated that 'the large-scale land job was entirely given to Canadian soldiers.'[7] He made it clear that the raid 'has resulted in our first heavy casualties'. In the fighting 'our men, tasting battle for the first time against the Germans of today, behaved bravely and brilliantly'. He went on to place the action in the sacrificial tradition of the previous world war, judging: 'The Battle of Dieppe will go on Canada's honour roll with Ypres, Vimy, the Somme and Passchendaele . . .' Their gallantry would be reflected a few weeks later in a rich crop of awards including sixty-one MCs and MMs, and twelve DSOs. There was a Victoria Cross for Cecil Merritt, and later another for the Reverend John Foote who though urged to try to re-embark chose to go into captivity with his flock.

Griffin's article also emphasised that the losses were suffered in a higher cause. One of the 'definite objectives' was 'what might be called the establishing of a beachhead on the continent by troops on a considerable experimental scale'. This legend of Dieppe as a military laboratory for the great invasion was repeated everywhere. Within a few days *The Times* was referring to it as a 'dress rehearsal' for a second front.

The groundwork for the exegesis was laid even before Jubilee was launched. A briefing prepared for editors a few days beforehand had raised the possibility of 'substantial losses'. However, it went on: 'No losses . . . can be compared with the value of the essential experience and military information gained . . . and the importance of this to our future policy'.[8] This claim would henceforth provide the bed-rock justification for Jubilee, repeated not only by those who conceived it but also by many of the men who had to carry it out.

Despite Mountbatten's remarks about the incoherence of the Germans' public reaction, Dieppe handed them a huge propaganda opportunity from which they wrung every drop of advantage. As expected, they presented the raid as a failed invasion attempt. The first considered bulletin, issued by the high command, went out in the evening and was fairly faithful to the facts, even underestimating the Allied casualties. It concluded: 'The enemy has suffered a decisive defeat. His attempt at invasion served only political purposes and was contrary to all military common sense.'[9]

A few weeks later, thousands of four-page pamphlets fluttered down over English south-coast towns and villages, some of them landing on the Canadians' camps. Titled 'Dieppe' they carried twenty-nine pictures laid out like a photo album depicting the after-math of the raid. They showed burning landing craft and bodies crumpled up beside wrecked tanks, soldiers in their underwear hob-bling over the pebbles, a grateful captive accepting a light from a helmeted German infantryman and German medics loading wounded onto a lorry. Apart from brief American and British press quotes apparently validating the contention that the raid was in fact an in-vasion attempt, no supporting text was considered necessary and the Germans let the images speak for themselves.

The pamphlet was a reasonable reflection of reality. Those prison-ers able to walk were marched off to collection centres in town before being put on trains for camps inland, prior to going east. German casualties got treated first but thereafter the wounded were mostly shown basic decency and the army censors scrutinising letters home noted the 'constant repetition of praise for the treatment they have received in hospital . . . from the Germans'.[10]

Forbes West was carted off Blue Beach to a makeshift first-aid post in a small hotel on the clifftop behind Puys. He lay there with about thirty other wounded, listening to the crash of falling RAF bombs. Later they were moved to the Hôtel Dieu hospital in Rouen where forty-eight hours after sustaining his leg wound he finally got treatment. It was 'good but it was rough . . . no rougher for me than for what they did to their own people. Anaesthetic was pretty short and their substitute was two strong Germans who held you down while the doctor did whatever he had to do.'[11]

The reaction of the Vichy press was slavish and predictable. *Le Réveil du Nord* presented the raid as 'a desperate action ordered by Moscow' and crowed that while the British public had been led to believe that the invasion of the continent was imminent, '*Londres a jubilé trop tôt*' ('London has celebrated too soon').

Dieppe underwent its own harrowing ordeal that day. The 12,000 or so men, women and children still in the town lived the most terrifying hours of their lives, caught between the bombs and shells and bullets of attackers and defenders. Some managed to reach air-raid shelters provided by the town's efficient Défense Passive civil defence organisation. Nonetheless twenty-six people were killed and six died later of wounds. Most of the victims lived in Janval on the southern edge of Dieppe where there were fewer shelters. They included a father of seven, a mother of five and twin fifteen-year-old boys. The oldest fatality was eighty-nine-year-old Alexandre Claire. Another ten civilians were killed in the Pourville area, including Claude Freville, just turned three. Seafront hotels like the Royal, the Brighton and the Regina were smoke-blackened or gutted and the tobacco factory was burned to the ground.

The population accepted their fate stoically. They showed only compassion to the defeated men who brought war to their town, helping them whenever they could and muttering words of support and even thanks. Some went further and put their own lives at risk. Lieutenant Commander Redvers Prior, who led the flotilla carrying the South Saskatchewans into Green Beach and ended up helping to organise the rearguard party, was wounded four times during the day but still managed to jump out of the hospital train taking him to Rouen.[12] He walked through the night, then hid in a barn. The penalty for aiding Allied soldiers was death, yet the farmer sheltered him for three days while he recovered, then gave him civilian clothes and 1,500 francs before handing him on to a Resistance network who passed him down an escape line to Spain. Several other evaders had the kindness of French strangers to thank for avoiding capture and making it back to England, including the artillery spotter on Blue Beach George Browne, and Lucien Dumais of the Fusiliers Mont-Royal. Dumais afterwards joined the escape and evasion organisation MI9 and would return to France.

Despite the many acts of sympathy and support, the Germans portrayed the French as having taken their side. The high command's official report which appeared ten days afterwards claimed that 'the attitude of the French population was more than correct . . . they helped the German forces during the fighting with all sorts of services'.[13] There was no evidence that this was the case but the occupiers were determined to present the event as an important test of Franco-German solidarity that the Dieppois had passed with flying colours. Two days after the raid the mayor René Levasseur was called to a meeting with the sub-prefect Michel Sassier, the commandant of the 571st Regiment Oberstleutnant Bartelt and the head of the local *Kommandantur*. He was told that due to the damage suffered and as a reward for the 'neutral conduct' of the population, a grant of 10 million francs would be given to help the town's recovery. Levasseur seized the chance to exploit this access of goodwill. He replied that though the grant was welcome, the return of the soldiers from the area taken prisoner in 1940 would be even more appreciated. The request was immediately approved by Hitler, evidence of the excellent humour that Jubilee's failure had generated at the top. The first batch of 984 prisoners arrived to a joyful welcome at Dieppe station on 12 September to be followed later on by another 601.

In Canada initial satisfaction soon gave way to apprehension. Details of the dead, the wounded and the captured were released in dribs and drabs and every day the list grew longer. The slow release of the figures was not the result of a deliberate policy of softening the blow, but simply because the administrative machinery of the Canadian Army in Britain was overwhelmed with the task of gathering the information. It was not until 15 September that a comprehensive list was published. Until then the total numbers released amounted to 925. Now the figures leaped to 3,350. It was 'the longest one-day casualty list in Canadian history' and ran to 134 pages, so long that many newspapers published it in instalments.[14] That meant a casualty rate of more than 67 per cent. The final reckoning would show that of the 4,963 Canadians who sailed for France, 907 were killed or died of their injuries and 1,946 were taken prisoner, of whom at least 568 were wounded.[15]

This was the Canadians' first battle with the Germans in this war and the results seemed every bit as dreadful as the great bloodbaths of the previous one. The announcement had 'shocked and dismayed every Canadian' declared the *Globe and Mail* in Toronto. The scale of the trauma diminished willingness to accept the official portrayal of Jubilee as a success and the claim that the losses were justified. Three days after the casualty list appeared the defence minister James Ralston published his official report. It stated the objectives of the raid were to 'gather information and experience vital to the general offensive program' and explained that heavy casualties 'were to be expected in amphibious operations of this type'. There were more details which corrected the optimistic picture painted earlier so that Canadians now knew that contrary to the first impression created, the town had never been captured. But there were still obvious gaps in the story and while the statement that 'no public analysis of the lessons learned is possible' was understandable on security grounds, it did little to support the thesis that the suffering had been worth it.

The goodwill of the press had already started to fray. The well-known British-born broadcaster John Collingwood Reade used his column in the conservative *Globe and Mail* to question the official line and make shrewd though commonsensical observations that blew holes in the logic of the military experts. In an article headlined

'Many Grave Doubts Raised by Official Report on Dieppe' he pointed out that any lessons learned by the attackers would be offset by the knowledge gained by the defenders, and concluded: 'No useful purpose is ever served by puffing up a doubtful experiment and magnifying it into a great victory.' The *Ottawa Journal* reflected that had the Germans attacked a British port with the same outcome the government would be claiming a major victory. To some extent the controversy was conducted along political lines. The *Globe* and the *Journal* were conservative-supporting and naturally unsympathetic to Mackenzie King's Liberal administration, while the Liberal press took a neutral or sympathetic line in their treatment of Dieppe.

Beyond political concerns the government had to contend with the effect on public morale. The devastated regiments sprang from the little towns and settlements of the plains, and cities like Hamilton and Windsor small enough to feel a shared identity. With Dieppe a tidal wave of grief rolled across the country, engulfing communities where everybody could put faces to the names on the list and remember them as they were when they marched away, barely out of boyhood and full of life and hope. Once the telegrams began to arrive families lived in a state of dread, readying themselves for the worst. In Windsor, Ontario, Mrs Elizabeth Murphy received four telegrams in the space of twenty-four hours informing her that three of her sons were now prisoners of war and one was dead.

The stream of letters home from the camps in Germany kept the memory of Dieppe alive and raw. They were monitored by the Prisoners of War Section of the Department of Foreign Affairs which in December 1942 issued an analysis of the contents. The feelings the writers poured out to their loved ones were a mixture of bitterness and pride. 'The general impression . . . is that of an operation which completely lacked the element of surprise,' the report noted. 'It looks as though the raid was a hopeless task from the outset. There is no indication whatever that any substantial progress away from the beaches was achieved or that the men on the beaches ever had a chance of coming to close grips with the enemy or achieving any useful purpose at all. This impression may be mistaken but it is the only impression left by these letters.'

The testimony amounted to an indictment of 'the hopeless character of the raid as a military operation' and by extension of those who
conceived it. On the other hand, there were 'hardly any complaints
about any other units or forces having failed to do their part'. The
only hint of criticism was that 'the air force did not give the support
that was expected of it'.[16] The prisoners struck a cheerful tone, no
doubt to try to calm the anxieties of their families and friends and
this was taken as evidence of the resilience of their morale. 'Faith in
their officers is freely expressed in many letters,' ran another report.[17]
'Regrets are not shown, but just enthusiasm, satisfaction and pride in
achievement, and the Canadians' share in the raid . . .'

The prisoners' plight had been made worse by a tit-for-tat dispute that
broke out between the German and British authorities over the
treatment of prisoners. The Germans were keen to maintain the idea
that, on the Western Front at least, war was still conducted according to an honourable code. During the surrender they seized part of
a set of orders which Brigadier Southam had taken ashore in defi-
ance of regulations and then inexplicably failed to destroy before his
capture. It included the directive that 'wherever possible prisoners'
hands will be tied to prevent destruction of their documents' – the
commando practice that Roberts had opposed.

The Germans announced that Dieppe prisoners would be shackled
in reprisal but relented after the War Office responded that if such an
order had been issued it would be 'cancelled'. A few weeks later, the
commandos launched a minor raid on the Channel Island of Sark in
which prisoners were taken and hands bound. The following day,
Canadian prisoners had their hands tied, shackles later replacing
rope. Britain then responded in kind, and against the advice of the
Canadian government ordered a number of German prisoners of war
in camps in Canada to be manacled. The issue went back and forth
with the Swiss government and International Committee of the Red
Cross mediating. It was not until November 1943 that the Germans
stopped the practice. By then observance of it had largely become a
formality. In one camp handcuffs had to be worn only briefly twice a
day. At the outset, though, the punishment had meant discomfort

and humiliation for many. Captain Walter McGregor of the Essex Scottish was one of 300 prisoners in one camp who were manacled from 08.00 to 21.00. 'Finished our second month in fetters yesterday,' he wrote. 'Resigned to having them on till the end of the war so anything short of that will come as a pleasant surprise . . .'[18]

The Canadian prisoners adopted the same array of coping mechanisms as every other prisoner of war. Some tried to fill the limitless spare time learning languages, broadening their education or aquiring unlikely skills. Bob Labatt took up embroidery. Some threw themselves into trying to escape. According to Fred Jasperson, the captured COs discussed Dieppe 'to some extent but nobody wanted to talk about it too much'.[19] The memory, then and thereafter, provoked a tangle of emotions, of pride, bewilderment, anguish and also bitterness.

More than thirty years later, Leo Lecky, the intelligence lance corporal who accompanied Brigadier Southam, was asked 'what sticks in your mind about Dieppe?' He replied: 'The absolute needless slaughter . . . the feeling that we had been bamboozled as guinea pigs'. They had been told on the crossing that before they arrived an air and sea bombardment 'was going to batter all resistance'. On landing there would undoubtedly be some 'sticky situations but with the commando training you've had it should be nothing . . . it will be more or less mopping up'. He concluded sadly: 'Oh boy, were we taken in.'[20]

The censors scoured the mail to gauge the damage to morale. They were relieved to find that 'there does not appear to be a hint of any desire to avoid further action'.[21] Their conclusion was that most men felt they had done their units and Canada proud and proved themselves better soldiers than the Germans, and had gained priceless personal experience for when the next time came. A report cited approvingly the comment of one anonymous participant that 'I learned more at Dieppe than the army could learn me in ten years.'

It was unlikely that the survivors would impart their true feelings in letters to their loved ones that had passed under the eyes of the authorities. The recollection of Lieutenant George Buchanan of the South Saskatchewans was that the relief of having made it back home was quickly replaced by feelings of dejection and disillusionment.

Two day after his return he was in the regiment's makeshift orderly room in a tented camp in Sussex going through the company rolls and trying to work out 'who to write to, who got back, who didn't' when a fellow officer who was a veteran of the First World War came in. He had decided to abandon his duties and head to the hospital in Birmingham where some of the unit's wounded were being treated and invited Buchanan along. When Buchanan pointed out that their superiors would regard this as having gone absent without leave his friend replied: 'To hell with them – they sold us down the river . . . So we just left the regiment. Neither of us cared whether we got court-martialled . . . that was the feeling of everybody at that point.'[22]

Dieppe, for all its trauma, did not seriously threaten the confidence of Canadians in their leaders. Public opinion seems to have been robust enough to accept that things went wrong in war and that there was little to be gained by raging about it. There would be no contentious inquiry like the one that followed the Hong Kong debacle of December 1941. No political heads rolled and the main reputational damage would be borne by the man most visibly associated with Jubilee, General Andy McNaughton. Nonetheless, for a while at least, it led young Canadians to think twice about joining up. Before the raid about 3,000 new recruits were volunteering each week. In the months after, the numbers dipped, and fell below 2,000 one week in October before starting to recover.

British public reaction was muted. The raid did little to reduce pressure to help Russia, with *The Times* declaring Dieppe would not 'dispel the impression that the British war effort is inadequate at a moment when Russia is facing her gravest crisis'.[23] Churchill would have to say something about what had happened and he dealt with the matter in a passage in a long speech to the Commons on 8 September.

It was the first session after the month-long summer recess and, as he reminded members, his first appearance since he emerged victorious from the vote of censure of early July. Since then there had been 'several important operations of war'. He started with Operation Pedestal, the epic effort of 9–15 August to fight a convoy through to relieve Malta. Next came Dieppe, which he dealt with in fewer than

300 words. It was a 'most gallant affair', the military credit for which went to 'the Canadian troops, who formed five-sixths of the assaulting force, and to the Royal Navy, which carried them all there and which carried most of them back'. The raid was to be 'considered as a reconnaissance in force' and was 'a hard, savage clash such as are likely to become increasingly numerous as the war deepens'. It was mounted because 'we had to get all the information necessary before launching operations on a much larger scale.' Apart from its reconnaissance value, the raid 'brought about an extremely satisfactory air battle in the West which Fighter Command wish they could repeat every week. It inflicted perhaps as much loss upon the enemy in killed and wounded as we suffered ourselves.' He made clear his own endorsement of the exercise, stating: 'I, personally, regarded the Dieppe assault, to which I gave my sanction, as an indispensable preliminary to full-scale operations.' He would give no more detail as it was best that the enemy 'should be left to his own ruminations, unassisted by British or American advice or comment'.[24]

This brief mention raised several contentious points. What did he mean by a reconnaissance in force? As generally understood, a reconnaissance was an attempt to discover enemy dispositions without getting into a fight, which seemed the opposite of what was intended at Dieppe. The claim that the RAF would welcome weekly repeats of the Dieppe air battle was equally baffling if the best that could be said was that losses had been equal on both sides.

However, neither of these matters gave concern to the Labour opposition leader in the Commons Arthur Greenwood when he rose to reply. He accepted 'the assurance that this was a reconnaissance in force' and had 'no doubt myself that it provided experience in combined operations which will be needed in the further stages of the war'.

Little more was heard about Dieppe in the Commons that year and it seemed that the episode had barely ruffled the surface of public debate. There was one notable exception to the newspapers' largely indulgent attitude. Lord Beaverbrook's Canadian blood was fired by what he saw as the scandalous waste of his countrymen's lives. He had used his newspapers to boost and flatter Mountbatten but now he turned on him, attacking him in public and in private. This was hurtful but not too professionally damaging given Beaverbrook's well-known vindictiveness.

More worrying to Mountbatten was the attitude of his peers. When the chiefs of staff met the day after the raid there was no mention in the minutes of any discussion of Dieppe. Nor was it raised in the meetings that followed. The discussion was completely dominated by Torch, the date of which had now been provisionally set for mid-October. COHQ would be closely involved in the planning and when Mountbatten made his first post-Jubilee appearance at the committee on Saturday 22 August his contribution was to point out the effect that the diversion of landing craft and crews to the project would have on major cross-Channel operations for the rest of the year.[25]

Things did not remain quiet for long. Brooke was absent from these meetings as he was travelling back from the Middle East with Churchill. On Saturday 29 August he and Mountbatten were invited down to Chequers. At dinner Brooke spoke freely and critically about the raid. Two days later Mountbatten wrote him a letter whose tone of high indignation reveals how seriously his composure had been shaken:

> Dear CIGS
>
> I was absolutely dumbfounded at dinner last Saturday at Chequers, when you made your very outspoken criticism of the manner in which the Dieppe raid was planned. I had meant to come and see you about it after leaving the dining room but, before I could do so, the prime minister sent for me on the terrace and said: 'I heard CIGS complaining that the planning was all wrong for the Dieppe Show. What did he mean?'

Mountbatten then gave a comprehensive defence of his role, one that he and his supporters would repeat often in the years ahead. He told Brooke that he had replied to Churchill that the raid had been 'planned in accordance with the chiefs of staff's own instructions' and that he had 'no idea on what [Brooke's] complaint is based unless it is a fundamental objection to having a CCO and a Combined Operations Staff'. When Churchill asked him to 'explain how the military side of the Dieppe raid was planned' he gave a lengthy account carefully apportioning responsibility, which he laid out in the letter. Dieppe had been chosen to satisfy General Paget's view that it should take place under adequate air cover. The exact location was selected by a search committee consisting of a soldier, sailor and airman of the COHQ staff in conjunction with the senior planning officer at Home Forces.

After examining the proposal himself he and Paget agreed that the Canadians and 1st Airborne Division should carry out the raid. He then obtained the chiefs of staff's approval, which of course included Brooke. After Roberts and the 2nd Canadian Division were selected, Paget had nominated Montgomery as his representative for the operation who had 'thereafter attended all the principal planning meetings and personally supervised the military plan while General Roberts was preparing it'. As a matter of policy he had got the navy and air force to fit in with the military plan and left General Montgomery an 'absolutely free hand'.

Mountbatten took responsibility for the decision to remount the raid following the cancellation of Rutter, claiming that he had 'obtained the concurrence of the C-in-C Home Forces [Paget] and C-in-C Portsmouth [James] to be the final authority to mount and launch the operation. The chiefs of staff approved . . .'

After Crerar replaced Montgomery for Jubilee, he 'attended the principal planning meetings and passed the revised plan in person . . .' He emphasised that far from being solely a COHQ enterprise 'from beginning to end the army were given complete freedom in regard to the military operations and the force commanders signed their own operation orders'.

He finished stiffly:

> I have always made it a practice to report to the chiefs of staff any conversations of consequence which I may have with the prime minister. Since, however, in this instance, the conversation arose out of a personal but direct criticism of me which you made at the dinner table, I have thought it better to report this to you alone in the first instance . . . I should very much hope that after reading the account of the planning arrangements for Dieppe . . . you will feel able to withdraw your criticism and assure me that the planning was, in fact, done with due regard to the army's special responsibilities.

If not, Mountbatten 'should have no option but to ask the minister of defence [i.e. Churchill] for a full and impartial inquiry into the planning and execution of the raid and the conduct of all concerned'.[26]

This seems to have been enough for Brooke to back off. The spat may have sharpened Mountbatten's awareness of the need to get COHQ's version of events abroad as soon as possible, for work immediately began on a long and detailed 'Combined Report on the Dieppe Raid' which appeared on 15 October in which the history was laid out as Mountbatten had explained it to the PM on the terrace at Chequers.

Even so, in December Churchill returned to the subject. His continued interest was perhaps the result of Beaverbrook's disparagement campaign, or his dual concern as both historian and statesman about how the episode would be regarded when the war was over.

In a memo to Ismay he mused that 'although for many reasons everyone was concerned to make this business look as good as possible, the time has now come when I must be informed more precisely about the military plans.'[27] Who had made the plans? Who approved them? What was Montgomery's part in them, and General McNaughton's? What did people think of Roberts? Did the General Staff approve the plans? When, in Brooke's absence, was the Vice CIGS told that the raid was on again? This was a reference to General Archibald Nye who had apparently heard that Dieppe was being attacked only when the first communiqués were issued.

Churchill was concerned with not only the origins of the operation but the quality of the plan itself, for 'at first sight it would appear to a layman very much out of accord with the accepted principles of war to attack the strongly fortified town front without first securing the cliffs on either side, and to use our tanks in frontal assault off the beaches by the casino, etc., instead of landing them a few miles up the coast and entering the town from the back.'

Ismay was told to get the answers, after which Churchill would consider whether a more formal inquiry was needed. On 22 December Ismay wrote to Mountbatten asking him for the information. He was apologetic, saying he had 'no idea for the reason for this. It may be that adverse criticisms have reached [Churchill's] ears; or again, it may be that he wishes to ensure that false deductions have not been drawn from the results, possibly with an eye to future operations on the continent. Yet again, it may be that his mind is harking back to the incident at a dinner party at Chequers when CIGS made a number of allegations . . .'[28]

Everything in Mountbatten's record to date had led him to believe that embarrassing episodes could be passed over smoothly with no adverse consequences for his career. He might have thought that having delivered a personal account to the PM as well as a long written report to Brooke, the post-Dieppe debris had been tidied away, yet now he was being asked to return to a subject he would rather forget.

It seemed clear from the prime minister's questions that he was looking for culprits. In his replies Mountbatten made sure that blame was spread wide and Montgomery in particular took his full share of responsibility. Monty was 'the senior army officer concerned with the raid from about the end of April onwards' and was 'present at all the important meetings of the planners'. McNaughton, on the other hand, 'having delegated his authority to General Crerar, took no direct part in the planning'. His assessment of Ham Roberts was less than effusive and also inaccurate given the Canadian's tendency to roll over when challenged by his British colleagues. He was a 'brave man who was always prepared to give a definite opinion and who was tenacious in holding to his views'. The query about whether the Vice CIGS was told Dieppe was on again produced a crisp admission that he 'was not specially informed of the operation'. Mountbatten perhaps felt that he was covered on this point by the approval he told Churchill and Brooke he had obtained from Paget and James to relaunch the raid on his own authority and which he claimed had been subsequently confirmed by the chiefs.

As to the plan itself, Mountbatten accepted there had been gaps in the intelligence picture. While photographic reconnaissance revealed much of the enemy defences they did not 'disclose the type or calibre of the guns in the eastern headland, nor did they show what ultimately proved to be the fact, that there were similar pillboxes built in the cliffs on the western headland'. Nor did they reveal the anti-tank guns behind some of the roadblocks into town due to the fact that they were removed during daylight.

Explaining the reasons for 'attacking a strongly fortified town without securing the cliffs at either side' he referred the prime minister to the paragraph in the report which showed that the plan was for the flank attacks to neutralise the headlands before the main assault went in.

While willing to accept a degree of responsibility for the various shortcomings, he was not going to let COHQ take the blame for the fatal flaw at its heart. On the key question of landing the tanks on the main beaches rather than on the flanks of the town he pointed to sections of the report which made it clear that the Combined Ops proposal had been to put the armour ashore on either side of Dieppe. They had been overruled by the Home Forces team who argued that the tanks would take too long to reach the town and might be held up if the bridges over the Scie and Sâane were blown.

In his version, COHQ had been the voice of prudence and caution, with the naval staff warning that 'a frontal attack was hazardous'. It was only after assurances that the assault would be preceded by 'a bombing attack on the town . . . of maximum intensity' that the Combined Ops team conceded and the army plan carried the day.[29]

Thus the main elements that had raised Churchill's hostile curiosity were laid at the door of the army – and Montgomery. The prime minister decided to leave things there, at least for the time being. There was no further talk of an inquiry and no possibility of any sort of censure of the main participants. Montgomery was now probably the most celebrated man in Britain having turned the victory at Alamein in November into a personal triumph. Mountbatten and COHQ had played an important part in the success of Torch and would soon be enmeshed in the Sicily landings. At the same time they were at work on the preparations for the cross-Channel invasion. Here Mountbatten had suffered a setback. His ambition to play a leading role was unlikely to be realised. The planning would be directed by the holder of the newly created post of chief of staff to the as yet unnamed Supreme Allied Commander. While he was struck down by pneumonia in March 1943 it was given to General

Frederick Morgan, and Mountbatten's allotted role in the great adventure would be essentially advisory. This was a blow but, following a familiar pattern, his disappointment was diminished by another vertiginous leap upward when in August 1943 he was appointed Supreme Allied Commander, South East Asia Command. His replacement was the former commando chief Bob Laycock, now a major general, who took over an organisation whose scope for independent action was much reduced. The time of large-scale raids was at an end. There were to be no more after Jubilee and henceforth all major amphibious operations would be invasions, in Sicily, Italy, Normandy and the South of France, requiring much bigger inter-service staffs and structures than COHQ could provide.

For the British Dieppe was a painful embarrassment. For the Americans it was sobering evidence of the difficulties involved in cross-Channel operations. The immediate memory of it would soon be washed away by the rush of events in North Africa. For the Canadian Army it was a catastrophe. 'Little was left of the 4th Brigade,' wrote Stacey, 'not much more of the 6th.'[30] Of the 554 Royals who sailed to France only two officers and six men returned. Exactly half of the force was killed. Of the 582 Rileys who fought, 197 died. Somehow a new 2nd Division would have to be rebuilt from the remains of the old.

Yet unit pride and identity reasserted itself with remarkable speed. George Buchanan remembered that among the South Saskatchewans, 'after about a month, a real *esprit de corps* developed again.' The new CO, Lieutenant Colonel Fred Clift, 'used the boys who came back as the core', lauding their achievements to the fresh troops arriving to fill the ranks. 'All the COs were doing the same thing, talking up the Dieppe veterans. All the privates became NCOs and all the NCOs got promotions.'

It was some time before the repercussions of the raid rippled to the top. McNaughton and Crerar may have had nothing to do with the raid's conception, but once involved, they had supported it to the hilt. Crerar had operational oversight of Jubilee while McNaughton looked on from above. But when the reputational reckoning inevitably came, it was McNaughton who suffered. At home his prestige was dented. In Britain his authority was undermined. The process was abetted by Crerar who emerged from the episode unscathed.

Brooke's admiration for McNaughton was already limited and he regarded him as touchy and uncooperative. McNaughton had made himself unpopular with his insistence that Canadian troops fight as one formation rather than being broken up and parcelled out to suit Allied needs. His performance in a major exercise, Spartan, in March 1943, run to simulate a continental invasion, dealt another blow to his standing, confirming Brooke's fears that he was 'quite incompetent to command an army'.[31]

Crerar was content to have his rival's reputation undermined by the British and McNaughton's enemies at home. The dignified soldier-scientist lingered on until the end of 1943 when he resigned, returning to Canada to eventually replace Ralston as defence minister. In February 1944 Crerar led the 1st Canadian Corps to Italy, then returned to take over the 1st Canadian Army to prepare it for D-Day, with Mann as his chief of staff.

Somebody at the top had to pay the price of failure and Ham Roberts was the perfect candidate. Stoical, passive, honourable and unimaginative, he was made for the role of scapegoat. It was some months before the blow fell. In April 1943, following what Crerar judged to be an inept performance in the Spartan war games, Roberts was relieved of command of 2nd Division and moved to a backwater post in charge of organising reinforcements. He left the army and Canada soon after the war and retired to the Channel Island of Jersey.

By the end of the war Mountbatten's achievements in South East Asia, overseeing the recapture of Burma and reversing the humiliation of Singapore, had gilded him with success and fame. The glow was not enough to dispel the shadow of Dieppe. In 1950, having just taken up an appointment as Fourth Sea Lord at the Admiralty, he found himself once more having to answer questions from Churchill, relayed again by the faithful Ismay. The great man was out of office and deep in writing his history of the war. Considering Dieppe, his interest now centred not so much on the planning and military responsibility as on the question of 'who took the decision to *revive* the attack after it had been abandoned and Montgomery had cleared out'. Specifically he wanted Ismay to find out 'did the chiefs of staff, or the Defence Committee or the War Cabinet ever consider the matter of the *revival* of the operation (a) when I was in England, (b) when I was out of England, or was it all pushed through by Dickie [Mountbatten] on his own without reference to higher authority?'[32]

Ismay could find nothing in the Cabinet Office files to clear the matter up, perhaps because 'in the vital interests of secrecy, nothing was put on paper'. However, he suggested Churchill must have known Jubilee was on as he used the code word in a cable from Cairo two days before it went ahead, and indeed had received another on the evening it was launched.

Churchill proceeded with a draft that made it clear that it was Mountbatten who revived the raid and that while he was 'in principle favourable to an operation of this character at this time', there was no written record of the revised plan being reconsidered by the chiefs or the War Cabinet.

When Mountbatten was consulted he reacted with something like panic. He browbeat Ismay, deluging him with answers and insisting on an interpretation of the casualty figure so it reflected only the 18 per cent dead rather than 67 per cent in all categories as in normal military accounting, and producing his own complete rewrite of the draft. According to David Reynolds's study of Churchill as a historian of the war, Churchill in the end 'lost interest . . . he simply nodded through Mountbatten's rewrite', which passed responsibility back to Churchill and the chiefs, played down the Canadian losses and played up the benefits of the operation.[33]

No matter how much time passed or how busy he was, on hearing of any book or programme on Dieppe, Mountbatten would swoop to assert his version of events. When in 1958 the Admiralty began preparations for an update of its Battle Summary No. 33, *The Raid on Dieppe*, he contacted Hughes-Hallett, Haydon, Skrine and Henriques of the old COHQ staff asking them to dredge their memories for recollections that matched his own. Bernard Fergusson's 1961 history of Combined Operations *The Watery Maze* was compiled and written under Mountbatten's supervision. In a Canadian Broadcasting

Corporation documentary for the *Close Up* series, produced to mark
the twentieth anniversary of the raid, Mountbatten was at its centre,
confident and smooth as he brazenly assured the audience: 'The old
Duke of Wellington has been credited with the saying that the Battle
of Waterloo was won on the playing fields of Eton. I am quite sure
that the Battle of Normandy was won on the beaches of Dieppe. For
every one man who died at Dieppe at least ten or more were spared in
the invasion of Normandy two years later.'[34] Once again he peddled
his own soothing formula for reading the casualty figures which
showed that of the Canadians who took part 'nearly 82 per cent
survived'.

The programme assembled almost everyone who had had a hand
in Dieppe. Even Ham Roberts was persuaded to make a rare public
appearance. Compared with the foxy evasiveness of Monty, the thin-
lipped hauteur of Hughes-Hallett and the stiff self-righteousness of
Crerar, he made a dignified and slightly tragic figure as he admitted
that 'earlier I did feel a bit bitter' about his treatment. In his soft,
English-sounding accent he went on: 'I don't like the word scapegoat
very much, but I think . . . that a lot of people think that I was to
blame because I was in command. But I was only a small man in those
days. A small cog in a big machine.' Then, smiling ruefully, he spelled
out the appalling dilemma that fate had prepared for him: 'I could
have refused, I suppose, but it wouldn't have done any good, from
the point of view that somebody else would have taken it on.'

The idea that he was the main culprit for the catastrophe was as
ignorant as it was unfair. As Colonel Stacey observed on the programme,
'given all the conditions of the time, I suspect if the Emperor Napoleon
had been in command off the Dieppe beaches that day he couldn't have
done very much more.' The one criticism that could justly be made of
Roberts was his decision to reinforce failure and commit his reserves. In
Stacey's opinion 'Napoleon would probably have done something that
General Roberts didn't do – he probably would have cut his losses and
abandoned his troops onshore rather sooner . . . But that is the sort of
judgement one can make years later. It's not an easy judgement to make
at the moment when the guns are firing.'

No one could have won the Battle of Dieppe except the Germans.

As an operation of war it was hare-brained and as the enemy judged, 'contrary to all military common sense'. The scale of the disaster reinforced the belief, especially among the Canadians, that there must have been a leak and that the defenders knew when and where they were coming. The subsequent inquiries produced nothing definitive and there is no reason to disbelieve the statement of the Puys sector commander Richard Schnösenberg on *Close Up*: 'No, we did not expect an attack.'

The existing state of high readiness in place along the entire Channel coast was enough to wreck the premise on which Jubilee rested: that it was possible to achieve a significant level of tactical surprise. Landing in darkness might catch the defenders off guard but the confusion was unlikely to last long. For the plan to work required the Royals and the South Saskatchewans to get ashore, overcome the beach defences, march for a mile and attack and capture wired-in batteries all in the space of half an hour. The success of the main beach landings was therefore dependent on adherence to a minute-by-minute timetable that experience told was unlikely to survive the first contact with the enemy.

Much would later be made of the gaps in the intelligence picture which failed to identify the guns in the headlands and the streets leading into the town. It was true that the intelligence was inadequate and would have been greatly improved by the undelivered report prepared by the Resistance agent Roger Hérissé and his local helpers. But the guns were impervious to bombardment and knowing about them would have made little difference to the outcome, unless the knowledge was enough to get the whole thing called off.

Nor would the massive air raid envisaged in the first version of the plan have necessarily done much to improve the attackers' chances. As Ham Roberts had rightly concluded, inaccuracy rather than accuracy was to be expected from the bombers. The dislocating effect would be temporary and once the aircraft departed the guns would probably still be there. A battleship or cruiser might have made a difference. Given the extreme vulnerability of capital ships to air attack and the huge materiel and propaganda costs of another sinking, the Admiralty's vehement opposition to the idea was not surprising.

In his *Close Up* appearance Monty suggested the Canadians' lack of battle experience was a major factor in the failure. He claimed to have had a conversation with Paget 'in which I said to him, I don't think it's right to use them for this very tricky operation . . . not because they're not fine chaps. They are! But because they're totally inexperienced.' Paget's 'view was that the Canadians had been a long time in England. They were very well trained. And they were becoming impatient . . . they wanted to go fighting. And if they weren't allowed to go fighting, there would be trouble. Not only with the soldiers [but] with the Canadian headquarters in England under General Andy McNaughton . . . so having expressed my fears and having done what I could, I said no more.'

Leaving aside Montgomery's contentious role in the selection of the Canadians, this was a distortion and a slur. The point of all raids at this time was to 'blood' soldiers and give them and their commanders battle experience. Where they were able to get to grips with the enemy the Canadians fought with skill and everywhere showed heartbreaking determination, and the idea that seasoned troops could have succeeded where they did not was insulting nonsense. According to Schnösenberg who commanded the defenders at Blue Beach, 'I don't believe that any troops, no matter what nation, could have taken Puys under [the] circumstances.' In Lord Lovat's opinion, 'The defences of Dieppe town and harbour were impregnable, no matter how well trained you were. And that I'm sure of. Nobody could have taken Dieppe.'[35]

Whether the original Combined Ops plan to land armour on the flanks might have fared better we can never know. Mountbatten and his team did not fight very hard for it and Hughes-Hallett conceded that 'the original plan would not have captured the town. There wouldn't have been time.'[36]

The recklessness and implausibility of the Dieppe plan has prompted a tendency among historians to find some hidden explanation for its genesis and execution. The Canadian historian David O'Keefe has developed a thesis presenting Jubilee as a gigantic cover operation to mask the main purpose of the raid: the seizure of Enigma machines, settings and codes.[37] Certainly this was one element in the plan, but skilful and engaging though O'Keefe's arguments are, it seems unlikely that military chiefs would hazard enormous human and materiel resources for the primary purpose of gathering intelligence matter which, vital though it was, previous experience showed could be obtained more cheaply and easily.

Extraordinary as the project seems, it was only one of several desperate ventures under serious consideration in the spring and early summer of 1942. Rutter was no more risky than Sledgehammer or Imperator, none of which would have been contemplated in calmer times. But a combination of political, military and domestic pressures meant that the men controlling the British war were prepared to give the go-ahead to the development of wild schemes that would have been rubbished if proposed in a peacetime staff college exercise. In war, the outlandish gets a respectful hearing and it is important to remember the fevered atmosphere in which Rutter was conceived. Some sort of major cross-Channel operation was inevitable that summer. Thanks to Mountbatten and COHQ it was Dieppe that was chosen, otherwise a crazy march on Paris or a catastrophic attempted seizure of the Cherbourg Peninsula might now be remembered in place of Jubilee as a great disaster of the Allied war.

The pressure for action goes some way to explaining the succession of bad decisions taken as Rutter progressed. Everyone involved bore a share of the responsibility. For Jubilee, one man has to take most of the blame. By his own admission it was Mountbatten who forced it through. How far he bent the rules to get his way is lost in the welter of claim and counterclaim, but without him Dieppe would surely have gone the way of the other parlous cross-Channel schemes in play during the entr'acte as Britain moved from defence to attack.

It was this realisation that perhaps underlay his campaign to bind Dieppe to D-Day with links of steel, thereby sanctifying the slaughter on the beaches as a tragic but necessary sacrifice. There is little evidence in the Rutter plans to support the claim that it was intended as a test bed for a great amphibious landing and a 'rehearsal for

D-Day'. The notion only began to gain traction when Jubilee was subsequently sold to press, public and politicians. There was a cursory examination in the Combined Report of 'lessons learned' which amounted to little more than statements of the obvious. The 'Lesson of Greatest Importance' was the 'need for overwhelming fire support including close support, during the initial stages of the attack'. It also found that 'had suitable day bombers such as American Fortresses been available in sufficient numbers, the decision might well have been different.'[38]

This was not much return for the lavish expenditure in lives and equipment. By now the final tally was more or less clear. It would end up showing combined military casualties of 3,625.[39] That included 169 commandos of whom thirty-seven were killed, and seventy-six Royal Marine commandos of whom twenty-nine died. Of the fifty US Rangers who took part, seven were killed and six wounded. Twenty-nine Churchill tanks and ten armoured cars and carriers were lost.

The navy total was 523 casualties of whom 148 died. One destroyer and thirty-three landing craft were sunk. The RAF losses were sixty-six aircrew, fifty-three of whom died, and 106 aircraft. They had in turn inflicted painful damage to the Luftwaffe but not affected the basic strategic situation. The day had illustrated the shortcomings in coordinating air and ground operations in a tight battle space. However, the development of command and control methods that got air support where it was needed in the shortest possible time was not as a result of Dieppe but the accumulated experience gained in North Africa and Italy.

Total German losses for all three services were 357 dead and 280 wounded with the Hess battery the major material loss. Thirty-seven prisoners, none of whom had much of value to impart, were taken back to England.

The meagre gains made it all the more important for Mountbatten to magnify Jubilee's significance. He was supported by the Canadian high command who although they had not personally initiated the revival, threw their weight behind Mountbatten's efforts. The legend received its greatest boost on the eve of D-Day when Crerar told the men of the

3rd Canadian Infantry Division: 'The plan, the preparations, the method and technique which will be employed are based on knowledge and experience bought and paid for by 2nd Canadian Division at Dieppe. The contribution . . . cannot be overestimated. It will prove to have been the essential prelude to our forthcoming and final success.'[40]

The experience of Dieppe certainly stimulated several developments that contributed greatly to success on 6 June 1944. One was the design of heavily armed and armoured landing craft capable of suppressing defences when close inshore and offering some protection to the troops inside. Force J, as it was known, apparently after 'Jubilee', was the creation of Hughes-Hallett who went on to become one of the main naval planners for Overlord. He was also credited with a major role in the adoption of the Mulberry prefabricated floating harbour which removed the need to capture a port. Even Mountbatten did not claim that this was a child of Jubilee. The Mulberry concept was well developed before the raid took place, though Dieppe underlined its necessity.

The impossibility of capturing a port intact by direct assault was already strongly suspected. Dieppe provided the brutal proof. The raid demonstrated how not to do things, such as attempt a landing without massive fire support. Thus it was that the invasion was launched across the broad open beaches of Calvados and the Cherbourg Peninsula supported by huge air and sea armadas and then resupplied through a harbour that the Allies brought with them. But did it take a bloodbath to acquire this knowledge and spur the developments that followed?

Many of those who fought both at Dieppe and in Normandy reacted forcefully to suggestions that the sacrifice was wasted. Denis Whitaker, eloquently critical of many aspects of Jubilee, wrote: 'I am appalled when people with little or no operational experience attempt to dismiss the lessons learned at Dieppe as inconsequential. These lessons, both strategic and tactical, saved countless lives . . . The courage and sacrifice of our men of Dieppe was clearly not in vain. The men of D-Day landed with a strong umbrella of air and artillery support. Their assault equipment – landing craft, armour and weapons – were superb. Their intelligence was accurate.' Echoing Crerar he concluded: 'These assault skills and technical innovations were "bought and paid for" by 2nd Canadian Division at Dieppe.'[41]

That, however, is not the same thing as saying that the lessons had to be paid for in blood, and it is hard not to agree with Montgomery, expressing himself rather mildly for once, that 'the lessons learned at Dieppe were very valuable, but I think they could have been learned without the loss of those splendid soldiers.'[42]

It was Mountbatten who put a number on the value of Dieppe in the currency that mattered most. Addressing the Dieppe Veterans and Prisoners of War Association in Toronto on 28 September 1973 he pointed to the casualties sustained on D-Day which were much lighter than expected. 'Of the 156,000 men who took part in the assault, there were only 2,500 casualties [i.e. dead] or one man in sixty,' he said. 'At Dieppe . . . the comparable loss was about one in five. So twelve times as many men, including of course many thousands of Canadians, survived the D-Day assaults and I am convinced that this was directly the result of the lessons we learned at Dieppe.'[43]

Mountbatten never stopped trying to get people to see Dieppe his way. The men in front of him did not need to be persuaded of the value of what they did. They were not there to pillory him.

Reading his words it seems the person he was trying hardest to convince was himself. For Rutter, everyone at the top from Paget down was culpable to some extent, and even then there were powerful non-military pressures for pushing the project forward that could be cited in mitigation. The responsibility for Jubilee rested largely on Mountbatten's shoulders. By the time Rutter was cancelled, Torch had been agreed and the political impetus for action was easing. Why then had he been so intent on bringing it back to life? The only answer that fits is that he was unable to countenance the abandonment of a project in which he and his organisation had invested so much prestige. It was the triumph of the vanity, wilfulness and ambition that were always the dark counterpoint to his great ability and considerable humanity. Yet a surprising degree of self-knowledge was also one of his qualities, and beneath the surface show of righteousness can be glimpsed a deep uneasiness that he carried to his grave.

Epilogue

Sometime after breakfast on 1 September 1944 a strange silence fell on the town. At about 09.20 the first tricolours appeared in windows and the news jumped from house to house and street to street. 'They're here!'[1] At 10.10 two soldiers on motorcycles appeared at the top of the rue Gambetta, the main route south. By the time they reached the war memorial in the place des Martyrs near the seafront the crowd was so dense they could get no further. 'Twenty women, mad with joy, jumped out and hugged and kissed them,' the local paper reported. The motorcyclists were carried off to the town hall where this time it was the turn of the mayor René Levasseur to kiss them, whereupon the crowd burst into the 'Marseillaise'. After four years and four months of fear, suffering and humiliation, Dieppe was free again.

The men of the Royal Hamilton Light Infantry arrived at Rouxmesnil-Bouteilles on the southern edge of the town in the afternoon. They had landed in France a month after D-Day with the rest of the 2nd Division. Since then they had fought in the great battle for Caen and the rout of the German army at the Falaise Gap. The division had been remade since 1942. There were fewer than 300 Dieppe veterans in the Canadian ranks and many of them had since died. Just a few days before, fourteen men had been killed or were missing and twenty-seven wounded clearing out machine-gun posts south-west of Rouen. Mercifully it seemed that the Germans had decided not to make a stand in Dieppe and had already retreated, leaving behind only booby traps and mines and a few snipers who were dealt with by the local Resistance fighters.

From their holding position at Rouxmesnil-Bouteilles, the Rileys 'caught the first glimpse of the English Channel and . . . the outskirts of Dieppe'.[2] Alongside them were the Essex Scottish and the Royals, their brothers-in-arms from the beaches of 1942. The Fusiliers

Mont-Royal and the South Saskatchewans were backed up on the road behind. The whole 2nd Division were there. Their diversion from the main path of the Allied advance was, as Matthew Halton, a CBC reporter with the troops put it, 'a gesture. But it was a gesture demanded by Canadian history.'[3]

As they waited for the order to move, word reached them that there were some old comrades nearby. The Rileys had halted only a mile or so away from the cemetery at Les Vertus where the dead of 19 August 1942 lay. Two men who had been on the beaches that day, Major Jack Halladay and Major Joe Pigott, slipped away. The graveyard was surrounded by fields and woods. The graves were arranged in eleven rows. Each was marked by a wooden cross with a number corresponding to a name written in a list kept in a hut nearby. The lawns between the rows were neat and clipped. Halladay and Pigott went down them, pausing at the graves of special friends, taking photographs to send back to the dead men's families. Then they returned to the road where the troops stood smoking and talking quietly in the warm, apple-scented evening.

It was not until the following day that the town was put in bounds. The Rileys entered to the same ecstatic welcome that greeted every man in uniform. The veterans showed the others the sites of the carnage, and they 'swarmed over the German defences, smashed by their own demolitions and broken by Allied bombings'.

That night the new mayor, Resistance leader Pierre Biez who had taken over following the honourable departure of M. Levasseur, hosted a dance for the officers in the town hall while the men fanned out through the town's bars. 'One could not help but notice the mixture of strange emotions that night on the faces of personnel who had visited the town previously,' the Rileys' war diary recorded. 'Some were gay. Some were lost in reverie, but all enjoyed the real hospitality of the French people. Dieppe was avenged and this celebration was a fitting close to the agonised scenes of two years ago.'[4]

Next day was the time for remembrance. At 11.00 there was a memorial service at the cemetery. Two hours later the division marched six abreast through streets packed with cheering civilians and past their commander General Crerar. There was a day to reorganise. Then on the morning of 5 September the 2nd Division mounted their jeeps and lorries and went back to the war.

The Canadians would always return, along with British commandos who fought with them and the sailors who carried them all over. Every year on the anniversary of the raid the town filled up with veterans and their families. The survivors are almost all gone now but the anniversary is still a big event in Dieppe and probably always will be. On the morning of the 19th a crowd gathers at Les Vertus for speeches and prayers, then they stroll among the graves and summon up the young faces behind the names on the white headstones. Before he died George Buchanan of the South Saskatchewans talked of the struggle he had to retain his composure, a battle he always lost. 'I try to steel myself,' he said. 'I'm fine until I see some names I know and before long I'm bawling like a kid . . . you see us guys we all joined together, in the Depression from the prairies . . . we bunked together and we went up the ranks together. We were buddies . . .'[5]

It is a French as much as an Allied occasion. The cemetery is the creation of the people of Dieppe. They joined in the grim work of collecting the dead and the carts that carried the catch from the fishing boats to the markets were loaded up with corpses scattered over the beaches. More arrived on the tide for days afterwards. The bodies were put first in mass graves around the town then exhumed a few days later and reburied at Les Vertus. The site had been selected in 1940 as a cemetery for the dead from the Allied military hospital. It was no more than a cow field but over the next few years, encouraged by the sub-prefect Michel Sassier and tolerated by the Germans, the local people turned it into the green and peaceful space it is today.[6]

It became a place of reconciliation as well as remembrance. From 1960 onwards men of the 302nd Division returned most years to lay a wreath at Les Vertus and to visit the graves of their own dead. There were very few of them left. After the raid the division was sent to the Russian front and by the end the war had been reduced to 200 men.[7]

Jubilee lasted a long morning but the scar it left on Dieppe will never fade. The town has reverted to its old identity as a genteel resort, and the surrounding villages are peaceful and prosperous. The innocent backdrop makes the plaques and little monuments dotted around on street corners and crossroads all the more poignant. In these innocuous corners one hot summer morning, young men died in their hundreds. At least they have their memorials. Millions of others do not. The last service of the dead of Dieppe is to remind us for ever of a simple truth: that peace is sweet and war an abyss of sorrow and waste.

Acknowledgements

As the Second World War recedes in the rear view mirror of history there are ever fewer participants around to tell us first hand what it was like. Almost no one who took part in the Dieppe Raid is still alive so *Operation Jubilee* rests on the evidence mined from official documents, contemporary accounts and post-facto recollections and memoirs.

That was fine until the pandemic struck. The mass shutdown and the travel bans that followed made me unusually dependent on the resourcefulness and goodwill of others. I want to start therefore by thanking my young assistant in Montreal, Michael Black, for battling through the obstacles, aided and abetted by the can-do attitude of Canadian librarians and archivists, in particular Christina Parsons and Shannyn Johnson at the Canadian War Museum, Jane Harkness and Isabella Sun of the Department of National Defence's Directorate of History and Heritage, Stan Overy of the RHLI Museum, Hardy Wheeler of the Essex and Kent Scottish Regiment Association and Martin Bédard of Library and Archives Canada, who pulled out all the stops to get material to me in time for the project to continue without delays.

The same resourceful spirit was shown in Britain by Karen Robson and the team at Southampton University's Hartley Library, where the Mountbatten archives are held, and the staffs of the National Archives and the London Library. Rebecca Jallot, archivist at Epsom College, searched the records for details of Ham Roberts' boyhood in England.

I was particularly interested in the French aspect of the story (almost entirely overlooked in English language accounts), that is, the experience of occupation and how the raid impacted on people in and around Dieppe. I was lucky to meet early on Bertrand Edimo of Dieppe Ville d'Art et Histoire who generously shared his deep knowledge and enthusiasm for the town and its history and helped greatly in unearthing material. Olivier Nidelet guided me through the holdings in the Médiathèque Jean Renoir.

It was a pleasure to meet Sophie Tabesse-Mallèvre, who passed on her deep research on the social fabric of the town during the war years. I was given encouragement and help by members of the historical society Les Amys du Vieux Dieppe, particularly Guy Turquer and Anne-Marie Alexandre. One research visit was spent at the lovely Hôtel de la Terrasse at Vasterival, which looks today much the same as it must have done when the men of 4 Commando crept past it in the early morning light of 19 August 1942. Apart from making the stay so enjoyable the owner François Delafontaine also passed on his copy of Gérard Cadot's wonderfully evocative account of his boyhood under the occupation.

I met generosity everywhere. The historian Andrew Lownie made life much easier by sending me a wealth of material from the research for his terrific book *The Mountbattens*, published in 2019.

I was a Brit, tackling a very Canadian story the emotional charge of which is still felt in the country today. Canadian experts could not have been more welcoming. Tim Cook, the master-historian of Canada's involvement in the two world wars gave encouragement and also took the trouble to read the manuscript, adding many insights and saving me from many errors. Jeff Noakes of the Canadian War Museum kindly pointed me towards much useful material.

My understanding of Canadian culture and attitudes was greatly helped by a friend from Paris, Jim Black. Another Paris friend, the Australian historian Paul Ham, author of a superb study of Passchendaele, taught me much about 'colonial' attitudes to British military supervision.

Throughout the process I was buoyed up by the support and engagement of my editor at Penguin, Daniel Crewe, whose idea this book was. His enthusiasm was inspirational and his guidance invaluable. I was equally fortunate to be working with Alpana Sajip, whose calm efficiency and good nature smoothed the path into print. The final product benefited from the painstaking and creative copyediting of David Milner. After reading and re-reading the manuscript umpteen times a sort of blindness sets in and errors go unnoticed. I was saved from multiple clangers by the eagle eyes and profound knowledge of Stephen Ryan who read the proofs. *Merci mille fois*, Stephen. I am also very grateful for the warmth and energy of Doug Pepper and the rest of the team at Penguin Random House Canada. My agent and dear friend Annabel Merullo was her usual smiling, dependable self. Thanks a million, Belle.

This was my nineteenth book but no matter how many you write it never gets any easier. Thankfully, Henrietta and Honor were once again there in support. Love you.

Notes

Abbreviations used:

ADM   Admiralty Records, The National Archives

BA   Broadlands Archives, University of Southampton

CAB   Cabinet Office Records, The National Archives

DEFE   Ministry of Defence Records, The National Archives

DHH   Directorate of History and Heritage, Department of Defense, Canada, interviews from the Terence Macartney-Filgate and William Whitehead fonds

GRO   Papers of Vice Admiral H. T. Baillie-Grohman, National Maritime Museum

IWM   Imperial War Museum

PREM Prime Minister's Office Records, The National Archives

Introduction

1 Private Papers of Major General J. C. Haydon, IWM 2397

2 John P. Campbell, *Dieppe Revisited: A Documentary Investigation* (Frank Cass, 1993), p. 1

3 G. F. Krivosheev, *Soviet Casualties and Combat Losses in the Twentieth Century* (Greenhill Books, 1997), pp. 85–97

Prologue: 'Tommy kommt'

1 George Guibon, *Á Dieppe, le 19 août, 1942*, IWM K.652.55

1. Now or Never

1 Field Marshal Lord Alanbrooke, *War Diaries 1939–1945*, ed. Alex Danchev and Daniel Todman (Weidenfeld & Nicolson, 2001), pp. 243–4

2 *Spectator*, 'Braced and Compact?', 6 March 1942

3 Peter Clarke, *The Cripps Version* (Allen Lane, 2002), p. 262

4 Brian Loring Villa, *Unauthorized Action: Mountbatten and the Dieppe Raid 1942* (OUP, 1989), p. 55, quoting Mary Soames, *Clementine Churchill: The Biography of a Marriage* (Houghton Mifflin, 1979), p. 415

5 Villa, op. cit., p. 54, quoting Lord Moran, *Churchill* (Houghton Mifflin, 1966), p. 29

6 Harold Nicolson, *Diaries and Letters*, 3 vols, ed. Nigel Nicolson (Collins, 1967), vol. 2, p. 223

7 Helen Peacocke, 'Food that Fuelled Churchill's Wartime', *Oxford Mail*, 28 May 2015; Will Noble, 'How to Eat, Drink and Smoke like Winston Churchill', londonist.com 2019

8 Clarke, op. cit., pp. 263–4

9 Steven Fielding, 'The Second World War and Popular Radicalism: The Significance of the "Movement away from Party"', *History*, vol. 80 (February 1995), pp. 38–58

10 One survey from November 1941 showed Anthony Eden as the public's favourite replacement, with Cripps backed by only 1 per cent. By April 1942, Eden stood at 37 per cent and Cripps second at 34 per cent. See Hadley Cantril (ed.), *Public Opinion, 1935–1946* (Princeton University Press, 1951), pp. 279–80

11 *Pathé Gazette*, 16 February 1942

12 Alanbrooke, op. cit., p. 243

13 www.moidigital.ac.uk

14 Ivan Maisky, *The Maisky Diaries: Red Ambassador to the Court of St James's 1932–1943*, ed. Gabriel Gorodetsky (Yale University Press, 2015), p. 414

15 Ibid., p. 419

16 Alanbrooke, op. cit., p. 243

17 Winston Churchill, *The Second World War*, Vol. III (Cassell, 1950), p. 568

18 David J. Bercuson and Holger H. Herwig, *One Christmas in Washington* (Weidenfeld & Nicolson, 2005), p. 137

19 Churchill, *The Second World War*, Vol. III, p. 585
20 Colonel Charles F. Brower, 'George C. Marshall: a Study in Character', www.marshallfoundation.org
21 Alanbrooke, op. cit., p. 236
22 Unpublished Memoir of Vice Admiral John Hughes-Hallett, IWM 14370
23 Alanbrooke, op. cit., pp. 237–8

2. *Lord Louis*

1 Arthur Marshall, *Life's Rich Pageant* (Hamish Hamilton, 1984), p. 155
2 Winston Churchill, *The Second World War*, Vol. IV (Cassell, 1950), p. 106
3 Philip Ziegler, *Mountbatten: The Official Biography* (Collins, 1984), p. 170
4 *The Economist*, quoted in the introduction to Alanbrooke, op. cit., p. xv
5 Alanbrooke, op. cit., p. 53
6 Ibid., p. 236
7 Ziegler, op. cit., p. 169
8 BA MB1/B17
9 Robert Henriques, *From a Biography of Myself* (Secker & Warburg, 1969), p. 54
10 Ziegler, op. cit., p. 136
11 Ibid., pp. 132, 137
12 Adrian Smith, *Mountbatten: Apprentice War Lord* (I. B. Tauris, 2010), p. 134
13 Quentin Reynolds, *Dress Rehearsal* (Random House, 1943), p. 20
14 Ziegler, op. cit., p. 152
15 Bernard Fergusson, *The Watery Maze: The Story of Combined Operations* (Collins, 1961), p. 87
16 Winston Churchill, *The Second World War*, Vol. II (Cassell, 1949), p. 217
17 Lord Lovat, *March Past* (Weidenfeld & Nicolson, 1978), p. 184
18 Fergusson, op. cit., pp. 84–5
19 CAB 121/364
20 Ibid.
21 Fergusson, op. cit., pp. 87–8
22 Ziegler, op. cit., p. 156

23 Mountbatten's comments on the manuscript are recorded in the Haydon Papers, IWM 2397

3. HMS Wimbledon

1 Fergusson, op. cit., p. 90

2 Marshall, op. cit., pp. 155–6

3 Haydon Papers, IWM 2397

4 Quentin Reynolds, op. cit., pp. 27, 30

5 Goronwy Rees, *A Bundle of Sensations* (Chatto & Windus, 1960), p. 147

6 Lovat, op. cit., p. 238

7 Fergusson, op. cit., p. 120

8 Ibid., pp. 122–3

9 Hughes-Hallett, op. cit., p. 112

10 GRO/29

11 Lovat, op. cit., p. 239

12 James Dunning, IWM Sound Archive 19927

13 Irving 'Bill' Portman, IWM Sound Archive 9766

14 George Cook, IWM Sound Archive 9977

15 John Carney, IWM Sound Archive 22927

16 Lovat, op. cit., p. 234

17 Donald Gilchrist, IWM Sound Archive 10792

18 Will Fowler, *The Commandos at Dieppe* (HarperCollins, 2002), p. 40

19 Donald Gilchrist, *Castle Commando* (Oliver and Boyd, 1960), pp. 16–7

20 Denis Whitaker and Shelagh Whitaker, *Dieppe: Tragedy to Triumph* (Leo Cooper, 1992), p. 73

4. An Unpleasant Military Problem

1 DEFE 2/306

2 Rees, op. cit., p. 148; General Sir Bernard Charles Tolver Paget, entry in *Dictionary of National Biography*

3 CAB 121/364

4 Hughes-Hallett, op. cit., p. 117

5 Ibid., pp. 117–18

6 Following the raid on Vaagso, Hitler moved 30,000 reinforcements to Norway and ordered the strengthening of coastal and inland defences (Wikipedia)

7 John Durnford-Slater, *Commando* (William Kimber, 1953), pp. 56, 70, 77, 79–81, 83–4, 88

8 Lovat, op. cit., p. 201

9 David O'Keefe, *One Day in August: The Untold Story of Canada's Tragedy at Dieppe* (Knopf Canada, 2013), p. 133

10 British and German scientists were both aware of the effect of aluminium strips but had refrained from using them to prevent revealing the secret to the other side. As the British bombing campaign got under way it was decided that the benefits outweighed the disadvantages and Window was used for the first time, with devastating effect, in Operation Gomorrah, the fire-bombing of Hamburg in July 1943.

11 F. H. Hinsley et al., *British Intelligence in the Second World War*, Vol. II (HMSO, 1981), p. 192

12 CAB 121/364

13 Hughes-Hallett, op. cit., p. 123

14 As it turned out this would have little strategic significance. Hitler had already decided there was no need to risk *Tirpitz* in the Atlantic, where the Kriegsmarine's U-boats seemed to be on the point of closing down the convoys.

15 CAB 121/364

16 David O'Keefe has shown that hidden under the suspiciously cloudy objectives lurked another 'pinch' operation, aimed at capturing cipher material from ships in Bayonne harbour. Though the prize would be of great value in the battle being fought at Bletchley Park, the scale of raid still looks excessive. That, it could be argued, was part of the stratagem. A big production with multiple targets would help disguise the real object of the exercise, and mask the progress that the decrypters had made in penetrating the Enigma codes.

17 CAB 79/87/5; Hughes-Hallett, op. cit., pp. 127–8

18 Hughes-Hallett, op. cit., p. 135

19 CAB 121/364

20 Colonel C. Stacey, *Six Years of War: The Army in Canada, Britain and the Pacific* (Edmond Cloutier, 1957), p. 326

21 Hughes-Hallett, op. cit., p. 118

22 BA MB1/B67

23 Fergusson, op. cit., pp. 168–9

24 PREM 3/256; DEFE 2/337

25 Captain S. W. Roskill, *The War at Sea, 1939–1945*, 2 vols (The Naval and Military Press, 2004), vol. 2, p. 240

26 Campbell, op, cit., p. 197

27 Mountbatten, speech to the Dieppe Veterans and Prisoners of War Association, 28 September 1973, IWM

5. Les Doryphores

1 Alanbrooke, op. cit., p. 257

2 Madame Ménage interview, 'Dress Rehearsal for D-Day', BA MB1/B67

3 *La Vigie Nouvelle*, 23 August 1940

4 Ibid., 28 August 1942

5 Jean Bellocq, *Dieppe et sa région face à l'occupant nazi* (Dieppe, 1979), p. 54

6 *La Vigie Nouvelle*, 14 February 1941

7 Bellocq, op. cit., p. 60

8 Daniel Pégisse and Gérard Cadot, *Enfance de guerre sur les falaises* (Éditions Bertout, 1998), p. 92

9 Roger Lefebvre, *Zone côtière: journal d'un secrétaire de Mairie sous l'Occupation* (Imprimerie Dieppoise, [1946]), p. 28

10 Terence Robertson, *Dieppe: The Shame and the Glory* (Pan, 1962), p. 222

11 DEFE 2/330

12 BA MB1/B67

13 GRO/29/2041

14 Bernard Dupuy, *Opération Jubilee – Dieppe 19 août, 1942* (privately printed), pp. 94–7

15 Norman Franks, *The Greatest Air Battle* (Grub Street, 1992), p. 29

16 Interview with General Linder, 'Rehearsal for Dieppe', ABC 1967, Mountbatten Archive MB1 B/67

17 DEFE 2/324, p. 9

18 *La Vigie Nouvelle*, 28 April 1942

19 DEFE 2/324

20 Ibid.

21 Quoted in Richard Hargreaves, *The Germans in Normandy* (Pen and Sword, 2006), pp. 4–5

6. Rutter

1 GRO/22

2 Letter from Laycock to Casa Maury, 9 December 1942, BA MB1/B26

3 Hughes-Hallett, op. cit., p. 120

4 O'Keefe, op. cit., pp. 178–80

5 Campbell, op. cit., p. 214

6 Rees, op. cit., p. 152

7 DEFE 2/542 2687

8 PREM 3/256

9 Colonel C. Stacey, *Arms, Men and Governments* (The Queen's Printer for Canada, 1970), p. 257

10 Haydon Papers, IWM 2397

11 DEFE 2/542

12 Ibid.

13 Ibid.

14 The mast spotted by Hérissé was soon afterwards shifted the short distance to Bruneval

15 'Rémy', *Mémoires d'un agent secret de la France Libre*, Vol. I (Éditions France-Empire, 1983), p. 340

16 Dupuy, op. cit., p. 346; 'Rémy', *Mémoires d'un agent secret de la France Libre*, Vol. II (Éditions France-Empire, 1983), p. 113

17 DEFE 2/550, 'Notes on Military Situation on Northern Coasts of France, Belgium and Holland'

18 Ibid.

19 Ibid.

20 Ibid.

21 DEFE 2/542

22 DEFE 2/335, 'Combined Report on the Dieppe Raid', p. 2

23 CAB 121/364

24 DEFE 2/337

25 DEFE 2/335, 'Combined Report on the Dieppe Raid', p. 2

26 Hughes-Hallett, op. cit., p. 152

27 Fergusson, op. cit., p. 170

28 The Canadian official historian Colonel Stacey states that initially the plan was for the main eastern flank attack by an infantry battalion, plus tanks, to be aimed at Criel-sur-Mer. See D E F E 2/337 and The Admiralty, Battle Summary No. 33, The Raid on Dieppe, reprinted as *The Dieppe Raid: the Combined Operations Assault on Hitler's European Fortress, August 1942* (Frontline Books, 2019), p. 4

29 DEFE 2/335, 'Combined Report on the Dieppe Raid', p. 2

30 Ibid.

31 Haydon Papers, IWM 2397

32 Hughes-Hallett, op. cit., p. 153

33 Ibid., p. 154

34 Nigel Hamilton, *Monty: The Making of a General, 1887–1942* (McGraw-Hill, 1981), p. 38

35 Brian Bond, 'Gort', in *Churchill's Generals*, ed. John Keegan (Weidenfeld & Nicolson, 1991), p. 34

36 Quoted in Norman F. Dixon, *On the Psychology of Military Incompetence* (repr. Pimlico, 1994)

37 PREM 3/256, Churchill to General Ismay, 21 December 1942

38 David L. Roll, *The Hopkins Touch: Harry Hopkins and the Forging of the Alliance to Defeat Hitler* (OUP, 2013), p. 183

39 Ibid., p. 184

40 Alanbrooke, op. cit., p. 249

41 Roll, op. cit., p. 191

42 General Albert C. Wedemeyer, *Wedemeyer Reports!* (Henry Holt, 1958), p. 108

43 Quoted in Roll, op. cit., p. 192

44 Alanbrooke, op. cit., p. 250

7. 'You bet we want it'

1 RHLI War Diary, 20 September 1941

2 J. L. Granatstein, *The Weight of Command* (UBC Press, 2016), p. 72

3 RHLI War Diary, 4 September 1940

4 Interview with Kenneth Curry, Veterans Affairs Canada Archive

5 Robertson, op. cit., p. 66

6 *Hampshire Telegraph and Post*, 17 April 1942

7 Stacey, *Arms, Men and Governments*, p. 40

8 Whitaker and Whitaker, op. cit., p. 76

9 Ibid., p. 75

10 BA MB1/B67

11 Ted Glass, 'General McNaughton – A Canadian Son of Martha', *IEEE Canadian Review*, September 1990

12 Ibid.

13 Granatstein, op. cit., p. 94

14 Ibid., pp. 43, 74, 87, 120, 133

15 Ibid., p. 74

16 'Crerar, Henry Duncan Graham', Paul Dickson, *Dictionary of Canadian Biography*

17 Ibid.

18 Quoted in Chelsea Sambells, 'The Battle of Vimy Ridge: History, Myth, Memorial and Remembrance' (chelseasambells.com), from Tim Cook, *Vimy: The Battle and the Legend* (Allen Lane, 2017)

19 *Life* magazine, 18 December 1939

20 Ibid.

21 Stacey, *Six Years of War*, p. 59

22 Ibid., p. 212

23 Quoted in Hamilton, *Monty: The Making of a General*, p. 506

24 David Fraser, *Alanbrooke* (Collins, 1982), p. 188n

25 Alanbrooke, op. cit., p. 164

26 Hamilton, *Monty: The Making of a General*, p. 507

27 Stacey, *Six Years of War*, p. 256

28 Ibid., p. 260

29 Ibid., p. 261

30 Ibid., pp. 269, 271–2

31 Ibid., p. 282

32 Dickson, *Dictionary of Canadian Biography*

33 Ibid.

34 Stacey, *Six Years of War*, p. 308

35 Quoted in Whitaker and Whitaker, op. cit., p. 73

36 Lovat, op. cit., p. 269

37 Quoted in Whitaker and Whitaker, op. cit., p. 73

38 Stacey, *Six Years of War*, p. 243

39 Stephen Grenfell, quoted in Hamilton, *Monty: The Making of a General*, p. 515

40 This account appears in Terence Robertson's *Dieppe: The Shame and the Glory*, based on an interview with Crerar

41 Stacey, *Six Years of War*, p. 329

42 Rees, op. cit., p. 139

43 Nigel Hamilton, *The Full Monty: Montgomery of Alamein, 1887–1942* (Allen Lane, 2001), p. 434

44 CBC, *Close Up*, 9 September 1962

45 Hamilton, *Monty: The Making of a General*, p. 551

46 Ziegler, op. cit., p. 189. Whitaker and Whitaker, op. cit., p. 75, tell a different story. They write that sometime in April before McNaughton's return to England, Crerar and his senior staff officer Guy Simonds met Mountbatten, who revealed the Dieppe plan to them. Crerar urged that the Canadians be given the job and Mountbatten did not object. It was decided 'for reasons of military protocol . . . to keep quiet about the plans for the Canadians' until a formal request had been made to McNaughton.

47 DEFE 2/227; Robertson, op. cit., p. 107

48 Rees, op. cit., p. 142

49 DEFE 2/337

8. Simmerforce

1 Interview with Forbes West, BA MB1/B67

2 *Connaissance de Dieppe et de sa région*, Médiathèque de la Ville de Dieppe

3 RHLI Diary, 6 March 1942

4 Granatstein, op. cit., p. 149

5 Ibid., p. 125

6 Ibid., p. 196

7 RHLI Diary, 15 May 1942

8 Whitaker and Whitaker, op. cit., p. 70

9 Canadian War Museum, Papers of Colonel R. Labatt

10 RHLI War Diary, 22 May 1942

11 Interview with the Rev. John Foote VC, BA MB1/B67

12 Lucien Dumais, *The Man Who Went Back* (Leo Cooper, 1975), pp. 9–10

13 Robertson, op. cit., p. 111

14 Hugh G. Henry, 'The Calgary Tanks at Dieppe', *Canadian Military History*, Vol. 4, No. 1 (1995), p. 72

15 DEFE 2/330

16 Henry, op. cit., p. 66

17 DEFE 2/330

18 Interview with Stanley Edwards, 17 July 2017, Veterans Affairs Canada Sound Archive

19 Hugh G. Henry and Jean-Paul Pallud, *Dieppe Through the Lens of the German War Photographer* (After the Battle, n.d.), p. 5

20 DEFE 2/306

21 Lucian K. Truscott Jr, *Command Missions* (Quid Pro Books, reprinted from 1954), p. 30

22 Leo Amery, *Diaries* (Hutchinson, 1988), p. 814

23 Truscott, op. cit., p. 44

24 CAB 79/56/36

25 CAB 79/56/48

26 GRO/22

27 Zeigler, op. cit., p. 87; GRO/29

28 GRO/29

29 Robertson, op. cit., pp. 118–20

30 Ziegler, op. cit., p. 189

31 GRO/22

32 GRO/30

33 Robin Neillands, *The Dieppe Raid* (Aurum, 2005), p. 96

34 Haydon Papers, IWM 2397

35 DEFE 2/550, 'Notes on Military Situation on Northern Coasts of France, Belgium and Holland'

36 Ibid.

9. Surprise

1   Stacey, *Six Years of War*, p. 336

2   DEFE 2/335, 'Combined Report on the Dieppe Raid', p. 2

3   CAB 121/364

4   DEFE 2/335, 'Combined Report on the Dieppe Raid', p. 3

5   CAB 121/364

6   Robertson, op. cit., p. 127

7   Major General George Kitching, quoted in Granatstein, op. cit., p. 37

8   GRO/29

9   Rees, op. cit., pp. 146–7

10   Ibid., p. 157

11   GRO/29

12   Mountbatten, memo to CBC, Haydon Papers, IWM 2397

13   Mountbatten to General Ismay, 24 December 1942, BA MB1/B18

14   GRO/29

15   Hughes-Hallett, op. cit., p. 160

16   GRO/28

17   BA MB1/B67

18   DEFE 2/542

19   GRO/22

20   BA MB1/B67

21   Letter to Haydon, Haydon Papers, IWM 2397

22   Rees, op. cit., p. 156

23   GRO/24

24   Robertson, op. cit., pp. 144–5

25   This veiled remark is seen by the Canadian historian David O'Keefe as proof that the real purpose of Rutter and Jubilee was the seizure of Enigma material from the German naval HQ at Dieppe

26   Interview with J. S. Edmondson, DHH

27   Sandy Antal and Kevin R. Shackleton, *Duty Nobly Done: The Official History of the Essex and Kent Scottish Regiment* (Walkerville, 2006), p. 392

28   Quoted in Arthur Kelly, 'A Battle Doomed to Fail for All the Wrong Reasons', *National Post*, 17 August 2012

29   Stacey, *Six Years of War*, p. 335

30 Churchill, op. cit., Vol. IV, pp. 343–4, 390

31 Hughes-Hallett, op. cit., p. 164

32 Ibid., pp. 165–6

33 Stacey, *Six Years of War*, p. 335

34 Robertson, op. cit., p. 159

35 RHLI Diary, 7 July 1942

10. *Resurrection*

1 ADM 223/299

2 CBC, *Close Up*, 9 September 1962

3 Hughes-Hallett, op. cit., p. 167

4 Rear Admiral J. Hughes-Hallett, 'The Mounting of Raids', *Royal United Services Institution Journal*, Vol. 95, No. 580 (1950)

5 Mountbatten, speech to the Dieppe Veterans and Prisoners of War Association, 28 September 1973, IWM

6 CBC, *Close Up*, 9 September 1962

7 Ibid.

8 Robertson, op. cit., p. 172

9 Hinsley et al., op. cit., p. 696

10 Truscott, op. cit., p. 55

11 Roll, op. cit., p. 208

12 Ibid.

13 Ibid., pp. 211, 214, 217, 219

14 Oliver Stone and Peter Kuznick, *The Untold History of the United States* (Simon & Schuster, 2012), pp. 106–7

15 GRO/22

16 Hamilton, *Monty: The Making of a General*, p. 555

17 Hughes-Hallett, op. cit., p. 169

18 Stacey, *Six Years of War*, p. 344

19 The Admiralty, Battle Summary No. 33, The Raid on Dieppe, reprinted as *The Dieppe Raid: the Combined Operations Assault on Hitler's European Fortress, August 1942* (Frontline Books, 2019), p. 4

20 DEFE 2/335, 'Combined Report on the Dieppe Raid', p. 9

21 Durnford-Slater, op. cit., p. 92

22 Also known as 'Eurekas', R-boats were designed by Miami shipbuilder Andrew Higgins. In the hunt for landing craft that followed Mountbatten's accession at COHQ they were gratefully snapped up.

23 Lovat, op. cit., p. 236

24 Ibid., p. 242.

25 DEFE 2/330

26 DEFE 2/324

27 DEFE 2/330

28 Robertson, op. cit., p. 227

29 DEFE 2/335, 'Combined Report on the Dieppe Raid', p. 210

30 Robertson, op. cit., p. 227

31 Quoted in Robertson, op. cit., pp. 198–9

32 BA MB1/B67

33 Private Papers of Captain D. H. H. Turner, IWM 9865

34 A. B. Austin, *We Landed at Dawn* (Gollancz, 1943), p. 58

35 BA MB1/B67

36 Whitaker and Whitaker, op. cit., p. 230

37 IWM Sound Archive 9977

38 Austin, op. cit., p. 53

Passage

1 Truscott, op. cit., p. 67

2 Hughes-Hallett, op. cit., p. 178

3 Quentin Reynolds, op. cit., p. 74

4 'Narrative of Experiences at Dieppe, Lieutenant Colonel R. R. Labatt', Canadian War Museum

5 Durnford-Slater, op. cit., p. 95

6 Austin, op. cit., p. 78

7 BA MB1/B67

8 Private Papers of Lieutenant M. L. Bateson RNVR, IWM 711

9 DEFE 2/335

10 Durnford-Slater, op. cit., pp. 103–4

11 DEFE 2/335

12 DEFE 2/337

13 DEFE 2/335

14 Truscott, op. cit., p. 67

15 The Admiralty, Battle Summary No. 33, The Raid on Dieppe, reprinted as *The Dieppe Raid: the Combined Operations Assault on Hitler's European Fortress, August 1942* (Frontline Books, 2019), p. 4

16 Hughes-Hallett, op. cit., pp. 180–81

17 Admiralty Report, p. 79

18 Interview with Richard Schnösenberg, DHH

19 DEFE 2/335

20 BA MB1/B67

21 Quoted in Franks, op. cit., p. 26

22 Lovat, op. cit., p. 249

23 Pégisse and Cadot, op. cit., p. 179

24 DEFE 2/337

25 IWM Sound Archive 10694

26 IWM Sound Archive 9977

27 Quoted in Fowler, op. cit., p. 163

28 Lovat, op. cit., p. 259

29 BA MB1/B67

30 DEFE 2/337

31 Lovat, op. cit., p. 251

32 Austin, op. cit., p. 89

33 IWM Sound Archive 19927

34 BA MB1/B67

35 Details taken from Jim DeFelice, *Rangers at Dieppe* (Berkley Caliber, 2009), the best and fullest account of the American role in Operation Jubilee

36 BA MB1/B67

37 DEFE 2/337

38 IWM Sound Archive 10060

Blue and Green

1 Admiralty Report, p. 27

2 DEFE 2/335, 'Combined Report on the Dieppe Raid', p. 84

3 BA MB1/B67

4 Stacey, *Six Years of War*, p. 364

5 BA MB1/B67

6 Interview with Richard Schnösenberg, DHH

7 DEFE 2/337

8 Later, other stories would emerge. Terence Robertson wrote that three days after Jubilee an informal inquiry took place at naval headquarters in Portsmouth into the events at Blue Beach with twelve naval officers giving evidence. Several testified that when the bow doors went down soldiers in the rear ranks had been extremely reluctant to move. One stated: 'When the soldiers started to jump onto the beach everything opened up. A number of casualties occurred before the troops reached the shelter of the wall. This discouraged the rest from landing, and only a firm handling of the situation by the naval officers in charge . . . succeeded in compelling the rest to follow their comrades.' The 'firm handling' involved 'revolvers having to be used as a threat' (Robertson, op. cit., p. 298).

9 Quoted in Dupuy, op. cit., p. 166

10 Mann Papers, Library and Archives Canada, 'Op' Jubilee: Personal Accounts Generally, RG24, Vol. 10873, File 232C2 (D53)

11 DEFE 2/337

12 Mann Papers

13 Ibid., 'Memorandum dealing with Blue Beach'

14 DEFE 2/337

15 Interview with Jack Poolton, Veterans Affairs Canada

16 DEFE 2/337

17 Ibid.

18 Ibid.

19 Ibid.

20 IWM 9865

21 DEFE 2/337

22 DEFE 2/338

23 DEFE 2/328

24 Of 554 from all ranks who embarked, 209 died then or later of wounds sustained on Blue Beach. Another eighteen died in captivity. Stacey, *Six Years of War*, p. 368

25 BA MB1/B67

26 Interview with Jack Poolton, Veterans Affairs Canada

27 Quentin Reynolds, op. cit., p. 108

28 DEFE 2/335, 'Combined Report on the Dieppe Raid', pp. 122–3

29 DEFE 2/337

30 All radio signals taken from ADM 223/298–9

31 Interview with J. S. Edmondson, DHH

32 DEFE 2/337

33 Robertson, op. cit., p. 333

34 Jack Nissen and A. W. Cockerill, *Winning the Radar War: A Memoir* (St Martin's Press, 1987), p. 152

35 BA MB1/B67

36 DEFE 2/335

37 Captain F. W. Hayter RCAMC, 'Evacuation of Casualties from Dieppe', Mann Papers

38 Reprinted in Bellocq, op. cit., p. 124

39 GRO 22

40 'Report of Intelligence Officer attached to Camerons of Canada', Mann Papers

41 'Comments by Sgt Hawkins and Flt Sgt Nissenthall', Mann Papers

42 Lefebvre, op. cit., p. 54

43 Terence Robertson quotes three soldiers who happily owned up to shooting prisoners, though it was claimed in mitigation that some were 'pointing out our positions to snipers'. Robertson, op. cit., pp. 337–8

44 'Report by Captain H. B. Carswell', Mann Papers

45 Interview with George Buchanan, DHH

46 DEFE 2/337

47 Interview with Lieutenant Nesbitt, DHH

48 Interview with J. S. Edmondson, DHH

49 DEFE 2/337

50 BA MB1/B67

51 Nissenthall, op. cit., p. 174

Red and White

1 Quoted in Franks, op. cit., p. 40

2 Rees, op. cit., p. 164

3 BA MB1/B35

4 Stacey, *Six Years of War*, p. 375. In his first report Hughes-Hallett calculated 'ten to twenty minutes'; 'Reports by Force Commanders on Operation Jubilee', DEFE 2/328

5 Admiralty Report, p. 33

6 All after-action reports taken from DEFE 2/328 unless otherwise stated

7 Other reports say it kept on firing

8 Whitaker and Whitaker, op. cit., p. 252

9 Interview with Archie Anderson, DHH

10 Antal and Shackleton, op. cit., p. 204

11 Interview with Leo Lecky, DHH

12 DEFE 2/328; interview with Fred Jasperson, DHH

13 'Narrative Experiences at Dieppe, 19 August, by Lieutenant Col R. R. Labatt OC, RHLI', Canadian War Museum

14 Whitaker and Whitaker, op. cit., p. 242

15 *Connaissance de Dieppe et de sa région*

16 Hughes-Hallett, op. cit., p. 182

17 See DEFE 2/328, Section II, p. 42

18 All signals taken from ADM 223/298–9

19 Whitaker and Whitaker, op. cit., p. 257

20 DEFE 2/335, 'Combined Report on the Dieppe Raid', p. 142

21 Interview with David Hart, Veterans Affairs Canada

22 Hughes-Hallett, op. cit., p. 185

23 'Mon Raid Sur Dieppe, Un officier Canadien français explique ce qui fait le courage du soldat', in *Connaissance de Dieppe et de sa région*

24 DEFE 2/328, p. 36

25 ADM 223/298–9

26 DEFE 2/328

27 Quoted in Whitaker and Whitaker, op. cit., pp. 254–5

Vanquish

1 Truscott, op. cit., p. 70

2 Admiralty Report, p. 163

3 DEFE 3/328, Part II, p. 50

4 BA MB1/B67

5 DEFE 3/328

6 DEFE 2/335

7 BA MB1/B68

8 Labatt, Canadian War Museum

9 Interview with Elmer Cole, Veterans Affairs Canada

10 DEFE 2/328

11 Rees, op. cit., pp. 166–7

12 IWM 9865

13 Quoted in Franks, op. cit., p. 112

14 Air Vice Marshal 'Johnnie' Johnson, *Wing Leader* (Goodall, 1995), p. 145

15 Interview with J. E. Johnson, IWM Sound Archive 10347

16 DEFE 2/337

17 DEFE 2/338

18 Admiralty Report, p. 46

19 Antal and Shackleton, op. cit., p. 415

20 DEFE 2/337

21 Labatt, Canadian War Museum

22 Stacey, *Six Years of War*, p. 367

23 IWM 711

24 DEFE 2/337

25 ADM 223/298–9

26 Rees, op. cit., pp. 170–71

27 BA MB1/B67

28 Interview with Jack Poolton, Veterans Affairs Canada

29 *Connaissance de Dieppe et de sa région*

30 Quentin Reynolds, op. cit., p. 121

31 Admiralty Report, p. 310

32 Labatt, Canadian War Museum

33 DEFE 2/335

34 BA MB1/B67

35 Interview with Archie Anderson, DHH

36 Interview with Richard Schnösenberg, DHH, CBC, *Close Up*, 9 September 1962

37 Guibon, op. cit., p. 15

38 *Connaissance de Dieppe et de sa région*

39 IWM 711
40 IWM 9865
41 BA MB1/B67

Aftermath

1 DEFE 2/330
2 PREM 3/256
3 DEFE 2/330
4 Alanbrooke, op. cit., p. 299
5 Quoted in Maisky, op. cit., p. 461
6 Alanbrooke, op. cit., p. 307
7 DEFE 2/329
8 Ibid.
9 David Ian Hall, 'The German View of the Dieppe Raid, August 1942', *Canadian Military History*, Vol. 21, No. 4 (Autumn 2012), p. 5
10 DEFE 2/335
11 BA MB1/B67
12 DEFE 2/335
13 Quoted in Dupuy, op. cit., p. 340
14 Timothy John Balzer, 'Selling Disaster: How the Canadian Public was Informed of Dieppe', MA thesis (University of Victoria, 2004), p. 40
15 Stacey, *Six Years of War*, p. 387
16 DEFE 2/324
17 Stacey, *Six Years of War*, p. 395
18 DEFE 2/328
19 Interview with Fred Jasperson, DHH
20 Interview with Leo Lecky, DHH
21 DEFE 2/324
22 Interview with George Buchanan, DHH
23 *The Times*, 27 August 1942
24 Hansard, House of Commons, Vol. 383, Col. 84
25 CAB 79/15/8
26 BA MB1/B18
27 PREM 3/256

28 BA MB1/B18

29 PREM 3/256

30 Stacey, *Six Years of War*, p. 387

31 Alanbrooke, op. cit., p. 388

32 David Reynolds, *In Command of History: Churchill Fighting and Writing the Second World War* (Allen Lane, 2004), pp. 345–6

33 Ibid., p. 347

34 CBC, *Close Up*, 9 September 1962

35 Ibid.

36 Ibid.

37 O'Keefe, op. cit.

38 DEFE 2/335, 'Combined Report on the Dieppe Raid', pp. 38–51

39 Admiralty Report, Appendix D, pp. 67–70

40 Quoted in Campbell, op. cit., p. 197

41 Whitaker and Whitaker, op. cit., p. 304

42 CBC, *Close Up*, 9 September 1962

43 Mountbatten, speech to the Dieppe Veterans and Prisoners of War Association, 28 September 1973, IWM

Epilogue

1 *La Vigie Nouvelle*, 2 September 1944

2 RHLI War Diary, 1 September 1944

3 CBC Report, 2 September 1944

4 RHLI War Diary, 2 September 1944

5 Interview with George Buchanan, DHH

6 Sophie Tabesse-Mallèvre, *Un jour sans soleil: 19 août 1942 sous le regard des Dieppois* (Au Petit Bonheur, 2011), p. 164

7 Interview with General Linder, BA MB1/B68

Index